Thomas W. Whigham

D1201432

The
Politics
of River
Trade

The Politics of River Trade

Tradition and Development in the Upper Plata, 1780–1870

Thomas Whigham

University of New Mexico Press
Albuquerque

Library of Congress
Cataloging-in-Publication Data

Whigham, Thomas, 1955–
The politics of river trade :
tradition and development in the
Upper Plata, 1780–1870 /
Thomas Whigham. — 1st ed.
      p.   cm.
Includes bibliographical references
and index.
ISBN 0-8263-1312-4
1. Rio de la Plata Region
(Argentina and Uruguay)—
Commerce—History.
2. Rio de la Plata Region
(Argentina and Uruguay)—
Economic conditions.
3. Exports—Rio de la Plata Region
(Argentina and Uruguay)—History.
I. Title.
HF3375.W48   1991
382'.0982'12—dc20   91-3493

*For
Edgar A. Ray,
with respect
and
affection.*

Contents

Maps

Illustrations appear following page 90

Tables

xi

Acknowledgments

In putting this study together, I have accumulated a great many debts, intellectual, material, and personal. I can hardly begin to thank all those friends and colleagues who have helped me over the years, though I recognize that what is good in the following work is a direct result of their kindness and advice.

Research in South America was made possible by grants from the Fulbright Hays Doctoral Research Program, the Sarah H. Moss Fellowship, and the University of Georgia Faculty Research Program.

I am especially grateful to the staffs of various archives, libraries, and historical institutes, including the Archivo Nacional de Asunción, Archivo General de la Provincia de Corrientes, Archivo General de la Nación (Buenos Aires), Archivo del Banco de la Provincia de Buenos Aires, Archivo Histórico y Administrativo de Entre Ríos (Paraná), Arquivo Histórico de Rio Grande do Sul (Pôrto Alegre), Museo Mitre (Buenos Aires), Instituto de Investigaciones Geo-Históricas (Resistencia), and the Centro Paraguayo de Estudios Sociológicos (Asunción).

Scholars in several countries gave me encouragement and counsel. In Argentina, Roberto Córtes Conde, José Carlos Chiaramonte, Juan Carlos Nicolau, Samuel Amaral, Alberto Rivera, and Ernesto J. A. Maeder provided valuable insights at various stages of research. I owe an equal debt to my Paraguayan colleagues, Alfredo Viola, Domingo Rivarola, and Juan Carlos Herken Krauer. In Montevideo, Juan Rial and Alicia Barán opened doors and were always ready with a friendly *cafecito*.

In the United States, I profited from the criticism of Meredith Dodge, Erick Langer, Lyman Johnson, Tulio Halperín-Donghi, Carl Vipperman, Peter Hoffer, and Jonathan Brown. My great appreciation also goes to

Frederick Bowser, Steve J. Stern, and Jerry W. Cooney, each of whom contributed in no small way to the realization of this project.

Finally, I am grateful to those many friends whose presence and personal support in ways known to each of them have helped me through some difficult times. In this context, I wish to mention Paul Copeland, Bruce Folsom, Jon McPherson, and especially my wife, Marta, and son, Alex, who showed patience, understanding, and love when I needed it most.

Preface

*La vida de los estados es el
comercio, como la sangre del
cuerpo humano, sin cuyas libres
circulaciones terminan en su
existencia.*
Estanislao López

For Latin America, economic development has always been linked with a stable political scene. It could hardly be otherwise, since tranquil political conditions make outside trade possible, and Latin America has always depended on overseas commerce for manufactured goods, investments, and technologies. Every interruption of trade has been costly, leaving the very forces necessary for internal development languishing, or committed to military ends. As with all human affairs, however, people find ways to advance their interests even in the worst of circumstances. When politicians and merchants find their standard options cut off, they must meet the challenge with new approaches and new resolve.

Independence presented the statesmen of Latin America with such a challenge. The breaking of ties with Spain in the 1810s and 1820s brought fullfledged nationhood to only a few areas; in most instances, the continent's lengthy history of chaos only gradually gave way to more stable patterns of governance. Regional economies in many areas suffered from this crisis for fifty years. Merchants, store owners, and even itinerant peddlers had to struggle tenaciously to remain active throughout this era. The new regimes, which subsisted on revenues from commercial transactions, were keenly aware of the need to bolster production and exchange. Yet how were merchants and state authorities to realize such a goal when political order was so tenuous?

Most recent studies of nineteenth-century Latin America argue that economic life was little affected by independence. The British, who controlled the international trade network, replaced the Spaniards as overlords of the continent. They reinforced Latin America's ties to the global economy, but as an unequal partner, fit only to supply the dockyards and factories of Europe with raw materials.

The Latin Americans themselves, according to this argument, remained backward. An elite of local merchants and landowners appropriated the few profits remitted to the New World, which they wasted on imported luxury goods while the masses continued to live in poverty. In the final analysis, the continent's dependent relationship with Britain determined the inner workings of Latin American society and ensured its continuing underdevelopment.

This dour appraisal of Latin American realities in the first phase of the national period has been the subject of debate for some twenty years.[1] Critics of both the left and the right have found this dependency paradigm wanting in terms of historical methodology. Few critics, however, have supplied empirical data to counter one key feature of the argument—the historical plausibility of autonomous development in Latin America.

In the following chapters, I will examine whether locally based development was a real option for one region frequently cited by dependency theorists as being an exception that proves the rule. Was it in fact an exception? Ostensibly nationalist economic agendas often mask a short-term response to limited trade conditions. Was an export-oriented development formula even possible given the degree of political disorder? If not, what alternatives did merchants and governments have?

The geographical setting is the Upper Río de la Plata, a region that today comprises Paraguay, the Argentine provinces of Corrientes and Misiones, and the adjacent Brazilian borderlands. It is an area fed by large rivers that link the region with outside markets. In times of conflict, the rivers became barriers rather than bridges. The Upper Plata then turned in upon itself, sometimes in resignation and sometimes with relief.

The economic history of the Upper Plata in the nineteenth century has had a surprising importance in the recent historical literature. Scholars working within the dependency paradigm have argued that Paraguay enjoyed an autonomous economic development that promoted social justice and permitted a more comprehensive degree of national sovereignty between 1811 and 1870. Paraguay, they claim, was a special case in a region where the pull of the Atlantic market undermined local manufacturing and promoted rural exports.

In order to test this thesis, Paraguay must be placed in its greater historical and geographical context—thus the utility of examining development in the entire Upper Platine region. Expanding the focus beyond national frontiers introduces certain organizational problems. Platine historiography is dominated by nationalist perspectives that deemphasize cross-regional phenomena, and it is sometimes difficult to restore the frayed ends of a complex history. For every weakness in organization, however, this perspective offers the reader the reward of greater breadth and a richer conceptualization of historical trends. Reference to regional structures allows us to ask whether development in the Plata owed more to extracontinental demand or to the needs of medium- and long-distance markets within Latin America itself. Did supplying these needs through interregional exchange provide the motor for economic growth?[2] Or was development generated from within, as the dependency writers suggest?

The Upper Plata never constituted a coherent region of the sort usually encountered in regional histories of Latin America. It was neither province, nor district, nor a political subdivision of a larger whole. After 1810, its constituent parts looked not to one government but to several. Local prejudices, moreover, cancelled out the forces that might otherwise have encouraged regional integration. The Upper Plata can, nonetheless, be examined as a spatialization of economic relations.[3] What Corrientes and Paraguay had in common in this regard was an unfavorable relation with the provinces of the south, especially Buenos Aires. Trade links with the latter were crucial to the economic development of the Upper Plata, far more so than any contacts with Europe. By its geographic placement, Buenos Aires commanded access to the river provinces; the port city also formed the largest market in the southern half of the continent. The lure of commerce with Buenos Aires and the lower provinces, however, carried a political price that many in the northeast found unpalatable.

In their rejection of Porteño dominance, governments in the Upper Plata attempted to safeguard their own economic interests, often looking to merchantile solutions. Mercantilism, with its preoccupation with exports, its conviction that demand is inelastic, and its concern with the terms—as opposed to the volume—of trade, supplied the instinctively conservative regimes of the region with appropriate, if expedient, rationalizations. In times of political uncertainty, the governments chose to stress the acquisition of specie over all other economic goals. These various endeavors provide a central focus for this study of Upper Platine trade and economic development.

In the pages that follow, I will explore the external trade of the region from the onset of the Bourbon Reforms in 1780 through the end of the War of the Triple Alliance in 1870. These two dates provide excellent benchmarks. The Bourbon Reforms, which were designed to modernize trade throughout the Spanish empire, effectively made economic development possible in the Upper Plata. The Triple Alliance conflict, on the other hand, saw Brazil, Argentina, and Uruguay combine their military forces against Paraguay in a desperate campaign that came close to destroying all the economic progress the region had made. I will touch on domestic commerce only to the extent that it informs the larger picture. In contrast to previous portraits of the Upper Plata as a stagnant hinterland, the evidence presented here suggests a region of real potential, intermittently realized, for a thriving export economy. This potential, however, was powerfully and repeatedly disrupted by politics. The ability of merchants and governments in the Upper Plata to contend with these tribulations constitutes an adventure in a real sense, an adventure that could have wider implications for studies of economic development in Latin America and elsewhere.

PART ONE

Commerce and Regional Politics 1780–1870

1

Trade and Conflict on the Rivers, 1780–1840

*Es preciso confesar que los
paraguayos y correntinos son
unidos entre si . . . no son tan
ladrones, borrachos y jugadores,
sino conocidamente más econó-
micos, instruidos y aplicados.*
Félix De Azara

The Upper Plata owes much of its historical diversity to its landlocked character. The region's poor geographical position relative to its external markets has always conditioned the otherwise remarkable productivity of its plains and forests. Hence any study of Upper Platine trade must necessarily focus on its great rivers—the Paraguay, the Uruguay, and the Paraná. Providing an outlet to Buenos Aires and the Atlantic Ocean, these waterways hold the key to the economic development of the Upper Plata. Throughout its history, leaders in the region feared that any closure of these vital arteries of commerce would force the region farther into isolation; and because Upper Platine commerce did not operate in a political vacuum, more often than not the ebb and flow of political affairs did in fact open or close the rivers, frustrating the economic potential of the area.

The commerce of the Upper Plata gravitated between two extremes, depending on whether unencumbered river passage was possible. When the rivers were open, the region actively participated in a trade that connected it with most parts of South America. Though the variety of its commodities was limited to tobacco, hides, timber, and the fragrant green tea called *yerba mate*, demand was always sufficient to promote their exportation. Both native and foreign-born merchants were generally ready to invest and join in the commerce. When the rivers were

3

closed, however, the Upper Plata became a collection of isolated, self-contained entities that displayed little need to trade even with each other. This semiautarchical arrangement found its partisans among the small farmers and peasants of the region, just as open trade found its supporters among the merchants and large landowners.

The inhabitants of the Upper Plata were well aware that the unrestricted flow of commerce downriver depended above all on the disposition of an outside power—Buenos Aires. The port city constituted the Upper Plata's most important market, a reality as necessary as it was resented. Moreover, the location of Buenos Aires at the mouth of the Río de la Plata gave its merchants and fiscal authorities control over trade to and from the inland provinces. The power of the Porteños to make or break the external trade of the Upper Plata, and their willingness to control it as their interest dictated, spurred no end of enmity in the northeast. These tensions colored relations with Buenos Aires throughout the colonial period, while the issue of free river passage provided a context for attempts at reconciliation after independence.

The Geographic Dimension

The Paraná-Paraguay river system runs southward along the eastern half of a broad, low plain and juts across the edge of this plain on its way to the sea. Unlike the Mississippi, which it closely resembles in continental location, the Paraná-Paraguay draws the bulk of its flow from the eastern part of its basin. In the far northeast, an extensive network of streams that have their common origin in the Brazilian highlands of Minas Gerais feeds the Alto Paraná. This turbulent river runs so swiftly in its deep channel that vessels moving upstream skirt its banks to avoid the force of the current. South of its great westward bend near Candelaria, the river is almost two kilometers across, but downriver, from the rapids (salto) of Apipé to the delta, it is somewhat shallow, presenting an obstacle for year-round passage.

The muddy Paraná, with its shallow, winding, and island-strewn course, offers a poor channel for navigation. The eastern bank below Corrientes does not lend itself to the founding of ports. Some stretches of the eastern bank are high and well defined, but marshes prevent contact between the populated centers in Corrientes and the main river channel. The western bank as far south as Santa Fé is regularly inundated; settlements on that side of the river are established at some distance from the water. As a commercial artery, the Paraná's chief disadvantage lies in affording relatively poor access to the surrounding territory.

The russet-colored Río Paraguay closely resembles the Paraná. It flows

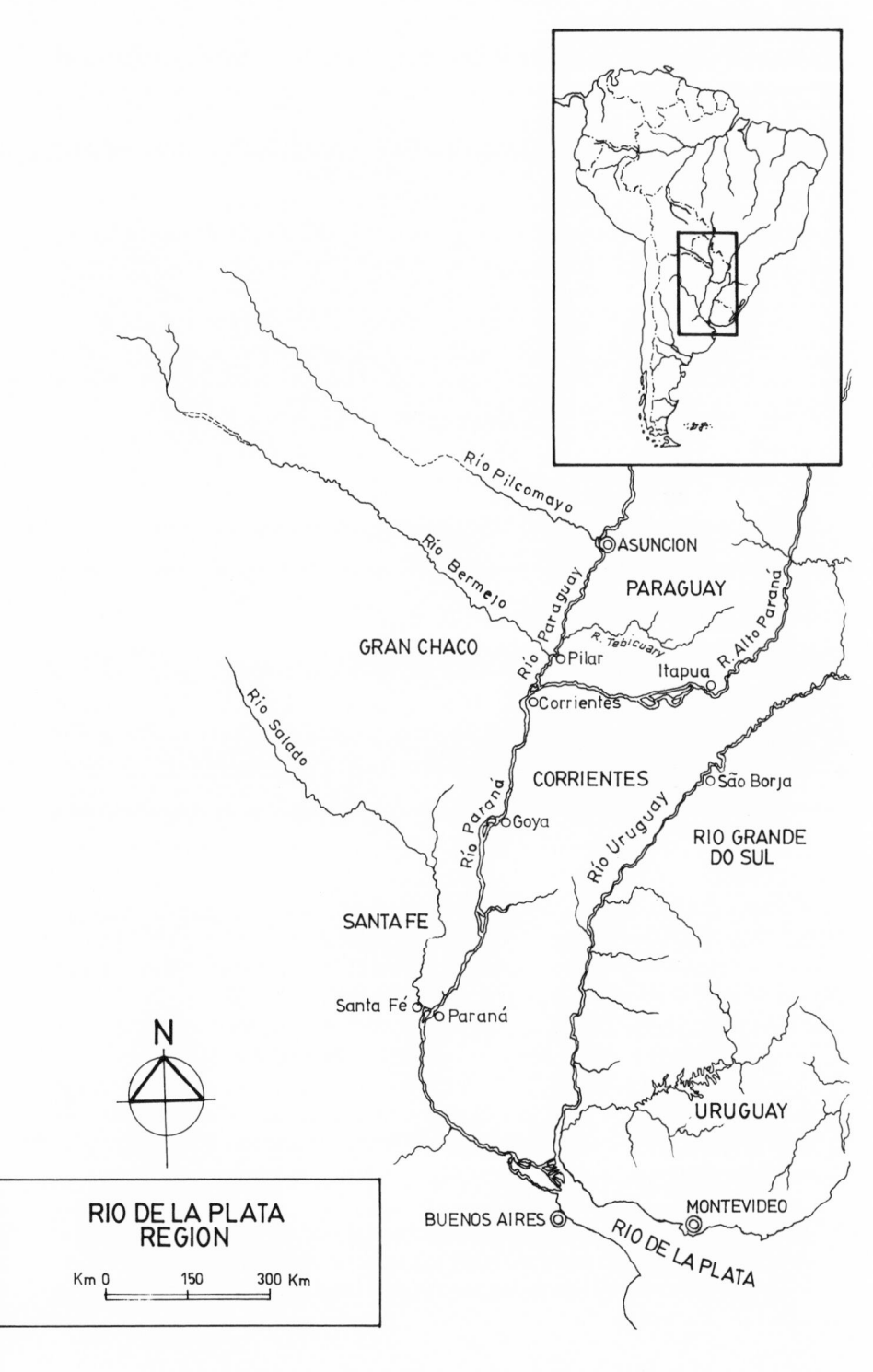

N

RIO DE LA PLATA
REGION

Km 0   150   300 Km

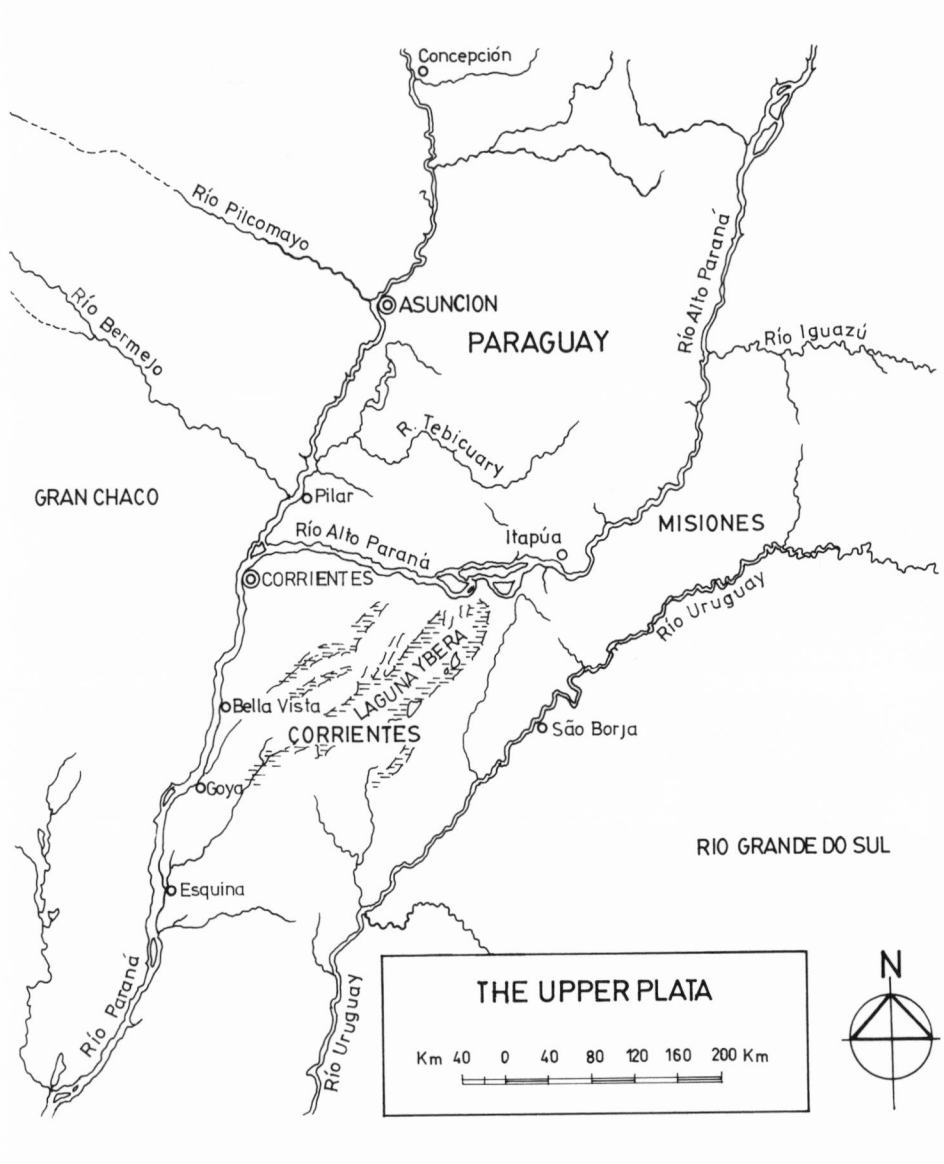

Concepción

Río Pilcomayo

Río Bermejo

ASUNCION

PARAGUAY

Río Alto Paraná

Río Iguazú

R. Tebicuary

GRAN CHACO

Pilar

Río Alto Paraná

Itapúa

MISIONES

CORRIENTES

Río Uruguay

LAGUNA YBERA

Bella Vista

CORRIENTES

São Borja

Goya

RIO GRANDE DO SUL

Esquina

Río Paraná

Río Uruguay

THE UPPER PLATA

Km 40   0   40   80   120 160 200 Km

N

from the edge of the sandstone plateau of Mato Grosso into a plain so flat that the river overflows its banks all the way to Asunción and beyond. Below Asunción, immense marshes characterize the area to the east of the river. One deep-channeled tributary, the Río Tebicuary, provides a passage through this swampland into central Paraguay.

The Paraná and Paraguay rivers combine their flow to set the annual rhythm of the Plata system. High waters rising on the Alto Paraná in January and February reach Santa Fé by early April. The Paraguay rises to its Asunción maximum in May and its flood reaches the Paraná later in that month, prolonging the autumn highwater period. During the rainy season from November to January, the flood of the Alto Paraná joins with that of the Paraguay to produce extraordinarily high waters to the south.[1]

The hydrographic features of the Río Uruguay differ markedly from those of the Paraná, the only navigational similarity being that each river has a fall barrier. In the period under discussion, the shoals of the Río Paraná at Apipé interfered little with downriver trade because the principal ports were all located well below the salto. The Uruguay, on the other hand, possessed extensive rapids at Butuí, situated between Itaqui and São Borja, and at Santa Rosa, just above the town of Salto. The succession of cascades served as a major block to early development and greatly interfered with regular river passage. They created no insurmountable problem during the rainy season, when the river was high. During the dry season, though, cargo had to be unloaded at one end of the rapids and repacked aboard another vessel on the other end, a time-consuming and expensive procedure.[2]

A peculiar feature of the Río Uruguay is the precipitous rise and fall of its waters, which influences navigation all along its course. Many of the river ports along its course were established on tributary streams to offset the effects of this fluctuation.

Social Divisions

The isolation of the Upper Plata and the relatively small number of European colonists there resulted in a thorough intermingling of Spanish and *Guaraní* Indian people by the mid-1500s. At the end of the eighteenth century, in an effort to make some sense of the results of continuing miscegenation, the viceregal government recognized six separate racial categories, each with its own socioeconomic prerogatives and responsibilities.

By far the smallest of these groupings was the white European (*peninsular*), who apparently constituted no more than 1 percent of the total population. These individuals were almost exclusively royal officials, merchants, and their families. As much as anything, they fulfilled a bureaucratic role in Upper Platine society, making the limited presence of Spain and Buenos Aires felt in a region that otherwise would have been totally isolated. They collected taxes and tithes and governed in the name of the Crown. In general, the local "whites," who made up the largest portion of the population, despised the peninsulares.

Termed *criollos* (creoles) or *españoles americanos*, the American-born whites were, in fact, more mestizo than white and numbered in the 1780s perhaps 58,000 individuals, 55 percent of the total population of Paraguay and 60 percent in Corrientes.[3] These were the ranchers and subsistence farmers of the region, frontiersmen who fended off Portuguese and Indian incursions and who kept the Upper Plata part of the Spanish realm. Some creoles held *encomienda* grants from the Crown that gave them control over Indian laborers (and technically made them responsible for Indian assimilation into colonial society). With or without an encomienda grant, however, few creoles could boast of anything more than modest material circumstances. While their agricultural efforts contributed tobacco, hides, and some cattle by-products to the external trade, in general they had little interest in outside commerce and greatly preferred their self-sufficient lifestyle to the entanglements of open relations with peoples farther to the south.

The colonial government divided the settled Indian population of the Upper Plata into three groups: *originarios, mitayos,* and *indios criollos.* Of the three, the originarios were fewest in number. These Indians resided permanently on a Spaniard's estate and were obliged to perform whatever task he set them to, whenever he wished it, without distinctions of age, sex, or other obligations. Though the legal position of these Indians closely resembled that of slaves, in fact there existed an important mitigating factor: Because they shared the same space with their overlord (*vecino feudatario*), the Indians became more Hispanicized and thus found it easy eventually to obtain a legal writ listing them as white. Also, the government invariably recognized any child born to an originaria and her Spanish master as being criollo. Because of these elements, the category of originario began to disappear in the late colonial era. There were only 753 originarios left, just 1 percent of the population of Paraguay, when the Spanish border commissioner Félix de Azara passed that way in the 1780s.[4] Official documents in Corrientes omitted the term originario, and it seems safe to say that by that time this group of Indians no longer existed south of the Alto Paraná.

The largest category of Indians (some 27,970 individuals in 1780s Paraguay) were the mitayos, who lived in outlying towns under the care of a government administrator. The mitayos can also be subdivided into three groups: those who had been under Jesuit supervision until 1767 and inhabited Misiones; those who received Franciscan tutelage in the Correntino pueblos of Itatí and Santa Lucía; and those who had been governed by Dominicans or lay clergy in nine villages of east-central Paraguay. These latter communities regularly provided labor services for outsiders or for the colonial government.

The final grouping of settled Indians, indios criollos, seems to have been a residual category of Native Americans who lived in such Spanish towns as Villarrica, Corrientes, or Asunción, but who did not live under the thumb of an *encomendero*. Presumably these individuals, who constituted around 3 percent of the population, worked as day laborers, sawyers, and sometimes stevedores.

The last official category of race mentioned in Upper Platine colonial documents is that of blacks or *pardos*. These individuals, both slave and free, were important economic actors within the urban setting. In Asunción, they even formed a majority, while for Paraguay as a whole, according to Azara, people of color made up almost 12 percent of the population (some 10,480 individuals). In Corrientes, the percentage seems to have been slightly higher.[5] Blacks acted as servants, couriers, and artisans. In the Paraguayan towns of Areguá and Tabapý, blacks were the slaves or *amparados* (slaves who could not be sold) of religious orders.

"Savage" Indian groups like the *Payaguá, Guaicurú*, and *Toba*, because they only rarely participated in the Upper Platine economy, did not figure in the colonial categorizations; they perhaps added another 20,000 to 30,000 individuals to the population of the Upper Plata as tallied by Azara. This yields a total figure of nearly 150,000 inhabitants for the entire region. This was half again higher than that of the province of Buenos Aires at roughly the same time, and gives some indication of the productive capacity of the northeastern region.

The Early Years

Settlement patterns on the Paraná-Paraguay rivers owed little to commerce in the early phases of colonization because little potential for trade existed in the Upper Plata. Before the eighteenth century, the Spanish empire regarded the whole of the Río de la Plata as peripheral, scarcely worth the funds necessary to maintain it. This meant that towns such as Corrientes, Goya, and even Asunción remained mere outposts of Spanish authority surrounded by a vast wilderness. Outside support for defense of the region proved almost nonexistent. Peasant militiamen had to furnish their own mounts and arms and even then were seldom paid for their services. Consequently, river boats in the region were forced to sail in convoys as protection against Indian canoe raids.

While the lack of adequate protection did little to foster trade, it encouraged a sense of self-reliance among the Paraguayans and Correntinos, who became accustomed to thinking of themselves as separate from the people of the lower provinces. This notion of uniqueness, reinforced by the widespread use of the Guaraní language instead of Spanish, had great consequences for the region. Though political realities never favored the creation of a single Hispano-Guaraní state in the Upper Plata, some sense of sociocultural indivisibility always pervaded life there.

The absence of precious metals in the region consigned the Upper Plata to two-hundred years of imperial neglect, during which time the regional economy hardly moved beyond a subsistence level. Barter dominated the marketplace. Wealth and social status were determined not so much by landownership as by access to Indian labor, at first through an indigenous system of reciprocal commitments, and, by the 1550s, through the encomienda. In the process, a regional elite evolved that was outwardly indistinguishable from the small farmers and ranchers. In Paraguay, this creole elite consisted of interrelated families that traced their origins to the sixteenth-century conquerors. These included the Bogarín, Yegros, Benítez, Iturbe, Cabañas Ampuero, and Montiel clans. Elite status was indicated by membership on the Asunción town council (*cabildo*), by holding a commission in the militia, or by the possession of an encomienda grant. In sparsely settled Corrientes, the situation was only slightly more fluid. Landholdings remained small in both provinces.

The peasants differed from the elite in few essentials. They married within their own caste and seldom ventured beyond the frontiers of the Upper Plata. They rarely questioned the decisions of the traditional power brokers. Men and women bred in this environment of monotony and isolation manifested strong feelings of rigidity and exclusiveness that the visits of strangers rarely affected. Yet, for all of its inbred conservatism, Upper Platine society could respond to commercial overtures when such opportunities appeared.

Cracks in the veneer of isolation first appeared in the late 1600s. The most significant element in this process was the development of an external market for yerba mate. Earlier in the century, Paraguay had exported cereals, sugar, and wine to Brazil in small quantities, but the lack of direct river routes limited trade between the two colonies.[7] Yerba provided a sounder base for growth than the other commodities, because Paraguay and the Jesuit missions had long constituted the only sources of this herb. In those areas, yerba even served as the principal medium of exchange, preferable to every commodity except coin. As the demand for yerba grew in the seventeenth century, Upper Platine producers used their monopoly position to overcome high transportation costs. The ports of Asunción, Candelaria, and Concepción had relatively easy access via the Paraná-Paraguay to the markets of Buenos Aires and Montevideo (trade in the latter market was initially far greater than in the former). The largest consumers in far-off Tucumán and Potosí were also supplied from these rivers, the yerba being transshipped through the town of Santa Fé. Between 1655 and 1675, the annual export of Upper Platine yerba soared from a scant 2,500 *arrobas* to more than 26,000.[8] The fame of the tea eventually spread to other parts of the continent until, by 1700, it gained popularity in Quito and Santiago de Chile. By then, total yerba exports from the Upper Plata had risen to 50,000 arrobas annually.[9]

Yerba maintained its preeminence in the export trade of the region until the end of the colonial era. Though yerba permitted the Upper Plata to participate in the broader economy of Spanish America, conditions for internal commerce as a whole remained poor during most of the eighteenth century. Government indifference was the chief impediment. The colonial administration of the Plata, as elsewhere in the New World, concerned itself less with the promotion of commerce than with the generation of revenues for defense.

One especially damaging feature of this short-sighted attitude was the operation of the *puerto preciso* at Santa Fé. The government had established the puerto preciso in 1662 to help the town raise funds for arms to fend off Indian attacks. Under this formulation, the Santafecinos could tax all traffic coming from Paraguay and Corrientes. They could also force the sale of Upper Platine goods at market prices in Santa Fé, even if the goods were destined for Buenos Aires. From the viewpoint of the Upper Plata, the puerto preciso was emblematic of Spain's indifference. What had been a stopgap measure to underwrite frontier defense remained on the books long after the Indian menace subsided, without serious consideration of the commercial consequences. Under this burden, little incentive existed for anything more than periodic trade between the Upper Plata and Las Conchas, a landing point near the northern edge of Buenos Aires. Certain merchants, especially in the port city, realized that substantial profits could be made from direct trade with Corrientes and Paraguay, but they made little headway in pressing their case with colonial authorities.[10]

The Viceregal Period

The government enacted few economic and administrative reforms before 1776, when the Crown, as part of a larger Bourbon reform movement, ordained the creation of the viceroyalty of La Plata. Previously, all Spanish territories in South America, from Panama to Patagonia, were linked within the massive viceroyalty of Peru, which had its administrative hub at Lima. The economic center of this old subdivision was the vast silver complex of Potosí in Upper Peru. This massive enterprise involved not just the mining and processing of ore but also transport and provisioning of miners. Provisioning brought Potosí into regular contact with many parts of the Plata, and from these connections grew an illegal traffic in silver, wine, mules, and other trade goods. The authorities were unable to stem this flow of contraband. In time the Crown, faced with the drain of silver eastward from Potosí and the consequent loss of revenue, accepted the inevitable and gave permission for individual shipments of imports from Montevideo and Buenos Aires to Upper Peru and for the export of silver that had paid the royal fifth, the Crown-assessed tax on silver. Then followed the establishment of the Platine viceroyalty, which included Potosí within its boundaries. The creation of this administrative unit signaled Spain's recognition of economic potential in a hitherto ignored part of the empire as well as the government's willingness to defend that region against foreign encroachment. It also signalled the emergence of Buenos Aires as the Plata's chief emporium, the focus for the modernization of the entire region (this despite the superiority of Montevideo's port). Buenos Aires henceforth acted as a catalyst in the economic transformation of Corrientes and Paraguay.

Other shifts in colonial commerce confirmed Buenos Aires as the principal market of southern South America. One contributing element in this regard was the adoption in 1778 of *comercio libre* as the linchpin of imperial trade. Not to be confused with the free trade of later years, the policy of comercio libre was designed to garner revenues for Madrid, not so much through new taxation as through an increased total volume of transactions with the colonies. The new policy aided commerce by streamlining taxation, by ending the strict licensing system of the past, and by allowing direct and unfettered trade between different regions of the empire. This last was particularly significant for the Upper Plata, because it made it easier for northern merchants to respond to growing external demand for their exports. In 1780, the puerto preciso of Santa Fé was abolished, eliminating the last obstacle to open trade on the rivers.

Certain commodities, such as timber, hides, and, of course, yerba, responded in dramatic fashion. The quantity of Upper Platine yerba to reach Buenos Aires in 1781 amounted to 114,000 arrobas. Eight years later the figure had risen to 188,215 arrobas.[11] Not only did the traditional sources of yerba production in Paraguay grow to meet the new demand, but the Guaraní towns of the Misiones area, under secular administration after 150 years of Jesuit rule, rapidly abandoned their subsistence economy in favor of an outward-oriented yerba commerce.

Within the Upper Plata, the new trade was largely confined to the ports of Asunción, Corrientes, and Concepción, the latter being important only as a transit point for yerba. Candelaria, the Jesuit port on the Alto Paraná, lost significance after the 1767 expulsion of the Jesuits and, as the Indian population fell, became increasingly less important to Misiones exports.

Asunción was the principal port of Paraguay. Located at a protected bend of the Río Paraguay near its confluence with the Pilcomayo, the town also was the oldest Spanish outpost in the region, having been founded in 1537. In 1782, it possessed only around 5,000 inhabitants, of whom 2,703 were blacks, both slave and free.[12] Only eleven years later, the population had grown to 7,088, doubtless the result of internal migration stimulated by rising commercial prosperity.[13] Trade there was apparently brisk; in 1798, yerba exports from the port of Asunción alone amounted to over 200,000 arrobas.[14]

Although the commerce of the Paraguayan capital was impressive, Asunción remained a rustic community. The government buildings were simple affairs, fashioned from adobe bricks and reinforced with heavy wooden beams. Stone was rarely used as a construction material. Unlike most Spanish American towns, Asunción was not organized on a grid pattern. Its unpaved streets ran in an erratic fashion from a central plaza dominated by the cabildo offices, the small cathedral, and the government house. Wharves and other port facilities were temporary constructions in the beginning, built from whatever wood was readily available. Given the sandbars and the river's periodic flooding, permanent docks seemed impractical to the Asunceños. Workers ferried freight to the shoreline in tiny skiffs or rafts. Indian *peones* or black slaves would then transport goods by oxcart to the customs house to be weighed and taxed, and from there shipments were sent on to the marketplace, warehouse, or residence of the consignee. Except for contraband, which was loaded secretly onto ships passing at some distance from the town, all Upper Platine river traffic was handled in this routine manner.

Unlike Asunción, the small northern port of Concepción was of recent foundation. Established in 1773 as a bulwark against Portuguese incursions into the area, Concepción stood on a plain twenty feet above the riverbank. In 1793, the population of the town numbered 1,551, the majority of whom were involved in the yerba commerce.[15] Concepción was situated at the terminus of trails leading eastward into the yerba forests (*yerbales*) and, as a consequence, was the first link in a long chain of production and consumption leading to Buenos Aires and beyond. Because the local yerba workers (*yerbateros* or *yerberos*) required meat for sustenance and hides for packing, settlers brought large herds of livestock to Concepción in the 1780s. There the animals thrived, and soon that port also began to export hides.

The town of Corrientes sat high on a bluff just below the point where the Alto Paraná and Paraguay rivers join to form the Paraná. The elevation of the town above the riverbank gave it an aspect different from that of either Asunción or Concepción. Unlike Asunción, Corrientes had streets regularly arranged, though unkempt and muddy. Its few public buildings were modest even by Upper Platine standards. The single exception was the former school of the Jesuits, a sturdy, tile-roofed building with two interior patios. After 1772, the building housed the office of the cabildo, the royal tobacco monopoly (estanco), the treasury and post office in addition to a primary school.[16]

The port of Corrientes also differed from that of Asunción. A broad, baylike formation at Asunción shielded the docking area from the swift current of the Paraguay's main channel. The port of Corrientes, on the other hand, was formed simply by the natural bank of the river. This lack of protection posed no problem for commercial traffic, however, because the anchorage permitted a close approach to the riverbank, where vessels were free from the currents. Though temporary wharves were present during the 1700s, the process of unloading merchant ships at Corrientes was still commonly accomplished by canoes.[17] The port suffered from its lack of a decent pier, adequate retaining walls, and sufficient space in its few warehouses. As for population, Corrientes paralleled the patterns of composition seen elsewhere in the Upper Plata. The total number of inhabitants—Indians, blacks, mestizos, and whites—was 4,500 in 1793.[18]

These three sites provided the Upper Plata with its main trade centers during late colonial times. Merchant groups composed of Basque and Catalan immigrants congregated at these points, transforming the sleepy backwaters into bustling communities.

The peninsular merchants made up a new kind of elite, one with liquid capital and access to government patronage. As a group, they were only moderately well-read, though some had absorbed the mercantilist writings of the Spanish thinker Gerónimo de Uztáriz, as well as the physiocratic doctrines of the French philosophes. As most had spent some time in Buenos Aires, Montevideo, and other areas of Spanish America, they intimately understood the conditions under which they labored. Above all else, they were willing to take risks. Every aspect of Upper Platine trade depended upon extension of credit to customers large and small, and this left merchants in a knotty position as both creditors and debtors. Nonetheless, they sometimes made sizable fortunes.

The most successful among them was Joseph Coene of Ghent, a man who had spent over a decade in South America before the establishment of the viceroyalty. He, wisely, married into the traditional Paraguayan elite and was granted an encomienda of Indians. Coene operated one of the largest commercial houses in Asunción; he handled wine, perfume, and other luxury items and exported yerba and tobacco on his own account to the lower provinces. Having reached the ripe age of sixty-five in 1804, Coene made an official accounting of his possessions, which included "three ranches stocked with cattle, a house, a farm, a ship currently in commerce to Buenos Aires, and forty odd slaves."[19] He bequeathed his business acumen to his son Manuel, who also distinguished himself as a militia commander in the 1790s. Coene's granddaughter Josefa married Fernando de la Mora, another member of the creole elite and a major figure in the Paraguayan independence struggle.[20]

Coene's career was exceptional among merchants in the Upper Plata. More commonly, they failed to bridge the obvious social gap between themselves and the old elite. The influence of the newcomers derived from their prominent place in the structure of commerce, yet, paradoxically, this proved their greatest weakness. Because the power of the merchants rested on a specific pattern of trade with the viceregal capital, they had little to fall back on once that pattern was disrupted. Further, as so many of the merchants were foreign-born, they could claim no long-term commitment to regional interests but only to their own narrowly conceived commercial interests. This ultimately made them easy targets for their political opponents in the post-independence era.

The merchants counted among their adversaries not only many small ranchers and farmers, but some members of the old creole elite as well. I must avoid positing too much enmity, however, between the old elite and the merchant groups, because the two did not necessarily stand in opposition. Some individuals born into the traditional order benefitted tremendously from the new mercantile connection by diversifying their economic activities, buying land, and investing heavily in the yerba trade. Other creoles proved unable to adapt to the changed circumstances or were simply less fortunate. They feared the merchants, suspecting that the traders would undercut their authority in the Upper Plata.

The struggle between peninsular merchants and the long-established creoles for political ascendancy was counterproductive for both groups. On some issues, such as the desire for open trade, the two shared a common outlook, but competition arose regarding political power in the region. The merchants tacitly acknowledged the authority of Buenos Aires in its dealings with the interior provinces and tended to regard the locals as poor cousins. For their part, the Upper Platine creoles resented the prominence of the merchants in the regional economy and especially their influence with Crown officials. This competition kept the two dominant groups of the Upper Plata effectively divided, and led, after independence, to a major political confrontation, into which moved the imposing figure of José Gaspar de Francia.

As we have seen, the liberalization of trade along the rivers gave great impetus to Upper Platine exports beginning in the 1780s. Table 1.1 reveals a far wider variety of exports from Asunción during these years than was the case earlier in the century. In the late 1740s, for instance, the only commodity regularly exported from the Paraguayan capital was yerba—around 40,000 arrobas a year in this period.[21] Forty years later, Asunceño yerba exports had shot up to more than 195,000 arrobas a year, most of which earned twice its local value in Buenos Aires, where yerba sold for three pesos the arroba. The Paraguayan export market had also diversified to include rope, sugar, sweets, cotton, hides, tobacco, salt, *aguardiente*, and all kinds of wood products. The trade earned Paraguay nearly 172,000 pesos a year, an impressive enough return, but this was only a fraction of what it might have been had the commercial infrastructure been more flexible.

The same trade pattern continued into the new century. A fairly complete listing of exports exists for 1800. As one might expect, yerba predominated, with some 218,000 arrobas being dispatched in that year. The 1800 totals also recorded 16,000 arrobas of tanbark, 1,576 of sugar, 1,432 of honey, 1,264 of sweets, and small quantities of wood, hides, oranges, salt, crockery, and starch.[22] As tobacco was a royal monopoly, licenses (*guías*) were not issued for its sale outside Paraguay, so it was excluded from the computations. Perhaps as much as 18,000 arrobas of tobacco, including cigars, was legally shipped from Paraguay at this time.[23]

A similar upturn in trade occurred in Corrientes. Records indicate that an average of forty merchant ships a year left Corrientes for ports in the lower provinces between 1792 and 1797. These vessels carried cargoes of hides, cotton, woods, honey and other foodstuffs. Tanbark, from which was extracted tannic acid for use in leather curing, became a major export of Corrientes. It proved so popular in Buenos Aires tanneries (*curtidurías*) that in 1797 alone nearly 20,000 arrobas were received from the province.[24]

The import picture was more varied, with British and Dutch woolens, Cordoban ponchos, Spanish wines, perfumes, and iron goods heading the list of items shipped into the Upper Plata. Merchants regularly used invoices and letters of credit (*facturas* and *libranzas*) to facilitate the sale of these goods in Corrientes and Asunción. They considered a markup of 20 to 80 percent normal. When overstocking periodically occurred, however, the merchants had to cut their prices drastically, thereby losing much of their investment. Even in the best of times, such an import market was risky. Credit and the trust born of kinship and social ties could not easily overcome the uncertainty of commerce. The economic growth in the region, though real enough, was decidedly fragile.

Traders in the Upper Plata nonetheless considered the first decade of

TABLE 1.1: Average Yearly Exports of Asunción, 1788–92

Item	Quantity	Price (in *reales* or *peso*)	Value
Yerba	195,102 arrobas	12 r./arroba	292,653 pesos
Tirantes (tie beams)	17,890 varas	7 r./vara	15,653 pesos
Vigas (beams)	1,746 varas	12 r./vara	2,619 pesos
Trozos (logs)	7,299 varas	21 r./vara	20,997 pesos
Rollizos of petereby (logs for masts)	30	10 r.	37 pesos
Masts for ships	1	50 p.	50 pesos
Yards for masts	1	11.5 p.	11 pesos
Tablones of lapacho	187 varas	6 r./vara	140 pesos
id. of cedar	1,829 varas	4 r./vara	914 pesos
id. of yvyraró	93 varas	8 r./vara	93 pesos
Tablas	37 varas	8 r./vara	93 pesos
Atravesaños (cross timbers)	23	6.5 r.	20 pesos
Ship *ligazones* (futtocks)	34	4 p.	136 pesos
Carts	9	40 p.	360 pesos
Cartwheel hubs	300	5 p.	1,500 pesos
Cartwheel axles	164	2 p.	328 pesos
Cartwheel pieces	25	2 p.	50 pesos
Cartwheel spokes	30	1 p.	30 pesos
Palm logs	4,187	6 r.	3,140 pesos
Bamboo	862	3 r.	325 pesos
Canoe paddles	2	4 r.	1 pesos
Tables	2	20 p.	40 pesos
Chairs and stools	36	10 p.	360 pesos
Desks	2	40 p.	80 pesos
Fine boxes for needlework	2	10 p.	20 pesos
Towropes	2	40 p.	40 pesos
Sugar	441 arrobas	4 p./arroba	1,764 pesos
Honey	1,397 arrobas	12 r./arroba	2,095 pesos
Sweets	157 arrobas	3 p./arroba	471 pesos
Starch	39 arrobas	3 p./arroba	117 pesos
Salt	1,262 arrobas	8 r./arroba	1,262 pesos
Clay jars	184	2 p.	368 pesos
Linen	1,534 arrobas	8 r./vara	479 pesos
Cotton	3,328 arrobas	12 r./arroba	4,992 pesos
Hides	201	12 r.	301 pesos
Aguardiente	2 barrels	22 p./barrel	44 pesos
Wax	3 arrobas	6 p./arroba	18 pesos
Whetstones	3	3 p.	9 pesos

(continued)

TABLE 1.1: Average Yearly Exports of Asunción, 1788–92 *(continued)*

Item	Quantity	Price (in *reales* or *peso*)	Value
Tobacco (royal monopoly)	n/a	n/a	47,773 pesos
Total			395,018 pesos
Costs			
11 percent due to commissions, *alcabalas*, *mermas*, *almacenes*, and import fees from Las Conchas to Buenos Aires			43,761 pesos
Handling			24,000 pesos
Total costs			67,461 pesos
Net value of exports			327,646 pesos
Value of imports			155,903 pesos
Difference			171,743 pesos

Source: Azara, *Descripción e historia del Paraguay*, 1:313–14.

the new century a time of great opportunity. Demand for northeastern commodities had risen steadily in Buenos Aires, and credit flowed liberally into the north to underwrite ever-bigger ventures. The Napoleonic wars had opened the viceregal capital to neutral shipping. A heavy volume of trading ensued. The situation grew rosier still when the British invaded Buenos Aires in 1806 and gave the port city a taste of free trade for the first time.

With Buenos Aires as much a part of the Atlantic economy as any European port, the complete commercial integration of the Upper Plata with the rest of the viceroyalty became a reality. Even earlier, as a result of the monopolistic policies of the royal tobacco estanco in the 1790s, specie had become an important part of the economic life of the region. In some locales, coin took on the quality of a fetish. Peasants, who had until recently been outside the market economy, now demanded coin in exchange for goods and services.[25] They much preferred cash to payments in yerba, which, after all, easily rotted in the tropical sun. Men and women began to operate retail shops out of their homes in some of the most remote villages. The eagerness with which many peasants embraced the cash nexus supports the idea that, even in the Upper Plata, the *mentalité* of the marketplace was never far removed from people's thoughts.

Everyone understood that the key to regional development was Buenos Aires. Though small by European standards, the Porteño market effectively encouraged modernization in the riverine or Litoral provinces by absorbing the greatest share of Upper Platine exports. Porteño merchants and moneylenders were well aware of their pivotal role in this trade and acted accordingly. Profits from yerba were so high that the

Buenos Aires *consulado* and the viceroy thought it advisable in 1806 to appoint a representative of that guild to faraway Concepción.

At about this time, Spanish officials first reported some contraband dealings in hides and tallow at a small *estancia* fifty-two leagues below Corrientes at the confluence of the Río Paraná and Riacho de Goya. From these obscure beginnings, the village of Goya was born and quickly evolved into the principal commercial center of southern Corrientes.[26]

All these developments served to nudge the Upper Plata out of its isolation. A Bourbon administration keenly interested in the expansion of trade had replaced the indifference of earlier days. Commercial linkages, both legal and contraband, began to knit the region together and ensure the inflow of profits.

Economic development carried a price, however. I have already mentioned the frustrations felt by the creole elites; their tribulations and anger were matched by those of the smallholders (*chacreros*) who found a "boom" mentality as upsetting as it was attractive. Though they could obtain an array of costly luxury items hitherto unavailable, the Upper Platine peasants often had to abandon much of what had been socially meaningful to them. Young men worked seven months of the year in the yerbales, far from family and the stabilizing effect of the community. The Indian populations in particular displayed a reluctance to sacrifice their precapitalist way of life to the uncertainty of the market economy. Thus, despite the fact that they shared in the overall material gain, many people in the Upper Plata were uncomfortable in their newfound economic role.

An outward-oriented development also involved obvious asymmetries with the lower provinces. The Upper Plata exercised only minimal influence over the terms of the river trade. As a prime example, in the last years before independence, the traders of Asunción attempted to raise the price of their exports and to create a legal monopoly over yerba similar to the tobacco estanco. By this means, the Asunceño merchants hoped to displace the growing influence of yerba speculators in Concepción as well as garner new profits at the expense of Porteño consumers. The viceregal government, pressured by the consulado of Buenos Aires, rejected this plan, and all the efforts of the Paraguayans in this matter went unfulfilled.[27]

The Porteños had the viceroy's ear, as well as the trading capital, and whether it was a question of yerba pricing or the admittance of foreign traders onto the interior rivers, the merchants of Buenos Aires always carried more weight with the authorities than those of the Upper Plata. This circumstance annoyed all segments of northeastern society, not just the merchants, and contributed to an already deeply felt suspicion and jealousy of the port city. The politico-economic rivalries so often associated with the early national era were thus present in every sense during the final decades of the colonial period.

Independence

The 1810s found the merchants of Asunción mired in problems caused by their own success. Their frustration at the hands of bureaucrats in Buenos Aires was already much in evidence; with independence, they also felt the full brunt of long-standing resentment from the creole elite. Animosity focused not only on the merchants but on their local allies (mostly petty bureaucrats associated with the trade) and on the Porteño connection generally. The merchants wielded an important measure of authority in the Upper Plata while the Paraguay and Paraná rivers were open. With the closure of the rivers, however, first by royalist warships from Montevideo, and then by the troops of the *gaucho* chieftain José Gervasio Artigas (1764–1850), the activities and influence of the merchants began to wane. Yerba, tobacco, and other produce rotted on the wharves of Upper Platine ports after 1816 because safe transport to Buenos Aires proved next to impossible during the civil war that engulfed the vital river routes to the south. The Asunceño merchants faced commercial disruption from without and political opposition from within. Thus, even at this early stage, politics constrained development in the Upper Plata.

In 1810–1811, Buenos Aires and the Upper Plata had a foretaste of the difficulties that would haunt them for the next forty years. When the cabildo of Buenos Aires renounced the regency of Cádiz in May, and in effect separated from the Spanish empire, the Upper Plata responded in a hesitant manner. News of the Porteño move for independence came in June when emissaries of the new government of Buenos Aires arrived with a plea that the region recognize its authority. Corrientes, through its cabildo, approved this appeal almost immediately. The merchants and ranchers who controlled the cabildo clearly hoped that their acquiescence would safeguard the status quo. Corrientes had always been labor-poor and could only generate a small export economy. Correntino commerce depended on the province's status as a transit point for Paraguayan tobacco and yerba. If this Carrera del Paraguay commerce (as it was called) was to be maintained, a regime friendly to Porteño interests had to be established in Asunción. If such a government could not be immediately created, then surely, the Porteños reasoned, Paraguayan resistance would last only a matter of months.

Events did not come to pass in this manner. The Paraguayan cabildo, hoping to avoid conflict with both Spaniard and Porteño, declared for fidelity to the regency and for good relations with Buenos Aires. The Porteños promptly rejected this legalistic sleight of hand and made preparations to compel the Paraguayans. A military force under Manuel Belgrano pressed northward from Buenos Aires and crossed the Alto Paraná at Itapúa in late December of 1810. The overconfident Belgrano, though, met two successive defeats and was forced to withdraw in March 1811. The Paraguayans established an independent state a few months later.

A militia commanded by members of the creole elite had defeated Belgrano, but these men did not favor the Spaniards and the colonial system per se. Instead, they feared that domination by Buenos Aires would mean their extinction as a political force in the region. In ensuing years, they rarely deviated from this position, and usually supported any regime that promised them control over their affairs in the countryside.

The failure of the Belgrano expedition did not signal the end of Porteño attempts to court or compel Paraguayan support. After the new government came to power in Asunción, it tried to accommodate the Porteños. An agreement was signed in October between Buenos Aires and Paraguay that bound the two in an alliance against the royalists, yet left the issue of political unification unsettled. The first article of the treaty abolished the tobacco monopoly and noted that Paraguay would sell the tobacco then held by the treasury in order to finance a defense against the "machinations of all interior and exterior enemies of our system."[28]

The second article provided that taxes on Paraguayan yerba formerly levied in Buenos Aires would henceforth be levied in Asunción, with the proceeds to be used for the general welfare of the province of Paraguay. The port city was allowed a moderate impost on the introduction of Paraguayan commodities only when urgent necessity required.

Article three also dealt with trade matters. This measure stressed that the sales tax (*alcabala*) would be levied only in the city of final sale, be that Asunción or Buenos Aires. Under normal circumstances, such a reform would have vastly facilitated the exchange of goods along the rivers.

Several articles on boundaries and other outstanding issues were appended to these three, together with a separate clause, apparently added later, that stated:

> The most excellent junta of Buenos Aires may establish some moderate impost in case of urgency on the introduction of the fruits of this province of Paraguay in Buenos Aires. . . . this imposition should be one and one-half real a *tercio* of yerba and another real and one-half an arroba of tobacco, and no more, until in the General Congress of the Provinces, without prejudice to Paraguay, this imposition is modified.[29]

The October treaty was little more than a truce. The document assured Paraguay a more equitable commerce with the lower provinces and gave Paraguayans semiofficial recognition of their independence. In return, the Porteños forged a temporary military alliance on terms so nebulous that the Paraguayans never had to provide much service or matériel. The treaty had little effect on trade because political circumstances ultimately did not permit it. Indeed, the Porteños soon attempted to regain all that had been conceded to Paraguay in the October agreement. Within a year, when the fortunes of Buenos Aires had improved, the port city tried to reassert its authority over Paraguay through economic and diplomatic pressure.

In pursuing this end, the Porteños could count on the help of officials in Corrientes and the lower provinces, who were instrumental in interfering with Paraguayan shipping on the Río Paraná. This led the Asunción *junta* in January 1812 to address a sharp note to Elías Galván (1774–1843), the popular governor of Corrientes, demanding that he immediately release several Paraguayan merchant vessels then being held in the port of Corrientes. The official reason for their detention was the presence of Spanish raiders on the river.[30] Forays by the royalists proved very much a part of the commercial scene in the Upper Plata at this time, and the Paraguayan junta on several occasions had to order ships to port to prevent their capture by the Spaniards. Corrientes, however, also suffered from Paraguayan competition, and Galván, himself a Porteño, thought he had good reason to adopt a policy of harassment against Paraguay. He did not hesitate to use what leverage he had. The Upper Plata had divided into separate and mutually antagonistic entities only two years after independence.

Santa Fé was another irritant to Paraguayan trade. Santafecino authorities wrote the treasury minister of Corrientes in February 1812 to inform him that they had detained a shipment of Paraguayan yerba because its transporters had not paid the alcabala at "the approved (rate) of twelve pesos the arroba."[31] The Santafecinos knew that the October treaty precluded alcabala payments except in the city of final sale, and that the rates, even during emergencies, were to be moderate. Twelve pesos the arroba was sheer extortion, since the yerba could not have been worth more than four.

Such incidents strained trade relations on the Paraná-Paraguay rivers. The Paraguayans usually blamed the Porteños for the contrary attitude of governments in intermediate provinces even when they were not, in fact, at fault. The Portuguese in Brazil took advantage of the troubles within the former Spanish possessions and began to push their own claims all along the frontier. At one point, they seized and temporarily occupied the Paraguayan outpost of Borbón, high on the Río Paraguay just south of Mato Grosso.[32] The Indians of the Chaco to the west took advantage of the confusion in the Upper Plata and attacked Paraguayan and Correntino settlements with impunity.

In an effort to find any friend amidst so many enemies, the junta of Paraguay reluctantly opened negotiations with Artigas, whose troops had already occupied parts of Corrientes, Misiones, Entre Ríos, and the Banda Oriental (as Uruguay was initially called). Unfortunately, Buenos Aires regarded these diplomatic overtures as an affront to its own authority in the anti-Spanish struggle. Relations between the Paraguayans and Artigas never amounted to much (the former were only interested in keeping the rivers open), but for the Porteños, the attempt at detente smacked of Paraguayan disloyalty.[33]

To force the issue, in September 1812, the Porteños decreed a double duty (three pesos an arroba) on Paraguayan tobacco and, to give their point emphasis, they also established a customs post at the port of Corrientes.[34] The 1811 treaty clearly forbade such elevated duties, but the Porteños felt justified in employing any means to reestablish their control over Paraguay.

Those opposed to Buenos Aires found their champion in José Gaspar de Francia (1766–1840), perhaps the most singular figure in the history of the region. Francia, himself a member of the creole elite and the son of a foreigner, was nearly fifty years old at the time of independence and had lived through all the changes that the Upper Plata had undergone since the 1780s. Trained as a doctor of theology at the University of Córdoba, he had returned to Paraguay to practice law. He brought with him a reputation for honesty and a visceral contempt for the Porteños, many of whom had purchased high positions in the university. Though his cold, publicly acknowledged deism gave him a gloomy outlook on life, he nonetheless possessed an appetite for hard work, which in turn brought him material success. By 1811, Francia already enjoyed the support of many in the *campo*, peasants and chacreros alike. Their suspicion of outside influences closely paralleled his own, and he was able to take advantage of this, first to isolate and then to destroy his adversaries.

The uncertain months during the first year of independence gave Francia the opportunity he needed, since, as one of the few educated men in Paraguay, his presence in the new government was almost universally deemed necessary. His skillful political maneuvering as a member of the first junta left the pro-Porteño faction in disarray. Francia then resigned and withdrew to the countryside, where he spent time making contacts with ranchers, Indian representatives, and all who might increase his base of support. He ignored the merchants and the few large landowners and, in so doing, made determined enemies in both camps. Francia's calculations were just as determined, however, and in the end, he made sure that Paraguay's future would be defined not by interelite rivalries but by his fiat alone.

The 1812 impasse with Buenos Aires settled the issue once and for all. Fernando de la Mora, the only remaining proponent of compromise on the Paraguayan junta, was forced to resign. (He later died in prison.) Francia had busily fomented discord in the rural areas, and he and his supporters were about to reap their reward. An unconditional separation from Buenos Aires had long been their goal, and since that situation now presented itself on a de facto basis, they sought to make it de jure as well. In November 1812, the two junta members then in Asunción bowed to public pressure and begged Francia to come back into the government. Francia set some high conditions: A batallion of infantry responsible only to him was created; he appointed all its officers; and he received one-half of the province's munitions. More important still, Francia received a virtual veto over future junta decisions: "No order or action will come from the government without being signed by the three individuals [i.e., junta members Fulgencio Yegros, Pedro Juan Caballero, and Francia] who contract this agreement."[35]

Although the establishment of Francia's supreme dictatorship was still nearly two years away, for all intents and purposes he had already assumed control. In September 1813, a special congress convened in Asunción to decide the character of the Paraguayan state. Dominated as it was by Francia's rural partisans, not surprisingly, the doctor of theology won the day. Francia became Consul of the Republic in association with Fulgencio Yegros. The same congress gave official sanction to the rupture with Buenos Aires. Francia's support within Paraguay remained solid and, in 1814, another congress elected him Dictator for five years. Two years later, he was named Dictator for life.

The onset of Francia's Perpetual Dictatorship in 1816 marked the end of easy commercial entry into the Upper Plata. Trade had proved difficult for several years, and though there would be some bright spots to come, in general, the days of open trade were over. The viceroyalty had brought hope for a large export economy, but the collapse of overall authority, together with credit structures and legal bureaucracies, had stripped away optimism along the rivers. Commercial prospects, in consequence, remained difficult to gauge and even more difficult to act upon. Many foreign-born merchants abandoned the Upper Plata entirely at this time and took up residence in the lower provinces. Others left for their ranches and *chacras* in the countryside, where they hoped to seclude themselves and wait for better times. Some reappeared many years later when the opening of the Paraná and Paraguay rivers again promised a trade boom.

In the short period since independence, the Upper Platine regimes had tried without much success to maintain the earlier levels of trade. The new governments understood that commercial decline also meant a decline in state revenues. They were at pains, therefore, to limit the damage, and even attempted to attract new trade to the region, much as Buenos Aires had succeeded in doing. A few of the old peninsular merchants, such as Andrés García Viñan, Emeterio Velilla, and Cayetano Yturburu, managed to weather the storm in the Upper Plata, though they found it increasingly difficult to keep alive the former lines of credit. One merchant of the older generation, José Tomás Ysasi, made himself commercial agent for the Paraguayan government and prospered as a result. His good fortune was short-lived, however; when Francia discovered in the mid-1820s that Ysasi had smuggled a massive quantity of coin out of the country, he placed a price on the merchant's head. Ysasi escaped the Dictator's fury by staying in Buenos Aires.

Ysasi was an exception. Few of the old traders retained sufficient cash to stay in business. An infusion of outside capital was necessary for economic development, but the old sources had none to give. The arrival of European merchants—mostly Britons and Italians—promised some relief in the form of new commercial contacts in Buenos Aires and perhaps even in the Atlantic trade. Such contacts, however, were fraught with risks for the European merchants. The Upper Plata was not easily reintegrated into the global market. John Parish Robertson provides a case in point.

Robertson, a young Scots entrepreneur, first visited the Río de la Plata in 1807 in the wake of the British invasions. After a number of adventures in Brazil and Buenos Aires, he made his way to Paraguay in December 1811, and there disposed of a large consignment of merchandise. Though not yet twenty years old, he immediately parlayed the earnings from this first sale into a large Paraguayan venture that included commission agents, retail shops, several warehouses, and a number of ships that regularly made the passage between Asunción and Buenos Aires.

At first regarded with apprehension, Robertson soon won the trust of Paraguayan officials, who gave him a free hand in the province. Even Francia was impressed. The Scotsman had seemingly rejuvenated the river trade by sealing commercial alliances with other British merchants in the lower provinces and by indirectly employing hundreds of workers in Paraguay. If later transactions, when 200 pesos worth of salt in Buenos Aires sold for 4,000 pesos in Asunción, are any guide, his earnings must have been substantial. His younger brother, William, arrived from Scotland to join him in 1814, and together they looked to still greater profits.[36]

The Robertson brothers were not magicians, however, and in the end, they took too many risks in Paraguay. Having promised the Dictator a precious cargo of arms, they did nothing to discourage his naive belief that commercial relations and perhaps recognition would be forthcoming from Britain. At the very least, Francia felt, the Robertsons should be able to arrange that Paraguayan river traffic be cloaked in the Union Jack. To this end, in 1814, he gave John Parish Robertson specimens of yerba, tobacco, sugar, and cloth, and ordered him to present them at the bar of the House of Commons and announce that Paraguay wished to sign a treaty of commerce and alliance.[37] The elder Robertson, who failed to take Francia's commission seriously, got no farther than Buenos Aires, and on his way back lost his cargo of arms and almost his life at the hands of the Artiguistas. Upon his empty-handed arrival in Asunción, he also lost the confidence of Francia. Peremptorily expelled, he took up residence in Corrientes. There he was joined by William, who brought with him what they had salvaged from the Paraguayan venture.

After the departure of the Robertsons, the curtain began to fall on Paraguay's trade. Total Paraguayan exports fell in value from 391,233 pesos in 1816 to 291,564 pesos in 1818, to 191,852 pesos in 1819, and then to a mere 57,498 pesos in 1820. Likewise, imports, as reflected in duty registers, fell from 83,640 pesos in 1816 to 58,480 pesos in 1818, and to 42,643 pesos in 1819. They rose to 69,647 pesos the next year owing to a brief lifting of the blockade against Paraguay, but in 1821 resumed their downward spiral to 44,346 pesos, finally reaching a low point of 4,824 pesos in 1822.[38]

The decline in Paraguay's export trade resulted primarily from political disorders in the lower provinces. Porteño and Artiguista intransigence made passage from Asunción next to impossible into the early 1820s. Another factor also contributed to the commercial decline: Francia's elaboration of a policy that closed Paraguay to almost all outside trade.

Despite claims in the dependency literature that Francia was a revolutionary, his thinking was fundamentally conservative. Like any absolutist in the Bourbon mold, he regarded trade, and all other economic activities, as subordinate to one paramount political goal: the enhancement of state power vis-à-vis internal classes and other competing states. This mercantilist stance stressed political consolidation over economic growth. Merchants were still regarded as outsiders in Paraguay, as powerful men with contacts in Buenos Aires, and therefore automatically suspect in Francia's eyes. In order to assure the survival of his regime, the Supreme Dictator drove most of them from Asunción, even though this resulted in a major loss in revenues earned on commerce. As J. P. Robertson, who doubtlessly overstated the case, explained:

> On some frivolous pretext he would declare the port of
> Assumption to be rigorously shut, and all active trade was
> immediately paralyzed. With as little ostensible cause he would,

after a season, open the ports. Then all were on the alert to load their vessels, and get off their produce to their different markets. But again, just perhaps as the first vessel was ready to sail, down would come a fresh order to shut the ports, the vessels were to be unloaded, heavy expenses incurred; and the produce, instead of rewarding the merchant for his capital employed, and risk ruin in supplying the republic with its wants, was remanded to his warehouses, there to deteriorate in value and perhaps to be altogether lost.[39]

As subsequent events were to show, Francia had no desire to see the total collapse of commerce. Rather, he wished to subject this diminishing trade to controls that would exact maximum revenues while simultaneously displacing potential opponents. He realized that this stance involved certain contradictions, but he willingly paid the price for political unity. Within these limits, he sought every fee, toll, and duty owed his government. This fiscal orientation was evident in his strict system of licensing (another remnant of the colonial era), his careful policing of the port district, and his overtly mercantilist prohibition on specie exports.[40] To be sure, he was never able to totally suppress the clandestine export of coin and other contraband, but like an efficient colonial governor, he did his best to stamp it out.[41]

Another effect of the commercial breakdown was a reorientation of much of the Paraguayan economy away from cash produce and toward subsistence farming. One can speculate that the rise of the ranching industry was tied to the decline of yerba production; large populations of yerbateros and other peones, who previously had supplied the export market with yerba, became ranch hands and agriculturalists.

Francia's Paraguay has provided dependency literature with its most frequently cited example of an alternative development model. The proponents of this interpretation count among their number Eduardo Galeano, E. Bradford Burns, Vivian Trías, and most strikingly, Richard Alan White, whose 1978 study, *Paraguay's Autonomous Revolution, 1810–1840*, continues to be regarded as the best revisionist treatment of the Francia period. White boldly asserts that the Dictator launched a radical social revolution:

In dismantling their traditional dependent society, the Paraguayans denied both the Spanish and creole elites their dominant social, political, and economic status, thus preventing them from continuing to direct the affairs of the nation in their upper-class interests. Along with eliminating the domination of the oligarchy, Paraguay refused to yield to the aggressions of

Argentine imperialism, thus escaping the new dependency
suffered by the other provinces. . . . Through stringent state
control and a sweeping land reform, moreover, Paraguay
diversified its traditional monocultural economy and developed a
balanced economy designed to provide adequately for the
fundamental needs of all the pepole—the first nation in all of
American history to achieve such a radical goal.[42]

Seen in the light of the 1970s, White's uncompromising stance had
much to recommend it. It was well timed, following closely in the wake
of André Gundar Frank's spectacular assault on traditional historiography.
It was thoughtful, aiming to flesh out the story of those forgotten by
historians wedded to a "great events" interpretation. It was also thorough, being based upon a careful reading of secondary works and a wealth
of archival documentation (much of which White incorporated into useful statistical graphs and appendices).

For all of its virtues, however, White's treatment has a basic flaw: It
allows the dependency theory to overwhelm the historical evidence.
White was not alone in this tendency. Many North American writers,
myself included, saw in the dependency paradigm the most salient way
to connect present injustices in the Third World with their antecedents
at the beginning of the last century.[43] The accumulation of new historical evidence (along with rising skepticism among Latin American scholars) has made these connections seem less palpable.

This is not the place to open a wide-ranging debate on the strengths
and weaknesses of the dependency perspective; here I am concerned
solely with the issue of autonomous development. In this respect, White
maintains that "profound structural changes" under Francia engendered
a broad transformation of society. Did any meaningful development
occur, however? Nowhere does White provide indices with which to
measure the alleged advances made by the Paraguayan masses.

In fact, Francia was uninterested in changing the socioeconomic
structure of Paraguay, except for those features that were relevant to the
legitimation of his regime. He displaced the merchants and seized the
properties of his creole opponents, though in no greater proportion than
was the case in other Latin American nations at the time. He pointedly
went no further. Slavery and the labor draft for Indians remained in place,
and the rural elites (except for native-born Spaniards) largely retained
their privileged status with regard to the peasants. In fact, because wage-
earning activities such as yerba processing drastically declined under
Francia, the number of dependent peones actually increased.

Although Francia entertained few democratic principles as such, he
was shrewd enough to manipulate the chacreros and certain members

of the creole elite. Despite the arguments of White, Burns, and Galeano, the Dictator was never a "popular" leader. Like many of his contemporaries in Buenos Aires, he occasionally used radical rhetoric in the early years, but his words were conventional in tone, drawn in the main from French sources. In practice, he had no commitment to egalitarianism. The mass congresses that gave birth to his dictatorship were composed of appointees—rural people who willingly left all the decision-making to Francia. They gave him the support he needed, and thereafter he saw little need for political adjustment. He called no further congresses. In legal matters, he usually relied on the colonial legal code, the *recopilación de Leyes de las Indias*. And with the exception of the cabildo, all of the institutional structures of the old intendancy survived on a reduced scale; these included fiscal, judicial, and military frameworks. Francia showed little penchant for innovation in such matters.

As for the Dictator's "sweeping land reform," no fundamental change took place. The much-lauded *estancias de la república*, for instance, were nothing more than an extension of an earlier system of royal ranches.[44] Francia also supposedly increased the number of leaseholds (*arrendamientos*) in the country by proclaiming as state property all unclaimed lands and then leasing them at moderate rates to peasants. Even if this story is accurate (and it is probably an exaggeration), little meaningful change could have taken place since the peasants involved had already squatted for years on these same lands without paying a fee to the government. Seen in this light, Francia's land policy was simply a device to increase revenues.

The Dictator's famous isolationism also found its motivation in political expediency. It kept Paraguay immune from the anarchy of the lower provinces, but it also kept out capital, foreign expertise, and any idea that Francia cared to reject. That a program of economic development could be constructed on such a base has yet to be convincingly demonstrated.

More than anything else, the Francia years represent a continuation of certain colonial patterns. The Dictator himself differed little in outlook from Lázaro de Ribera, Pedro Melo de Portugal, or any other late colonial governor, save that they were peninsulares with an expressed loyalty for the Crown, whereas Francia, a creole, favored local interests over those of the metropole. All agreed, however, that Paraguayan society was best organized from the top down in patrimonial fashion, with leaders guiding and arbitrating between social sectors to assure overall harmony. According to this notion of statecraft, the leader was above factions, with duties and responsibilities to society as a whole. Bourbon officials also took to heart the desire to make Paraguay pay for itself, to raise new revenues and new defenses against outside interlopers.[45] Francia had these same concerns, and in the same way, though his political circumstances were less favorable than those of his predecessors.

The Dictator's politics were consistently conservative and authoritarian. He never gave in to idealistic whims. He took pride in an image of aloofness and austerity. Even his dress, with the heavy coat and out-sized shoebuckles, was more reminiscent of Bourbon times than of any revolutionary era. Francia regarded the Paraguayan nation not so much as his creation but as his trust. This explains his strong defense of independence as well as his insistence on the primacy of state sovereignty, an attitude that had as many economic implications as political ones. The dependency writers have largely forgotten that the Bourbon regime favored an activist role for the state in the Platine economy; Francia simply took his lead from these earlier efforts. He improvised where he had to, but he preferred to follow precedent.

Francia seemed more arbitrary and more paternalistic than others only because he was more successful. In an era dominated by young military chiefs and opportunists, Paraguay was ruled by a well-educated, middle-aged civilian who combined in his person all executive and legislative power. Like Napoleon and Peter the Great, Francia believed himself the Man of Providence, and he acted accordingly. In the process, he took Paraguay out of the mainstream of Latin American development.

The Artiguista Occupation of Corrientes

Paraguay's example was not followed elsewhere in the Upper Plata. Having lost its role as a port of transit for Paraguay, Corrientes had to content itself with its own tiny export trade in hides and timber. Despite the limited opportunities that this presented, Correntino merchants persevered. By provincial standards, their wealth had been impressive; the 1814 census revealed that the average merchant of Corrientes owned 2,835 pesos in property and goods, more than twice that of the average clergyman and four times that of the average rancher.[46] This privileged position failed to insulate the Correntino merchants from the vagaries of politics, and their hold even on domestic commerce remained conditional at best. Some foreign speculators joined them in the river trade, including the Robertson brothers. All of these traders, however, were vulnerable to political disorder, such as the region experienced during the Artiguista occupation of 1814–20.

The career of José Gervasio Artigas was closely tied to the rise of federalism in the Argentine Litoral. A centralist regime operated by and for Buenos Aires had governed Corrientes since independence. Though Governor Elías Galván was personally well liked, few Correntinos trusted the Porteños. The rebellion of Artigas in the Banda Oriental gave hope to many in the Upper Plata who sought autonomy within an Argentine federation and who perceived that Porteño interests were manifestly not their own. Responding to these concerns, Correntino ranchers revolted in March 1814 and swept the pro-Porteño regime from power. Led by the alcoholic Juan Bautista Méndez, these insurrectionists lost no time in affiliating with Artigas's political coalition, the *Liga Federal*.

Local tradition has stressed the negative impact of the Artigas years, but this judgment is superficial at best. Little of substance changed in Corrientes. Méndez, as garrison commander, was the logical choice for governor, but the composition of the cabildo remained basically the same. By switching sides, the ranching and mercantile elites increased their room to maneuver in the Upper Plata; no one seriously contemplated imitating the isolationism of the Paraguayans. Instead, in seeking to manipulate the cabildo, Artigas often ended up being the one manipulated. On specific issues, such as the stationing of Indian cavalry in the provincial capital, the Correntino elites challenged Artigas and won. Unlike the Francia regime, the government of Corrientes could boast of little relative autonomy from the class structure of the province, and thus, even during the turbulent revolutionary period, the state remained an elite institution.

For all of his republican impulses and his emphasis on the welfare of his rural supporters, Artigas could never afford to ignore the powerful merchants. His grand scheme called for the creation of new trade structures that would offset those of Buenos Aires. To make this goal a reality, he clearly required outside help. The trade regulations elaborated for Corrientes therefore proposed a low, 4 percent export duty, the better to attract foreign—especially British—trade. The Robertson brothers, though ill disposed toward Artigas, were happy to explore the market in Corrientes, where they received favorable treatment from Governor Méndez.[47]

Both Artigas and Méndez understood that British imports were inevitable, whatever their provenance. They could arrive legally, and pay duties to the government, or they would come anyway as contraband. The Robertsons also realized this, and from their arrival in May 1815, enjoyed conspicuous success in their enterprise. The warehouses they maintained in Corrientes and Goya did a brisk business in hides, which other British merchants in Buenos Aires incorporated into the overseas trade. These Correntino hides earned four times their purchase price in Buenos Aires and nearly nine times when resold in Liverpool. The Robertsons also later claimed to have singlehandedly introduced specie to regional commerce, though this was surely an overstatement. Silver coinage had circulated freely in Corrientes since the time of the colonial tobacco estanco, and what the Robertsons observed was more likely a temporary shortage caused by the civil wars than an absolute dearth.[48]

The same conflicts continued to disrupt the Correntino export trade.

J. P. Robertson, in another probable exaggeration, asserted that Correntino exports earned 500,000 pesos a year during peacetime, but that the struggle with the Porteños had reduced this figure appreciably. All this he blamed on the lawless ways of the Artiguista troops who occupied the province. Though Robertson witnessed little of the cruelty he described, his picture of turmoil was appropriate.

Foreign merchants with less resolution might have abandoned the field at this point, but the Robertson brothers, armed with Artigas's license, persisted in the Upper Plata. They wisely established an alliance with Peter Campbell, an Irish deserter from the 1806 British expedition who had become a trusted agent of Artigas. Campbell was godfather to a son of Governor Méndez and thus in an excellent position to protect the Robertsons' business interests. This he proceeded to do for the modest annual fee of 1,200 pesos. He guarded with federalist schooners the river approaches to the ports of Corrientes and Goya, organized oxcart caravans (tropas) into the interior, and arranged appropriate bribes at either end. Through such methods, Campbell made it possible for the Robertsons and their associate, John Postlethwaite, to establish a small commercial empire.[49]

The British merchants in the Upper Plata successfully adapted their entrepreneurial talents to the traditional marketing practices of the region. Using a formula they had perfected in Paraguay, the Robertsons extended credits (habilitaciones) of cash and goods to ranchers on the condition that they be repaid in hides. The price of providing such credit was chronic insecurity, but given the potential profits, it was clearly a risk the Robertsons were willing to take. Unlike their Basque predecessors, the brothers charged low rates of interest on their advances and paid top prices for hides. This innovation in the etiquette of credit attracted even small ranchers and many minor shopkeepers (pulperos) who could not pass up the potential profits. Campbell aided in collecting the promised hides by providing military escorts to and from the cattle zones of the south. Through such contacts, the Robertsons managed to export over 50,000 hides between 1815 and 1816.[50]

The magnitude of their operations, however, aroused the enmity of the older merchants, who spread the tale that the Robertsons were swindlers who used debased coin. The falseness of this report was easily demonstrated, but because the Britons also had problems in receiving regular remittances in gold from Buenos Aires, they started to lose the confidence of the Correntino ranchers.[51] The brothers also had to contend with the competition of smugglers. Though they themselves were probably involved in such activities, their memoirs, written thirty years later, spoke of the phenomenon with disgust:

Smuggling, in the smaller communities of the colonies, assailed the honesty of the guardians of the public purse in many insidious shapes; bottled stout and benicarlo wine for their tables, handsome ornaments for their salas [parlors], satin dresses for their wives and daughters, doubloons tendered in the way of loan, never expected to be returned. . . . Thus, in all parts, were poachers allowed to infest the domains of the public revenues, and rarely did I hear of any serious affray between the officers of the Patria preserves and these said poachers.[52]

Despite such annoyances, by late 1816, the Correntino treasury showed a surplus of over 25,000 pesos, due in large part to duties paid by the Robertsons. Méndez decided to spend this cash on rebuilding the cabildo offices and on munitions to aid Artigas in his war against the Portuguese. Even in this latter transaction, the Britons registered a gain, since they provided the armaments.[53]

The remaining years of Artiguista rule in Corrientes were less beneficial for the region. Raids by pro-federalist troops in the disputed Misiones region to the south of the Pasaná river had made enemies for Artigas in Francia's Paraguay. The Portuguese attacks in the east proved more serious, stretching to the limit the military capacities of the Liga Federal. Méndez tried to keep the commercial line open without much success. The Robertsons relocated to Goya for a time and then decided to give up their Correntino operation entirely. Postlethwaite stayed on until 1820, when he, too, fled.[54]

In the meantime, Francia dispatched a small flotilla to Corrientes to take revenge for Artiguista attacks on Paraguayan shipping. Though few shots were fired, the result was a paralyzed commerce.[55] To the south, a greater danger to Artigas arose when his erstwhile lieutenant, Francisco Ramírez (1788–1821) launched a rebellion and, aided by the Porteños, halted all river traffic bound for Corrientes. In quick order, Ramírez began a general invasion of the province, driving his former master into Misiones. Even there, the troops of Ramírez tracked him down. In September 1820, after abandoning Méndez, Artigas crossed into Paraguay, where Francia had offered him an isolated asylum in the far northeast. There he remained in exile for the final thirty years of his life.[56]

Ramírez, meanwhile, had established a dictatorial government in Corrientes that united the province with his native Entre Ríos. While this resulted in a measure of stability, the Correntinos had had enough of being used by outsiders. A shocking level of brigandage had followed Artigas's departure, and the region showed little interest in a future dictated by the authors of such violence. Fresh revolts allowed the much-chastened cabildo to secede from the "Republic of Entre Ríos" after only one year. Thereafter, Corrientes was free to concentrate on its three main priorities—peace, trade, and open rivers.

The Pilar del Ñeembucú Connection

Francia never completely shut the door to outside commerce. Though he closed Asunción, he still maintained two "free ports" in the south of the country, the most important of which was Pilar del Ñeembucú, located just above the Río Paraguay's confluence with the Paraná. The town had been founded in 1779 to help repulse Indian raids in the area, and by the mid-1790s its population amounted to almost 2,000.[57] Francia transformed this tiny waystation into Paraguay's focal point for commerce with Buenos Aires, Montevideo, and the lower provinces.

Even during the most confused periods, some trade items made their way from Pilar to downriver ports and vice versa. In 1818, for example, Porteño duty ledgers recorded the arrival from Paraguay of large cargoes of yerba, sweets, tobacco, and other produce. At least thirteen other vessels made the hazardous journey between the two ports during the next year.[58]

A positive trend in the Pilar trade was discernible by 1822. At the beginning of that year, Francia received a message from the reform-minded governor of Corrientes, Juan José Fernández Blanco (1778–1825). Noting the defeat of the royalists throughout the Plata, Fernández Blanco extended the hand of friendship to the Paraguayan leader and offered to open trade on the rivers. The Correntino was as good as his word, and on January 30 a Paraguayan ship arrived at Pilar from downstream with a large cargo of goods.[59]

Fernández Blanco combined executive talent with circumspection and honesty. He had spent many years in the river trade, having served with his brother, the chief customs officer for the port of Corrientes during the last years of the colony. The governor, moreover, owned one of the largest tanneries in Corrientes and had done business in Buenos Aires on many occasions. His intimate knowledge of commerce thus made him an excellent spokesman for the cabildo, now resurrected as the *Honorable Congreso Provincial*, dominated, as always, by merchants and ranchers. Fernández Blanco knew that if he could not find a friend in Francia, he might still be able to find a business partner.

With Francia's regularization of the Pilar trade, ships were no longer permitted to approach Asunción. Instead, a pilot and escort at Curupayty met all ships clearing Corrientes for Paraguay and escorted them from there to Pilar, where trade goods were inspected and duties paid. Samples, along with invoices and price lists, were sent on to the capital for

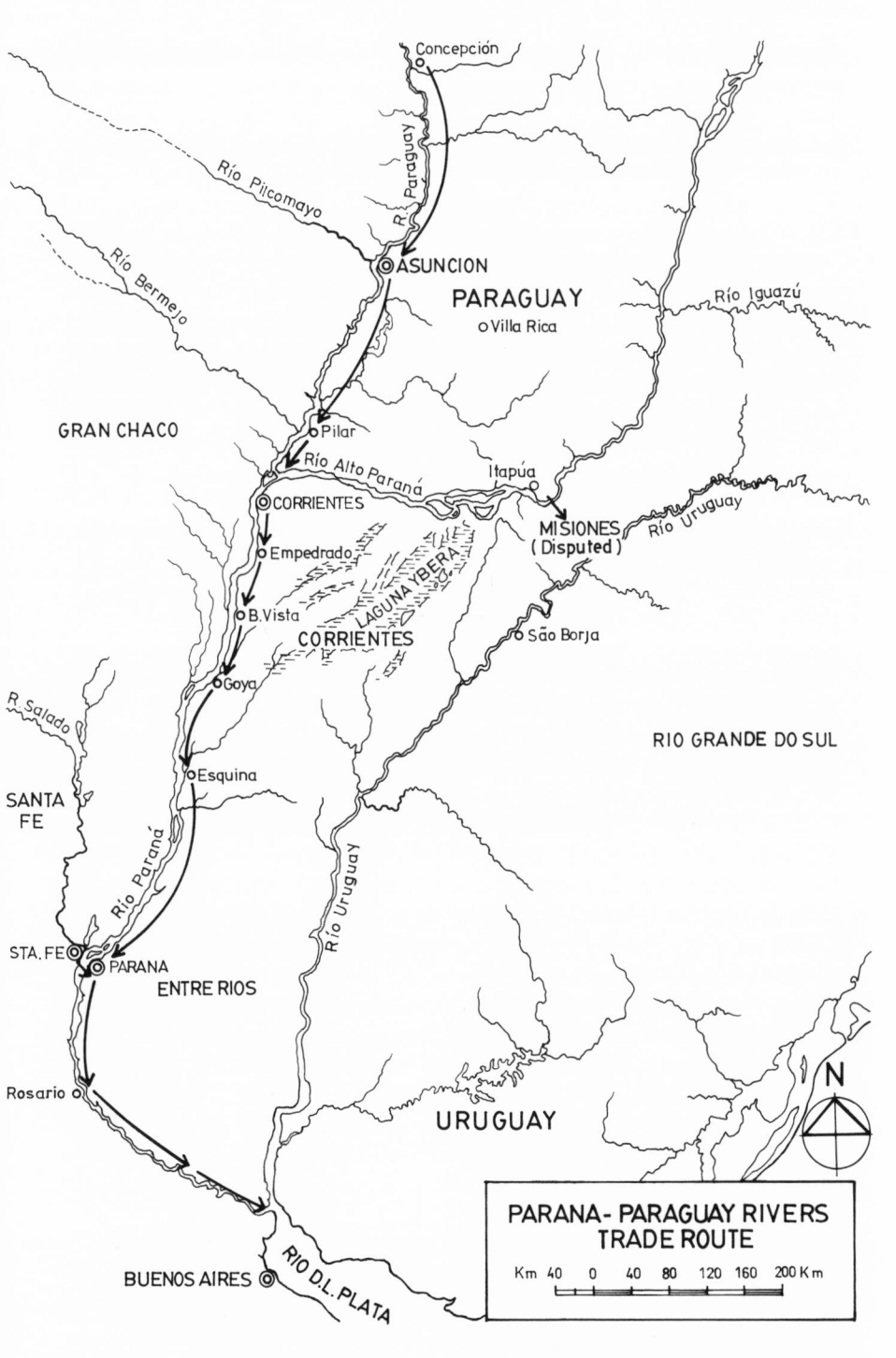

Concepción

Río Pilcomayo

Río Paraguay

Río Bermejo

ASUNCION

PARAGUAY

o Villa Rica

Río Iguazú

GRAN CHACO

Pilar

Río Alto Paraná

Itapúa

CORRIENTES

MISIONES
(Disputed)

Río Uruguay

Empedrado

LAGUNA YBERA

B. Vista

CORRIENTES

São Borja

Goya

R. Salado

RIO GRANDE DO SUL

Esquina

SANTA
FE

Río Paraná

Río Uruguay

STA. FE

PARANA

ENTRE RIOS

N

Rosario

URUGUAY

PARANA- PARAGUAY RIVERS
TRADE ROUTE

Km 40   0   40 80 120 160 200 Km

BUENOS AIRES

RIO D.L. PLATA

Francia's perusal and his permission to unload. The most common state purchases were arms, munitions, paper, and books and journals from abroad. Paraguayan-born shopkeepers, some of whom had come from settlements as remote as Villarrica and Ybytymí, were eager to buy ponchos, oil, chocolate, vinegar, wine, cloth, and iron implements.[60] Francia himself judged the quality of such goods, at times lowering their prices arbitrarily, at other times rejecting them altogether.[61]

The 1820s marked the commencement of a limited but fairly regular commerce that was to outlast Francia. Aside from the profits created in the process, the Pilar-Corrientes connection suited the political interests of the Upper Platine governments and confounded the desire of the Porteños to keep the two provinces divided. In fact, Corrientes was generally regarded as a member of the Argentine "family." It had shown little interest in independence, but the provincial government at the port of Corrientes could seldom make its presence felt even in its own hinterland. Thus, the ranchers and chacreros of the Correntino interior pursued their own interests, and, despite the fact that they had no Francia to unite them, they nonetheless shared his distate for the Porteños. The weakness of the Correntino state meant, though, that an autonomous existence was untenable in the long run.

Buenos Aires, understandably, saw Paraguay as a breakaway province and, thus, a dangerous example. Trade between the former viceregal capital and a rebellious province could never be tolerated officially, but fewer legal restraints impeded the trade between Corrientes and Buenos Aires. Therefore, large quantities of Paraguayan produce were loaded onto vessels at Pilar, ferried the short distance to Corrientes, and reexported to Buenos Aires under Correntino label. Imports moved northward in a like manner.[62] The political instability of the times, in effect, brought together the forces favoring regional coherence in the Upper Plata. As long as immediate needs were met, no one in the lower provinces need be the wiser, at least for the record. Merchants could make profits on both sides of the Paraná.

By the mid-1820s, trade was running smoothly at Pilar, and a small community of foreign merchants operated there under Francia's protection. These men counted among their numbers Correntinos, Porteños, Genoese, and an occasional Englishman.[63] They must have found Pilar a primitive place, where the port guards amused themselves by roping crocodiles (the fat of which was used as a medicine), and the inhabitants of the town, both men and women, spent the hotter days of the year bathing naked along the riverbank.[64]

The extant commercial registers give the impression that trade remained active at Pilar throughout the decade. In 1827, yerba was selling for twice as much an arroba in Corrientes as in Asunción, and eager merchants from the south were ready to barter arms and goods of all sorts to obtain the herb.[65] In August of that year, three ships arrived from Buenos Aires with wine, firearms, and tin, all exchanged for yerba and tobacco. A few weeks afterward, the commandant of Pilar reported the appearance of four more ships from downriver, noting that "all those coming from Corrientes now want only yerba."[66]

As the legitimate trade grew, so did contraband transactions. In 1826–27, illicit trade resulted in the arrest of several Spanish merchants, five of whom were shot for their transgressions.[67] Seven more were fined 41,200 pesos for their contraband dealings, a sum equal to nearly 50 percent of state revenues that year. Despite such massive fines, the illegal trade was simply too lucrative to be totally quelled.

Two items imported at Pilar deserve special mention—cotton and ponchos, both from Corrientes. The autonomous development model assumes a high degree of self-sufficiency for Paraguay in the Francia period, but these imports, which appeared in some volume during the 1820s, suggest that the Paraguayans lacked even basic material for clothing.[68] That Correntinos were still handling native-made ponchos at this time calls into question yet another precept of the dependency school: that local handicraft production was undermined by the inflow of cheap British textiles. While this phenomenon did occur, its effects were less pronounced in the Upper Plata than the dependency writers would have us believe.

While 1827 stands as the peak year for trade during Francia's time, commerce at Pilar endured on a limited basis over the next decade. Table 1.2 indicates the level of exports in this period and their subsequent rise, a result of better trading conditions on the Paraná. It is clear that although Francia never completely prohibited trade on the rivers, he showed no interest in its expansion to the high levels of the late colonial period. Commercial activity on that scale would not return to Paraguay until 1852, long after the Dictator's death.

Although Francia favored a Paraguayan economy that was essentially closed, he retained some place for an external trade that served the interests of the state. Accordingly, commerce assumed a decidedly political guise: it was used to obtain the specie and paper required for government bureaucracy and, more important, armaments and other materials necessary for defense. At Francia's death in 1840, the socioeconomic structure of the country still largely resembled that of 1820. As for foreign policy, by fostering a general isolation from the outside world, Francia prevented the reassimilation of Paraguay into a Porteño-dominated sphere and established a different political agenda for the Upper Plata. Having initiated the Pilar trade on an ad hoc basis, Francia refused to make it more than a secondary focus in his effort to gain recognition. He did

TABLE 1.2: Exports of Pilar del Ñeembucú

	1829	1832	1835	1838	1845[a]	1847–48[b]
(*In arrobas*)						
Yerba	7,525	2,562	6,286	5,317	81,988	28,455
Tobacco	1,592	798	1,388	1,557	23,072	125,708
Salt	1,913	1,121	3,410	1,884	1,791	
Honey	1,256				2,175	3,320
Starch					2,003	
Sugar					228	
Sweets					3,172	7,099
Cigars					120	780
Horsehair						2,716
(*In absolute numbers*)						
Barrels of aguardiente	1,645	1,231	1,305	1,900	4,140	
Rawhides						14,076
Tanned hides					1,076	9,740

[a]Another archival source quotes a much lower export figure for 1845, but the document appears to be incomplete. See Mapa de exportación de la república del Paraguay en el año de 1845, ANA-SH 267.
[b]This figure covers March 1847 through September 1848.
Sources: Resumen de exportación (1845), ANA-SH 274; Frutos extraídos del Pilar, 30 September 1848, ANA-NE 866; White, *Paraguay's Autonomous Revolution*, pp. 239–41, 243.

not live to see the Asunción commerce supplant that of Pilar. He had long shown himself ready to deal with merchants coming from Corrientes and elsewhere, but specific political considerations, such as the recognition of Paraguayan sovereignty and independence, were always uppermost in his mind. This unrelenting posture he bequeathed to succeeding regimes.

The Itapúa Trade

Though possession of the Misiones area remained in dispute until the War of the Triple Alliance, the area still managed to support some commerce, even during the worst of times. Trade centered on the small Paraguayan port of Itapúa, high on the Alto Paraná and just across from Candelaria. The latter village had once been the Jesuit capital, and the bulk of the Order's yerba exports had passed through it. Like its sister communities to the south, Candelaria had fallen on hard times since the Jesuit expulsion of 1767. Half a century later, it was laid waste by the troops of Artigas and his Indian allies. Shortly thereafter, Portuguese

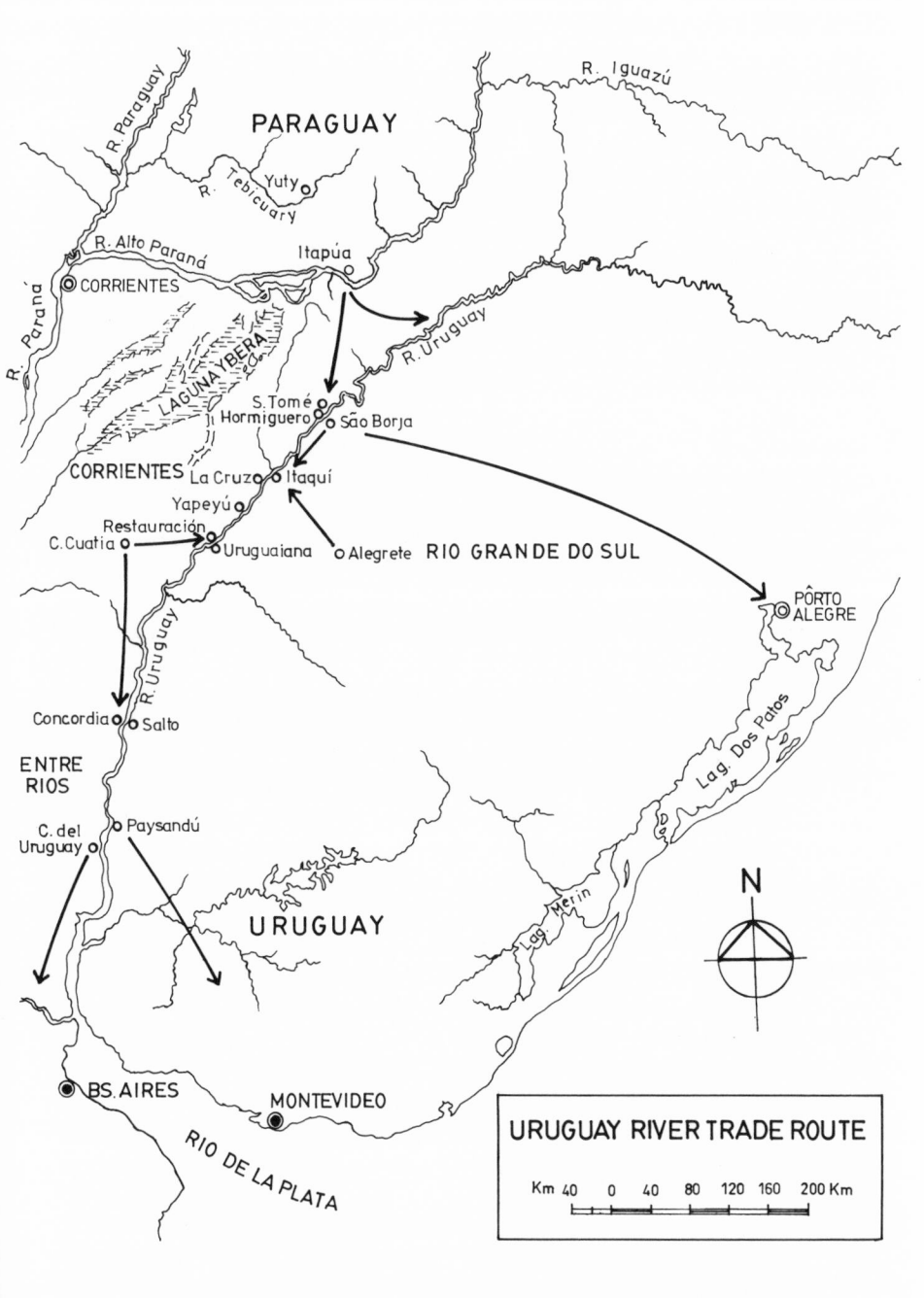

R. Iguazú

PARAGUAY

R. Paraguay

Yuty o

R. Tebicuary

R. Alto Paraná   Itapúa

R. Paraná

◎ CORRIENTES

LAGUNA YBERA

S. Tomé o
ı Hormiguero o o São Borja

CORRIENTES   La Cruz o o Itaquí

R. Uruguay

Yapeyú o

Restauración
C. Cuatia o   o Uruguaiana   o Alegrete   RIO GRANDE DO SUL

R. Uruguay

PÔRTO
◎ ALEGRE

Concordia o o Salto

ENTRE
RIOS

Lag. Dos Patos

C. del
Uruguay o   o Paysandú

URUGUAY

Lag. Merin

N

◎ BS. AIRES   MONTEVIDEO ◎

RIO DE LA PLATA

URUGUAY RIVER TRADE ROUTE

Km 40   0   40   80 120 160 200 Km

forces opposed to Artigas swept through the district and destroyed what remained of the mission communities, leaving not a single structure standing. The Paraguayans withdrew, but they retook the southern bank of the Alto Paraná three years later. By then, few traces of the once-proud Jesuit capital remained.

The Paraguayan occupation of Candelaria made possible a relatively secure overland trade with São Borja. To ensure Paraguayan authority along this route, Francia built an immense wall, two meters high, running some 1,200 meters across a small peninsula that jutted into the river opposite Itapúa. The wall was formed with stones taken from the ruins of nearby missions. It was heavily reinforced with battlements and trenchworks, and a large garrison was permanently stationed there. Francia named this fortification San José, but it soon assumed the more common appellation of Trinchera de los Paraguayos.[69]

The construction of the Trinchera was not the only measure Francia took to secure this area. In 1822, he established another fort at Tranquera de Loreto on the southern or left bank of the Alto Paraná, fifteen leagues west of Itapúa. The spot was well chosen. Located just above the salto of Apipé, Tranquera stood at the narrowest point of dry land between the river and the swampy Laguna Yberá directly to the south. The Jesuits had left a series of rudimentary levees in this quarter, which Francia greatly widened and extended. In an emergency, the floodgates could be opened to unite the waters of the Yberá and Alto Paraná and form an insurmountable barrier to any large military force approaching from the west.[70]

Because these fortified positions alone were insufficient to dominate the disputed areas between the Alto Paraná and the Uruguay, the Dictator also marshalled resources to patrol the zone and offer escorts for merchant caravans. A small force stationed in the ruins of Candelaria supplied troops for temporary posts at Santo Tomás, San Carlos, and, periodically, at Santo Tomé. While none of these steps assured absolute Paraguayan sovereignty over the Misiones area, they did make trade feasible, and the Upper Plata benefitted accordingly.

Brazilian merchants also operated in Itapúa as early as 1819, although Francia strictly regulated their activities. He wished to restrict contacts between Paraguayans and foreigners and thus protect his regime from foreign (especially Porteño) influences. The Brazilian presence in Itapúa represented a departure from Francia's general predilection for a closed economy for Paraguay, but this link with São Borja served his government well. This commercial "vent" permitted the passage of Upper Platine tobacco and yerba in exchange for needed armaments, paper, and manufactured goods. Providing an alternative when the Paraná was closed, this eastern route kept alive Upper Platine trade with Brazil and the lower provinces while simultaneously solidifying regional interests in the face of outside pressure. Nevertheless, Itapúa always represented an expedient trade, a substitute for the normal, more profitable, commerce via the Paraguay and Paraná. An overland route was both more expensive and more dangerous, with the inevitable result that the Brazilian merchants passed on their expenses to Paraguayan consumers.

Unlike the commercial network associated with Pilar, that of Itapúa received some sanction through diplomatic channels. In January 1822, Pablo Machado, an envoy of the new Brazilian empire, arrived in Asunción to discuss the possibility of formal commercial relations. Francia was pleased with this de facto recognition of his regime and agreed to a one-year opening of Itapúa to Brazilian commerce, but he restricted trade to that one port.[71] Because Brazil had rendered São Borja safe for Paraguayan merchants, Francia decided to allow the trade to remain open indefinitely, and in response, the commerce grew quickly. In the five-week period between late July and early September 1823, Itapúa customs officers registered export licenses for 1,680 arrobas of tobacco and more than 8,000 arrobas of yerba.[72]

In dealing with Francia, the Brazilian empire inherited a specific strategic outlook from the Portuguese. A major aim of this approach in the Plata was to prevent the consolidation of a united provinces of Argentina under Porteño aegis. To accomplish this, the Brazilians wooed Paraguay with promises of expanded commerce and official recognition. Since Rio de Janeiro desired, at the least, Francia's neutrality in the coming conflict in the Banda Oriental, the Itapúa trade began to assume great importance. In 1824, the Brazilian court named Antonio Manoel Correia da Câmara commercial agent to Asunción. Arriving in the Paraguayan capital one year later, Correia da Câmara attempted to convince Francia of the good intentions of Brazil and, in the process, promised more than he should have. He agreed with the Dictator that Brazil should recognize Paraguay and that indemnities should be paid for the Brazilian-inspired Indian attacks in the Río Apá area of the far north. Correia da Câmara even consented to procure a large load of armaments for the Paraguayans as a sign of good faith.

The failure of the Brazilian diplomat to make good on any of these promises ruined chances for close relations between the two governments. Although Correia was allowed to reenter Paraguay in September 1827, a disillusioned Francia refused to allow him to proceed beyond Itapúa. Correia remained at that port for nearly a year, hoping that the Dictator would relent, in the meantime busying himself with the growing commerce. He finally departed the Upper Plata in mid-1828.

The Cisplatine War of 1825–28, which pitted the Argentine provinces against Brazil in the Banda Oriental, reduced but did not stop the flow of Paraguayan produce from Itapúa to São Borja. The Paraguayans endeavored to remain neutral in the conflict, but military engagements between Corrientes and Brazil interfered with the traffic. An allied force occupied São Borja for a time, and it was only at the conclusion of the fighting that active trading resumed. At war's end, ports along the Río Uruguay again found themselves well stocked with Paraguayan yerba and tobacco.[73] Table 1.3 demonstrates the size of the export trade during the 1830s. The figures exclude the cash returns for exports at Itapúa, because the documentary evidence is extremely fragmentary. It is known, however, that yerba exports from Itapúa in the one year of 1838 exceeded 35,000 *pesos*.[74]

The Itapúa commerce aided the development of eastern Paraguay between the 1820s and 1840s. The better part of the produce exchanged in the trade was drawn from the Yuty area, some 100 kilometers to the north of the Alto Paraná. Both yerba and tobacco were available there in large quantities. A number of government estancias in the same locale provided the livestock and hides for much of the state's share of the trade. Yuty, however, was so isolated from the rest of the country as to invite smuggling on the part of both outsiders and its own residents (*vecinos*).[75]

Itapúa was the scene of much activity, both legal and illegal. Possessing only 2,000 inhabitants in the mid-1820s, the town nonetheless became a key entrepôt, handling a large portion of Paraguay's imports— not only armaments and paper, but cloth, ponchos, vinegar, oil, wine, hats, drugs, musical instruments, and iron goods.[76] A series of cart trails connected the town with various districts of the Paraguayan interior. These same trails served hundreds of retail merchants (or their agents) who arrived in Itapúa yearly to restock their wares.[77]

The Brazilian merchants based in Itapúa were a practical lot. Although few in number, they exercised an appreciable influence over the affairs of this section of the Upper Plata, so much so that Portuguese soon became the lingua franca of Itapúa, surpassing even Guaraní. As in colonial times, the merchants made wide use of libranzas and other credit arrangements.

As for their personal lives, the Brazilian traders enjoyed an official toleration not normally allowed the Paraguayan residents of the town. One interesting document preserved in the Archivo Nacional de Asunción tells how Francia, in 1831, admonished his representative in Itapúa to ignore the women who accompanied some of the merchants:

> These merchants and the women they bring are not subjects of
> this state . . . and have come only temporarily to Paraguay [in the
> course] of their business affairs. It is not right that the
> government or anyone else bother to enquire about their
> friendships or their private lives . . . nor judge if the women some

TABLE 1.3: Exports of Itapúa, 1826–39

Year	Yerba[a]	Tobacco[a]	Cigars[a]	Dulce[a]	Starch[a]	Hides	Carts	Livestock
1826	1,422	8,977				1,091	23	
1829	3,698	4,863		162				2,565
1830	184	2,094	27	25		155	36	1,952
1831	2,120	3,457	37	11	9	422	35	
1832	23,457	5,378					35	1,435
1833	400	810		21	20	6	4	
1835	5,392	22,628				7,843	83	
1837	6,830	10,495				9,347	123	
1838	7,375	2,359				2,874	88	
1839	4,651	1,117				918	8	

Note: Exports also included small quantities of timber, sugar, corn, aguardiente, rice, honey, soap, cheese, onions, ponchos, dried manioc (*popí*), crockery, and bacon.
[a] In arrobas.
Sources: Cuaderno de derecho de extracción (1830), ANA-NE 2928; Cuaderno de derecho de extracción (1831), ANA-NE 2936; Cuaderno de derecho de extracción (1833), ANA-NE 2951; White, *Paraguay's Autonomous Revolution*, pp. 246–52. (There is some confusion in White as to what proportion of the Itapúa trade was in private hands and what proportion was directly in the hands of the state.)

bring are legitimate or concubine. . . . The commandant of São Borja is their rightful judge. . . . what is worse still is that, as a result of this persecution, there will be merchants who will refuse to come. Yardin has already departed with all his goods, which annoys me greatly. This only cheats the treasury out of customs receipts and the populace out of an abundance of wares. See the trouble you have caused with your imprudence and thoughtlessness![78]

The Dictator's favor did not go unnoticed by the merchants, who generally accorded him every support and service, regularly reporting, for example, on the movement of Correntino troops in the area. The merchants' regard for Francia was based on their common desire to keep Itapúa and Misiones open to trade. Overall, their efforts proved successful.[79]

There were, however, many impediments to a secure passage across Misiones. While the Paraguayans frequently provided military escorts for merchant caravans, they sometimes left the traders to fend for themselves on the dangerous journey from São Borja to Itapúa. Assaults by Indians or Correntino brigands were common, especially between the Aguapey and Uruguay rivers, where neither the Paraguayan nor the Correntino government offered much protection. One band of highwaymen, led by a notorious cutthroat named Carabí, was responsible for a series of major thefts in the late 1830s and early 1840s. During one raid in 1840, Carabí captured two Brazilian merchants coming from Itapúa, stripped them naked, and then allowed them to return on foot to the Paraguayan outpost. Seeking redress from the Paraguayan commandant, the outraged merchants were told to refer instead to Correntino officials, in whose territory the incident supposedly had taken place.[80] In refusing to be held accountable, the commandant simply admitted that it was impossible to police the disputed area.

The Itapúa commerce in every way reflected the fiscal-minded mercantilism of Francia. As at Pilar, the trade was hardly free, being regulated at every juncture by a jealous state. As is clear from the export records, moreover, the state sector of the economy had necessarily grown to include a large portion of foreign trade. All this was in the interest of the Dictator, who organized commerce so as to strengthen his authority, to ensure internal unification with minimal threat from the outside. The Brazilian merchants tolerated his strictures because they were basically given a monopoly position. In this, too, there existed an obvious colonial precedent.

In common with the rest of Upper Platine trade, the fundamental drawback to the trans-Misiones traffic was political. As long as border demarcation remained unclear, commerce never ran smoothly. In the beginning, this mattered little since the Paraguayans almost always had the upper hand, but, as time passed, Correntino interest in Misiones and the Río Uruguay grew to the point where conflict with Paraguay became inevitable.

Both Paraguay and Corrientes benefitted from the Río Uruguay commerce, but in unequal measure. The Paraguayans were chiefly interested in keeping the line open between São Borja and Itapúa, and the trade in the latter town continued despite border disputes. The Correntinos cared less about the Uruguay trade as such, since their markets were quite distant from the river. The main centers of Correntino population lay to the west of the Yberá marshlands, a nearly impassable zone that remained as it had been described during the 1770s, "a wasteland of wild horses and jaguars."[81] Merchants bound from Brazil to Corrientes had to take a circuitous route to the south, passing the customs station (receptoría) of Curuzú Cuatiá, and working their way around the swamps to reach Goya and Bella Vista. From these points, their goods were packed aboard small vessels for transshipment up the Río Paraná to the port of Corrientes.

Paraguayans were thus in a better position than Correntinos in the Río Uruguay trade. Political aspirations did not always yield to geography, however, and the process of Correntino expansion toward the east ultimately challenged Paraguayan authority in the area. During the early 1820s and again during 1832–34, skirmishes occurred between these two claimants. Francia regarded control over Misiones as absolutely necessary to his commercial strategy; the Correntinos regarded the same area key to the renovation of their provincial yerba industry. As Misiones seesawed back and forth, trade languished.[82] In the end, the Paraguayans managed to reestablish their contacts with São Borja. The Correntinos, in turn, gained possession of all the lands from the Río Uruguay port of La Cruz southward to Entre Ríos.

The rivalry between the two governments over Misiones obscured the fact that both had much to gain from the Río Uruguay connection and that both could share in its benefits. Politics—the constant hindrance to Upper Platine integration—overrode this option.

Adjustments and Limitations: The Corrientes Trade

Corrientes invariably appeared little better than a shadow of its northern neighbor. Paraguay had an abundant, sedentary labor force. Lacking adequate manpower, Corrientes was unable to construct a wide-scale commerce of its own and had to depend on the whims of merchants in Buenos Aires and Paraguay. Because of its weak commercial position,

Corrientes always proved susceptible to market fluctuations in downriver ports. All this explains why trade assumed a fiery political aspect in Corrientes throughout the early 1800s.

Juan José Fernández Blanco (1778–1825) was an unlikely standard-bearer for Corrientes, yet this prudent governor had a record of success that was worthy of emulation. His quiet negotiations with Francia had opened the Pilar traffic. Similar arrangements with the other Litoral provinces, especially the Quadrilateral Treaty of 1822, set the stage for unencumbered commerce on the Paraná and the restoration of Correntino properties that had been seized by Ramírez. Fernández Blanco invariably acted at the behest of the same elite of merchants and landowners that dominated the province's economy in colonial times. Like them, he was a conservative who rejected many of the changes that had taken place since independence. Though he could do nothing to stop it, he abhorred the ongoing militarization in the southern provinces. Still, he tried to maintain good relations with all parties, especially with Buenos Aires. His was not a de facto regime, and, though he had military experience, he was no *caudillo*. Fernández Blanco set a pattern for efficient administration in Corrientes that endured until the late 1830s, long after his three-year mandate had expired.

In trade matters, Fernández Blanco proved nearly as mercantilistic as Francia. He forbade specie exports starting in 1823 and meted out harsh penalties for smugglers.[83] Nevertheless, the governor's interpretation of mercantilism was less restrictive than that of the Dictator. Following Spanish tradition, Francia advocated state monopolies (as with timber) and strict fiscal controls on all imports and exports. Fernández Blanco's vision was more growth-oriented, stressing the protection of local industries through high tariffs. Without such intervention, he argued, Corrientes stood little chance in the face of foreign competition for markets in the lower provinces.

Fernández Blanco bequeathed his protectionist outlook to his successor, Pedro Ferré (1788–1867), who, in turn, made it the cornerstone of Correntino trade policy. The son of Catalán immigrants, Ferré eschewed the usual route to power via the colonial militia. He rose through the levels of the local shipbuilding industry, married well, and by the 1820s, owned one of the Upper Plata's largest shipyards. His work as a master shipwright gave him access to the merchant elite of Corrientes, who recognized in him a potential spokesman. He also caught the eye of Fernández Blanco, and thanks to the latter's early sponsorship, the provincial congress elected Ferré governor on three occasions (1824–28, 1830–33, 1839–42). In turn, Ferré represented the interests of the tradesmen, ranchers, and artisans of the province. He came to symbolize the Litoral's opposition to Buenos Aires. His hopes for the modernization of Corrientes expressed themselves curiously in a combination of eloquence, irascibility, and a stubbornness that rivaled that of Francia.[84]

Ferré took a hard line in favor of protectionism. Corrientes, he reasoned, could never hope to offset the tremendous advantage that Buenos Aires enjoyed in the overseas trade. The medium-distance trade, however, suggested a different picture: If the foreign share of the Porteño market could be limited somehow, then Corrientes and the other Litoral provinces could supply Buenos Aires with locally produced goods. In this fashion, Argentines alone would benefit, rather than having to share their bounty with Britons, Brazilians, and Paraguayans. Such a major economic shift, however, could only be accomplished through heavy tariffs. For those consumers who might complain of the shortages and high prices created by such tariffs, Ferré had a forceful answer:

> Yes, without a doubt a small number of men of fortune will suffer, for they will be deprived of drinking luxurious table wines and liquors. . . . the less wealthy classes will not find much difference between the liquors they presently drink, except in the price, and will diminish their consumption, which I do not believe to be damaging. Our countrymen will not be able to buy English-made ponchos; they will not carry *bolas* and rope made in England; we will not dress in foreign-made clothing and other items we can produce: but on the other hand, the condition of the Argentine people will be less unfortunate, and the consciousness of widespread misery that today is condemned will not haunt us.[85]

This argument was never calculated to win support in the lower provinces. The merchants and cattlebreeders of Buenos Aires had gained much from their government's policy of free trade. These men felt that the high cost of production would make Ferré's plan untenable and that, in any case, the consumer should not be abused in order to promote the welfare of the farmers. With the Porteños thus opposed, Ferré could not gain national support for his position, and it was ultimately doomed to failure.

Protectionism, it should be remembered, stood at the heart of economic thinking in both Britain and the United States at that time, and it is hardly surprising that a responsible governor like Ferré should look for similar solutions. The Porteños themselves grudgingly passed protectionist measures in 1835 and 1837, but these were designed to help the artisans of the port city and only incidentally aided the Upper Plata. Half-hearted at their inception, the Porteño tariffs made little difference in practice.

Protectionism can best be understood as the economic expression of provincial federalism. Ferré also spoke in favor of other federalist demands, such as free navigation of the rivers and nationalization of the customs revenue, which until then had been controlled by Buenos Aires alone. In all fairness, he said, would not such policies better serve national interests? The "federalists" of Buenos Aires saw it differently, and refused to move on any issue that might weaken their privileges.

Despite Ferré's rancor, he could do nothing to force the hand of the Porteños. To the extent that he continued to mix in interprovincial affairs, the Correntino governor sided more and more with the enemies of Buenos Aires. This brought the elites of his province into more regular contact with liberals and centralists, individuals whose resolute promotion of outward-oriented growth made a deep impression on the Correntinos. Soon, they too began to think in terms of unlimited economic frontiers.

The reality was quite different. Corrientes was still a poor province with a population that numbered only 50,000 in 1828.[86] The provincial government had never effectively controlled the rural zones. The frequent incursions of Chaco Indians, bandits, and deserters from various armies made governance of the countryside precarious at best. Hence, while the biggest landowners lived in the town of Corrientes, the foremen and peones on their estates trafficked in hides and cattle by-products that entered the Porteño market as contraband. Neither the owners of the cattle nor the provincial exchequer benefitted from these dealings. The result, as revealed in Table 1.4, was hardly satisfactory for Corrientes. Despite the regularity of the province's commerce, Corrientes registered a negative balance of trade in nearly every year. The magnitude of this negative balance can probably be explained by the high incidence of reexportation to Paraguay, although the commercial registers do not state this specifically. In any case, because trade deficits had to be made up in silver, a shortage of specie resulted, and in the rural districts, the economy reverted to barter.[87] The prohibition on specie exports evidently made no difference, nor did the emission of paper money.

Along with the province's consumers, the Correntino government was a clear loser in these circumstances. Customs duties paid for nearly 70 percent of the province's administrative apparatus, and it was in Ferré's interest to increase exports. He and his associates looked for an answer in protectionism. Corrientes prohibited the importation of aguardiente (1839), clothing and footware (1831), "foreign goods" and furniture (1832), and yerba mate (1833).[88] A high level of smuggling soon rendered all of these measures ineffective; within a year after this last prohibition, the Correntino government again permitted the importation of yerba.[89] In the long run, protectionism failed to work in Corrientes because, unlike Paraguay, the province was coming into more contact with the outside world. Foreign goods could not be kept out.

TABLE 1.4: Trade on the Paraná River, Corrientes Province, 1825–43

Year	No. of vessels to enter province	Imports (in pesos)	Exports (in pesos)	Difference
1825	n/a	357,624	172,239	− 185,385
1826	n/a	391,074	258,322	− 132,752
1827	216	385,411	286,879	− 98,532
1828	153	196,801	206,549	9,748
1829	176	626,448	411,203	− 215,245
1830	159	462,934	241,967	− 220,967
1831	177	349,008	322,287	− 26,721
1832	179	426,243	332,324	− 93,919
1833	118	407,146	374,831	− 32,315
1834	107	394,952	223,733	− 60,219
1835	138	540,279	455,808	− 84,471
1836	149	399,967	435,386	35,419
1837	140	502,510	350,183	− 152,327
1838	121	308,640	213,088	− 95,552
1839	56	96,778	64,221	− 21,557
1840	52	387,990	202,987	− 185,003
1841	102	397,076	314,175	− 82,901
1842	n/a	n/a	n/a	n/a
1843	n/a	529,818	227,098	− 302,720

Sources: Capital introducido y exportado de la provincia de Corrientes, AGPC Expedientes Administrativos 1830, legajo 28; 1832, legajos 32–36; 1834, legajo 41; 1836, legajo 49; 1837, legajo 52; 1839, legajo 59; 1840, legajo 61, legajo 63; 1842, legajo 65; 1844, legajo 71; ROPC I:429, II:220, 33, III:434–35.

Nor could foreign merchants. Indeed, a substantial foreign presence in Corrientes was by then taken for granted. When the Robertson brothers established their business at Goya in the 1810s, their activities attracted considerable attention throughout the province. Two decades later, foreign merchants were living on a semipermanent basis in some of the smallest villages of Corrientes.[90] In 1830, the provincial government, eager to "increase the number of merchants" in towns along the Paraná, authorized the settlement of foreigners in several of those locations, including Bella Vista, which had only been founded a few years earlier.[91] Despite legislation restricting imports, conditions for foreign businessmen in Corrientes had become so favorable by the mid-1830s that some began to seek Argentine citizenship.[92]

At the time of Francia's death in 1840, the two subregions of the Upper Plata had evolved quite different approaches to commerce. Ferré had failed in his efforts to defend and expand the Correntino economy through protectionism, and instead the province actually promoted the presence of foreign traders. As it became more integrated with the economy of the south, Corrientes became less self-sufficient and less able to withstand the disruptions caused by the civil wars.

Paraguay, for its part, had gained its independence, but remained isolated and xenophobic. The country could boast a small foreign mercantile community only at Itapúa and Pilar; the rural elite, though still alive, failed to develop alongside the other creole elites of the Plata. Paraguay examined the possibility of foreign trade in a most tentative fashion and continued to regard political recognition as a necessary prelude to more open commerce. By the 1840s, however, the time had come for change.

2

The Growth
of Commerce,
1840–65

*In this world there is no
pleasure greater than coming
back to life after having been
torn to pieces.*
The Popul Vuh

The 1840s witnessed a conjuncture of events that led to better conditions for trade in the Upper Plata. This process of change drew its impetus from both internal and external pressures. The older generation of political leaders was passing from the scene, to be replaced by a more flexible generation, aware of world economic trends. These individuals had the vision and the desire to see the regional economy develop along modern lines. As these leaders consolidated their hold over the Upper Plata—in Buenos Aires and Montevideo—merchants began to look for new markets in the Litoral provinces. Where they could, they cooperated with like-minded governments in opening the way to those markets. Meanwhile, events in the Upper Plata itself increasingly favored commercial growth.

The Rise of Carlos Antonio López

The death of Francia, a critical event that signalled changes in the economic orientation of Paraguay, opened the decade. After several months of uncertainty, the republic adopted a consular regime headed by two men of varying talents. The first, Mariano Roque Alonso (1792?–1853), was a barely literate militia officer who had attained power through a barracks revolt. Finding it impossible to administer the affairs of state without more learned help, Alonso turned to Carlos Antonio López (1787–1862), one of the last graduates of the Asunción seminary. López quickly eclipsed his mentor in authority, and though a general congress in March 1841 named the two coequal rulers for a period of three years, the redoubtable López ruled alone.

López had spent the better part of his life as a country attorney and rancher in the small village of Rosario. The sense of timelessness in such rural areas obscured the real changes occurring in the country as a whole. The population of Paraguay had risen substantially—to over 238,000 inhabitants in 1846.[1] Yet the government made few adjustments to these changed circumstances; there was little political flexibility in Paraguay while Francia ruled. Any meaningful change had to await the arrival of López.

Though of modest birth, López married well and, by the social standards of the Paraguayan interior, rose high in the ranks of the rural elite. He avoided politics, but because of his education, both chacreros and ranchers saw him as an enlightened man. Like Francia, he used his reputation as a springboard to power, but unlike the Dictator, López allowed himself a degree of human weakness. This manifested itself in his vanity, his greed, and most alarmingly, in his nepotism. To López, his children could do no wrong. He appointed several to positions of high authority in the government. Later, after his power was secure, López transferred vast tracts of state land and other properties to his children.

For all his faults, Carlos Antonio López was a capable administrator. He designed a bureaucracy for the Paraguayan state, as well as a judiciary, and established an officer corps for the military. He filled these new posts with the most able among his supporters, a good many of whom came from the same propertied class as López. He self-consciously created a new state apparatus to replace the colonial structures that had been the mainstay of the Francia regime. Above all, the new leader was willing to experiment, to learn from his mistakes. If his basic impulses were as authoritarian as those of the late Dictator, he balanced them with a flexibility that was unmistakably "liberal."

In the beginning, López was open-minded on the issue of trade. Whereas the Dictator had been content to adapt the rigid mercantilism of the old Spanish system to his own ends, López sought a more modern balance between fiscal needs and mercantile interests. He knew that Paraguayan economic development depended on markets in the lower provinces, and he wished to see these contacts enhanced—though never at the expense of state power. This much he retained from Francia.

It should be stressed that the modern outlook of the new leader was possible only because of new influences from the outside. López evaluated these influences with great care, rejecting those that might too hastily involve Paraguay in radical ideas or external disputes. One of the first conflicts to engage his attention was already several years old when he came to power; it was centered east of the Uruguay River in Brazil.

Rebellions and Accommodations in the East

In the 1830s, while Francia was bemoaning the intrusions into Misiones of "that savage thief, the carpenter Ferré," trouble was afoot at the other end of the Itapúa route in Rio Grande do Sul. For years, the Riograndense *estancieros* had chafed under a system of interprovincial duties within Brazil that made it difficult for them to compete with Buenos Aires for the jerked beef market in Rio de Janeiro and São Paulo. The imperial government showed little inclination to enact protectionist legislation to shore up the southern cattle industry. With dim prospects for redress within the empire, the Riograndense estancieros broke their ties with Brazil in September 1835 and founded an independent republic. This touched off the Farrapo (Ragamuffin) Rebellion, a ten-year struggle that had a profound impact on the Río Uruguay commerce.

The Farrapo Rebellion brought a wave of migrants to the Upper Plata. Many families, fleeing the violence, crossed the Uruguay into Correntino and Paraguayan territory. These refugees, among whom were Indians and escaped slaves, were generally well received as new settlers. Numerous merchants also joined the exodus, relocating to the western or right bank of the river, there to reestablish their business ventures. This movement of refugees was the first step in the repopulation of Misiones, an area virtually uninhabited since the expulsion of the Jesuits.

São Borja fell to Farrapo troops in October 1835 and remained in their hands for nearly ten years. This did not remove São Borja from the struggle, however, because guerrilla forces remained active in the area. On many occasions, cavalry from one side would cross the river in pursuit of troops from the other, resulting in clashes with the Correntinos or Paraguayans.

In the 1830s, São Borja was little more than an open space surrounded by forests. Most of its 1,000 permanent residents spoke only Guaraní and concerned themselves with ranching and subsistence farming.[2] Even though there were no docking facilities at the port and only six box-like *chalanas* to ferry produce, this small village was the key link in a trade network stretching from Asunción and Corrientes to Montevideo. As a result, by the early 1840s, this primitive port serviced "upwards of 100 small vessels of from ten to thirty tons."[3]

Commerce with the Upper Plata was important to the Farrapos for the revenues it furnished the would-be republic; for the regular imports of yerba and tobacco; and, increasingly, for the horses and mules necessary to sustain the armed struggle. All sides recognized the strategic nature of mounts for the rebel cavalry. As one Paulista representative remarked in the Imperial Chamber of Deputies, "The rebels have 12,000 horses and 12,000 horses are nearly 12,000 men. . . . whoever has the largest herds of horses will win."[4] No reliable statistics are available on the number of horses and mules entering Rio Grande from the Upper Plata during the conflict, but a government report indicated an "abundance" of horses passing through the Alegrete and Missões districts (bordering Corrientes) in 1841.[5] When the acquisition of horses through legal trade proved difficult or merely inconvenient, combatants raided Correntino territory, taking whatever livestock they desired. After one such incursion in 1844, the governor of Corrientes petitioned the imperial commander on behalf of the ranchers of Santo Tomé and La Cruz, who claimed a loss of more than 10,000 pesos in stolen horses and cattle.[6]

The fighting sometimes hindered the harvesting of Riograndense yerba. There, as in other areas along the Río Uruguay, the yerba industry had declined since the end of the colonial period. The Farrapo Rebellion did not help matters. While the exploitation of yerbales in the north continued, such activity was subject to an uncertain labor supply, and it was, after all, in the interest of the Riograndense government to cultivate commercial ties to Paraguay. The importation of Paraguayan yerba thus played some part in a market traditionally dominated by the domestic product.

Receipts from Itapúa in the early 1840s suggest that commerce was less restricted by the war than one might suppose. Retail stores still held goods of all kinds, and new shipments arrived regularly from São Borja.[7] In 1841, a Riograndense merchant, Jordan Luiz de Araujo, operated one such establishment in Itapúa whose shelves displayed a large inventory of European imports valued at a striking 22,244 pesos. Araujo later owned a general store in São Borja, where he dealt primarily in Paraguayan tobacco and yerba.[8] Supplies of those two commodities remained plentiful because of the steady volume of trade. Francia's death had little impact on Itapúa.

The rebellion only momentarily threatened to change the balance of political forces within the region. The Farrapos were inconsistent in their attitudes toward their Spanish-speaking neighbors. Some envisioned a new state that would include Entre Ríos, Corrientes, Rio Grande do Sul, Uruguay, and perhaps Paraguay. Others, among them the republican chieftain Bento Gonçalves, continued to hope for some sort of federal relation with Brazil.[9]

These were only dreams, even at the high tide of rebel success. Francia had been crushingly cool toward the Farrapos, no doubt because he dared not risk the prize of ultimate Brazilian recognition of Paraguayan independence. His successor, López, sensing Farrapo defeat, likewise displayed no taste for adventure in Rio Grande do Sul.

The Correntino government also held aloof until the early 1840s, when a consuming desire to inflict revenge on an old enemy, the Porteño governor, Juan Manuel de Rosas (1793–1877), inspired a brief alliance with the Farrapo cause. Troops loyal to Rosas had murdered 800 Correntino prisoners after the battle of Pago Largo in 1839. Many elite families lost sons in the massacre. This bloodshed ushered in a decade of violence for Corrientes, only occasionally broken by short periods of calm. The quest for vengeance sent the Correntinos searching for allies, even among the Farrapos. In this case, the effort was doomed from the start, because the rebels were already in retreat and could offer no assistance to Corrientes. The Riograndenses, though, willingly arranged a common understanding of political interests within the Upper Plata. In January 1842, Farrapo envoys signed a secret convention with Governor Ferré that opened trading relations along the Uruguay, stressing the common need to eliminate smuggling. The convention obligated the Farrapos to disarm any opponents of Corrientes who might operate from Riograndense soil, and the Correntinos likewise were enjoined to expel any imperial agents from their province.[10]

These links proved impossible to maintain. Between 1841 and 1848, Corrientes had seven different administrations, none of which had much real authority within the province. In Rio Grande do Sul, the Farrapo cause was dying. Even with the aid of foreign adventurers, notably Giuseppe Garibaldi, the republican forces found themselves constantly on the defensive. In March 1843, São Borja and Itaqui fell to the imperial army, and the rebels transported all stocks of tobacco, paper, cloth, and other valuables to the opposite side of the river.[11] Exhausted and defeated, the Farrapos finally accepted the emperor's generous peace terms in February 1845, under which officers in the rebel army were allowed to reenter the imperial forces with the ranks they had held under the Farrapo regime. To satisfy Riograndense economic demands, the imperial government already had imposed a 25 percent import duty on Platine *charqui* (dried beef), a concession that rendered the Brazilian connection far more important to Rio Grande do Sul than any linkage to the Upper Plata.[12]

The settlement of the war in Rio Grande do Sul promised little in the way of a conclusive peace because the struggle between Corrientes and the Rosas forces continued to disrupt trade on the Uruguay. Yet the defeat of the Farrapos did signal a new trend in the political development of the Upper Plata. The empire was now firmly in control in São Borja and Itaqui, and this made easier the reorientation of economic life toward Brazil. The separatist tendency of the Riograndenses no longer meshed with that of the Upper Plata. Political union with their Hispanic neighbors now held less appeal for the Riograndenses, since their demand for increased trade could be realized under the empire. Nevertheless, Brazilians of all political persuasions still supported an independent role for Corrientes, Paraguay, and the Banda Oriental, because such an expression of autonomy prevented the resurgence of Buenos Aires.

The Río Paraná and the Struggle for Free Navigation

With Paraguayan commerce in the Río Uruguay region relatively untouched by the conflict, Carlos Antonio López viewed the 1845 demise of the Farrapo cause with outward indifference. In part, his attitude was rooted in a fear of alienating Brazil, but of greater weight was his preoccupation with policy and events on the Paraná, the more crucial river system.

In preceding decades, Francia had pushed the Paraguayan penchant for insularity to near-limits, insisting that any substantial trade on the Paraná be coupled with recognition of his country's independence. This was something the Porteños refused to grant. Those who governed Corrientes during the same years were less successful in resisting the pull of the south, favoring instead some formula for regional coherence based on a common need for free navigation on the rivers all the way to the Atlantic Ocean. Free navigation essentially meant the internationalization of the rivers on the model of the Rhine Convention of 1804–1805, which opened that river to all flags. If the European powers could be persuaded to recognize the rights of Corrientes in this regard, then the Europeans would be legally bound to challenge any future closure of the rivers by Buenos Aires.

Buenos Aires adhered to a standard policy on river transit that the inhabitants of the Upper Plata considered prejudicial. Merchants in the northeast wanted to receive foreign cargoes directly, without taxation by other provinces. Since few foreign vessels traveled beyond Buenos Aires, what the merchants in effect demanded was the right to transship cargo from the lower provinces without having to pay duty to the Porteños. This last concession Buenos Aires adamantly refused to grant.

With considerably less justification, the Porteños were also unwilling to concede foreign access to the interior rivers. Free navigation at that time was probably important only as a political symbol. Before the advent of the steamship, river transit to the Upper Plata was slow and costly; it could take 112 days to sail the 1,000 miles from Montevideo to Corrientes, and few foreign merchants were willing to bear the necessary expenses. As the British consul in Buenos Aires remarked:

> The people of those countries must not continue to deceive
> themselves with the dream of Dr. Francia, that it can answer the
> purpose of the merchants of Europe to incur the unnecessary

risks and expenses of sending their own vessels, so little adapted
for the navigation of rivers, so many hundred miles into the
interior of the South American continent in quest of a cargo that
is at all times to be had in the sea-ports of their mouths.[13]

During these years, Juan Manuel de Rosas embodied the stance of Buenos Aires on the question of Platine navigation. His long governorship
(1829–52) reinforced the resolve of the port city to bring the recalcitrant
northeast fully under its sway. Although Rosas's reality has been obscured
by a century of polemics, it is perhaps best to describe him as a skillful
proponent of coastal cattle interests. He put himself forward as a champion of provincial rights, and of a loose, federal interpretation of Argentine statehood. In fact, however, Rosas generally chose to ignore the rights
of provinces other than his own. He ruthlessly quelled all centralist
(unitario) opposition to his regime in Buenos Aires and then set out to
restore the authority of the port city throughout the former viceroyalty.
Rosas was a cautious man, however, and preferred whenever possible to
divide his enemies before moving against them. Hence, he saw river
trade as a tap to be turned on or off as he saw fit. After all, the Upper
Plata was not his first priority; the region never accounted for more than
6 percent of Porteño river commerce during his governorship.[14] The Upper
Plata may have needed Buenos Aires, but the reverse was never true,
and Rosas knew it. He was satisfied, as it suited his needs, to favor
Paraguay over Corrientes or vice versa, thus preventing the creation of a
regional front against him.

Beneath his diplomatic maneuvering, however, Rosas's policy on Upper
Platine commerce displayed remarkable consistency: There was to be
no free navigation of the interior rivers. The Porteño leader also insisted
that Buenos Aires be the only legal port of entry, and he used laws his
unitario predecessors had framed to confine customs to the port city.
Rosas's opponents argued that this policy denied Corrientes its just share
of the trade receipts; all provinces contributed to the commerce, they
argued, but only Buenos Aires saw any return.

Rosas could enforce his edict because many leaders in the Litoral, though
eager for a share of customs revenue, saw no immediate benefit from free
trade. Further, though they might resent Porteño control over the customs house, they had other problems—of a military nature—to resolve.

Circumstances changed in the 1830s, however. Awareness of foreign
trade options via the rivers was at first meager, but as news from Montevideo slowly penetrated governing circles of the Upper Plata, Rosas
was pressed more and more for consideration on this point. His allies in
the region began to wonder when they, too, would share in the profits
of growing trade.

The real test for the Upper Plata came early in the next decade with the death of the Supreme Dictator, a long-time enemy of Rosas. Eyes turned to that "famed fairy-land of Paraguay, so long guarded by that wondrous ogre, Francia."[15] The foreign mercantile community in Buenos Aires responded with interest to the new trading possibilities, as did the governments of Corrientes and Montevideo, and Rosas himself.[16]

Carlos Antonio López carefully considered the merits of these different suitors. Like Francia, he regarded commerce as largely a question of politics. No public outcry for increased trade had occurred since the Dictator's death, and his docile compatriots had given López carte blanche to deal with foreign states as he saw fit. After some reflection, he decided to deviate from the previous policy of isolation. He decided to confront Rosas.

One of López's first experiments was the negotiation of two treaties with Corrientes. The ruling elite of that province bore Rosas no love. Though López was as unwilling to commit his forces to their struggle as he had been to assist the Farrapos, he hoped that joining with the Correntinos would weaken the authority of the Porteño governor in the region. López also saw that the long-standing political stalemate in Misiones between Corrientes and Paraguay had benefitted neither side. He now found it convenient to receive Ferré's envoys, and in July 1841, treaties of commerce and boundaries were signed in Asunción that left Paraguay the territories north of the Aguapey River while assigning control of Apipé and the Río Uruguay settlements to Corrientes. The river fords of Itatí, Yabebirí, and Itapúa, all on the Alto Paraná, were declared open to Correntino trade, as was Pilar on the Paraguay. In recognition of the cultural and linguistic unity of the two parties, the treaty declared that "the sons of both states will be considered natives of one and the other . . . with free use of their rights."[17]

These agreements were probably viewed as temporary measures in both Corrientes and Paraguay. For Ferré, the main rationale was to limit disturbances on the northern frontier in order to concentrate fully on the Porteños. The Paraguayans, meanwhile, were eager to restore some commerce along the Paraná while keeping open the trade route to São Borja. To show good faith, the Paraguayans began to evacuate southern Misiones, and the population of this area, and presumably its trade, began to grow again.[18]

As a result of the treaties, 1841 ended as a good year for Paraná commerce in the Upper Plata. The Correntino state newspaper, *El Nacional Correntino*, expressed great satisfaction at the arrival of Paraguayan chalanas, "extremely overloaded" with produce of the country.[19] Pilar, too, enjoyed the benefits of the new arrangement. More than seventy Paraguayan merchants were listed as trading yerba for goods in that town between July and December, and some hard currency was sent from

Asunción to cover the cost of still other goods entering Pilar over the same period.[20] Since the resident foreign merchants could not legally export this specie, it, too, was doubtless converted to yerba and tobacco and sent south. Shipments of goods from Pilar to Asunción also rose, from only one in July to at least forty-five in December.[21]

The 1841 treaties infuriated Rosas. The agreements interfered with his self-proclaimed right to conduct the foreign affairs of all the Argentine provinces, and they also approved boundaries that were not to his liking. The treaties essentially recognized Paraguayan independence, a step that Rosas had vehemently opposed.

As López no doubt recognized, the 1841 agreements were of limited utility. They had the potential to stabilize conditions along the southern frontier of Paraguay and promote the entry of foreign trading ships into the Upper Plata.[22] But the treaties were tied to the strength of the Ferré government, a regime whose continued existence withered in the face of Porteño opposition. In December 1842, the Correntinos, together with some Uruguayan allies, suffered a massive defeat at the hands of the Rosistas at Arroyo Grande in Entre Ríos. The Rosistas fanned out into southern Corrientes and within a few weeks occupied most of the province. Ferré, fleeing from the collapse of his forces, passed through Paraguay on his way into exile in Rio Grande do Sul. López had gained a frontier even less secure than before.[23]

A new reason for optimism appeared at just this moment, in the person of George J. R. Gordon, a British commerical agent. This gentleman, consular official at the British legation in Rio de Janeiro, had traveled the overland route from São Borja to Itapúa and from there to Asunción, arriving in October 1842. His purpose in visiting the region was to secure information "as to the disposition of the [Paraguayan] government with respect to commercial intercourse . . . and, generally, the commercial resources and capabilities of the country." Gordon had no authority to conclude treaties. His reports to the Foreign Office confirm that López, though interested in outside trade, was suspicious of contacts arranged without prior recognition of Paraguayan independence. Gordon stayed in Asunción for several weeks and was shown all hospitality.

Toward the end of his visit, Gordon involved himself in a pet scheme to distribute smallpox vaccine to the Paraguayans, without having first secured government permission. Astonished that a foreigner would take such liberties, López had him expelled from the country. Gordon left without having obtained any trading concessions. Thus ended a brief episode in which part of the Upper Plata saw some renewed foreign interest in its trade, but again, as so often before, politics prevented the realization of concrete linkages. Gordon summed up his visit to the region by describing Paraguay as a land of great, if unrealized, possibilities. "Paraguay is nothing," he concluded, "worth nothing, and capable of nothing in its present state and under its present system of government."[24]

This was too harsh a judgment. Gordon had acted unwisely and unprofessionally. The Paraguayan state had good reason to suspect foreign intentions, and, after all, only two years had passed since Francia's demise. The new regime in Asunción had no experience with such overtures. The British remained skeptical, unwilling to risk diplomatic relations with Paraguay against the expressed wishes of the Porteños.

The mid-1840s was a time of political chaos in the Upper Plata. The pro-Rosas government imposed on Corrientes in December 1842 proved ephemeral, and within a few months, the province again found itself at odds with the Porteño governor. True to form, Rosas tried to maximize his gains from this situation by dividing his opponents in the region. To the Paraguayans he held out the hand of friendship, though not of recognition. In April 1843, Rosas pleaded in a note to López that good relations were in Paraguay's interest. Brazil and the unitarios he argued, were at that moment planning an invasion of Paraguay from Corrientes as a first step in the conquest of the lower provinces.[25] This spurious charge played well to Paraguayan sensibilities and fears. Nevertheless, for the time being, López maintained a policy of neutrality towards the south.

Toward the Correntinos, Rosas behaved with open hostility. Informed that ships from Corrientes had traded with unitario-held ports without paying duties to his agents, Rosas imposed a near-absolute blockade on the rebellious province, pointedly exempting the Paraguayans from its most severe strictures.[26] As Rosas expected, this differential treatment set Corrientes against Paraguay, and in October 1844, the Correntino government decreed that all vessels flying the Porteño ensign or trading with Buenos Aires could be detained indefinitely. This measure was obviously aimed at Paraguayan shipping.[27] López quickly retaliated by seizing all Correntino vessels then in Paraguayan waters.[28] For the moment, Rosas had succeeded in setting the two parts of the Upper Plata against each other.

This state of affairs lasted a mere two months, until Brazil entered the picture. Brazil had arranged terms with the Farrapos in Rio Grande do Sul, and turning its attention to the neighboring Upper Plata, the Brazilian Foreign Ministry offered to mediate between López and the Correntinos. An expanded struggle against Rosas was the Brazilian goal, and this they achieved with little difficulty. José Antônio Pimenta Bueno, a career diplomat, had arrived in Asunción some months earlier to arrange Brazilian recognition of Paraguayan independence, which came in October 1844.[29] In early December, he helped forge a Paraguayan accord with Corrientes that clarified visitation rights for trading ships and implicitly bound the two governments in an anti-Porteño alliance.[30]

This association became firmer some months later. Rosas had responded to the Paraguayan-Correntno détente by immediately blocking the trade of all Upper Platine states.[31] He tried to salvage as much of an understanding with Paraguay as he could, writing to López that "no one more than [myself] regrets the problematic situation of Paraguay, the difficulties it encounters in forwarding its industries and bettering its interests.[32] In fact, Rosas had received several Paraguayan envoys during the two preceding years, but had promised them nothing. Despite his words, he refused to cooperate in any meaningful way.

The Anglo-French Intervention: Repercussions in the Upper Plata

Rosas might have caused still greater mischief, but his principal foreign policy concern in 1845 centered not on the Upper Plata but on Uruguay and the Anglo-French blockade of Buenos Aires. The background to this particular struggle is long, complicated, and contradictory. It involved European efforts to protect a perceived balance of power in the Río de la Plata from the hegemony of Buenos Aires. This meant rescuing the unitarios at Montevideo and perhaps opening the Río Paraná by force. Foreign merchants in the south held differing opinions concerning the advisability of the blockade, though most professed an interest in the trading potential of the Upper Plata.[33]

After some hesitation, the blockading powers, in late 1845, opened the Paraná in spectacular fashion. Having already landed troops on the island of Martín García in the estuary, the British and French fleet commanders proposed forcing a passage up the Paraná, with the object of convoying perhaps as many as one hundred merchant vessels to ports in Entre Ríos, Corrientes, and Paraguay. Interested merchants were invited to participate.

Rosas vigorously disputed the passage of the allied fleet, sending troops from Buenos Aires to reinforce his garrisons along the river. He also decided to defend the mouth of the Paraná, at the Vuelta de Obligado, where the banks were high and the river eight hundred yards wide. To halt the enemy fleet, three heavy chains supported by twenty-four vessels were extended across the water from the mainland to an island; behind this obstacle lay another ten defensive fire-vessels, as well as a heavily armed schooner.

The French and British warships left Montevideo on November 17 and reached the barrier the next day. A battle lasting more than seven hours followed, in which the allies cut the chains and destroyed the Rosista batteries. While losses to both defenders and attackers were high, the British commander, Charles Hotham, elected to continue upriver, his warships serving now as escort for the merchant fleet. The convoy survived another engagement at San Lorenzo and anticipated a better reception in the unitario-controlled areas to the north.[34]

The merchant convoy included vessels from Britain, France, Prussia, Denmark, Uruguay, and the free city-state of Hamburg. Some foreign-owned business firms had invested their entire stock in the Paraná venture and expected considerable returns on their efforts. They were disappointed. In Entre Ríos the expedition learned that the Rosista general Justo José de Urquiza (1800–70) had already gained ascendancy over the unitarios and that no early possibility existed of an anti-Rosas alliance in the Upper Plata. Still, the fleet pushed on to Corrientes where the allies hoped to be well received.

Upon reaching that port in December, the traders began to unload their goods. Governor Joaquín Madariaga (1799–1848) was friendly enough, but in general the Correntino populace reacted with suspicion. A foreign presence of this magnitude had never before been seen in the region; the Correntinos hardly knew what to make of it. The foreign merchants soon tired of the lack of any real market. As one British naval officer later recounted,

> I should imagine that this mercantile speculation will turn out a regular failure. There is little or no money in the country. The women do all the work that is required, both for themselves and the men; and the men are too lazy by far to care about business. Besides . . . [people must] consider the difficulties attendant on a voyage up the Paraná to Paraguay or Corrientes, viz. that the wind, which is fair at San Lorenzo, for instance, becomes dead foul two miles beyond it; the numerous sandbanks which are continuously shifting their positions, from the great strength of the current, thereby rendering what was a safe passage in January a mass of sand in May. And then comes the difficulty of disposing of cargoes. One vessel with a cargo of salt, when we were there, finding it impossible to dispose of it, asked permission to throw it into the river, which was refused, and she at last got rid of it by presenting it to the government. Some of the vessels were at anchor for three weeks at a time, waiting for a fair wind. When all is considered, I think the attempt at trade will be given over.[35]

In addition to the above difficulties, the Madariaga administration promptly advanced its own interests by raising customs duties to exorbitant levels, which the merchants had no alternative but to accept. Some of the traders set up retail shops in Corrientes, but business proved exceedingly slow. One merchant, complaining of poor profits, noted that the Paraguayans ("those second Chinese!") had only purchased six to eight thousand dollars worth of goods at Corrientes.[36] What he failed to realize was that this sum, paltry by the standards of Buenos Aires and Montevideo, was substantial in Upper Platine terms. Most commerce in the region was still conducted through barter, and specie was jealously guarded in government vaults. That these practices still obtained in the Upper Plata had evidently escaped the attention of many traders based in Montevideo, who only knew that the Correntinos and Paraguayans suffered from a dearth of cash.

Rosas, who was well aware of their plight, openly celebrated the failure of the merchants' Paraná venture. His English-language newspaper, the *British Packet and Argentine News*, mockingly commented on the role played in this affair by William Gore Ouseley, British minister to the Platine states: "Pygmies seem to be in vogue everywhere now, and we suppose Mr. Ouseley pets this burlesque of a trade to keep in the fashion seeing that Tom Thumb has not yet turned his steps that way."[37]

If trade in Corrientes seemed sluggish to the backers of the convoy, there was also momentary frustration to be endured in Paraguay. Captain Hotham carried important letters from Minister Ouseley to Carlos Antonio López. Consequently, the naval officer stayed only briefly in Corrientes before pushing on to Asunción. He arrived in mid-January with other diplomats aboard the French steamer *Fulton*. This vessel of 800 tons caused a sensation in the Paraguayan capital. Although the *Fulton* "excited a degree of wonder" among the Asunceños, not one Paraguayan official accepted an invitation to come aboard. This lack of enthusiasm resulted from Hotham's inability to grant López's primary condition for joining the struggle against Rosas. López, again, wanted the intervening powers to recognize Paraguayan independence. Hotham could do no more than arrange several treaties in a tentative form and urge López to send agents south to meet with European and unitario representatives. Two such envoys left with the steamer, but they accomplished nothing in Montevideo.[38]

By June 1846, the British and French had decided that the intervention was a political as well as commercial failure, and they began to withdraw their forces. Negotiations with Buenos Aires continued for another four years, but the basic outcome was already understood in principle. Meanwhile, in the Upper Plata, the troops of Urquiza occupied the port of Corrientes, and the door seemed to shut again on the commerce of the region.

Was the Anglo-French intervention really the debacle that it seemed to contemporary observers? Clearly, the foreign merchants involved made less than they had expected to make on the sale of their goods, and all of the political gains of the expedition proved ephemeral. From the point of view of the Upper Plata, though, the intervention was crucial because it destroyed the myth of Porteño invincibility. Corrientes and Paraguay had joined together, at least for a short period, and every reason existed to assume that they would do so again. Free navigation on the Paraná and Paraguay rivers had been attained, and, though it had again been lost, renewed Porteño control over the rivers now rested on allies, such as Urquiza, that Rosas could trust less and less. Above all, the intervention focused the attention of the Litoral's people on a common goal: keeping the rivers open.

European intervention also reverberated positively for Upper Platine commerce, despite the complaints of merchants who were apparently dissatisfied with having tripled their investment.[39] When the convoy set sail downriver in May 1846, it carried from Corrientes 435,815 hides, 995 *varas* of various hardwoods, 25,583 arrobas of horsehair, 25,897 arrobas of tobacco, and slightly more than 40,000 arrobas of yerba.[40] The better part of the last two commodities was probably transshiped from Paraguay. With respect to revenues, Correntino customs receipts rose from 13,150 pesos in 1844 to 431,449 pesos two years later.[41] For Corrientes, an increase of this magnitude was next to miraculous.

The Paraguayans were unable to conclude any formal agreements with the British and French, but they derived considerable commercial advantage from what proved to be a porous blockade of Buenos Aires. The blockade stimulated Rosas to become uncharacteristically favorable to open trade. After all, his most urgent task was to diminish its impact, so he tolerated trade with Montevideo even though, in order to reach Buenos Aires, such goods brought customs duties to his unitario opponents. Both sides allowed favored merchants to trade clandestinely, and small craft carried on active blockade-running that evaded the patrolling squadron at night.

Buenos Aires still found it difficult to keep itself supplied in such bulk items as tobacco, timber, and yerba mate. Formerly, the port city received these items mainly from Brazil, but that source was now cut off by allied naval units. Paraguayan commodities, however, avoided the European patrols by taking a land passage from Santa Fé. The Paraguayans could also sell their produce at other ports within the lower provinces that Rosas had previously denied them. In this fashion, the López government, as the key purveyor of yerba, as well as individual Paraguayan merchants, made large profits and used the income to purchase a wide variety of imported goods. Between March 1847 and September 1848, for example, some 330,000 pesos worth of merchandise was unloaded at Pilar.[42] This was a far cry from the days of Francia.

In Upper Platine terms, therefore, European intervention brought substantial change. In the past, political exigencies had invariably frustrated the chances for regional and extraregional trade. For once, politics worked in favor of the Upper Plata. In far-off London, the Prime Minister, Lord Palmerston, might complain of the Paraguayans that "they want very little of what we can produce, and they have nothing to give us in return."[43] This blithe remark overlooked the remarkable consequences of the intervention: From now on, isolationism would not be a real option for the Upper Plata. The region had linked its economy to the outside world, and, for better or worse, there was no going back.

Confrontation along the Río Uruguay, 1845–52

Rosas successfully withstood the pressures associated with the Anglo-French intervention. He also made his enemies in the Upper Plata pay for their support of the unitario cause. Throughout the late 1840s, forces loyal to Rosas repeatedly invaded the region. They burned ranch houses, seized cattle, and cut off the supply lines to Brazil. Then, in November 1847, Urquiza defeated the remnants of Madariaga's army near the village of Caacatí and proceeded to place a nominal Rosista, Benjamín Virasoro (1812–97), in the governor's seat at Corrientes.

As might have been expected, these events disrupted trade, especially on the Uruguay. Commercial linkages with Brazil had been a priority of the Madariaga regime because they reinforced political ties, and the Correntino government dutifully reported new trading opportunities on the Uruguay whenever favorable circumstances presented themselves.[44] The arrival of Virasoro, however, ruined chances for renewed trade. The Brazilians, fresh from their victory over the Farrapos, refused to have anything to do with the new government in Corrientes. The Paraguayan state feared a Rosista victory, which left the west bank of the Uruguay under enemy control for the first time in years. López had aided Madariaga in an earlier campaign, and he wondered if Paraguay would be next on the Rosistas' list.

In framing a plan of defense, López failed to differentiate between Rosas and his clients in Corrientes; López adamantly refused to sit idle when outsiders threatened trans-Misiones commerce. In 1849, as Francia had done years earlier, López moved to assure Paraguayan sovereignty over Misiones by dispatching southward a column of more than 1,600 men under the command of Hungarian mercenary Franz Wisner von Morgenstern. These troops advanced into the disputed area in June, with instructions from López to secure the territory to the Uruguay River and, if possible, to purchase 2,000 muskets from Brazilian authorities.[45] By July 4, the village of Hormiguero had fallen to the Paraguayans. Wisner promptly sent word to the Austrian commercial attaché at Rio de Janeiro that Hormiguero was in Paraguayan hands and that the small port desired trade. Austrian merchants, he said, would be exempted from all duties since their emperor had seen fit to recommend the recognition of Paraguayan independence. This absurdly optimistic missive reflected the unrealistic tenor of the 1849 Paraguayan incursion.[46]

The purpose of the expedition was to reestablish the trade between Itapúa (called Encarnación after 1846) and São Borja, but the Brazilians did not wish to endanger their status as neutrals.[47] As a result, commerce continued to languish, and Wisner did not occupy Santo Tomé for any length of time. Instead, he deployed his troops in a restrained manner, limiting himself to minor forays against the Correntino Rosistas and their Entrerriano allies. These engagements all proved inconclusive. By 1850, the Paraguayans had returned to Tranquera, making only occasional raids against the Correntinos over the next two years. Within a decade, López considered the Itapúa trade important only for occasional armament acquisitions from Brazil. That commerce was significant enough for Paraguay to retain Tranquera de Loreto, but from then on, Itapúa counted for little in the nation's aggregate trade.

Though the 1849 Paraguayan expedition to the Río Uruguay was of short duration and little ultimate significance, it resulted in considerable destruction to the area. Deciding Hormiguero could no longer be held, the Paraguayans burned the small port town on evacuation. They also drove the entire livestock holdings of the Santo Tomé district, perhaps 11,000 animals, back to Paraguay.[48] The commercial consequence of these actions was severe for Corrientes, with total 1850–51 exports to the Brazilian port of Uruguaiana, for instance, amounting to only 869 hides and 1,170 cheeses, all the latter conveyed overland from Goya.[49]

Free Navigation Achieved

For a few years in the late 1840s, it appeared that Juan Manuel de Rosas had reasserted his dominance over Platine affairs. Though more desirous of outside trade than before, Paraguay under López remained nearly as isolated as in the days of Francia; the Rosistas held the Litoral provinces once more; the Anglo-French intervention was but a memory; and even Brazil appeared quiescent.

Rosista dominance proved to be an illusion. Rosas refused to let rest the issue of Uruguayan independence, which prompted Brazil to break diplomatic relations with Buenos Aires in October 1850 and to form an alliance with Paraguay two months later. Rosas might have weathered this turn of events, but then, stunningly, in May 1851, Urquiza, perhaps the ablest general in the Rosista army, suddenly turned on his master.

A man of great personal ambition, Urquiza commanded considerable authority in his native Entre Ríos and in Corrientes. Aside from his military achievements, he had spent the 1840s acquiring land, and was, by the end of the decade, the largest landowner in Entre Ríos and the province's leading *saladerista*. Urquiza could never hope to turn these possessions to further profit, however, as long as Rosas denied free navigation to the Litoral provinces.

Rosas realized that objective conditions favored a betrayal by Urquiza and began to regard his lieutenant with growing suspicion. Rather than wait for the fate usually meted out to rivals, the Entrerriano decided to act. First Entre Ríos and then Corrientes declared war on Rosas, and within a matter of weeks all the Litoral provinces, as well as Brazil, were united in a movement against the Porteño leader. Benjamín Virasoro conveniently switched sides, linking himself with his old mentor, Urquiza. Paraguay also gave its blessing to this alliance on the condition that the new Argentine government recognize its independence.

Military operations began in Uruguay, where the allies smashed the Rosistas by October. Rosas's long-term strategy based the security of his regime on the loyalty of provincial leaders, allowing him to concentrate his major defense on armies that he could not control. This was his final mistake because, in the end, he could not trust his own allies. Urquiza's troops crossed the Paraná in late 1851 and marched southward through Santa Fé and the northern Buenos Aires provinces. At Caseros, they met and soundly defeated the ill-prepared armies of Rosas in February 1852. Rosas fled to the safety of a British man-of-war, which conveyed him to a long exile in England.

In the truce that ended the fighting, Urquiza, himself a man of the Litoral, inserted provisions for freedom of navigation and abolition of interprovincial duties.[50] This soon became law as articles 12 and 26 of the 1853 constitution. In July, the new Porteño government officially recognized the independence of Paraguay, extending to inhabitants of that country the same right of free navigation enjoyed by Correntinos, Entrerrianos, and citizens of other Litoral provinces. This agreement also involved a boundary settlement between Paraguay and the Argentine Confederation whereby Apipé and Candelaria were assigned to the Confederation while free passage for the Paraguayans was guaranteed between Encarnación and São Borja.[51]

Despite the new order of things, the fundamental conflict of interests between Buenos Aires and the Platine states of the northeast still affected the economic life of the Upper Plata. Whether the relation with Corrientes (the only part of the region to remain within the confederation) might evolve in the direction of partnership or of Porteño domination soon made itself clear. After the fall of Rosas, the Argentine Confederation assumed a federal legal structure that gave Buenos Aires a political role no greater than that of the provinces. In terms of fiscal policy, Confederation authorities wanted to nationalize the customs receipts previously under the exclusive control of Buenos Aires. The Porteño elites, however, unanimously rejected the structure because it curtailed both their influence and profits. Within a year, they forced the withdrawal of the province of Buenos Aires from the Confederation. Buenos Aires and the Confederation, with its capital at Paraná, remained at odds for some years afterwards.

Still, the Upper Plata had finally attained two of its key political objectives. The Paraguayans had gained recognition from a government based in Buenos Aires, and Corrientes was now incorporated into a federal Argentine political structure that, theoretically at least, gave it the same legal status as Buenos Aires and the other provinces.

Peace guaranteed not only a more stable environment for trade but also the emergence of new commercial patterns in the region. The governments of the Upper Plata had spent more than a decade defining what their trade policy would be if free navigation became a reality. In 1842, Corrientes had adopted the Spanish commercial code of 1829 almost in its entirety. This body of legislation, more modern than anything that preceded it, still smacked of mercantilism in that it stressed the acquisition of revenue over all other elements.[52]

Carlos Antonio López's approach was more complex; he was constructing not just a trade policy, but a completely new state apparatus that would have to respond to changed realities. Far more than Francia, López was a creature of his class. Except at the beginning, he rarely sought the active support of the chacreros, but concentrated instead on the wealthier landowners. The periodic congresses that sat during his tenure, for instance, were composed of landholders alone. Ultimately, the commercial policies he developed favored, first, the Paraguayan state (oftentimes construed as the López family); second, the landed gentry of the interior (who had the most cattle to dispose of); third, the foreign merchants (whose expertise made trade possible); and lastly, the chacreros, who had so loyally followed the late Dictator. The landless peasants and Indian populations concerned López only in their role as laborers.

In 1842, López passed a series of customs regulations that mirrored these priorities. He set import duties at a high 40 percent for items that could be produced in Paraguay. Silk, jewelry, and pocket watches paid 25 percent import duty, while salt paid three reales the *fanega*. All other imports paid 15 percent, except scientific instruments and maps, which entered duty-free. As for Paraguayan commodities, López ordered a tiny duty of two reales for every hide exported and a 5 percent duty for other exports. He went further with those exporters who might discover "useful inventions" and those who dealt in manufactured items such as Paraguayan spirits, snuff, vegetable oils, and soap. These commodities could be exported duty-free. The prohibition on exports of coin (or any metallic wealth) stayed in force. López affixed these regulations to minute and pedantic instructions to port commanders and customs officials on how duties and incidental fees were to be collected.[53]

Unlike Ferré and the other Correntino governors, whose mercantilist inclinations expressed themselves mainly through the elaboration of protective tariffs, López followed a monopolistic commercial policy that harkened back to Bourbon models. He felt that strict controls on trade were good in their own right; the fiscal health of the Paraguayan state was more important than considerations of private enterprise. This attitude explains the thrust as well as the detail of his 1842 regulations.

Six years after the enactment of these decrees, the Paraguayan government incorporated the twenty-one autonomous Indian communities (pueblos de indios) into the national patrimony. Ostensibly, this measure made citizens of the thousands of settled Indians in the country. In reality, the seizure of the pueblos vastly enhanced the commercial potential of the state, not only by unleashing a large, hitherto underutilized labor force, but also by turning over to government control some of the finest ranches, farmlands, and yerbales in Paraguay.

In essence, then, an archaic institution was abolished in order to make room for commerce. Paraguay's closed economy, nurtured under Francia, was, by 1852, almost wholly restructured in favor of open trading relations with the lower provinces. New opportunities existed for both the state and private speculator, and neither showed any interest in a return to isolation.

The New Paraguay

Paraguayan exports had suffered in their traditional markets since the 1820s. This was particularly true of yerba, which had to face competition from Brazil. Though inferior, Brazilian yerba was readily available in Buenos Aires and other middle-distance markets. López coped with this situation by creating state monopolies for yerba, timber, and, intermittently, hides and cattle by-products. In this fashion, López made official something that went unstated in Francia's time: The state meant to control national trade in all its aspects. The mercantilist origins of this attitude were clear enough. Whatever else occurred, the state intended to reap its share of profits from commerce.

The government monopolies never constituted the regressive institutions that they seem to have been at first glance; because the monopolies paid their many employees at least partly in coin, they swelled the ranks of Paraguayan wage earners, while simultaneously decreasing the number of people held in peonage. Their primary function, however, was to assure an inflow of revenue to the treasury.

López realized that the economic development of Paraguay depended to some extent on foreign entrepreneurs and the capital that they would bring into the country. By the mid-1840s, enough foreign merchants were resident in Pilar for the government to publish a decree defining their status. Among other things, the decree stressed that the property of foreigners was to be considered inviolate, even in time of war. Departing from Francia's strict observance of the *droit d'aubane*, by which the state automatically seized the possessions of foreign nationals who died in Paraguay, López announced that the property of any foreigner dying without a will would be held for legal heirs or creditors and only after two years would be adjudged to the treasury.[54] And, if this were not enough to reassure foreign merchants, López took a personal interest in the welfare of certain of their number. At the beginning of the new decade, he helped North American investors establish a cigar-rolling factory, a sawmill, and other concerns. Though López eventually withdrew these privileges, he by no means discouraged foreign enterprise. The British and French, eager to exploit a huge, virtually untapped market, entered the Upper Plata in great numbers, there to be welcomed by both the Paraguayan and Correntino governments. By the late 1850s, almost all of the larger import houses in the region were foreign-owned.

The López family also engaged heavily in commerce, with the children of the president often acting as middlemen and earning substantial commissions. They took advantage of their position to buy at prices below market and to sell above. Having started life in fairly mean circumstances, the López sons lost no time in establishing themselves as key figures in landholding, ranching, and the yerba trade. Their father's generosity made possible their large-scale entry into the yerba workings of San Pedro, Concepción, and Río Estrella. One son-in-law, Vicente Barrios, exploited the rich yerbales of San Estanislao. Another, Saturnino Bedoya, ran one of the largest auction and wholesale houses in Asunción. Even the female relatives of the president profited by purchasing ragged banknotes from the public at an 8 percent discount and exchanging them at full value from the treasury. No one dared complain about the business ventures of the López family.[55]

These shady activities failed, however, to keep out other native merchants. Upper Platine businessmen, many of whom had suffered under Francia and the Rosistas, returned from exile during these years to claim a share of the export trade. One, Juan Andrés Gelly, later achieved distinction as Paraguayan foreign minister. Another, Pedro Nolasco Decoud, was a forebear of several important Paraguayan politicians of the post-

1870 era. These individuals were often joined in their commercial enterprises by friends and relatives who had stayed behind. Native talents and entrepreneurial skills (not to mention the impact of technological improvements such as steam-powered vessels) were, in a small way, reunited in fomenting commercial growth. In many respects, the Upper Plata of the 1850s was finally beginning to fulfill the promise of the late colonial period.

As a result of the opening of the rivers and the signing of commercial treaties with Argentina, Britain, France, the United States, and Sardinia in 1853–54, Paraguay underwent a substantial transformation. At the time of the Anglo-French intervention, the country was so isolated that most Paraguayans had never seen a foreign vessel—much less a steamer— sailing the Río Paraguay. By the 1850s, however, scores of merchant ships visited Paraguay, expanding foreign trade at all levels. Specific figures for exports of the four chief Paraguayan commodities will be examined later, but taken as a whole, Paraguayan exports during the years 1857, 1858, and 1860 realized nearly two and one-half times the value of those realized between 1852 and 1854. The import statistics for the same period suggest a growth of at least 100 percent.[56]

In the new scheme of things, Pilar lost its standing as the only legal port of entry on the Río Paraguay, and Asunción resumed its role as the focal point of the Paraguayan yerba trade. Yerba in the 1850s accounted for 40 to 50 percent of the total value of exports, recalling the late colonial era and early Francia years. In relative terms, tobacco was even more successful. The value for annual tobacco exports tripled between 1854 and 1858, and in volume the totals sometimes outstripped those for yerba. Though the Argentine provinces consumed most Paraguayan tobacco, some small amounts apparently reached the European marketplace.[57]

Wine, perfumes, cloth, arms, and munitions were imported, in addition to finished goods. The López government constituted the sole customer for arms and munitions, along with huge quantities of iron and construction materials. Such purchases were made possible by revenues derived from customs duties, stamped paper, shopkeepers' licenses, the *diezmo* (a tax on crop production that Francia had abolished and López reinstated, much to the detriment of the chacreros), and, of course, by profits from state monopolies. Government purchases amounted to around one-quarter of Paraguay's total imports, though they rarely figured in the official returns.

López also used state revenues to hire foreign engineers and machinists, most of them British, to work on a number of ambitious state projects, including a railroad, arsenal, shipyard, new docking facilities at Asunción, an imposing fortress at Humaitá, and an iron foundry. In the 1970s, these innovations gained some attention from writers, including myself, who saw in them clear proof of autonomous development. Standards of proof have grown stricter on this point since then, however, as well they might, for what looked impressive at first glance turns out to be a much more modest change than many historians initially thought. To be specific, a balanced program of economic modernization was the furthest thing from López's mind. His coffers registered a surplus that he used to bolster the Paraguayan military; all of his major projects were directed toward that basic goal. Other effects were incidental.[58]

It should be noted, moreover, that Paraguay was hardly alone in pursuing a limited kind of "development." Most Latin American states aided the establishment of manufacturing in one way or the other. In Colombia, state loans to private manufacturers and limited industrial monopolies were common in the 1850s.[59] In Mexico, the government financed the establishment of textile mills, carpet factories, and iron and paper manufacture.[60]

López was unique only in that he placed military preparedness ahead of overall economic growth. And even limited growth, he realized, depended above all on outside trade. In Paraguay, no one, least of all López, spoke of modernization in isolation from the rest of the world.

The economic stance of the López government remained an odd blend of the old and the new. López recognized that his country needed trade, but he was not so sure that it needed many traders. A suspicious man, López was loathe to let outsiders have much commercial influence in his country. His treatment of individual foreign merchants remained arbitrary, which surely deterred many from a long stay in Paraguay. Foreigners were forbidden to own land, and all commercial transactions were subject to a complex series of regulations that discouraged foreign participation. Overseas traders especially complained of inconsistent portage fees and of the length of time (sometimes a matter of weeks) spent in evaluating payment of duties. Writing in 1856, the British consul, Charles Henderson, summed up merchants' complaints by stating that the López regime had much to learn about economics:

> The commerce of Paraguay is susceptible of a vast increase. Were the government to abandon its monopolies and restrictive policy, freely admit foreigners and foreign improvements, stimulate the native population to habits of industry by allowing them to reap the advantage of their exertions, and encourage useful enterprises for which the country offers a splendid field, a most beneficial change would soon take place, and industry and commerce would bring vigor and prosperity where poverty and indolence are now paramount.[61]

In fact, at least in the case of yerba, López's conservative approach may have resulted in an optimal return for the Paraguayans. Because state interests remained paramount, López wanted no interference from merchants who might wish to reform fiscal procedures. As it was, the Paraguayan government had to deal with increased smuggling, which had grown almost as fast as the legal trade, and which also frequently involved foreigners.[62]

Despite the difficulties, López needed the foreign traders. Domestic trade had also grown, but few Paraguayans possessed the capital, talent, and business experience to branch out into the overseas trade. Retail sales remained in the hands of Paraguayans, but licenses were expensive, and native merchants were often dependent on the foreigners for credit. The few Paraguayan entrepreneurs who surfaced at this time soon tired of commerce and applied their profits to the more prestigious acquisition of land. This left foreigners in a commanding position in the country's trade. In January 1855, only three British commercial houses operated in Asunción, but between them they handled a third of the goods imported into Paraguay. Paraguayan commission agents and Correntino and Italian merchants brought in the remaining two-thirds.[63]

Typical of the foreign merchants entering Paraguay during these times was David Bruce, captain of the Porteño vessel *Buenos Aires*. Landing at Asunción in July 1855, he unloaded 500 large boxes of "general merchandise," 8 kegs of wine, 20 kilos of iron, 22 large flasks of olive oil, 3 large rolls of paper, 10 copper bars, and 10 cases of champagne. Bruce had already spent a number of years in the Paraná trade and knew the Upper Platine market well. He would have earned a massive profit on his venture had it not been for the discovery of over one hundred arrobas of yerba concealed on his vessel beneath packages of tobacco. Though the police soon demonstrated that the Italian officer of the *Buenos Aires* had hidden this contraband, the Paraguayan government decided to fine Bruce as well, who paid a penalty of 1,368 pesos. Humiliated, the Briton decided to remain outside of the Paraguay trade thereafter.[64]

In any case, the import-export totals for 1851–61 suggest that López, operating under the old mercantilist system, had managed to produce a healthy balance of trade, slipping into deficit only once (see Table 2.1). Over this eleven-year period, Paraguay earned more than 4,000,000 pesos from commerce, a considerable sum by Upper Platine standards and far better than that achieved by Corrientes. Even though Henderson argued that under an "enlightened system of commerce" the country's production would increase tenfold, López's trade policies clearly reaped some benefit for Paraguay. I remain hestitant, however, about official statistics that pointedly excluded arms purchases in an age of military buildup. Moreover, under the mercantilist system of López, the import market

TABLE 2.1: Value of Paraguayan Trade, 1851–61 (in pesos fuertes)

Year	Exports	Imports	Difference
1851	341,616	230,917	+ 110,699
1852	470,010	715,886	− 245,876
1853	690,480	406,688	+ 283,792
1854	777,861	595,823	+ 182,038
1855	1,005,900	431,835	+ 574,065
1856	1,143,131	631,234	+ 511,897
1857	1,700,722	1,074,639	+ 626,083
1858	1,205,819	866,596	+ 339,223
1859	2,199,678	1,539,648	+ 660,030
1860	1,693,904	855,841	+ 808,063
1861	1,344,542	1,013,246	+ 331,296
Total	12,573,663	8,392,353	+ 4,181,310

Source: Marbais Du Graty, *La república del Paraguay*, pp. 346–48; Schmitt, *Paraguay und Europa*, p. 146.

was largely limited to a small elite that could afford fine wines, perfumes, and other luxuries. The bulk of the Paraguayan population had little contact with imports of any kind, outside of an occasional machete or a bolt of cheap cloth. The state was content to stress only exports and let imports take care of themselves. While this attitude brought larger revenues to the government and profits to a few individuals, it clearly failed to foster any real economic development.

Another change associated with the opening of the rivers should be noted: The trans-Misiones trade between Encarnación and São Borja had become obsolete. Some caravans still made the trip during the 1850s, but the direct river contact with Buenos Aires made the secondary route unnecessary. While this commerce was dying, however, another was being born—with the Brazilian province of Mato Grosso via the Río Paraguay.

The Opening of the Mato Grosso

Mato Grosso was probably the most isolated area of Brazil. Lying just north of the Upper Plata, it was in some respects more a part of the Platine region than of the Brazilian empire. Overland communication with the rest of Brazil had always been nearly impossible. In the colonial period, the population of Mato Grosso amounted to only a few hundred Portuguese military personnel, gold prospectors, and partly acculturated Indians. Things changed little until the 1850s. No one ever delineated the

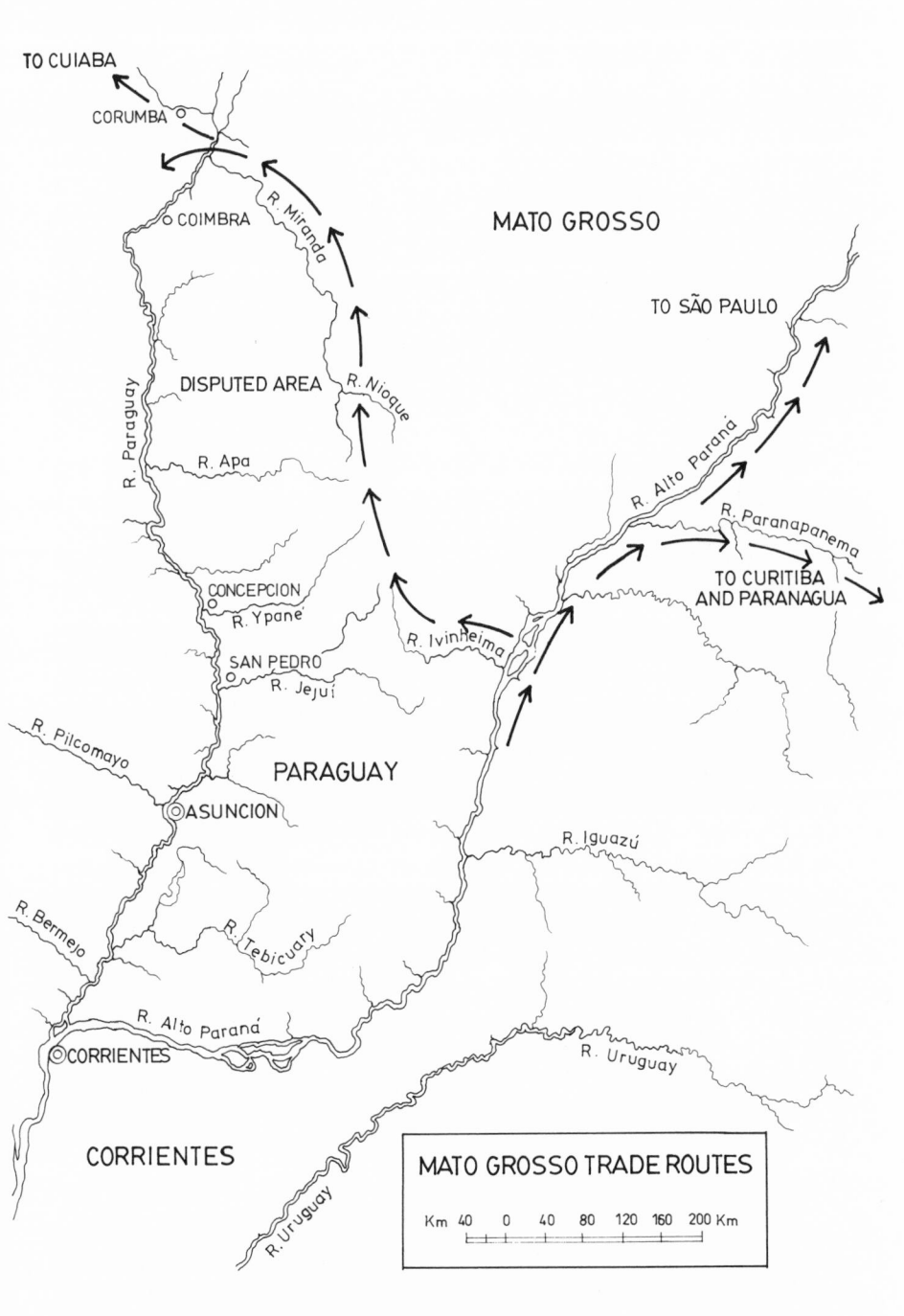

TO CUIABA

CORUMBA

COIMBRA

MATO GROSSO

R. Miranda

TO SÃO PAULO

R. Nioque

DISPUTED AREA

R. Apa

R. Alto Paraná

R. Paraguay

R. Paranapanema

CONCEPCION

R. Ypane

TO CURITIBA
AND PARANAGUA

SAN PEDRO

R. Jejui

R. Ivinheima

PARAGUAY

R. Pilcomayo

R. Iguazú

ASUNCION

R. Bermejo

R. Tebicuary

R. Alto Paraná

CORRIENTES

R. Uruguay

CORRIENTES

R. Uruguay

MATO GROSSO TRADE ROUTES

Km 40   0   40   80   120   160   200 Km

border with Paraguay, and try as they might, imperial authorities failed to obtain permission from Asunción to use the Río Paraguay as their main link with the tiny settlements of the Brazilian far west. As for direct commercial contacts between Mato Grosso and Paraguay, these were vetoed by Francia, who loudly rejected what he saw as a "contemptible trade in bagatelles, which amounts to no more than some hammocks, a little bit of cotton, and some bolts of very ordinary, crude cotton cloth," all of which he suspected would provide a pretext for spying.[65]

Frustrated Brazilian officials responded with a plan to create a mixed fluvial-overland route leading to the Mato Grossense capital of Cuiabá from the Atlantic port of Paranaguá via Curitiba and the Paranapanema, Alto Paraná, Ivinheima, Brilhante, Nioque, and Miranda rivers. With the exception of a short stretch between the headwaters of the Brilhante and the Nioque, the route was entirely navigable for small craft from Curitiba on. The government actually founded several military colonies in the south of Mato Grosso in the early 1850s to help facilitate this plan.[66] Like the trans-Misiones route, however, this new passage was still cumbersome and artificial, and when López finally agreed to open the Paraguay to Brazilian traffic in 1858, the colonies on the banks of the Brilhante and Nioque rivers began to stagnate.[67]

The 1858 agreement stipulated that no more than three ships could ascend the Paraguay from its mouth at any one time. This allayed the fears of López, who, because the treaty ignored the issue of boundaries, still suspected Brazilian intentions. In spite of this drawback, some trade was generated at Mato Grossense ports in the late 1850s and early 1860s. Unfortunately, Brazilian customs regulations plagued this interchange from the start, since vessels were required to discharge their goods for duty payment at the town of Corumbá, more than 400 miles below Cuiabá, the chief market. Brazilian ships could proceed to Cuiabá, but Paraguayan vessels were not allowed beyond Corumbá and had to send their cargoes on in canoes at great expense and risk. The exorbitant price for canoe transport, when added to the high freights paid from Buenos Aires, raised prices almost to a par with those of goods conducted by land from Rio de Janeiro.[68] Despite this impediment, the Mato Grosso trade proceeded in a fashion, and the towns of the province soon received merchant vessels from Buenos Aires, Corrientes, Italy, and Uruguay, as well as from Paraguay and Brazil.

Corrientes in 1850s

Corrientes also took advantage of the new trading opportunities gained from the opening of the rivers. The population of the province had grown to over 82,000 by 1850, and many Correntinos eagerly prepared to meet the challenge of an enhanced export trade.[69] Sadly, exact figures for this commercial growth are wanting for the period after 1855. Two years earlier, the new constitution nationalized the provincial customs service, and its records were no longer kept as regularly as before. That a great deal of economic progress was attained in Corrientes, however, is beyond doubt.

Much credit should be given to the efforts of Governor Juan Gregorio Pujol (1817–61). The son of a peninsular merchant, Pujol had the advantages of wealth and education. Like Francia, he was a product of the University of Córdoba, but, whereas the Paraguayan had dedicated himself to the study of theology, the Correntino made jurisprudence his occupation and unitario politics his passion. Assuming office after the defeat of Rosas at Caseros, Pujol came to symbolize the innovative spirit of his times and class, for the elites of Corrientes, more so than those of Paraguay, had taken modernization to heart. Pujol favored an open system for Corrientes, one in which provincial economic development would parallel that of Buenos Aires, without the province becoming subservient to the port city. Although this vision proved naive in the long run, Pujol tried to further its possibilities during his administration. He gave the impression of shrewd judgment and integrity and, armed with these qualities, convinced many Correntinos of the rightness of his thinking. Pujol even managed to gain control of the countryside, suppressing vagrancy in his quest for modernization and social order.[70]

His predecessor, Benjamín Virasoro, had limited his economic policies to the enactment of various protectionist measures, such as 50-percent duties on the importation of foreign tobacco, cigars, honey, and starch.[71] Virasoro doubled the fee required for commercial licenses and anchorage and tripled that for navigational permits.[72] He never went beyond such traditional mechanisms for bolstering the fiscal well-being of Corrientes.

Pujol was of a different stripe. He started his administration by inaugurating a foreign-run steamship line that served the Correntino ports on the Paraná. With an eye to future commerce, he also authorized the exploration of the Bermejo River, a tributary of the Río Paraguay that might offer an opportunity to link Corrientes with the town of Oran in Salta province. Pujol opened two new ports, Empedrado and Yahapé, to outside trade and arranged for the dredging of the Riacho of Goya to accommodate more shipping.[73]

Pujol correctly identified underpopulation as the key obstacle to Correntino economic growth. He proposed to overcome this problem by attracting foreign immigrants to the area through special subsidies, land grants, and other government aid. Pujol actually created an agricultural community for French colonists at San Juan.[74]

Some of Pujol's innovations, however, engendered opposition from the Paraguayans. In mid-1853, the Correntino governor imposed a 5-

percent transit duty on produce exported from Paraguay, apparently to raise extra funds to finance his many projects.[75] López angrily denounced the step as contrary to the terms of the 1852 recognition treaty. When this complaint failed to move Pujol, López closed Paraguayan ports to Correntino shipping and communicated this decision to all foreign representatives then present in Asunción.[76] This display of pique had the desired effect, with Pujol rescinding the transit duty early the next year. Amicable commercial relations between Paraguay and Corrientes resumed in March, after López revoked his own punitive decree. From that point on, Pujol had little trouble with the Paraguayans.

Visitors to Corrientes in the 1850s and 1860s reported a prosperous territory, well suited to commercial ventures and lacking only sufficient population to fully exploit its abundant resources. The population of the province had risen to 85,447 inhabitants in 1857, with 8,626 living in the capital city.[77]

More than one hundred merchants, a large portion of whom were foreigners, made their residence at the port of Corrientes in the mid-1850s. Such a sizable mercantile presence only three years after the opening of the Paraná suggests that trade had grown rapidly in the province; the state newspaper saw fit to advertise sales and auctions of imported goods on a weekly basis as well as the comings and goings of vessels and the arrival of consignments of merchandise. To take one example, on January 23, 1856, the schooner *Asia* arrived from Buenos Aires with goods for fifteen different merchants, including books, medicines, hardware, flour, sugar, hats, paper, yerba mate, paint, and a machine for shelling maize.[78]

Merchants long-established in Corrientes had advantages not available to newcomers. They knew the territory and had the right local connections to smooth the way for any venture. Many were first-generation Argentines with as many links to the old world as to Buenos Aires. Yet even these individuals could put on a Correntino face. The career of Roberto Guy Billinghurst provides the clearest case. Born in Buenos Aires in 1819, Billinghurst made his earliest appearance in the Upper Plata as an agent of a Porteño firm. He later married a relative of Governor Virasoro and set up his own retail and wholesale shop in the provincial capital. Together with his brother Mariano, he opened a branch office in Pilar in the early López years. He spent more than a decade trading Manchester goods for Paraguayan yerba, growing rich in the process. Billinghurst owned at least two merchant vessels that ferried goods to and from Buenos Aires. Some ten years after the Anglo-French intervention, the British government named him vice-consul in Corrientes, a post that not only gave him partial immunity from political problems but also helped him secure recognition as a patron for all British commerce in the region. As much a modernizer as his friend Pujol, Billinghurst was a founding member of the Correntino chamber of commerce, which, in 1855, boasted a dues-paying membership of ninety businessmen.[79]

Since the Paraná remained the principal route for trade, few in the Correntino government gave much thought to the Río Uruguay, save for an occasional official argument for higher taxes. The right bank of the river had not recovered from the Paraguayan invasion of 1849, and eight years later, the Santo Tomé district still possessed only 864 inhabitants, making it the least populated district in the province.[80] In consequence, the number of merchant ships involved in the commerce above Salto never rose above one hundred between the mid-1850s and the early 1860s. Only one, the Brazilian vessel *Uruguay*, was a steamer, and it was apparently unable to service São Borja and Hormiguero because it could not pass over the Butuí rapids.[81] An expansion of trade did occur on the Río Uruguay during this period, but only in its lower reaches at Paysandú and Concepción del Uruguay. The success of this commerce was almost entirely due to the operations of General Urquiza's nearby *saladero*.[82]

Background to War: The Early 1860s

Carlos Antonio López died in 1862, having survived his counterpart Pujol by only thirteen months. These two men had provided the Upper Platine states with insightful, if sometimes eccentric, leadership and had overseen the transformation of the region from an isolated backwater to a place of relative prosperity. For Paraguay in particular, trade links had been reestablished with Corrientes, Buenos Aires, and Montevideo, and had extended, in a tentative way, to Europe. The 1852 agreements opened more than just the Paraná and Paraguay rivers—it also created the conditions for sustained growth in the Upper Plata. Self-sufficiency and protectionism had yielded to an outward-looking pattern of economic growth based on stable markets in the lower provinces. As long as the housing boom in Buenos Aires lasted, there would be a demand for Upper Platine timber. Yerba from the region would continue to quench the thirst of Porteño consumers, and the demand for hides from the northeast remained stable in the tanneries of Buenos Aires and Montevideo. López and Pujol saw all this clearly and adjusted their policies to take advantage of favorable trade.

There seemed little reason to assume that these trends would change after 1862. In Paraguay, Carlos Antonio López was succeeded by his eldest son, Francisco Solano López (1826–70). The chief beneficiary of his father's favor, the younger López had had all the material advantages that his country could offer. Overindulged in every way, he was imperious, conceited, and had decided ideas about the proper relations of rank and class.[83] He fancied himself a military genius, an appraisal that had tragic consequences.

As regards the economy, López was perhaps more astute than his father. He had visited Europe in 1853–54 and brought back some sound ideas for promoting Paraguayan trade. For example, he tried to diversify the export market by subsidizing overseas shipments of national products. One of these products was cotton, the development of which López saw as a key objective. With the southern ports of the United States block-aded after 1861, Britain cried out for other sources of cotton; López sought to meet this demand by improving the Paraguayan harvest through the use of North American seeds and new techniques.[84] Ultimately, as will be seen, he had little chance to exploit any new markets. In other respects, Francisco Solano López continued the trade policies of his father.

Corrientes fared less well after Pujol left the governorship in 1859. As part of the Argentine Confederation, the province was overtaken by the larger political struggles of the nation. Buenos Aires had withdrawn from the Confederation only one year after the battle at Caseros, leaving the other thirteen provinces, Corrientes among them, to follow Urquiza and the ideal of federalism. Free navigation of the rivers had been achieved, but this alone had failed to resolve the issue of the port city's proper place within the Confederation, leaving Buenos Aires and the Litoral locked in conflict.

Urquiza's goal during the 1850s was to bring trade to the Litoral prov-inces via the Río Paraná ports, especially Rosario. He had some luck with this, though hardly enough to balance the Confederation's lack of access to the Porteño market, which was booming thanks to increased European demand for wool. It proved difficult to attract foreign ship-ping to the Paraná when merchants could deal with Buenos Aires and save themselves the added expense of a upriver voyage. The Porteños also had sufficient collateral to obtain European loans, whereas the Con-federation government barely made ends meet. To meet this fiscal chal-lenge, Urquiza tried lowering import duties, but even this did not work. By the end of the decade, he was desperate and ready to resort to force.

The struggle between Buenos Aires and the Confederation caught the Upper Plata at a disadvantage. For the rivers to remain open, it was nec-essary for the region to have good relations with both sides. The Cor-rentinos had seen their percentage of the Porteño trade nearly double in the 1850s, and no one wished to see that commerce disrupted. The Paraguayans, happy in their new prosperity, also proved eager to fore-stall any outbreak of hostilities. Thus, in 1859, when violence first broke out between the Confederation and Buenos Aires, it was Paraguayan medi-ation that contained and momentarily defused the crisis.

Pujol sided with the Confederation, though he was in no sense Urquiza's puppet. If anything, like his predecessors, he represented the independent commercial interests of Corrientes—the shipwrights, immigrants, and potential investors in the province. Some ranchers supported him in this and in his admiration for a laissez faire interpretation of the economy. Others, such as Nicanor Cáceres (1812–70) of the cattle district of Curuzú Cuatiá, remained suspicious of this approach. When Rosas left the scene, these men switched their loyalty to another caudillo, Urquiza.

Ever since independence, the provincial authorities at the port of Corrientes had tried to bring the southern ranching zones under the fiscal sway of the government. They had made some progress under Pujol, but many ranchers still resented the favoritism shown merchants and foreign entrepreneurs. If these trends had gone unchanged, the political power of the ranchers surely would have been eclipsed. As it was, the dispute between Buenos Aires and the Confederation gave new hope to Cáceres and the other rural caudillos. The resulting cleavage in the body politic of Corrientes created new instability in the province during the 1860s.

Pujol, promoted to national senator, had left the governorship to José María Rolón (1826–62), a cleric of mediocre talents and little imagination, who proceeded to reverse economic policies. Rather than encourage the yerba mate industry through subsidies or reduced license fees, Rolón hindered it with new taxes.[85] He reestablished the internal passport, making noncompliance a serious crime. He also restricted the sale of horses outside of the province and, in as many ways as possible, tried to resurrect the administrative and fiscal structures of the pre-Pujol era.[86] In this, he had ongoing help from Cáceres and other rural bosses, who opposed the Correntino merchants. In large part, these attitudes were irrational, since the ranchers gained from the more open economy after 1852. Nevertheless, they thought the merchants could not be trusted to safeguard the interests of the campo. Sadly for Corrientes, this local conflict was quickly subsumed—and transformed—by the greater struggle between Buenos Aires and the Confederation.

The overall political picture in the Plata took on a new aspect in September 1861, when the Porteño militia gained the advantage against Confederation troops at the battle of Pavón in the province of Buenos Aires. Though Urquiza held his ground, he was disillusioned by the failure of his forces to overcome those of the port city. He elected to abandon the field. Urquiza retired to Entre Ríos, there to brood over his poor fortune and to hope for better days. Even in his retirement, however, he still maintained a wide influence in the Litoral.

Pavón signalled the rise to power in Argentina of Bartolomé Mitre (1821–1906), governor of Buenos Aires. As much a man of letters as a man of the sword, Mitre had cleverly exploited the difficulties in Corrientes to carve out a base of personal support in the Upper Plata. After Pavón, he quickly secured the presidency and, from that high position, attempted to manipulate national policy in favor of Porteño interests. Mitre had a broader vision of Argentina's future, however, than either Rosas or Urquiza. As historian H. S. Ferns explains,

> The economic significance of the victory of General Mitre consisted in the recognition at the center of authority of the advantages to the mercantile and landowning class of securing capital and labor from Europe, both of which were cheap by comparison with the capital and labor available in Argentine itself. It was assumed correctly that both would flow to the River Plate if security was offered, and security was a matter of political action. Once Argentina had demonstrated a capacity to protect the lives of foreign immigrants and to pay a fixed rate of interest and debt service charges, both workers and investors, the first mainly in Spain and Italy, the second mainly in Britain, were willing to try their luck in Argentina.[87]

Of course, for Mitre's scheme to come to fruition, he had to eliminate any rival center of power around which provincial opposition might gravitate—and he had to do this quickly, before his enemies in the Litoral could regroup.

The Upper Plata felt immediately the effect of Mitre's ascendancy. In Corrientes, Rolón resigned in December 1861 under pressure from urban liberals who had supported Mitre against Urquiza. Rolón was replaced by two Mitristas, José Pampín (1861–62) and Manuel Ignacio Lagraña (1862–65). Amidst the political confusion, these two men attempted to advance Correntino trade through closer ties to Buenos Aires. In addition, Lagraña lowered the yerba tax, though he did not abolish it; opened a series of roads into the yerbales; and established several mills in Misiones to facilitate processing. He also promoted the cultivation of cotton and tobacco in Corrientes by distributing seeds and free land to interested speculators.[88]

Despite these advances, neither Pampín nor Lagraña managed to win the sympathy of the cattle interests in the south. Under the influence of Cáceres, who spent part of the mid-1860s in exile, this powerful sector remained opposed to any ties to Mitre and the Porteños. Urquiza, sulking in Entre Ríos, gave tacit support to this opposition. Thus, on the eve of the War of the Triple Alliance in 1864, Corrientes was still a divided polity, with one foot striding toward liberal, capitalist, outward-oriented economic growth and the other planted in a tradition of mercantilism and de facto rule.

The Maelstrom

The events that finally sparked the war were straightforward enough. The Brazilian leadership had had longstanding difficulties with Uruguay, a country whose ranching elite had several times supported rebels in Rio Grande do Sul. Aside from this general animosity, certain Brazilian landowners held property on both sides of the Brazil-Uruguay frontier without ever having bothered to establish clear and legal title. By the early 1860s, these hazy claims and counterclaims resulted in a major international dispute that Brazil was willing to settle by force. The Uruguayans had some allies, however. Neither Francia nor Carlos Antonio López had cared much about the far-off Banda Oriental, and they had never thought to intervene in Uruguayan affairs in favor of one cause or another. The younger López convinced himself, however, that the political status of the other Platine buffer state was intimately tied to that of Paraguay. Through diplomatic channels, he let it be known that his government would not countenance any outside interference in the affairs of that state. This argument was a completely new—and erroneous—interpretation of balance-of-power arrangements in the Plata.

In fact, outside of López's imagination, no balance of power had existed in the Río de la Plata and therefore no possible threat to such a balance. If there was a preeminent power in the greater region, clearly it was Brazil. Since the defeat of the Farrapos, the empire had followed a clear policy of territorial aggrandizement on its southern borders. Boundary disputes between Paraguay and Brazil, having their roots in colonial times, had resurfaced during the time of the elder López. Through negotiations, he had managed to delay any showdowns. His son, however, dreamed of Paraguay as the great arbiter of South America, a posture that set him on a collision course with neighboring states. Even if López was sincere in his estimation of the political realities, anything more than a rhetorical attack against the powerful empire seemed absurd and was discounted by all observers. The Brazilians simply chose to ignore the Paraguayan threat and proceeded against Uruguay through a military intervention. An enraged López responded with a general mobilization, sending his troops upriver into Mato Grosso. A few months later, trying to force a passage south to Uruguay across Correntino territory, López also incurred the ill-will of Argentina. He ended by going to war with both countries, and ultimately with Uruguay, by then under the control of forces friendly to Brazil.

In order to keep their autonomous development model for Paraguay consistent, dependency writers such as Trías and José Alfredo Fornos Penalba have portrayed the War of the Triple Alliance as a conspiracy designed by Britain and its local proxies to destroy an alternative economic system that threatened the capitalist order in South America. Eduardo Galeano, more a figure of the Latin American literary world than an historian per se, nonetheless provides a cogent summary of the dependency position on the war:

> British commerce did not hide its concern [over Paraguay], not only because this last bastion of national resistance in the heart of the continent seemed invulnerable, but also and especially because of the dangerous example set to its neighbors by the Paraguayan obstinacy. Latin America's most progressive country was building its future without foreign investment, without British loans, and without the blessings of free trade.[89]

Such, we are told, was the underlying cause of the conflict, with British monies and political support arranged in favor of the Allies.

The Paraguayans, however, were neither obstinate nor particularly progressive in their dealings with the wider regional economy. Indeed, no structural contradiction existed between the economy of Paraguay and that of its neighbors that had to be resolved through war. By the 1860s, almost nothing remained of a closed economy in the region. Protectionism had been scrapped, duties generally had been reduced, and European manufactured goods, capital goods, and merchant houses had become the dominant features of the trade, in Buenos Aires, Corrientes, and Asunción as well. As for the British, they already understood that the Paraguayan market was too small to warrant their attention in any meaningful way. Some British banks issued loans to Brazil and Argentina to finance military expansion in the early stages of the war, but this was private speculation, arranged with the expectation that the conflict would end in a quick Allied victory. When months turned into years, the bankers began to regret their earlier enthusiasm. The politicians at Westminster, for their part, were completely indifferent as to who won or lost the war.[90]

Ironically, the dependency theorists have fallen for the self-serving tales of Mitre and other Allied propagandists, who claimed that their war against López would result in open rivers. That was nonsense; the rivers were already open to as much traffic as the market could bear. Mitre, a consummate politician as well as a major proponent of the war, had reason to thank López for the latter's foolhardy attack in 1865. After all, the occupation of Corrientes left the Litoral provinces with no alternative to Porteño leadership. Buenos Aires could count on Brazilian arms to prosecute a war that many in the Argentine interior otherwise would have opposed. As for the argument that Mitre went to war to eliminate the threat posed by the statist model of government, this, too, misses the point.[91] Mitre attacked the authoritarianism of the López regime because that feature of the Paraguayan political order was least acceptable to European public opinion. To help carry out the war, Mitre wanted to attract potential backers across the Atlantic with the idea that he was motivated solely to overcome tyranny. His real aim was to consolidate Porteño rule in Argentina and annex as much of Paraguay as possible, but this goal he carefully enclosed in a mask of liberalism.

During the first months of the war, trade was left undisturbed, except in Mato Grosso. Immediately after the capture of the Brazilian steamer *Marqués de Olinda* in November 1864, López dispatched some 3,500 men by river and another 2,500 by land to take the southern reaches of Mato Grosso as far as Corumbá. This expedition was wildly successful. Taking the main centers of the province within weeks, the Paraguayan army sent south a large cache of military stocks encountered at Coimbra, Miranda, Albuquerque, and Corumbá. These arms and munitions proved of inestimable value to the Paraguayan war effort, since, with some few exceptions, they constituted the only military supplies López received after 1864. During the Mato Grosso campaign, the Paraguayans captured several merchant vessels that they ultimately converted into warships. Only one foreign vessel, the British steamer *Ranger*, was permitted to descend from Mato Grosso, and this solely because the British decided to sell the ship to López.[92]

The small commerce of Mato Grosso disintegrated rapidly under the Paraguayan occupation. One observer, then living in Asunción, remarked of the former mercantile community of Mato Grosso that

> all the foreigners [the Paraguayans] could find were brought down as prisoners, after having been stripped of everything they possessed; they were principally Germans, Italians, and Frenchmen. I saw many poor fellows working as laborers or begging in the streets, who, a few weeks before, had been wealthy merchants or landowners.[93]

Fresh from his victory in the north, López rashly turned his attention to Corrientes. The Paraguayan leader assumed that provincial separatism would keep the Argentines from making any serious response until after he had defeated the Brazilians in Uruguay. In this, López particularly counted on Urquiza, who he mistakenly believed would reject Porteño pleas for a united front.

In April 1865, a small Paraguayan fleet captured the port of Corrientes, and within a few days López disembarked the better part of his army at that point. His troops moved southward in two columns, one along the Uruguay and the other along the Paraná.

For all intents and purposes, the Uruguay River campaign had already started in January, when a 10,000-man Paraguayan expeditionary force passed over the Alto Paraná into Misiones to prepare for a possible advance to the south. In late April, the column began its march. The Correntino inhabitants of the west, or right, bank of the Uruguay fled in panic at the approach of López's army. On May 10, when the Paraguayans entered Santo Tomé, they found the place abandoned, "except for a few families and merchants, the majority of whom were foreigners."[94] The merchants apparently took advantage of the circumstances and appropriated a large number of cattle and horses left behind by fleeing Correntino ranchers.

In early June, advance elements of the Paraguayan army crossed the Uruguay at São Borja and swiftly consolidated a bridgehead. On reaching the town, Paraguayan officers told local citizens that López expected aid from Urquiza in Entre Ríos that would enable their troops to divide and undertake the capture of Montevideo and Pôrto Alegre.[95] Unfortunately, help from Urquiza never materialized.

As the Paraguayans pushed south, they lost contact with the supply base at Encarnación. This necessitated foraging on a wide scale, which quickly reversed the stock gains made in the region since 1852. Citrus orchards were destroyed and ranch houses sacked in the process.[96] In the end, the Paraguayan columns advanced as far as Uruguaiana, where Allied forces cut them off in August. After one bloody engagement on the right bank of the river, the Paraguayan commanders decided that their situation was hopeless and surrendered. The Río Uruguay played no role in the struggle thereafter.

The fortunes of the Paraguayan column on the Paraná also proved dismal. López had seriously miscalculated the possibility of aid from Urquiza and the latter's Correntino allies. In fact, six days after the attack on Corrientes, Urquiza sent a letter to Mitre offering full support against the invaders.[97] For the moment, the entire nation rallied to the leadership of Buenos Aires and made Mitre's job of sealing an unpopular alliance with Brazil all the easier. Dissension within several of Argentina's provinces occurred intermittently during the course of the war, but Mitre won enough time to gain the advantage against the Paraguayans and drive them back across the Paraná.

The occupation of Corrientes had not reflected well on the Paraguayans. The Correntinos apparently entered the war with little fear of the Paraguayan soldiery, on many occasions welcoming them.[98] The troops of López, however, failed to acquit themselves with distinction. They freely looted the ranches of Goya and Bella Vista, destroying what they could not carry off. The large herds of livestock in the province were put to the knife to prevent their falling into Allied hands, leaving "the country for miles round white with the bleached bones."[99]

The commercial establishments of the province, even those owned by foreigners, fared no better. The towns of the Correntino hinterland received brutal treatment, and witnesses recorded no end of atrocities.[100] The tanneries, retail stores, port facilities, and government buildings of Goya, Bella Vista, and Empedrado were all pillaged and put to the torch.

The town of Corrientes proper came through the occupation in better condition. López had sent his foreign minister, José Berges, from Asunción to organize a provisional regime with the aid of three Correntino collaborators. This group eventually gained control of the situation and halted looting by Paraguayan troops. Reparations were paid to the most important merchants of the town. For example, T. H. Mangels, an English shopkeeper, received a full 10,000 pesos from López for the abuses he had suffered.[101]

Others were less fortunate. The Correntinos were ordered to accept Paraguayan paper currency, which was valued at thirty-four pesos to the gold ounce.[102] Some merchants expressed unwillingness to regard these bills as legal tender until the day the Paraguayan commander ordered the detention of an entire community of Chaco Indians upon their refusal to take the paper money in exchange for horse fodder and firewood. He had them all shot in full view of the merchants.[103] Though no further resistance from the shopkeepers was forthcoming, these actions did little to inspire confidence in the Paraguayan administration's stated desire for continued open trade, which was by then a hopeless goal in any case.

The details of the 1865 military campaign in Corrientes are well known. The Paraguayans pushed southward to Goya without opposition save for an occasional raid against them by cavalry units under Cáceres. A successful Allied raid on the port of Corrientes in late May brought about a temporary withdrawal of Paraguayan forces. López then decided to seize or destroy the Brazilian fleet ascending the river near Bella Vista. This decision resulted in the disastrous battle of the Riachuelo, which crushed any hopes López might have entertained for a quick victory. Paraguayan losses proved so heavy that their navy remained inactive for the rest of the war. One month later, when news of the Uruguaiana disaster reached López, he ordered his remaining troops to retreat across the Alto Paraná to fortified positions at Humaitá. The remainder of the conflict was fought on Paraguayan soil.

The Allies used the province of Corrientes as a staging area for their operations against Paraguay, and their activities and the need for provisions of all kinds led to a rebirth of commerce in this part of the Upper Plata. Yet it was an imbalanced phenomenon. Articles of clothing and manufactured goods commanded any price and were eagerly sought by soldiers of the Allied armies. Correntino produce, on the other hand, proved difficult to obtain. A large portion of the rural population had been uprooted or killed, and few were left to harvest the tobacco and cotton. The oxen needed to transport yerba from Misiones were used to haul war matériel. Moreover, only the ranches of the east escaped the ravages of the Paraguayans; all the rest were burnt and their livestock taken.[104] Some of the eastern estancieros, including Cáceres, profited from the Allied demand for meat. So did Urquiza, who by then had elected to sit out the war at his estancia in Entre Ríos. As a British officer serving with López noted,

> when the Allies invaded Paraguay [in 1866, Urquiza] sent a few hundred men, who mutinied on board the steamers, and were ultimately disbanded. He also sent a few old guns, which he had formerly taken from Buenos Ayres. He was not heard of again during the war, except as selling large quantities of cattle and horses to the Allies, and thus amassing immense wealth.[105]

All in all, the Correntino trade occasioned by the war benefitted the province only incidentally. Goods were brought from Buenos Aires or Montevideo and sold on account to the Allies, but little of the profit accrued to Corrientes. Some foreign merchants came to the port of Corrientes at this time and, in the manner of carpetbaggers, attempted to wring some earnings from the place. The 1869 census revealed 415 individuals engaged in trade at the port, of whom 181 were foreigners, including three Swiss, one Austrian, and one Mexican![106] The number of native Correntinos in this listing cannot be determined because only the denomination "Argentine" was used.

This designation—"Argentine"—indicates one important consequence of the war. Corrientes had been overwhelmed from several directions and was incapable of expressing a position independent of Buenos Aires. To be sure, Urquiza and Cáceres continued to exercise some influence in the province through puppet governors, and, as a whole, the Correntino population remained hostile to Mitre. The Correntinos, however, were in no position to defy Buenos Aires, and in 1868, Mitre used the pretext of internal dissension to expel the pro-Cáceres governor, Evaristo López, and replace him with men more favorable to Buenos Aires. In October 1869, Santiago Baibiene, the most fervent of the Correntino Mitristas, won out against other contenders and was named governor.[107] The victory of Buenos Aires was complete. Never again would the province of Corrientes reach out to Paraguay, seeking some sense of regional coherence within the Upper Plata. From then on, Buenos Aires and the Porteño vision of Argentine nationhood reigned supreme in Corrientes.

If the situation in Corrientes was bad, in Paraguay it approached savagery. A detailed examination of post-1865 events lies beyond the scope of this study. To summarize, after the retreat to Humaitá, the Allies subjected López's forces to a slow strangulation, broken periodically by extremely bloody engagements, the carnage of these nearly defying description.

Outside trade was out of the question. A number of foreign ships came up the Paraguay in the first year of the conflict to rescue the citizens of their respective countries: the Italian *Principe Oddone*, the French *Decidee*, and the British *Doterel* and *Flying Fish*. These were almost the only ships to reach Asunción during the war. Some Bolivian merchants arrived at the Paraguayan capital in 1867, but their influence was ephemeral at best. When the Allies took Asunción two years later, the city was a mere shell, and López's death in March 1870 came as an anticlimax.

The war that López had started in the name of an abstract notion, the balance of power, brought catastrophe to the people of the Upper Plata. For the region to prosper, it had to increase its trade with Buenos Aires and other ports in the lower provinces. It had to compete effectively in the yerba, tobacco, and hide trades. It had to attract outside investors who could help build a solid economy. The war made all of this impossible.

López had presented himself as a palpable, breathing symbol of the national cause, and therein lay the great tragedy of Paraguay. As the inhabitants of that country saw it, they had to choose between López and immolation. Aside from some members of the elite who had earlier taken refuge in Buenos Aires (and who subsequently fought on the Allied side), most Paraguayans followed López into the maelstrom. The peasant masses, when converted into soldiers, resolutely obeyed even the most impetuous orders of their officers. The results were terrible. Perhaps as many as 220,000 people died in battle or from disease and hunger—out of a total population of fewer than 450,000. Only 28,000 of the survivors were men; women were subsequently thought to outnumber men by more than four to one. Decades passed before a normal ratio between the sexes was reestablished.[108]

The shock delivered to the Upper Plata precluded any return to the thriving trade of the prewar years. Porteño expansion had reached its apogee, and, though the Brazilians prevented an outright Argentine annexation of Paraguay, they gave no such thought to the territories south of the Alto Paraná. Corrientes was never again able to elaborate a political role for itself separate from Buenos Aires. Economic development still resulted from the Porteño trade connection, but the prospects were in no sense good. Commerce would take long in recovering. The rivers, so long the key factor in expressing the economic identity of the Upper Plata, served the region only by defining borders.

Ruins of the Jesuit missions. (Courtesy: Archivo General de la Nación).

The Upper Platine countryside during the early 1800s. Land such as this provided hides and tallow for markets in the lower provinces (D'Orbigny, *Viaje a la América meridional*).

José Gaspar de Francia (1766–1840), Supreme Dictator of Paraguay, the first of that nation's three great authoritarian leaders. Francia proved willing to curtail trade with the lower provinces to consolidate his regime. The resulting long-term isolation of Paraguay drew the attention of many foreign observers. (Page, *La Plata, the Argentine Confederation, and Paraguay*).

Upper Platine *chacreros*, early nineteenth century.
(Demersay, *Atlas*).

The rapids (*salto*) at Santa Rosa prevented easy development of the Uruguay river as a commercial artery. (Courtesy: Archivo General de la Nación).

Juan Manuel de Rosas (1793–1877), the guiding force behind Porteño politics for a generation. As governor of Buenos Aires province, he attempted to control the entire Platine region, an effort which earned him many enemies in the Upper Plata (Alfred de Brossard, *Considérations Historiques et Politiques*).

Pedro Ferré (1788–1867), several times governor of Corrientes, and a strong advocate of protectionism and provincial rights in the face of pressures from Buenos Aires. (Courtesy: Archivo General de la Nación).

The port of Corrientes as it appeared during the Anglo-French intervention of the late 1840s. (Attributed to Ousely).

95

Yerbateros processing the *ilex* into tea in eastern Paraguay during the mid-nineteenth century. (Hield, *Glimpses of South America*).

Carlos Antonio López (1787–1862), consul and president of Paraguay during the mid-nineteenth century. López oversaw the reentry of his country into the Platine trade system after the opening of the rivers in 1852. (Du Graty, *La república del Paraguay*).

Roberto Guy Billinghurst
(1810–1892), in old age. A
major force in Upper Platine
trade in the 1850s and 1860s,
Billinghurst maintained warehouses and retail shops in
Corrientes, Goya, and Pilar.
(Courtesy: Federico Palma).

The Asunción riverfront in the
early 1850s (Demersay,
"Fragments d'un Voyage au
Paraguay").

A tobacco worker vear Villarrica in the 1850s (Demersay, "Fragments d'un Voyage au Paraguay").

(Facing page top) Rafts (*jangadas*) composed of hardwood trunks awaiting shipment to Buenos Aires (Courtesy: Archivo General de la Nación).

(Facing page bottom) The marketplace of Asunción was the center of commercial activity in Paraguay after the rivers were opened in the 1850s (DuGraty, *La república del Paraguay*).

The port of Corrientes and its shipyard in the early 1860s. (Bossi, *Viage Pinttoresco*).

Bartolomé Mitre (1821–1906), Argentine president during the Triple Alliance War. A master politician, Mitre succeeded in uniting his country under Porteño leadershp during the campaign against Paraguay. (Warren, *Paraguay: An Informal History*).

Francisco Solano López (1826–1870), Paraguayan president and field marshal, whose early plans for the modernization and expansion of Paraguay's trade were dashed by the Allied blockade during the 1864–1870 war. (O'Leary, *El Mariscal López*).

Paraguayan prisoners during the Triple Alliance War. (attributed to W. Bate).

Port scene in Corrientes, late nineteenth century. (Courtesy: Archivo General de la Nación).

(Facing page) Woodworkers camp in the Misiones, late nineteenth century. Such camps had been in operation, off and on, for nearly a century. (Bernárdez, *De Buenos Aires al Iguazú*).

The loss of life in Paraguay during the war had been so great that in the 1880s most hard labor in the ports of the country was still handled by women. Here, women porters ferry oranges to a river vessel. (Courtesy: H. L. Hoffenberg).

PART TWO

Export Commodities and Development in the Upper Plata

3

Yerba Mate

*Y decía un amigo mío que, de
arrebatao y malo mató a su
mujer de un palo porque le dió
un mate frío.*

Jose Hernandez

On the eve of independence, the trade of the Upper Plata revolved around the export of yerba mate. Since the herb was not grown elsewhere in Spanish America, with growing popular use, Upper Platine yerba enjoyed a near-captive market in Buenos Aires and throughout the southern half of the continent; at times this one commodity loomed so large in regional export totals that other products appeared marginal by comparison. It dominated the lives of poor laborers who spent six months of every year gathering it in the isolated forests along the northern frontier with Brazil and in eastern Paraguay. Yerba could also make or break the many merchants and speculators of Asunción whose livelihood depended on its export.

In part because of its key role, however, the "tea of Paraguay" proved sensitive to the political instability of the 1800s. Some of the finest yerba lands in Misiones and Corrientes were completely abandoned in the upheaval. In Paraguay, the post-independence regimes initially sought to curtail the influence of the yerba merchants and, in so doing, disrupted the economic chain that made yerba profitable. The establishment of a state monopoly over this commodity did nothing to stem the decline of exportation. As the decades passed, Brazilian yerba from the backlands of the Rio Grande do Sul and Paraná provinces claimed a larger share of a market once exclusively supplied by the Upper Platine product. This new competition weakened the Upper Plata's trading position in Buenos Aires; it also guaranteed that the city would suffer no want of yerba during the War of the Triple Alliance. State policies and the vagaries of war, therefore, worked to depress an industry in which the Upper Plata enjoyed a natural advantage.

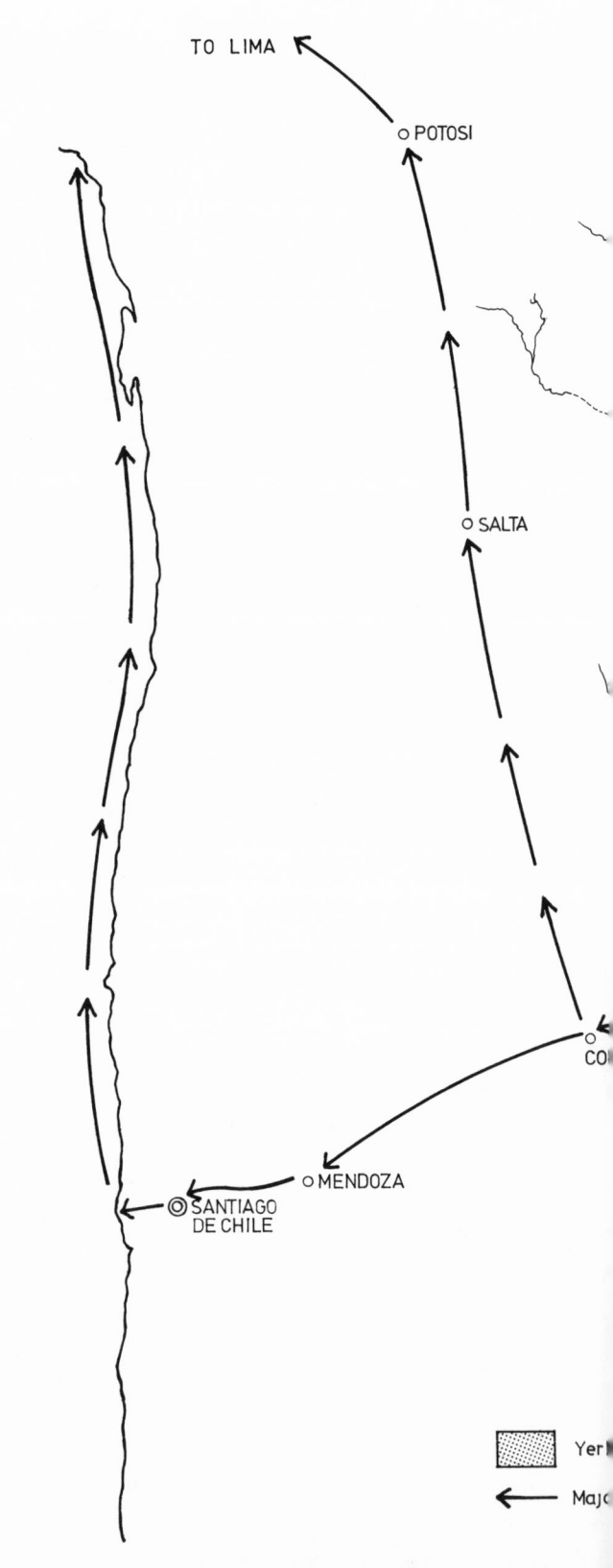

TO LIMA

○ POTOSI

○ SALTA

○
CO

○ MENDOZA

◎ SANTIAGO
DE CHILE

▨ Yer

← Majo

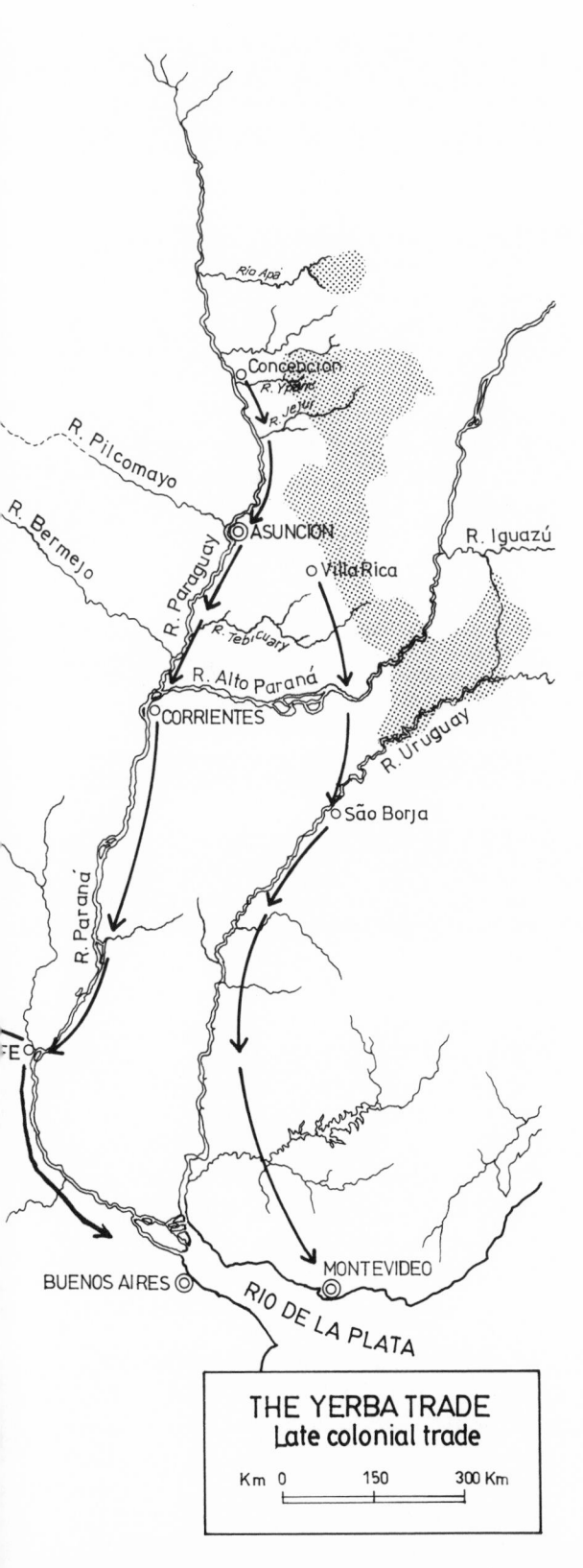

THE YERBA TRADE
Late colonial trade

Km 0   150   300 Km

Origins

The use of the herb *ilex paraguaiensis* to prepare a tea-like beverage originated in pre-Columbian times. Early Spanish settlers in the Upper Plata at first used the drink as a medicinal agent, but soon learned to appreciate its invigorating qualities—derived from a high caffeine content—in coping with the tropical climate. They prepared and drank the tea in much the same way as is done today. Boiling water was poured on a small amount of yerba placed in a gourd-like vessel called the *mate*. A straw (*bombilla*) of wood or silver was then used to suck the infusion into the mouth. At one end of the bombilla, a finely punctured metal globe acted as a strainer and prevented the passage of small leaves up the tube. The habit of taking yerba in this manner gradually developed into a social custom of consequence, whereby groups of men sat and passed the mate, periodically replenishing the gourd with hot water.

Settlers initially regarded the habitual use of yerba as a vice, but this view changed as the years passed and the economic possibilities of the herb became apparent. Because yerba was a spontaneous production of nature, it was treated under Spanish law as a mineral. As with other minerals, yerba fell under the heading of royal property that could be exploited by private persons under a licensing system, yet never owned outright by anyone other than the monarch. The Crown took a long time to recognize the potential value of this possession.

During the first three-quarters of the seventeenth century, the major focus of yerba production was in the far northeast of Paraguay, near the Mbaracajú range of hills. By the 1680s, as the use of yerba spread from the Upper Plata to most of Spanish South America, nearly 50,000 arrobas of Upper Platine yerba passed annually through Buenos Aires.[1]

As demand grew, yerba increasingly became associated with the Paraguayan mission establishments of the Jesuits. The widespread popularity of yerba mate caught the attention of the Society of Jesus, whose many mission communities, far to the south of the Mbaracajú hills and closer to downriver markets, were in a favorable geographic position for the development of a yerba industry. The Jesuits also succeeded in cultivating the yerba shrub, a feat never matched by their secular competitors in Paraguay, who clung to the pre-Columbian pattern of gathering the plant from wild stands, called yerbales or *minerales de yerba*. The hard-working Jesuits used the thousands of Indians under their care to transplant forest trees to mission fields. There the Indian workers set the plants in evenly spaced plots and carefully nurtured them. The Jesuits learned that if wild seeds were gathered just after ripening they could be easily divested of pulp and germinated more rapidly. These innovations, in tandem with favorable political and commercial connections, meant that Upper Platine yerba production would center on the Jesuit missions. This was not accomplished, however, without antagonizing the yerba speculators of Asunción.

In the beginning, the Jesuits cultivated yerba for domestic consumption and to help pay the annual tribute to the Spanish Crown. Only later did yerba become profitable for individual missions. Until the early 1700s, the colonial government, through the Audiencia of Buenos Aires, limited Jesuit yerba exports to 12,000 arrobas a year.[2] This restriction amounted to a political compromise between the Jesuit order and the Asunción yerba merchants, a compromise that did not long endure.

Indeed, an abiding enmity characterized relations between the Jesuits and the Spanish colonists north of the Río Tebicuary and in Corrientes. The settlers envied the Jesuits their political links, resented their dominance in yerba, and most of all, coveted their access to Indian labor. The Comunero rebellions of the 1710s and 1720s, which commenced in Paraguay and eventually coalesced in Corrientes, demonstrated the frustrations of the colonists against Jesuit influence. Though Spanish authorities sided with the Jesuits on that occasion, the times were beginning to change.[3]

The profitability of Jesuit yerba ventures was widely recognized by the beginning of the eighteenth century. Large markets had developed in Chile, Alto Peru, and as far away as Quito. More important, perhaps, the government began to ease restrictions on trade. In consequence, the missions tripled, then quadrupled their export totals. In 1673, for example, only 10,531 arrobas were shipped to downriver consumers via Santa Fé, but in 1734, nearly 44,000 arrobas were exported along the same route.[4]

In the end, however, the Jesuits faced too much opposition, and not solely on the local level. The later Bourbons, particularly Charles III, refused to extend the same patronage to the Jesuits as had earlier monarchs. Starting in the 1750s, a jealous Crown, acting on the advice of regalist courtiers, began to revoke Jesuit privileges in the empire. In the region of the Río de la Plata, the colonial government transferred some of the Jesuit lands east of the Río Uruguay to the Portuguese. In 1767 came the dramatic expulsion.[5]

After the Jesuits departed, the mission region passed into the hands of royal agents, an arrangement that theoretically safeguarded the interests of the Indians. In fact, the new administrators systematically looted the missions and, with the help of Correntino profiteers, reduced the Guaraní population to little better than slaves. The Spaniards' single-minded pursuit of profits from yerba production meant the neglect of subsistence agriculture, leaving the Indians chronically malnourished. The secular authorities within the Upper Plata showed little concern; in some cases, they even disregarded the Indians' need for clothing. Writing in 1799, Félix de Azara commented, "I believe I can positively say that not a single pueblo has been given a complete set of clothing, not even once, since the expulsion of the Jesuits, and I emphasize . . . that I do not exaggerate."[6]

Such callous treatment helps to explain the growing exodus of these Indians to the south, which approached wholesale abandonment of the region by the time of independence. The demographic decline in the Misiones region was unmatched even by the 1864–70 war.[7] In the process, the Indians left the meticulously nurtured yerba plantations to nature. The military campaigns of Artigas and the Portuguese general Francisco das Chagas Santos in the late 1810s, in destroying the few remaining mission communities, simply validated this already ugly state of affairs.[8] The Correntino and Riograndense yerba-raising zones were all contiguous to Misiones and generally shared its fate. Sadly, there is little statistical information available on yerba production in these areas during this period.

As the fortunes of Misiones deteriorated, the situation in secular Paraguay improved. With ready credit from Porteño moneylenders and unencumbered passage down the rivers, the yerba merchants of Asunción became the dominant exporters. They also constituted the prime actors in opening the northern frontier to yerba exploitation. By the 1780s, the center of yerba production had moved far to the north of Misiones, to new yerbales along the Apá, Ypané, and Jejuí rivers. Export totals from this area fell short of the old figures from the missions, but they rapidly multiplied with the discovery of new sources of yerba. Shipments of Paraguayan yerba amounted to only 27,000 arrobas in 1776.[9] As seen in Table 3.1, however, few years passed before the annual export reached hundreds of thousands of arrobas. The commercial reforms associated with the founding of the viceroyalty provided the catalyst in generating this massive trade, but also of importance was the growing demand in the lower provinces and the near-mania felt by merchants who dealt in this Upper Platine equivalent of gold.

Not only did exports increase dramatically, but production in the Upper Plata also expanded into areas hitherto untouched by the trade. An instance of this growth was seen at Concepción, the small but important port high on the Río Paraguay that served as a focal point for yerba export. By 1804, more than sixty speculators at Concepción controlled approximately 4,000 yerba gatherers (yerberos or yerbateros). The Viceroy considered these activities so important that, in the same year, he suggested that the consulado of Buenos Aires appoint a deputy for Concepción to regulate and report on the yerba trade. The appointment came two years later.[10]

Yerba also stimulated the settlement of the northern reaches of the

TABLE 3.1: Paraguayan Yerba Exports, 1781–1812

Year	Arrobas exported	Year	Arrobas exported
1781	125,271	1797	236,205
1782	n/a	1798	330,480
1783	247,290	1799	n/a
1784	111,533	1800	217,110
1785	n/a	1801	281,790
1786	161,258	1802	246,833
1787	166,207	1803	231,928
1788	120,353	1804	283,544
1789	169,875	1805	263,344
1790	148,837	1806	279,992
1791	142,245	1807	297,800
1792	234,787	1808	327,150
1793	116,145	1809	204,547
1794	130,163	1810	151,425
1795	154,058	1811	162,097
1796	210,172	1812	150,300

Sources: Libros de asientos de guías, tornaguías, y alcabalas, 1783–1812, ANA-NE 11, 80, 115, 188, 418, 1159, 1167, 1186, 1790, 2900, 3089, 3337, 3341, 3345, 3356, 3360; and Azara, *Geografía física y esférica del Paraguay*, p. 434.

Upper Plata. Around the Río Ypané, the colonial government granted a series of land titles to ranchers in the hopes of providing cattle sufficient to feed the yerbateros of Concepción and to supply hides to pack the tea. Similar settlement policies brought colonists as far north as the Río Blanco (now in Mato Grosso). On each occasion, this increased the commercial potential of Upper Platine cattle, since surplus hides from that zone were soon exported to the lower provinces. In this way, the yerba industry bolstered trade in other sectors.[11]

Processing: The Socioeconomic Structures

The gathering and preparation of yerba for market was difficult and demanding work:

> It was of so arduous a nature that, though very lucrative, it was generally conducted either by young beginners in the world, or by low men, who, like miners, having got entangled in a system of gambling, alternately made and lost fortunes; were always poor; and finally died in the yerbales. Exceptions to this rule there

were, but very few. Like their masters, the peons were almost invariably gamblers too. They were, therefore, no sooner out of the woods, than they were obliged to return to them.[12]

Yerba gathering proved more than physically arduous. It also depended upon credit arrangements that bordered on the exploitative. In Asunción, a merchant grubstaked a yerba speculator (*habilitado* or *beneficiador*), who in turn commanded between twenty and fifty yerbateros. The loan received by the habilitado consisted of a small amount of cash and many supplies (beeves, charqui, iron implements, and other items essential to the yerba-gathering operation), to be repaid to the merchant in yerba at a prearranged price and time.

In his turn, the habilitado advanced these supplies to the yerbateros, who generally entered the forests heavily in his debt, since he had charged them double for everything—machetes, ponchos, tobacco, liquor, packs of cards, and axes. More often than not, a yerbatero found his wages forfeited for two to three months before work had even begun.[13] Things were little better for the habilitado, who could lose his entire investment if his workers fled the yerbales—as they sometimes did, much to the consternation of merchants and speculators alike.

Simply getting to the yerbales often proved exceedingly difficult. An Indian scout was usually sent on weeks ahead to locate yerbales suitable for exploitation. Then the expedition would begin. The only animals capable of crossing the heavy brushlands were bulls and mules, and both helped in the conveyance of provisions, yerba, and men. The threat of snakes, jaguars (*yaguareté*), and venomous insects made a difficult trek dangerous as well and necessitated heavy clothing and tanned sheepskins to protect the face and limbs. At night, bonfires kept wild animals at bay. Making its way into the interior, the tropa had to guard constantly against Indian attack, especially from the Mbaya and Monteses, who lived in the immediate vicinity.

Upon arrival in the yerbales, the habilitado would select an appropriate location to build a camp. Setting up sheds, makeshift warehouses, and other structures could take several weeks. Preparations for yerba processing commenced with the construction of the *tatacuá*, a small, enclosed depression in the ground where the leaves and sprigs of the yerba tree were initially cured. Yerbateros would tamp down the soil here until its bottom formed a level foundation. Four strong stakes were then driven in at right angles to enclose the space, while upon its surface workers placed several large logs. They set these aflame to scorch the yerba brought from the adjoining woods. Since the branches of the *ilex* can be cut back every two to three years without seriously damaging the plant, yerbateros could completely strip the leaf-bearing branches, tie the leaves in bundles weighing up to seventy pounds, and heap them upon the tatacuá.

After some time, the scorched leaves were raked onto a heavy rawhide netting (raído) and carried to the next place in the curing process, the *barbacuá*. This was an arch of some fifteen to twenty feet square, supported by three strong trestles. The central trestle formed the highest point on the arch. Cross-bars were securely fastened to either side of the center support to make a roof for the arch. The half-dried material from the tatacuá was carefully placed upon this frame in quantities of fifty to 100 arrobas. A large fire was then kindled underneath, and workers spread out the yerba so the heat reached every bit of it. They took great care to prevent the yerba from igniting; the habilitado or foreman (urú) watched the drying process from a tall stand near the barbacuá.

The fires remained lit from dawn to early evening and the drying was generally complete within forty-eight hours. If dried properly, the yerba lost nearly half its weight. If it rained during this time, however, the material upon the barbacuá would have to be raked and dried again. The resulting product always proved inferior in quality.

When the yerba was thoroughly toasted, the fire was swept out from under the arch and the dried leaves were manipulated through the frame to the ground. The leaves would then be pounded with heavy mallets and ground to a coarse powder.

Ready for consumption, the yerba was removed to the storehouses for packaging. It was forced into hide bales, called tercios, which were made by trimming the edges of a bull's hide, moistening it, doubling it lengthwise, and sewing the sides with hide thongs. The bag was filled with yerba and the contents hammered down with a wooden pestle while the hide was still moist. The tercios contracted as they dried, ultimately forming a rock-hard bundle weighing approximately eight arrobas. These bales were loaded onto carts drawn by bulls and transported to the nearest waterway, where stevedores placed them on rafts for transport downriver to Concepción and Asunción.[14]

Ordinarily, two grades of yerba were produced. The cheaper, known as *yerba de palos*, grew only in hill country; it was usually pulverized on the bare earth. The other grade, *caamini*, sold at twice the price of yerba de palos. The shrub that produced this yerba grew in the flatlands, and it bore more and finer leaves that were more yellowish than the hill variety. Workers generally ground caamini in leather-lined tatacuá, thus yielding a product that was free of dirt, twigs, and stems.[15]

The methods of processing and transporting yerba changed little in the period under discussion. Contractual arrangements and payment procedures likewise underwent little alteration. Yerbateros usually worked in pairs, except when they hired a third man to aid them in the operation of the barbacuá. Yerbateros received a chit for every portion of yerba delivered to the habilitado, and at the end of their sojourn in the forests, they exchanged these receipts for a stipulated amount of cash and goods per arroba. In comparison with the large profit made by the yerba merchant, the average yerbatero garnered little, and even this was soon gone in the settlement of old debts. It was much the same for the habilitado:

> The peon's ruin is measured by tens: that of his master by hundreds and thousands. Both are slaves; slave alike of their vanity and their passions. Having for a season gratified these, they are both alike content to return to the arduous task of working in the yerbales, and of providing, by fresh sacrifices and fresh labor, for the renewed gratification of these habits. . . . [16]

The temporary settlements within the yerbales had the appearance and general tenor of mining camps. Despite their isolation, they offered an assortment of simple diversions, especially drink and gambling. Transporters or peddlers (changadores) from the outside were only too happy to provide demijohns of hard liquor in exchange for illegally extracted yerba. Try as they might, colonial officials failed to curtail the activities of these smugglers, who, one may assume, had their own profitable contacts with the province's merchants.[17] As for other passions, few women came to the yerbales, but homosexual relations evidently were common enough. One case from 1806 discusses this explicitly. Eight peones from Concepción fled nearby yerbales because, they claimed, their foreman had forced sex upon them, first offering to buy their favor with extra clothes and later demanding it without recompense. The investigation that followed revealed all sorts of sexual irregularities in the forest. The accused foreman was cleared of sodomy charges when it was shown that all eight peones owed him money and that he had previously forbidden them from playing cards.[18]

Among those who suffered the most in the yerba chain were the yerbateros of the several pueblos de indios located in eastern Paraguay. These Indian communities, like the former Jesuit missions farther south, were run by royal officials called administradores de naturales, who supposedly acted as general advocates for their Indian wards. In fact, the administradores, sometimes in collusion with outsiders, often would compel the Indians to purchase goods on credit at usurous rates of interest, all to be repaid in yerba, thus forcing the natives to work the yerbales for no further compensation. Félix de Azara, writing of the pueblo of San Estanislao in 1786, noted that the Indians owed "36,000 arrobas of yerba [to their administrador] in payments for various loans and another 6,000 to outside lenders."[19]

Credit and the Crisis of Independence

To local eyes, the Asunción-based yerba merchant seemed to be the key player in the colonial export trade of the Upper Plata, through his manipulations of credit. In actuality, he was only one link in a large and complicated network that reached all the way back to Spain. The yerba trade proved distinctive in that, unlike tobacco and hides, its maintenance required a considerable outlay of outside credit. This meant that the Upper Plata had to depend on Porteño merchant/moneylenders, the one group with sufficient capital and political influence to support yerba production and marketing. It is little wonder that these men garnered the greatest profits from the arrangement. As Governor, Agustín Fernando de Pinedo had remarked some years earlier,

> there is not a single merchant in [Paraguay] who trades with his own capital. The goods that they bring are borrowed on very expensive credit in Buenos Aires, and with the obligation of paying 8 percent interest upon all that remains in deposit in the marketplace. . . . experience has shown that [many] traders who bring goods to Paraguay do not finish paying for them in six, eight, ten, or more years. They arrive here with this heavy burden and with the possibility of heavy losses. The merchant thus sets a high price on these goods he carries from Buenos Aires and turns them over to a *beneficiador de yerba* who has nothing of his own. The beneficiador, looking to sell them, brings them to whom? To the miserable peons whose nakedness and misery forces them to offer what they cannot pay.[20]

The system of credit, and the intensive mercantile activity that it engendered, had the effect of partly proletarianizing small producers, bringing them out of a strict subsistence economy. Despite the cash and goods that the system made available to laborers, they doubtless paid a high social price. Far from family, they no longer felt part of a fixed community with traditional values and a sense of place. Some chose to live out their lives in the yerbales, like soldiers who had seen too much of combat to go home. Commonly termed *desarraigados* or *vagos*, they were without clear connection to their former lives in the small communities of the Paraguayan interior. Nonetheless, many laborers apparently felt that work in the yerbales, with all of its risks, was preferable to work on the farm.

The yerba trade helped force the Upper Plata out of its isolation. It ultimately generated high profits for merchants, moneylenders, and changadores, as well as considerable tax revenues to the colonial state. According to one source, between 1788 and 1792, Paraguay exported a yearly average of 292,653 pesos worth of yerba to Corrientes, Santa Fé, and Buenos Aires (more than three-quarters going to the latter). The state's share on this return was 11 percent, or 32,182 pesos a year. This figure, realized through the alcabala and various commissions, constituted a significant sum for the times.[21]

After taking imports into consideration, the return for Paraguay on the 1788–92 trade averaged nearly 137,000 pesos a year. While it is unclear how much of this stayed in the province, a good portion probably remained to be funneled into local commerce, to purchase land, and to stock that land with cattle acquired from Corrientes. In this way, the yerba trade affirmed economic growth in the Upper Plata, a region that previously had existed only as a distant periphery of the viceroyalty. In the lower provinces, the taste for the herb of Paraguay had grown greatly, and it had assumed a permanent place in the Porteño diet. Yerba prices in Buenos Aires varied greatly (normally from one and one-half to three pesos the arroba, according to quality), though demand remained high. In this way, the Upper Plata found itself firmly knitted into the economic fabric of the Spanish empire.

Independence ultimately resulted in a major restructuring of market possibilities in yerba. The system of credit that had flourished under the Bourbons fell apart because revolutionary forces failed to impede the royalist pirates sailing out of Montevideo. Later, the Artiguistas added to the chaotic situation. As shipping on the Río Paraná became progressively more dangerous, the yerba merchants in the Upper Plata became desperate. They voiced their concerns for security through the local cabildos and juntas in the region—all in vain. These weak institutions never marshalled sufficient political support or military reserves to stabilize a deteriorating situation, and they were soon replaced by regimes that were less interested in promoting the yerba trade than they were in retaining power.

The Francia government, of course, was archetypal in this regard. The Dictator certainly was eager for the revenue earned on yerba exports, which, as we will see, maintained a high volume until 1819.[22] Francia nonetheless regarded his main task as one of political consolidation. He subordinated all economic goals to this end. Yerba merchants had generally persevered up to this point. They had survived the collapse of the viceroyalty, along with its supportive correlate institutions—the consulado, the *intendencia*, and the libranza. The merchants survived the attacks of royalist pirates and Artiguista marauders. But they had little chance of surviving the Dictator's suspicion.

The yerba merchants normally depended on credit links with Buenos Aires—links that had become increasingly precarious. In Francia's eyes, this connection made them natural allies of the port city within the

Upper Plata. The peninsular origin of many merchants added to their predicament in the increasingly xenophobic atmosphere of Asunción. Their fortunes ever more uncertain, they conducted business only at the sufferance of the Dictator. Thus, local antagonism, combined with civil war to the south, made the yerba trade less attractive to those few merchants who stayed on in Paraguay after the late 1810s. They could no longer count on turning a profit.

The yerba trade had changed fundamentally. Habilitados could no longer rely on the availability of loans since most of the merchants issuing such loans had either left Paraguay or had gone into seclusion in the countryside. The frugal government of the Dictator only rarely offered credit, and yet the costly system of taxes and license fees was still in place, inherited almost in toto from the colonial period.

Given these practical difficulties, habilitados could find only makeshift and conditional sources of funding for their ventures. Because of this, and because the traditional markets for their yerba were now so constrained, speculators abandoned operations in the most distant yerbales. Certain Indian groups took advantage of the confusion in the north and initiated merciless raids against the remaining encampments during the 1810s and 1820s. On one occasion in 1815, they struck at Concepción, leaving thirteen yerbateros dead.[23] Francia initially responded by creating new military outposts and colonies, such as Tevegó, but these settlements did not thrive, as the Dictator was unwilling to spend much to support an unproductive area.[24] More and more, the harvesting of yerba was left to Francia's army, which, unlike the colonial militia, served year-round, requiring its own provisions of yerba.

The export of Paraguayan yerba, which until the mid-1810s had been relatively free of restrictions, now experienced rigid controls. Starting in 1823, Francia insisted that a minimum of one-third of all yerba exports from Itapúa be supplied out of stocks belonging to the municipal cabildo.[25] This decree supposedly left room for private exporters. Nonetheless, it tended to depress individual initiative in favor of state efforts. The Paraguayan state, like the Spanish Crown before it, technically owned the yerbales, yet Francia never made the export of yerba a state monopoly, in spite of his government's trading thousands of arrobas on its own account. One commentator has argued that Francia brought some balance to the internal economy of Paraguay through a more equitable redistribution of profits coming from this external commerce.[26] In reality, Francia had nothing of the kind in mind; his trade policies followed the simple mercantilist logic of guarding state revenues in the face of a shrinking export trade. And, indeed, as Table 3.2 shows, exports had fallen dramatically. The figure for 1816 reveals a yerba export in excess of anything recorded over the previous decade or so. After 1820, how-

TABLE 3.2: Paraguayan Yerba Exports—The Francia Era

Year	Arrobas	Percent of export total	Pesos fuertes
1816	239,920	74.1	289,920
1818	205,482	70.2	205,482
1819	109,520	57.0	109,520
1820	42,365	73.6	42,364
1829	11,222	24.2	15,845
1830	184*	n/a	n/a
1831	2,120*	n/a	n/a
1832	26,018	58.4	55,228
1833	400*	n/a	n/a
1835	24,016	11.4	17,283
1837	27,447	31.3	46,811
1838	28,196	48.7	55,915
1839	9,084	53.1	14,006

*Represents exports from Itapúa only.
Sources: Cuaderno de extracción, Itapúa, 1830, ANA-NE 2928; Cuaderno del derecho de extracción, Itapúa, 1831, ANA-NE 2936; Cuaderno del derecho de extracción, 1833, ANA-NE 2951; and White, *Paraguay's Autonomous Revolution*, pp. 227–37.

ever, the totals never rose above one-tenth of the earlier figure and sometimes, as in 1829 and 1839, dropped still more dismayingly. Clearly, the export of yerba from Paraguay became erratic and uncertain during the Francia years.

It is known that interest in Upper Platine yerba remained avid in Buenos Aires. Noting that demand for yerba was still high throughout the lower provinces, merchants continued to wait for a more open commerce. The few European merchants in Buenos Aires were eager to introduce textiles and manufactured goods into the Upper Platine market in exchange for yerba and tobacco.[27] These same merchants generally felt that their own interest in reconstructing trade was best served by supporting the Porteño position, regardless of the political consequences for Paraguay and the rest of the Upper Plata. The pro-Rosas *British Packet and Argentine News* made this position clear:

> The true interest of Paraguay . . . consists in the closest union
> with the Argentine Republic; it matters not whether as an
> independent state, or a province of the Federation, the benefits
> arising to it from such a connection would be immense:
> protecting duties, and all those measures generally adopted by
> wise Governments for the encouragement of domestic trade,
> would quickly restore that of Paraguay and crush all foreign

competition; whilst the incalculable advantages which may hereafter arise from steam navigation, and which can only be obtained through the same medium will indefinitely contribute to its prosperity—not only the cheap and expeditious transportation of its produce but in facilitating and promoting the intercourse between its inhabitants and those of the lower provinces, thereby breaking down the barriers which distance, peculiarity of manners, and the jealousy of present as well as former masters had played between them, and smoothing the way for civilization and refinement.[28]

Such a broad consensus, however, implied a common political culture and a set of shared interests that were not easily found in the Plata. The difficulties between Buenos Aires and the Upper Plata endured for some time, and the yerba trade, along with commerce as a whole, suffered for it.

Despite these problems, yerba mate remained a central feature of Upper Platine economic life during the early nineteenth century. All segments of society preferred it to other beverages. And while it now served the domestic market more than that of the lower provinces, its export from the northeast by no means ended. The various governments in the Upper Plata still granted concessions (beneficios) for yerba exploitation.[29] The governments also continued to issue licenses for the domestic yerba trade in considerable number.[30] As for the export trade, while it often proved difficult, it nonetheless occurred; yerba exports still reached consumers in the southern markets via Misiones. For instance, documents from February 1830 trace the passage of twenty arrobas of Paraguayan yerba from Itapúa across to São Borja, recrossing the Uruguay River, paying duties at Curuzú Cuatiá, then being reexported southward to Santa Fé from the small port of Esquina.[31] The complexity of such a route necessarily meant that only a few exports could get through.

New Developments

The scarcity of Upper Platine yerba in the lower provinces led to high prices there. In the late 1820s, an arroba of Paraguayan yerba selling for seven pesos in Corrientes realized fifty pesos in Buenos Aires.[32] High prices directly stimulated yerba exploitation in areas that hitherto had produced little of the herb for export. Certain peripheral regions of Brazil, such as the hinterland of Paraná province and several districts of Rio Grande do Sul, benefitted accordingly. There workers extracted a poor grade of yerba, rendered still poorer by the admixture of grasses and base materials when prepared for shipment. Despite the clear inferiority of the product, investors appeared from as far away as Montevideo, Buenos Aires, and even Santa Fé to participate in the Brazilian yerba speculation. As a result, by the mid-1820s, the Upper Plata could no longer depend on a captive yerba market in the south. To give one illustration of the effect of this new source (usually called *yerba de Paranaguá* after its port of embarkation), in 1828 some 19,000 oxen laden with yerba left Curitiba to supply ships leaving for the Plata.[33] If each animal carried 150 pounds, the total export of Paranaense yerba for that year probably approached seventy tons—a figure that dwarfed the Upper Platine totals. Some of the Brazilian yerba even entered markets in the Upper Plata itself.[34] As Brazilian yerba cultivation spread to Mato Grosso and elsewhere, the Paraguayans could not afford to dismiss the competition.

Another outcome of high prices for Paraguayan yerba was increased smuggling. Even where Brazilian yerba was available, the better-tasting Paraguayan variety was preferred, thus encouraging smuggling where no other means of export presented itself. For a brief period in 1833, the Correntino government attempted to stem the flow of smuggled Paraguayan yerba by prohibiting the sale of all but domestic yerba within the province.[35] Within a year, the authorities realized the futility of this decree and eliminated the trade barrier. Nevertheless, the Correntinos promptly levied new taxes (six to eight reales the arroba) on legally imported yerba, thus reinforcing the attractiveness of the smuggled product.[36] The Paraguayans also had difficulty with yerba smugglers, though the documentation in the Archivo Nacional de Asunción is scarcely conclusive on this point. Evidently Francia had as many problems with the internal smuggling of yerba as he did with anything that passed beyond Paraguay's borders.[37]

In any case, the Dictator's death in 1840 brought little immediate change. External commerce was almost nonexistent, though merchants from various countries still showed interest in obtaining Upper Platine yerba. Given the circumstances, these individuals showed considerable naiveté in their optimistic projections. The *British Packet* captured the essence of the problem:

> it is assumed that a radical change has taken place in Paraguay, and that this El Dorado of many daydreams is longing for the arrival of foreign adventures to relieve it of its superabundant riches . . . [but] the system of the Dictator outlives its founder, and . . . the principles which constitute its basis remain unchallenged. [No] material change has taken place in the Dictator's singular mode of levying and collecting the duties, nor in the patriarchal manner of transacting business generally.[38]

Yerba continued to be important domestically. In 1843, the Paraguayan government granted 147 beneficios, the great majority in the far north between Concepción and San Pedro.[39] As in colonial times, traders still used yerba in lieu of specie; they could even exchange it for cattle or for goods at state stores.[40] Though in its records the government always expressed these transactions in terms of pesos and reales, only rarely did contracting parties conduct an exchange in cash. On one occasion in 1844, for example, the treasury paid 604 pesos to the account of the northern Indian community of Belén in exchange for yerba at a set price of five reales the arroba. The state subtracted almost half of this total to pay for transport and various taxes. Moreover, the yerbateros of Belén generally could withdraw the balance only in goods whose value was preset by government fiat. If the community owed the state for various advances, this, too, was subtracted from the balance.[41] On many levels, the basic cycle of exploitation and usury associated with yerba underwent little change in independent Paraguay. The paternalism evinced by Francia with regard to rural landowners seemed not to extend to the yerbateros, who suffered much as before.

At roughly the same time, the sale of Riograndense yerba helped to underwrite the Farrapo Rebellion. Historians usually associate the Farrapos with the cattle-raising zones north of the Uruguayan frontier, but their republican government also controlled the rich yerbales of Alegrete and Cruz Alta in the Brazilian Misiones (Missões). The Farrapos favored the development of agriculture and instituted a series of protective tariffs against imported wheat, potatoes, and yerba.[42] Riograndense yerba, in a separate decree, was freed from all export duties.[43] The exploitation of local yerbales continued on a regular basis, and contributions to the Farrapo cause were sometimes made in that medium.[44]

As with the Paraguayans, smuggling constituted a problem for Farrapo authorities in the São Borja-Itaqui area, where rafts easily transported yerba across the river to Corrientes. Security for legal trade in this part of the Plata remained precarious until after the end of the 1835–45 rebellion. The only safe route for yerba exports was to Montevideo and from there to Buenos Aires. Riograndense yerba had proven its marketability and, as the years wore on, it became a major competitor in the Buenos Aires market.

By the mid-1840s, Carlos Antonio López had consolidated his hold over the Paraguayan government and turned his attention specifically to economic matters. Uppermost in his mind was maintaining state authority over the export trade. López had a more legalistic bent than the late Dictator and wished to legitimize the mercantilist control over trade that Francia had taken for granted. Among his earliest acts, he established a strict state monopoly on the export of Paraguayan yerba.[45] This measure headed off any future competition with foreign merchants who might wish to enter a resuscitated yerba trade. Contemporary documents have left no record as to the local reaction to the creation of the monopoly but, if the estanco's lack of popularity in the region provides any indication, potential yerba speculators were none too happy with a similar institution. State management of all yerba exports ultimately added to the uneven pattern of economic growth in the Upper Plata, though governments failed to recognize the pernicious effects of such monopolies for years to come.[46]

Events in the lower provinces had already created a new interest in Upper Platine trade. The Anglo-French blockade of Buenos Aires forced the Porteños to explore new sources of supply for yerba and tobacco. Rosas consequently liberalized tariff regulations to encourage the flow of both Upper Platine commodities into Buenos Aires.[47] As the rivers became more secure as commercial arteries, yerba and other Upper Platine commodities could profitably enter the markets of the lower provinces. Both the state and individual entrepreneurs prospered. Certain institutional impediments, however, still had to be overcome.

The "Liberation" of the Pueblos de Indios

The Paraguayan state saw one of these impediments in the semiautonomous character of the twenty-one pueblos de indios. The pueblos had always maintained a privileged relation vis-à-vis the state. For example, colonial officials restricted outside exploitation of community resources (though much of this did in fact occur). The government treated Indian-owned lands as inalienable. At least five of the twenty-one pueblos—San Estanislao, Belén, Yuty, Caazapá, and San Joaquín—controlled both the by-ways and the necessary labor to work several of Paraguay's most important yerbales.

López recognized the latent potential of this area and the possible windfall that could accrue to the state. Previously, with the yerba trade limited to a domestic market, little stimulus existed for an expanded exploitation of the Indian holdings. With outside demand rising, López saw an opportunity to increase the government's revenues from yerba. In October 1848, he issued a decree that disestablished the pueblos de indios, divesting each community of its cabildo and segregated status and making its men liable for military service. The terms of this decree stated that, beginning in 1852, the Indians were responsible for all agricultural and pastoral taxes, to be paid in yerba mate. Moreover, nearly all communal lands, as well as the substantial goods and properties owned by the cabildos, passed immediately into the hands of the Paraguayan state .[48] With the enactment of this decree, as many as 25,000 day workers entered the Paraguayan labor market. The Indians were declared citizens of the republic, but their lot was hardly enviable. They now became simple peones, much like other poor people of the interior. Without access to traditional mechanisms of communal support, the Indians had little choice but to pursue the only work open to them. This made renewed exploitation of the yerbales easy. With a stroke of his pen, López had ensured an adequate labor force to meet the needs of production and in so doing made possible larger yerba exports in the coming years. Researchers have yet to investigate the social changes occasioned by the dissolution of the pueblos. It seems clear, however, that production rose in the yerba zones.[49]

The "liberation" of the pueblos de indios and the Anglo-French intervention paved the way for a considerable yerba trade, but little permanent improvement occurred while warships continued to obstruct the rivers. The political impasse also had to be overcome.

A New Beginning: The 1850s and 1860s

The fall of the Rosas regime in 1852 meant that commercial vessels could ascend the rivers unmolested and return with full cargoes of yerba and other commodities. Credit arrangements with Porteño lenders also became possible again. The changed circumstances for trade impressed López, who wished to see yerba profit his family and his government in the same way it had benefitted colonial entrepreneurs. He established military posts in the yerbales of Villarrica and those of the far north, purportedly to fend off Indian attacks in those districts. His soldiers stayed on, however, to harvest much of the yerba destined for the Paraguayan export market. Military commanders routinely drafted workers from the nearest settlements to augment the number of laborers. As payment to these men, the state issued chits good at various public stores. The exchange rate set on these vouchers was highly disadvantageous to the workers.[50]

López concentrated on expanding production in the yerbales. A labor force under military command was clearly insufficient to this task, therefore López pointedly avoided eliminating the old private licensing system. To attract new speculators, he lowered taxes on yerba, a process he had begun in 1842 when he decreased taxes for public works from 15 to 5 percent.[51] López went still further in 1848, when he issued a Draconian measure against yerbateros, who, for fear of Indian attack, had abandoned their work in the yerbales. Such "deserters," he ordered, risked the death penalty "just as in combat."[52] More often, the government treated flight from the yerbales as a civil offense; the habilitado could collect substantial sums if the authorities captured escaped workers. If the latter could not pay, the government rarely failed to flog them.[53] Thus López sought to encourage private enterprise in yerba.

In spite of such efforts, yerba exports failed to match the unqualified success of other Upper Platine trade items, particularly tobacco. The picture for yerba, as Table 3.3 demonstrates, was erratic, yet it is clear that profits remained large enough to permit a steady fiscal return to the López government.

Several factors explain the spotty record of Paraguayan yerba exports at this time. In terms of total volume, the country's export of yerba had largely regained its pre-independence levels. Demand in the lower provinces, however, had risen sharply as the number of yerba drinkers had grown with the general population. Paraguayan production failed to meet this new demand, leaving Brazilian supplies to make up the difference. The yerbales of Rio Grande do Sul had fully recovered from the Farrapo conflict and were being worked more efficiently, sometimes under foreign contract. A French firm in isolated Itaqui processed sixty-six tons of yerba in 1858. Within seven years, exports from Itaqui exceeded sixteen times that amount.[54] Table 3.4 shows that Riograndense yerba found an avid market in the Platine states; since these figures exclude Paranaense exports, one can assume that the total Brazilian export to the Plata was much higher.

The former Jesuit yerba plantations in Misiones had been left to nature many years before, though speculators had continued to work them periodically as though they were natural yerbales. Now, even these sources began to affect the market. Before Argentine recognition of Paraguay's independence, no one had formulated the exact demarcation line in the Misiones. Governments generally assumed that the old settlements along the Río Uruguay belonged to Corrientes and that those lying between the Alto Paraná and the Río Aguapey were Paraguayan. With the precise border unclear, exploitation of yerbales during this period was informal if not exactly sub rosa.

However, the comprehensive 1852 treaty provided a guarantee of free access for Paraguay across Misiones to São Borja, thus alleviating the thorny transit issue.[55] The relaxation of tensions on this frontier made possible renewed official interest in yerba, and the Correntinos moved quickly. Aimé Bompland, the famous French botanist and one-time prisoner of Francia, acted as agent for the Correntino government in these endeavors. His many reports to Governor Pujol had an exuberant tone, outlining elaborate plans for the cultivation of yerba and the importation of machinery.[56] Though excessively optimistic, his hopes for the Correntino yerba industry had some success. By the late 1850s, the east-

TABLE 3.3: Paraguayan Yerba Exports—The López Era

Year	Arrobas	Pesos fuertes
1845	81,988	81,270
1846	n/a	n/a
1847	n/a	n/a
1848	28,455*	n/a
1849	n/a	n/a
1850	n/a	n/a
1851	85,923	233,204
1852	68,195	157,108
1853	123,449	304,378
1854	85,676	282,485
1855	168,000	336,000
1856	85,519	508,115
1857	124,951	749,820
1858	92,575	574,040
1859	130,540	781,210
1860	178,537	1,093,860
1861	254,513	674,367
1862	187,559	706,204
1863	191,836	965,435
1864	224,381	1,231,998
1865	78,606	531,065

*Incomplete figure (Pilar exports only).
Sources: ANA-SH 274, NE 866; El Semanario, 1 October 1853, 8 October 1953, 24 December 1853, 11 January 1855, and 16 February 1861 through 8 July 1965; Marbais Du Graty, La república del Paraguay, pp. 346–50; Herken Krauer, "Proceso economico," 83–116.

ern yerbales abounded with Corrientes-based workers; one operation, just outside of San Javier, turned out 3,000 arrobas in 1857, much of it for export.[57]

While the Brazilian and Correntino competition influenced the market, chief blame for the irregular showing of Paraguayan yerba must rest with López himself. The state, as sole distributor of yerba internally, maintained an artificially low price for the product within Paraguay. Though this had certain political advantages, it also limited potential earnings for yerba concessionaires and workers. No incentive existed to encourage private competition within Paraguay, and the internal market appeared static.

Not so the external trade. As distinct from its attitude toward tobacco and hides, the Paraguayan state actively manipulated yerba exports and, apparently believing itself the master of a captive market downriver,

TABLE 3.4: Yerba Exports, Rio Grande do Sul to Platine Region

Year	Arrobas*	Value in milreis
1850	97,958	142,133
1851	77,766	116,282
1852	128,195	191,943
1853	168,133	253,258
1854	124,926	223,997
1855	216,881	419,867
1856	268,879	960,241
1857	342,363	1,314,768
1858	317,547	1,060,358
1859–60	309,951	908,674
1860–61	308,957	925,170
1861–62	291,080	804,115
1862–63	397,398	818,202
1863–64	379,876	759,092
1864–65	437,912	787,159
1865–66	357,358	795,750

*The original citations were listed in terms of Brazilian arrobas (33 pounds to the arroba rather than 25 pounds for the Platine measurement). For clarity's sake, the Brazilian quantities have been converted to their Platine equivalents. Sources: Adapted from AHRGS, diversos pequenos grupos, caixa 90; and Camargo, *Quadro Estadístico*, 2:34–35, 39, 40.

set an exorbitant price on its yerba. This encouraged the Brazilians, who easily supplied a cheaper product to Buenos Aires. One British observer, in a letter to the son of the Paraguayan president, commented:

> I find the yerba market at Buenos Aires is *ruinously* bad—sales cannot be made more than 40 to 42 reales per arroba Plata!!! The fact is the yerba made in the Misiones or in Brazil is coming into favor on account of the low price—this quality of yerba is very much inferior to Paraguay yerba—but the price is about one-half. Consequently, the great mass of people take the cheap article, and *in turn they will like it;* this will have a serious effect on the commerce of Paraguay, and it will be well for your government to make arrangement to reduce the price of the yerba.[58]

López remained deaf to such advice. He preferred to control the terms of the trade, rather than its volume, and in so doing prevented the long-term growth of the yerba commerce. Between 1856 and 1860, the Paraguayan government fixed the export price of its yerba at six pesos the arroba, regardless of fluctuations in supply and demand.[59] Because Brazilian yerba sold at rates consistently lower than this in Buenos Aires, the Paraguayan pricing strategy was outwardly counterproductive; it assured Brazilian dominance in the Porteño market because the common folk of the port were unwilling to pay the higher Paraguayan price.

Still, the mercantilist policy of high pricing did meet the immediate requirements of an ambitious government. López needed ready cash to secure armaments from foreign suppliers. This was no small matter, since the inflow of cash on yerba regularly represented 40 to 50 percent of all foreign exchange earned on Paraguayan exports.[60] López either failed to see the long-term detrimental effects of high pricing or, as seems more likely, he concerned himself only with short-term political benefits. He evidently felt that the high quality of Paraguayan yerba would assure a ready market in the lower provinces despite competition.

One illustration of López's hazy market strategy came in 1860, when he grudgingly lowered his export price for yerba to two and one-half pesos the arroba. Despite certain modern claims to the contrary, he did not do this in order to undercut Brazilian competition.[61] Rather, as stated in the decree, López needed cash quickly to purchase cattle for his expanding military infrastructure.[62] In the same decree, he passed on his loss to the habilitados by lowering the state purchase price in Asunción to eleven reales the arroba, thus making certain that production would rapidly fall, since habilitados no longer could make a profit.

Cutting the price for Paraguayan yerba apparently had only a minor impact in Buenos Aires. It made little difference to Brazilian competition. In fact, the 1860–61 export figures suggest that Porteño demand was inelastic; the amount charged in previous years had been more reflective of market conditions. To increase overall profits to the Paraguayan state, the lower price would have had to induce a doubling of the volume sold, yet nothing of the kind occurred. By 1862, López decided to raise yerba prices to earlier levels (see Table 3.5). It may be that López failed to give the Porteño market enough time to adjust to new pricing policies, or possibly Porteño merchants had binding contracts for the receipt of Brazilian yerba.

In an apparent effort to placate the habilitados, López in mid-1862 permitted private parties to sell yerba within Paraguay.[63] This shift in policy freed the domestic market from most government controls, making commerce more responsive to demand. New profits for habilitados became possible. Production again rose, one measure of which was seen in the increased number of beneficios granted—from 269 in 1864 to 351 a year later.[64]

By that time, López had been succeeded by his son, Francisco Solano López. The latter had acted as a major force in bringing small quantities of yerba to markets in Europe. He took several bales to England dur-

TABLE 3.5: Paraguayan Yerba Exports, Price Changes in Asunción

Year	Pesos per arroba
1852	2.30
1853	2.47
1854	3.30
1855	2.00
1856	5.94
1857	6.00
1858	6.20
1859	5.98
1860	6.13
1861	2.65
1862	3.77
1863	5.03
1864	5.49
1865	6.76*

*This high price is based on the January-June 1864 exports, which were the last exports before the imposition of the Brazilian blockade.
Sources: *El Semanario*, 1 October 1853; 8 October 1853; 24 December 1853; 11 January 1855; and 16 February 1861 through 8 July 1865; Marbais Du Graty, *La república del Paraguay*, pp. 346–50; Herken Krauer, "Proceso económica," 83–116.

ing his 1854–55 European tour and continued to promote the herb over the next decade. Unfortunately for the Upper Plata, the Europeans never developed a taste for yerba as a beverage, and in England it was sold exclusively as a drug.[65] Upper Platine yerba remained important chiefly as a commodity in Buenos Aires, Montevideo, and other towns of the lower provinces.[66] The efforts of the younger López to stimulate demand for yerba in Europe, however, deserve attention. On a symbolic level, they demonstrated a new Paraguayan outlook as well as a desire to diversity markets and, ultimately, to break the dominance of Porteño consumers.

The 1860s never saw the full recovery of the Upper Platine yerba trade. The interrelated effects of high pricing and Brazilian competition kept exports from Paraguay at levels of the 1780s, generally well below 250,000 arrobas a year. Nevertheless, yerba still accounted for nearly 40 percent of total Paraguayan exports. The domestic market for yerba showed improvement only after the 1862 decree, but this made little difference to Paraguayan yerbateros, who rarely, if ever, earned any real profits.[67] Their lives remained precarious, with no immediate hope for change.

The situation for yerba production in underpopulated Corrientes was relatively stable. Although several entrepreneurs came forward with plans to advance the industry, their efforts met with little apparent success.[68] The only subregion of the Upper Plata to show an improvement over the colonial era was that area of Rio Grande do Sul bordering on the Uruguay River and extending eastward to Alegrete and Cruz Alta. This zone, by increasing its yerba exports to the lower provinces, took advantage of poor conditions for yerba production in Corrientes and the mistaken efforts of the Paraguayan state to maintain high prices despite Brazilian competition.

The War of the Triple Alliance dashed all hope for further Upper Platine expansion in the yerba markets of the south. The Brazilian river blockades effectively interdicted trade, and the region slipped promptly back into isolation. New supplies of yerba de Paranaguá arrived to meet the demand. The postwar world imposed a new set of conditions on the yerba mate trade. For one thing, yerba was increasingly cultivated in large plantations rather than extracted from yerbales, which became ever more difficult to locate. This occurred readily in Misiones, where European immigrant labor and private Porteño capital provided the incentive for a large-scale yerba industry starting in the 1890s. In returning to a system of yerba plantations, Misiones came full circle to the Jesuit example. The same phenomenon occurred in Rio Grande do Sul and Paraguay, though on a more limited scale.

The Paraguayan state abandoned its hold on the export of yerba at the conclusion of the war. By then, the labor force needed to develop the yerba industry was no longer available. Many yerbateros had died in the conflict; workers who might otherwise have entered the yerbales found greater opportunities in the foreign-owned tannin industry. By the mid-1880s, the impoverished Paraguayan government sold at auction all of the yerbales still under state ownership.

An Economy Built on Green Tea

During the late colonial period, yerba was the fuel that drove the engine of Upper Platine development. Even before the expulsion of the Jesuits, most inhabitants of the Southern Cone knew and preferred the green tea over other beverages. As demand grew, the Upper Plata responded with increased exports, built upon a more sophisticated system of credit and transport. Nearly all sectors of society were affected by the trade. Subsistence farmers found themselves converted to full-time yerbateros, while merchants and moneylenders all along the rivers earned high profits. The yerba commerce led to improvements in other areas of the Upper Platine economy. The need for oxen to haul yerba and the need for hides for packing material, for instance, brought an expansion of the cattle industry into the north of Paraguay. More important, yerba mate brought the Upper Plata out of its age-old isolation, allowing the region to join a commercial network that reached from Buenos Aires to Santiago de Chile and beyond.

The impact within the Upper Plata was tremendous. A new elite of merchants associated with the trade threatened to displace the traditional landowners as the dominant force in the region. This process of displacement was uneven, however, and created as many alliances as it did enemies. These divisions in the upper echelons of society had yet to play themselves out by the time of independence, and ultimately they cleared the path to power for José Gaspar de Francia.

The workings of the yerba trade went unaffected by independence. The Dictator refrained from interference as long as his government received its due share. He even allowed foreign merchants, like the Robertson brothers, to participate. He failed to reckon with what Artigas and the other provincial chieftains could do to disrupt the trade, however. Their actions to the south soon convinced him that isolation was preferable to the new, unsettled state of affairs in the Plata. The fact that many yerba merchants had opposed him in the first place made it easier for Francia to curtail their activities, until yerba exports became little more than a shadow of what they had been. Paraguay survived, but the formerly all-important commerce collapsed.

The Upper Platine yerba trade fell victim to the political chaos of the early nineteenth century. The closure of the rivers destroyed commercial links with the lower provinces that as late as 1818 had provided the northeast with a market for over 200,000 arrobas of its yerba. Even after 1852, the arbitrary practices of the Paraguayan state monopoly, along with a now fully established Brazilian competition, impeded the reestablishment of the trade. Nothing that Carlos Antonio López or his son could do would change the poor status of the yerba commerce. The War of the Triple Alliance was just another in a series of misfortunes. In the end, the old yerba mate trade did not survive this era of national hubris.

4

Tobacco

The goddess of nicotine is
worshipped by almost every
Paraguayan, irrespective of sex
and age.
W. H. Koebel

The political difficulties suffered by the Upper Plata after independence had a striking effect on the production and marketing of the region's tobacco. Tobacco had formed a major sector of the colonial economy and was the only noteworthy cash crop in the northeast. When trade collapsed after the mid-1820s, tobacco had no outlet except for a small domestic market. When circumstances permitted an open commerce, however, tobacco recovered rapidly, more than realizing its earlier promise.

Known as *pety* to the pre-Columbian Guaraní, tobacco was first grown commercially in the Upper Plata at the beginning of the eighteenth century.[1] By the 1770s, it had become one of the most important agricultural exports of the region, second only to yerba mate. Within the Upper Plata, tobacco and yerba were used as a means of exchange, for payment of taxes, and as essential items issued to contracted and slave labor.[2] Tobacco cultivation was concentrated in the more populous zones of east-central Paraguay: Itauguá was the dominant region during the colonial era, while Villarrica assumed greater importance after independence. These areas possessed abundant labor as well as rich red earth.[3] Since tobacco quickly exhausted the soil, it proved necessary to rotate its cultivation frequently. Some tobacco production also took place in the south, in the hinterland around Corrientes and in Misiones.

Cultivation

The mode of tobacco culture followed in the Upper Plata dated from the earliest days of the colony and remained basically unchanged throughout the nineteenth century. Sown in May or June, the young seedlings were ready for transplanting in about two months. This phase usually ended by September, though the operation sometimes continued for two more months. The plants were set from two to three feet apart, and in ten weeks they reached maturity. The maturation period in the Upper Plata was far more rapid than in Cuba, where the time varied between 90 and 110 days.

The lower leaves, which were very short, were gathered first; these formed the grade known as *pito*. Within a few days, the blossom appeared and was immediately pinched off. The plant by then measured more than three feet in height. The upper leaves were collected as they matured, supplying three grades, known as *buena, regular,* and *media* (these terms did not come into official use until the early national period; during colonial times, they were grouped together as *hoja*—large leafed tobacco). Each plant produced about four leaves of these several grades, all of which were favorably compared with Havana tobaccos. In January, from the September plants, and in February, from the October plants, a fifth grade was gathered; this was distinguished as *doble*, the wide leaf. Only five or six leaves were then left to be collected in March or April, yielding a grade known as *para*.[4] Tobacco growers (*cosecheros*) cured all grades of Upper Platine tobacco in the same manner. Stacked on makeshift racks inside open-air sheds, leaves were simply left to dry for some weeks before packing.

These cultivation and curing techniques differed in several respects from those used in other tobacco-producing areas. In Cuba, for example, the leaves were allowed to grow to full maturity and then the entire plant was cut down. A sucker would start from the roots, and from this, a second, and sometimes a third crop was taken. The Paraguayan system allowed the leaf to mature on the stalk; the Cuban procedure was to cut the stalk as soon as the leaf itself ceased to grow. The method pursued in Paraguay resulted in far stronger tobacco, possessing from 2.5 to 7 percent nicotine, while the Cuban variant rarely attained more than 2.2 percent.[5] To the inhabitants of the lower provinces, who were accustomed from childhood to smoking the strongest cigars, the potency of the Upper Platine product added to its attraction. Travellers often remarked that among the Paraguayans and Correntinos it was a common sight to see a new mother give her baby alternate sucks of a nipple and a fat cheroot.

The cosechero was generally a smallholder who owned his own acreage or leased it from the government.[6] Each cosechero worked these lands himself, together with his immediate family and perhaps one or two retainers. More often than not, tobacco took up only a portion of his fields, the rest being devoted to maize, manioc root, and other subsistence crops. The cosechero found tobacco cultivation attractive, as little capital or equipment was required to produce this cash crop. Profits from tobacco sales brought in needed farm implements and the occasional luxury item, though the initial lack of major outside markets limited the scale of potential earnings. In this, the Upper Platine cosechero resembled the small-scale tobacco growers of Costa Rica and Venezuela, who were likewise constrained by the lack of trade options.[7]

The Renta de Tabacos

In the colonial era, the cosecheros' desires were simple: stable markets, no limit on production, fair payment, and most important, unhindered transport downriver to Buenos Aires and Montevideo. Government officials, on the other hand, perceived tobacco principally as a source of revenue. One consequence of this outlook in the Upper Plata was the creation in 1779 of the *real renta de tabacos*, a privileged Crown monopoly (estanco) entrusted with the manufacture and sale of products made from the region's tobacco. The Platine renta was modeled after that of New Spain and, like its Mexican counterpart, was designed to produce a substantial fiscal return for the colonial regime.[8] While it clearly accomplished this goal, the institution also fostered resentment against Bourbon economic policies not just in the Plata but wherever the renta operated.

The state monopolies of the Spanish colonial empire acted under license from the Crown or, in the case of certain minerals, under a system of leases, with the concessionaire retaining the exclusive privilege of production and sale within the district. Some of the monopolies, such as mercury and salt, proved more an annoyance to the consumer than a profit to the treasury. The renta de tabacos, however, quickly became one of the most lucrative sources of public income in Spanish America and the Philippines. In New Spain, for example, revenue from this source came to nearly 1,500,000 pesos during the early 1770s; within two decades, the receipts had increased to three times that amount. It was much the same in Chile and Peru.[9]

In the Río de la Plata, the renta sought to assure the cultivation of high-quality tobacco, low purchase prices from the grower, uninterrupted production to meet demand, and complete authority over tobacco sales. Precisely the same aims were outlined by Visitor-General (and later Minister of the Indies) José de Gálvez when he organized the renta in New Spain.[10] In both cases, the government designed a complex administrative plan for the distribution of tobacco, and in both cases the renta faced stiff opposition from cosecheros and tobacco merchants.[11]

A government decree required Paraguayan growers to contract with the renta for the amount of tobacco they could deliver annually. All cultivators were ordered to register with imperial officials. The estanco, however, had to cope with the active opposition of many growers, voiced through their spokesmen on the cabildo of Asunción. The cosecheros objected to restrictions on sales of tobacco as a necessity in the Upper Plata, and any contracted amount due the renta could, in lean years, result in a local shortage. Likewise, any surplus that accrued could conceivably be destroyed under the forced contract system. Most of all, the cosecheros and the merchants of Asunción balked at any restriction on extraprovincial trade. Substantial profits from tobacco could be realized only in the lower provinces, but renta authorities decided that this commerce, and its profits, would remain the estanco's alone.[12]

The Upper Platine renta had its own José de Gálvez in the person of Director-General Francisco de Paula Sanz.[13] Like Gálvez, Paula Sanz was a peninsular bureaucrat who had come to the New World to help organize viceregal finances. Seen by his contemporaries as arrogant but highly competent, he learned early how to use favoritism to promote efficiency. His duties took him to Paraguay and Corrientes between 1778 and 1781 where, as chief officer of the renta, he came to know the tobacco situation firsthand. He particularly noted the political weight of tobacco merchants in the Asunción cabildo and, on at least one occasion, gave in to their demands. In May 1779, he grudgingly permitted an unlimited production of tobacco within Paraguay. No grower would henceforth be held to a contract, and any tobacco not purchased by the renta could be retained by the cosechero. Private sale outside the province, however, was again specifically forbidden.[14]

Despite the good intentions of Paula Sanz, his compromise added to the long-term difficulties of the renta in the Upper Plata. Unlimited production indicated a commitment on the part of the monopoly to purchase all tobacco grown. Also, the freedom to purchase and sell tobacco inside Paraguay ultimately encouraged the smuggling of contraband tobacco. The cosecheros remained unsatisfied with prices, as low as two pesos an arroba for pito and twelve reales for hoja. The estanco sold the same unprocessed tobacco at nine and one-half to twelve and one-half pesos the arroba.[15] Paula Sanz had prohibited the cultivation of tobacco in the lower provinces, however, so Paraguayan growers effectively operated under conditions of a guaranteed market.

The modus vivendi between renta and cosecheros worked well and allowed for some innovations in tobacco processing. The foremost change involved the introduction of black twist tobacco. *Torcido negro*, a pigtail twist of tobacco darkened and sweetened with molasses, was a popular chewing tobacco throughout the Plata. This commodity, however, was grown and processed across the frontier in Brazil and was commonly smuggled into the Río de la Plata. Viceregal authorities hoped that if tor-cido negro were produced in Paraguay, the local product would replace the Brazilian variety and needed specie would not be illegally exported.[16] Be-cause processing black twist required much labor, its production was con-fined to the pueblos de indios and Misiones, the latter area being subject in matters of tobacco to the Asunción renta. Private cosecheros, while encouraged to process black twist, never showed much interest even though the renta purchased it at a high twenty-five reales the arroba.[17]

The renta enjoyed wide discretionary powers in all matters concern-ing tobacco. Estanco officials had the right to confiscate illegal hoards and to arrest violators.[18] With these powers, the colonial authorities estab-lished the monopoly on a solid footing and overrode all resistance.

Cosecheros soon adapted to the demands of the monopoly. Even though cultivation of tobacco remained relatively free of constraints, sales and processing were strongly conditioned by the needs of the renta. The grower transported his ripe tobacco in carts to Asunción, where it was inspected and purchased by estanco officials. If he deemed the journey too troublesome, the grower sold his crops at a slight discount to a pass-ing merchant, who then transported it to the processing point. After purchase in the provincial capital, the unprocessed tobacco (en rama) awaited transport to Buenos Aires in private craft under contract to the renta. Tobacco not dispatched to Asunción remained in the interior for local sale.[19]

While Paraguayan cosecheros had reservations about the large differ-ence between purchase price and retail price, they showed little alarm as long as markets for their product remained assured. In 1789, how-ever, viceregal authorities ordered a complete cancellation of Paraguayan black twist production and a reduction in the purchase of unprocessed tobacco.[20] Because of poor quality, Paraguayan black twist had proven unpopular with Porteño customers, who preferred the smuggled Brazil-ian variety that could be had at a lower price. As a result, 20,000 arro-bas of black twist and other surplus Paraguayan tobacco en rama piled up in Buenos Aires warehouses and nearly bankrupted the renta de tabacos there.[21]

The effects of the 1789 decree were immediate and long-lasting. At no time during the remaining twenty years of the monopoly did the renta regain the confidence of the growers, and some cosecheros simply aban-doned the cultivation of tobacco. With purchases of the renta limited for a time to 7,000 arrobas a year, the risk of no return on time and labor was simply too great. Some growers turned to the only other profitable way out—smuggling.

Unlike cultivation, which was limited in the colonial period to Para-guay, the sale of tobacco, in both legal and contraband forms, occurred throughout the Upper Plata. Corrientes provided a prime example of what happened when estanco policy clashed with smuggling.

Between 1779 and 1812, the Correntino renta managed all legal sales of tobacco in the province. The monopoly maintained many offices and stores in the interior in such locations as San Roque, Saladas, and Goya.[22] Employees for those stores (estanqueros) proved exceptionally hard to recruit, given that their salaries were set at a paltry 5 percent of sales. As the provincial administrator of the renta commented in 1789: "the estanqueros of the countryside are all disgusted with the poor profits and are resigning. In many areas estancos have yet to be established because of the lack of willing subjects to administer them."[23] The reason for the poor return was not difficult to discern: Competition from smuggled tobacco was ruining estanco activities.

Contraband tobacco from Paraguay easily undersold the renta's product, and smuggling was evidently directed by many Asunción merchants. These men and their agents, the key promoters of the illegal traffic, paid the cosecheros a premium over the price offered by the renta. The illegal product was then shipped south to secret workshops for conversion into cigars. The grower enjoyed considerable advantages. He could sell an inferior grade of tobacco to private buyers and, if pressured to do so, still deliver superior tobacco to estanco officials. Over time, this practice had the effect of driving honest merchants out of business, since the renta generally refused to accept inferior tobacco from merchant middlemen.[24]

The southward shipment of contraband tobacco passed through Corrientes, first as a trickle in the 1780s. Paraguayan sailors received permission to transport three bundles of tobacco for their personal use on the voyage to Buenos Aires. Often the sailors pooled their bundles and sold the tobacco illegally at intermediate ports.[25] Later, when smuggling became a way of life along the rivers, ingenious methods of concealment and transport made their appearance. Larger vessels carried many arrobas of tobacco hidden under sleeping mats and between rawhides. Canoes loaded with contraband made the passage from Paraguay at night, avoiding the more populated Correntino shoreline above Santa Lucía. Tobacco smugglers sometimes plied their trade in Indian villages (tolderías) on the Chaco side of the river. The Indians, in turn, traded the tobacco in markets as distant as Tucumán and Santiago del Estero.[26]

Renta authorities were totally unable to stem the clandestine trade, though guardposts were established at the Paso del Rey, Curupayty, Itatí, and, in 1787, in Misiones at Tranquera de Loreto. At all these points, the smugglers escaped detection. In 1791, the renta provided an armed vessel, the Santa Bárbara, to patrol the area at the mouth of the Río Paraguay. Within two years, that craft was joined by another, the San

Antonio. Between September and November 1791, the *Santa Bárbara* seized 316 arrobas of tobacco, more than enough to pay for the vessel's operating expenses.[27] For every arroba taken, though, a good many more apparently got through, often with the connivance of corrupt renta officials and guards.[28]

Estanco policies did bring a small fiscal return in Corrientes, especially in the 1790s. The institution as a whole, however, had serious problems throughout the Platine basin. Corruption and smuggling plagued the monopoly, and an incentive never developed for growers to integrate themselves into a contract system. Even a plan, in 1800, to grant cosecheros exemption from militia service failed to placate the Paraguayans. With the price differential still in effect, smuggling continued unabated, and the only notable change was a demoralization of the militia.[29]

Though a thorn in the side of the bureaucracy, tobacco smuggling helped foster the economic integration of the Upper Plata by providing an outlet for cosecheros and merchants throughout the region. The real potential of tobacco could only manifest itself under conditions of open commerce, but such a policy was unthinkable for the colonial administration. Estanco officials, by expending their energy in revenue collection and in vain efforts to curb the illicit trade, lost an opportunity to increase the legal commerce in tobacco.

While the monopoly represented a shortsighted imperial recognition of the Upper Plata's commercial and fiscal possibilities, it was also indirectly responsible for the advent of a more modern economy in the region. For the first time, cosecheros received hard cash for their produce. Renta employees were likewise paid in silver and, starting in 1801 in Corrientes, all purchases of renta tobacco were conducted in that medium.[30] The spread of specie had important consequences for the Upper Platine economy and bolstered the system of credit that buttressed the more profitable yerba industry. This expanding money economy brought with it a growth of credit for new enterprises, especially small retail stores, and ended the economic isolation of the region. The elimination of the puerto preciso of Santa Fé in 1779 started the process; the introduction of specie completed it. By the turn of the century, little stood in the way of great profits for all concerned with the tobacco trade.

As seen in Table 4.1, the available statistics for Paraguayan tobacco exports indicate considerable variation in volume. This variation can be explained mostly by fluctuations in rainfall; the bumper crop of 1786, for instance, owed its success to favorable weather. The abnormally high export of 1810, on the other hand, resulted from last-minute efforts by the estanco to send buyers directly into the countryside, rather than wait for tobacco shipments to arrive at Asunción. The buyers evidently ob-

TABLE 4.1: Paraguayan Tobacco Exports*, 1780–1810

Year	Arrobas hoja	Arrobas pito	Total arrobas
1780			17,892
1781			14,417
1782			4,950
1783	3,457	10,359	13,817
1784	4,853	11,859	16,713
1785			18,010
1786	20,736	31,755	52,491
1787	18,594	16,373	34,968
1788	8,634	14,538	23,172
1789	n/a	n/a	n/a
1790	4,684	3,569	8,253
1791	3,419	3,812	7,231
1792	5,234	7,017	12,251
1793	10,997	13,807	24,805
1794	18,555	18,140	36,695
1795	10,814	13,197	24,011
1796	14,449	5,273	19,722
1797	6,177	6,812	12,990
1798	11,611	12,277	23,889
1799	12,060	11,920	23,980
1800	8,029	6,799	14,828
1801			32,957
1802	28,590	16,402	44,992
1803			17,456
1804			28,154
1805	n/a	n/a	n/a
1806	n/a	n/a	9,125
1807	4,254	4,811	9,065
1808	4,025	4,068	8,093
1809	2,463	2,312	4,776
1810	29,414	25,187	54,601

*These figures represent those quantities purchased by the Asunción renta and destined for export. A blank in the table means that no export at all was listed in the documentation; n/a (not available) means I haven't found the document or that it no longer exists.

Sources: Juan José González to Governor Joaquín de Alós, Asunción, 8 June 1790, ANA-NE 376; Juan Bautista de Achard to Governor Bernardo de Valazco, Asunción, 5 February 1810, ANA-NE 2901; "El monopolio de la real Renta," 68–72; and Cooney, *Paraguay and the Royal Tobacco Monopoly*, pp. 157–64.

tained that portion of the crop that normally would have been taken by smugglers. As compared to yerba, the volume of tobacco exported over these years seems unimpressive, but tobacco regularly earned three times the value of yerba per arroba in the Porteño market. If smuggled tobacco is factored into the export total, the figures are comparatively high.

Throughout the period of the estanco, tobacco cultivation was legally restricted to Paraguay. This exclusivity annoyed agriculturalists in other areas of the Upper Plata where tobacco had previously flourished, and on many occasions they made their grievances known to the renta. In 1785 and again in 1788, the cabildo of Corrientes requested authorization for tobacco cultivation in the province, noting that the quality of Correntino tobacco "greatly exceeded that of Paraguay." Moreover, it was argued, shipping costs from Correntino ports would be somewhat less than from Paraguay.[31] The negative response of renta authorities was unequivocal. Not only did they consider a production increase ill-advised, but they also were concerned that they could not prevent smuggling in the area.[32] No significant changes in the operation of the monopoly were contemplated. In the early 1800s, with Spain and the empire burdened by wartime revenue needs, no tinkering with the system in Paraguay was allowed.[33] Nonetheless, despite inefficiency, corruption, and contraband, the renta produced a profit and created many jobs.

Tobacco During the Francia Regime

The monopoly structure effectively came to an end in May 1811 with Paraguayan independence. Within a month, a provincial congress, summoned to deal with the new situation and to correct past grievances, resolved that "the estanco will be extinguished, leaving tobacco to a free commerce like other products of the province."[34] Corrientes followed suit a year later, leaving both production and sale of tobacco open throughout the Upper Plata.[35]

The instability of the newly independent regimes brought uncertainty to the trade. While farmers were free to plant as much tobacco as they desired, merchants were fearful that the commodity would fail to reach its market in the lower provinces. Until 1813, royalist forces periodically blockaded the river route and marauding bands frequently harassed river traffic, making the export trade both expensive and hazardous. Warehouses in Asunción and Corrientes often overflowed with produce ready to ship south, and yet ships were unable to sail because of political disturbances. The situation greatly jeopardized the sale of Upper Platine tobacco, since Buenos Aires and the lower provinces could just as easily obtain tobacco from Brazil and Cuba.

The uncertainty of the tobacco trade increased in the early 1810s when the Porteño government imposed an extraordinary tax on Paraguayan tobacco. Asunción chose to regard this new tariff as a violation of an 1811 treaty that mandated that tobacco would pay only one and one-half reales the arroba.[36] By 1812, the Buenos Aires revolutionaries had grown irritated at Paraguayan refusal to offer military assistance to the Platine independence movement, and chose to ignore the establishment of Paraguay's independence.[37] The ensuing trade war eased Francia's path to power. Though by the end of the decade the Porteños finally abandoned their discrimination against Paraguayan exports, they continued to claim sovereignty over the entire northeast.

During the Francia years, tobacco remained important to Paraguayan agriculture. Though the export sector deteriorated, domestic consumption of tobacco remained steady. Even though adversely affected by unstable conditions in the lower provinces, Paraguayan tobacco was in demand to the south. For example, the Porteño vessel *Santa Fé y Animas* brought some 351 bales of leaf to Buenos Aires from Pilar in 1819.[38] The early unitario governments in Buenos Aires during the 1820s, adhering to free trade principles, placed no discriminatory tariff on tobacco. The duty paid was a basic 10 percent ad valorem for unprocessed tobacco and 20 percent for cigars, the same as paid on those products from Corrientes or Misiones.[39]

During the last ten years of the renta, legal tobacco exports from Paraguay exceeded 20,000 arrobas a year on only four occasions. Despite claims to the contrary, the legal trade only rarely surpassed these totals after the early years of the Francia period.[40] The totals for the 1830s shown in Table 4.2 nevertheless suggest that demand for Paraguayan tobacco in the lower provinces had risen over earlier levels.

Table 4.2, obviously, contains no indication of contraband tobacco. Francia's internal spy network likely decreased the smuggling of this time, though it clearly never eradicated it. In the early days of his regime, Portuguese smugglers were quite active at Itapúa and in Misiones.[41] As mentioned earlier, in 1826–27 a rash of smuggling also occurred at the port of Pilar. Francia forced the offending merchants to pay a massive fine, but he was under no illusions that this would end all smuggling.[42] Such incidents demonstrate that the illicit trade still generated considerable profits for those willing to assume the risks.

Francia's mercantilist control of the export economy prevented any free trade in tobacco during the 1820s and 1830s. The detested estanco had been replaced by a theoretically open commerce, but cosecheros found Francia's export policies more arbitrary and more oppressive than the royal monopoly had been.

TABLE 4.2: Paraguayan Tobacco Exports—The Francia Era

Year	Arrobas	Pesos fuertes
1816	33,196	82,990
1818	27,139	67,846
1819	28,754	71,884
1820	5,476	13,690
1827	1,995 (minimum export)	
1829	6,455	28,292
1832	6,176	28,888
1835	24,016	115,406
1837	12,964	59,279
1838	6,090	26,619
1839	2,026	7,826

Sources: Adapted from White, *Paraguay's Automonous Revolution*, pp. 227–37. White's figures were obtained from treasury and alcabala records of the ANA. Williams, "Paraguayan Isolation under Dr. Francia," 108, provided the incomplete 1827 figure.

Given the difficulty of accommodating the export market, many Paraguayan cosecheros turned away from the cultivation of cash crops during the Francia period. As we have seen, this brought a reorientation toward subsistence agriculture. Maize and manioc were planted in increased amounts, along with cotton, rice, sugarcane, and vegetables.[43] Naturally, a good deal of tobacco was still grown, but it served domestic needs almost exclusively.

Tobacco: The Correntino Connection

In 1835, Juan Manuel de Rosas reversed the free-trade policy of earlier governments in an attempt to protect local enterprises and to further link the Upper Platine economy to that of Buenos Aires, without opening the inland waterways to direct foreign trade. He raised duties on foreign tobacco from 25 to 35 percent ad valorem, but for the Paraguay and Corrientes trade, the tariffs remained the same as before.[44] Paraguayan tobacco thus enjoyed a solid tariff advantage over Cuban and Brazilian tobacco in the Porteño markets.

Buenos Aires needed and wanted tobacco from upriver, as Rosas pointed out in an 1836 letter to the governor of Corrientes, who had complained about Correntino products having to pay the same duties as products from Paraguay. Rosas argued that Upper Platine yerba and tobacco suited the Porteño palate and that to discriminate between the two was to invite contraband. As for Upper Platine cigars, which paid a 20 percent import duty in Buenos Aires, Rosas cited the need to give consideration to the narrowly defined interests of his own province: "I had in mind the powerful consideration that there are many poor women [here] who live from this type of industry."[45] Rosas never bothered to mention that, by the logic of his own political claims, it would have been contradictory to differentiate between Paraguayan products and those of Corrientes. After all, he had stated consistently that Paraguay was just another province in the federation, not an independent state.

The situation looked different through Correntino eyes. Had it not been for the civil wars, Corrientes probably would have greatly increased its share of the Upper Plata's tobacco production. As it was, Correntino tobacco never developed an export market remotely as large as that of Paraguay. Some small room for optimism nonetheless existed. In 1828, for example, a French traveler, Alcides D'Orbigny, visited the Correntino interior and noted the importance of tobacco there. He stressed the interest of Corrientes-based merchants in creating solid trade linkages with cosecheros. No money ever changed hands. Instead, a "multitude" of agents and travelling merchants scoured the countryside, advancing credit to growers in the form of goods and, in accord with verbal agreements, carefully inspecting the growing tobacco before concluding any bargains. Repayment was made at harvest time in tobacco at a prearranged price. The merchant priced his stock to guarantee a 100 percent profit. He also made sure to inspect the tobacco again as workers packed it aboard oxcarts.[46] The tiny amounts of Correntino tobacco shipped south as a result of these exchanges appeared in the registers in such curious and unquantifiable units of measure as *bolsita, bulto, bocoy, cajon, saquito, rollo,* and *petaca.* This obviously complicates any analysis of export statistics, though clearly the total amounts involved were small indeed.

The Correntino government encouraged tobacco cultivation and even tried to set precise standards for production. In 1832, Ferré went so far as to regulate the blending of tobacco grades to make the crop more attractive in the export market. Under his decree, violators risked the confiscation of their entire harvest.[47]

Any expansion of tobacco production required two conditions that Corrientes could not easily meet: a reliable, plentiful labor supply and security for time and effort invested. Frequent military drafts in the tobacco-growing zones tended to depopulate an already underpopulated area. Given the uncertain circumstances, Correntino agriculturalists continued to favor subsistence farming. Beyond this, in 1841, when Corrientes needed allies in the war against Rosas, the Paraguayans obtained from their neighbors a treaty that allowed for the introduction of Paraguayan tobacco in Corrientes at a low 8 percent, an action not in the interest of Correntino growers.[48] In the mid-1840s, the war that raged on Correntino soil did nothing to encourage agriculture of any kind. Up to the 1850s, the tale of Correntino tobacco was one of optimistic projections that faltered and were destroyed by political events.

Free Trade and Tobacco

The stagnant state of Paraguayan tobacco production was underlined in the report of George J. R. Gordon, a British commercial agent who visited Paraguay after the death of the Dictator. He noted with great pessimism that "tobacco, which grown of various and some excellent qualities must . . . take long before it could be produced to any considerable extent and could scarce be so at all without European colonization or the introduction of the slave trade."[49] The immediate outlook for tobacco was, in fact, far brighter than Gordon had foreseen.

A North American, Edward Augustus Hopkins, who arrived in Asunción in mid-1845, may have been partially responsible for this change. Although only twenty-two years old, Hopkins had been appointed by President James K. Polk as "confidential agent to Paraguay for the purpose of obtaining information concerning the political condition and commercial resources of that country, with a view to the acknowledgement of its independence."[50] The new government of Carlos Antonio López was delighted with the possibility of support from so influential a nation as the United States. Hopkins lost no time in assuring López that the United States would definitely recognize Paraguayan independence. He also offered on behalf of his government to mediate Paraguay's longstanding difficulties with Buenos Aires. The North American, however, had no authority to promise recognition or to enter into mediation. He greatly exceeded the bounds of his commission, and his ill-advised enthusiasm ultimately brought about a serious confrontation between the United States and Paraguay.[51]

Hopkins's appearance nonetheless had positive consequences for Paraguayan tobacco. Having ingratiated himself with López, Hopkins obtained a series of valuable concessions, including permission to build a cigar-rolling factory on Paraguayan soil. Although tobacco had long been a key export crop, until that time it had, with the exception of black twist, generally been shipped en rama, to be processed into cigars in the lower provinces. Cigars for local consumption were manufactured in the home, usually by servants or female family members. The cigars smoked by Francia, for example, had been rolled by his own sister.[52]

Hopkins returned to the United States to acquire capital and equipment for his factory. In the meantime, the opportunities that he had outlined for a Paraguayan cigar trade had not escaped the attention of López and other potential speculators. As early as August 1845, the Paraguayan diplomat Juan Andrés Gelly announced his intention to invest heavily in cigar manufacturing. "I will see," he wrote, "if when they open the ports, we can find [markets] for 100,000 to 200,000 cigars."[53]

Markets of such magnitude soon appeared. In fact, tobacco production in the Upper Plata received a massive stimulation from the outside, an incentive so large in scope that it totally transformed the export structure of the region. From a nearly stagnant commerce, based as it still was on yerba mate, a tobacco trade that endured throughout the 1850s bloomed overnight.

The most important element in this metamorphosis was the Anglo-French blockade of Buenos Aires in 1845–48. Before this time, Buenos Aires and the lower provinces had imported Brazilian and Cuban tobacco. In contrast to his attitude toward foreign access to Upper Platine markets, Rosas had allowed the passage of Paraguayan exports along the Paraná, on his own terms. With the British and French at his doorstep, however, Rosas was inclined to see López as the lesser of several evils. The Porteño merchants, for their part, had little choice but to trade with Paraguay if they wished to continue to sell tobacco.

The Paraguayan product, unlike its Brazilian or Cuban competition, could avoid the Anglo-French blockade by taking a land passage from Santa Fé or the Bajada of Paraná. The Paraguayans took advantage of the blockade by selling their tobacco at ports in the lower provinces previously denied them.

Rosas also reduced import duties by one-third, hoping to encourage the flow of goods into Buenos Aires.[54] The results were dramatic. In 1845, the total Paraguayan export of unprocessed tobacco amounted to only 23,072 arrobas together with 120 arrobas of cigars, though relatively little of this export was bound for the Porteño market.[55] Between March 1847 and September 1848, the port of Pilar alone exported 125,708 arrobas of unprocessed tobacco and 780 arrobas of cigars, nearly all destined for Buenos Aires.[56]

The speed with which these events occurred startled all parties. In Paraguay, López remained suspicious. Though he was certainly pleased to gain the revenues accruing from a revival of the tobacco commerce, the thought of large merchant fleets entering the port of Asunción filled him with some dismay.[57] Meanwhile, the activities of Hopkins, who had returned to Paraguay, took on an obnoxious, even threatening character. In the United States, he had organized the United States and Paraguay Navigation Company, backed chiefly by Rhode Island financiers, including a U.S. senator. The company purchased a steamer, loaded it with goods and machinery, and sent it to the Upper Plata in March

1853. The vessel, rechristened *El Paraguay*, never reached its destination; gales so damaged the ship en route that it was forced to put into port at São Luis de Maranhao, where it was condemned by Brazilian authorities. All the machinery destined for the tobacco enterprise was sold. While this proved a considerable blow to Hopkins, it did not spell the end for his cigar-rolling operation.

The North American had obtained the services of five skilled cigar makers from Cuba, who informed him of the excellent quality of Paraguayan tobacco, "though the rude manner in which it had previously been cured had given it a very low price in the market."[58] In addition to the Cubans, finally in Asunción, Hopkins also had permission from López to employ as many Paraguayan peones as needed. The Cuban specialists lost no time in instructing their charges "how to convert their hitherto nearly valueless raw material into cigars that would bring a good price in any part of the world."[59] Hopkins's blustering personal style kept getting in the way, however. He frequently boasted to López of the power of the United States, and of his own influence in Washington. López was notoriously sensitive in matters of protocol yet he willingly ignored his instincts when Hopkins dangled before him promises of mediation with Rosas and of early U.S. recognition. It only slowly occurred to López that Hopkins's claims had little to back them up. Then, the North American made things still worse in an incident where, riding crop in hand, he brusquely demanded that López punish a Paraguayan soldier who had struck Hopkins's brother. Hopkins's undiplomatic behavior, together with his inability to fulfill his promises to López, soon turned the Paraguayan president against him. The Asunción government determined to rid itself of this foreign embarrassment. Bit by bit, López revoked the concessions granted Hopkins and, in 1854, expelled him from the republic.[60] By then, however, all the key changes relative to the tobacco industry had taken place.

The changing political scene in the late 1840s encouraged speculators who knew the potential for tobacco production in the Upper Plata. When a well-connected French entrepreneur, Blas Despouy, approached the Paraguayan government in 1848 to contract for 200,000 arrobas of tobacco annually, his was no idle or fantastic proposition. Despouy had worked in South America for decades and understood the intricacies of Platine politics. For him, the likelihood of great profits merely required investment and timing.[61] But Despouy could not interest López in a potential replay of the Hopkins fiasco, and there this one venture ended.

The defeat of Rosas and the subsequent implementation of free navigation on the rivers had a substantial effect on Paraguayan tobacco exports, as Table 4.3 indicates. The 1851 export statistic of nearly 29,000 arrobas of leaf together with 191,000 cigars resembled that of pre-blockade

TABLE 4.3: Index of Paraguayan Tobacco Exports, The López Years (1856 = 100. For absolute numbers, see Appendix I).

Year	Leaf Value (pesos fuertes)		Cigars Value (pesos fuertes)		Combined value (pesos fuertes)
1851	14	16	5	8	58,177
1852	60	46	13	21	165,292
1853	69	45	49	38	163,461
1854	50	42	124	74	160,745
1855	108[a]	120	116[a]	107	436,920
1856	100	100	100	100	366,510
1857	120	168	103	104	603,690
1858	131	143	98	98	516,770
1859	110	170	59	59	605,791
1860	60	77	142	133	292,830
1861	73	88	129	115	327,943
1862	155	259	93	58	913,885
1863	87	147	99	76	528,034
1864	155	235	380	183	852,824
1865	55	75	301	157	295,606

[a]Minimum figure.
Sources: *El Semanario,* 1 October 1853, 8 October 1853, 24 December 1853, 11 January 1855, and 16 February 1861 through 8 July 1865; Marbais Du Graty, *La república del Paraguay,* pp. 346–50; Herken Krauer, "Proceso económico," 83–116.

days. In fact, the anti-Rosas campaign impeded the transport of all but military supplies at that time. In the year following the battle of Caseros, tobacco exports to Buenos Aires more than quadrupled and stayed high throughout the 1850s and 1860s.

Changes in quality as well as quantity also occurred. Before the blockade of Buenos Aires, Carlos Antonio López was content merely to control exports through Pilar and Itapúa. Commercial regulation, export fees, alcabala receipts—these were the concerns of his government. He gave little, if any, thought to production and quality control. With opportunities in the late 1840s opening the way for greater exports, however, the state took a new interest in tobacco. If Paraguayan tobacco, not to mention yerba, was to retain any hold over the Porteño market after the lifting of the blockade, it had to be competitive; the fraudulent practice of blending good tobacco with inferior, sometimes decomposing, grades had to be stopped. Eventually the government ordered cosecheros to sell their produce in leaf rather than bundles so the product could readily be inspected by trade officials.[62] To encourage both productivity and high quality, the government freed cigars from all export taxes, and cigar makers whose product "approximated Havanas in form, size, and other qualities" received an award of four reales per thousand cigars.[63] Those who produced cigars of fair commercial quality received two reales per thousand. Carlos Antonio López wanted Paraguay to seize the Platine market for high profit, high quality, finished tobacco, as well as for the raw commodity.

In addition, throughout the 1850s, the Paraguayan government increased its purchases of private tobacco holdings. Ostensibly, the object was to meet the need for tobacco at the various public works. In fact, though he refrained from openly taking over the private sector, López had in mind a larger role for the state in the lucrative tobacco export trade. "No sensible person," López argued, "can fail to recognize the right of the state to purchase tobacco from the cosecheros in amounts needed for public projects—commerce will be unaffected by the occasional purchase of 40,000–50,000 arrobas."[64] Without monopoly control, this was the only option for a mercantilist regime, since cosecheros could sell to the highest bidder. Even with this new state interest concerning production and trade, the export of Paraguayan tobacco remained largely in private hands, though the national treasury benefitted from private export through taxes and special fees.[65]

During the 1850s, tobacco dominated the Paraguayan export market along with yerba mate. Increased demand caused tobacco cultivation to eclipse that of foodstuffs, which rendered the importation of such articles necessary. By 1857, foodstuffs rose almost to famine prices that were only partially offset by imports from Buenos Aires and by the harvest of new crops at the end of the year.[66] Imported food remained dear during 1858, with maize, for example, averaging four to six times its 1856 price.[67] Although cosecheros and export merchants realized profits on the tobacco crop, the population as a whole suffered from the food scarcity. No pressure, however, was placed upon the growers to raise foodstuffs instead of tobacco. The cosecheros, in fact, were now favored by the state, which needed the revenues supplied by tobacco export more than it needed an ample production of maize and manioc.

About this time, some Paraguayan tobacco began to appear in European markets under government sponsorship. In June 1853, López sent his son, Francisco Solano, on a European tour. The mission of the younger López was to confirm the recognition of Paraguayan independence and obtain treaties of friendship and commerce. Aboard the ship taking López to Europe were samples of Paraguayan tobacco, cotton, and yerba. These few bales, already mildewed by the time López arrived in Britain, constituted the first sustained effort to interest Europe in Paraguayan produce.

Although the European market represented only a tiny fraction of total Paraguayan exports, the effort to break into it was undertaken seriously. In 1855, Paraguayan tobacco earned a gold medal and an honorable mention at the Paris Exposition.[68] Two years later, one shipment of Paraguayan tobacco at London weighed in at over three English tons, each pound of which brought eight and one-half pence at auction.[69] European promoters of Paraguayan tobacco remained optimistic. The British agents of the López government went so far as to suggest an increased role for the Paraguayan state in the tobacco trade: "I strongly recommend that all this growth of tobacco should be secured by the Government as it is much approved here and will interfere much with the North American [tobacco] hereafter."[70] The Paraguayans displayed great interest in the European market, particularly after the U.S. civil war interrupted the flow of tobacco from that country. The death of Carlos Antonio López in 1862 brought no shift in policy. If anything, because the political apparatus passed into the hands of his European-minded son, Paraguayans appeared more determined than before to capture foreign tobacco markets. Representatives on the continent spoke glowingly of these possibilities, and in Britain in 1864, financial backing from the Baron Lionel Nathan de Rothschild was considered.[71] Buenos Aires, however, remained the largest consumer.

Isolation was no longer a feature of commercial relations in the Upper Plata. Both the state and private entrepreneurs garnered profits from the tobacco commerce, and the Paraguayan government worked steadily to bolster the trade and the revenues it earned. In 1858, for instance, the government moved to eliminate the shipment of inferior or spoiled tobacco by requiring export licenses. No one could thereafter sell tobacco without a written indication of quality. Failure to abide by this license system brought a fine of twenty-five pesos for each illegal arroba. The administration of Francisco Solano López also tried to assure the high quality of exported tobacco through classification by grade.[72]

Though demand for Upper Platine produce had reinvigorated the old trade networks, cultivation failed to increase uniformly throughout the region. As before, Correntino tobacco remained in the shadow of the Paraguayan product, at least in volume of exports during the 1850s and 1860s. In 1855, the port of Corrientes exported only six arrobas en rama, together with 40,000 cigars.[73] While the post-1852 provincial governments favored the development of tobacco, they left active encouragement to the private sector.

Tobacco cultivation in Corrientes was limited to the impoverished districts (or departments) of Lomas, Caacatí, Ensenadas, San Miguel, Yaguareté Corá, and San Roque. As a rule, the province consumed all it produced, though as one observer argued in 1857, the province could have exported as much as 80,000 arrobas of leaf a year if certain impediments were overcome.[74] Foremost among these was a lack of skilled and unskilled labor. The rural regions of Corrientes, in contrast to those of Paraguay, were low in population and most of that was transient. Many workers abandoned the area seasonally to work the cattle ranches of the south. Under such conditions, tobacco cultivation remained both primitive and limited.

This problem never prevented speculators from investing in Correntino tobacco. A 120 percent profit was projected in the first year, given sufficient initial investments. Such profits compared favorably with those of tobacco enterprises in North America and Brazil. In 1862, businessmen tried to introduce the cultivation of black tobacco in Corrientes, in hopes of overcoming Brazilian dominance in this product. Little came of the venture.[75] Investors continued to stress the potential of tobacco over the next few years, noting that the Correntino product would pay none of the customs duties faced by the Paraguayan product.[76] Though this seemed a reasonable argument, the risks involved outweighed possible benefits, and investment remained in the realm of talk.

The protracted War of the Triple Alliance severely affected tobacco cultivation. As a cash crop, tobacco depended on markets in the lower provinces, but after 1864, Paraguayan produce almost never penetrated the Allied blockade.[77] When available from the Upper Plata, tobacco brought a wartime price downriver, as much as six pesos, four reales the arroba, but few exports got through.[78]

During the war, Paraguay reverted to a level of exports lower than that of the Francia period. Except for the occasional merchant slipping through the lines, it proved impossible to carry on any export trade.[79] What tobacco was grown passed quickly to the front to provision the Paraguayan troops. As the war went on, the economy had to gear itself to the production of foodstuffs, leaving aside all other crops.[80]

Tobacco and the Chance for Development

Between 1780 and 1865, tobacco played a key role in the economy of the Upper Plata. Both legal and contraband tobacco always found markets in the lower provinces. Political variables could and did pose a threat to this trade, but given a chance, commerce in this commodity always managed to rebound. Paraguay clearly dominated sales to the south; Corrientes, try as it might, could never compete with its neighbor.

The defeat of Paraguay in the War of the Triple Alliance and the devastation of the regional economy did not favor a reestablishment of the old commercial structure. The small European market, fully supplied by North American and Egyptian tobacco, lost any interest it once had in an Upper Platine source. Buenos Aires refocused its attention on the Brazilian and Cuban product. The massive wave of immigration that came in the following decades, because it swelled the consumer base with individuals who were unaccustomed to the strong Upper Platine tobacco, only reinforced the overseas trade linkage.

The tobacco trade illustrates a fundamental theme of this study—that politics frustrated trading between producers in the Upper Plata and consumers in the south. The former had reason to lament the failure of the trade; tobacco was one of the only commodities that could be freely traded by its growers and the only one that remained relatively unencumbered by heavy export restrictions. The lack of such controls probably reflected a residual distaste for the workings of the old estanco (though, as we have seen, such feelings failed to impede state monopolies on other commodities).

In any case, tobacco offered a direct road to economic advancement for the smallholders of the region. Only stable politics could permit sustained growth, however. The connection with Buenos Aires depended on open rivers and, more broadly, on political harmony among the Platine states. Post-independence conditions permitted little of this. The old social elites never perceived how much real potential an open tobacco trade would have. They knew that tobacco showed resiliency as a trade item during periods of stability, but they never saw that resiliency in itself was insufficient for development. An export that might have crystalized economic growth in the Upper Plata was never given the backing needed to achieve that measure of success.

5

Cattle

*He knows each animal of a herd
as we do persons; and of the horse
he chooses for himself, he knows
the good and the bad, his qualities and moral defects, just as we
know the psychology of a friend.*
Paul Groussac

The subtropical lowlands of the Upper Plata, with their extremes of climate and foliage, did not easily lend themselves to stockraising. Hides,
tallow, and jerked beef, as articles of export, never surpassed yerba mate
and tobacco. Moreover, the competition presented by Entre Ríos, the
Banda Oriental, and especially the province of Buenos Aires prevented
the emergence of the northeast as a supplier in the large international
market for dried beef (charqui). This does not mean, however, that ranching had little impact within the Upper Plata. Quite the contrary; in some
areas, it was the dominant enterprise.

This was particularly true in southern Corrientes and along the Río
Uruguay. There, the grassy terrain resembled that of Entre Ríos, whereas
to the north, the waving grasses grew thinner. In Misiones, stands of
yataí palms (*Areca olerácea*) encroached upon the steppes, which ultimately gave way to dense forests in Paraguay. Before the advent of permanently settled ranches—estancias—this area was home to thousands
of wild cattle and horses who shared the plain with tapirs and anteaters.
The animals thrived on a rich diet of white clover, thistles, wild grasses,
and palm fruit; except for the jaguar, their only predator was man.

The excellence of the Correntino pastures permitted a vast expansion of the wild cattle population by the end of the 1500s, and in the
late sixteenth century, specialized cowpunchers called *vaqueros* emerged
to exploit the herds. As with the gaucho of the Pampas, the vaquero
had few possessions and these he kept close at hand: lasso, whip, sad-
dle, a sheathed double-edged knife (*facón*), and the inevitable *boleadoras*,

a weighted sling of Indian origin used to throw cattle and horses. A heavy poncho, a wide-brimmed hat, and a hide undergarment (*chiripá*) was the vaquero's complete attire. Aside from a higher consumption of meat, the vaquero's diet resembled that of other northeasterners and included yerba, cornmush, manioc bread (*chipá*), and occasionally fruit. In the main, the vaquero existed outside the money economy.

Range cattle were regarded as Crown property. By the mid-seventeenth century, the government awarded rights to individuals to round up and slaughter a specific number of cattle each year within a prescribed area. These forays, termed *vaquerías*, were conducted periodically until around 1750. Generally, these involved little more than the slaughter of the animals for their hides, tongue, and ribs, the last two items being standard fare for vaqueros in the Upper Plata.

By modern standards, the vaquería was a wasteful economic activity. The hunting parties left most of an animal's carcass to the jaguars and vultures and made no effort to preserve the reproductive capacity of the herd. During the 1700s, this practice made little difference due to the sheer size of cattle populations.

The right to conduct vaquerías was a jealously guarded monopoly organized under a licensing system. The frequency of expeditions into the rangelands remained low until the illegal export of hides started on a regular basis at the beginning of the eighteenth century. The growing economies of northern Europe required leather in substantial amounts for shoes, packing material, and tack. Buenos Aires could meet most of this rising demand through Portuguese smugglers along the Brazilian frontier and through sales to French and British slave traders. Though remote from this trade, Upper Platine vaqueros participated in it, an expanded exploitation of herds being the inevitable result.

Outside demand for hides increased in the eighteenth century, with vaquerías becoming more prevalent all the time. This engendered a serious depletion of range cattle by the 1720s, and little time passed before the wild herds were exterminated. Correntino entrepreneurs then turned to the domestication of cattle, a move that required estancias to contain the animals. This in turn brought a gradual transformation in the northeast, away from a concept of wealth based on the license to conduct vaquerías, to one based on the ownership of grazing land. A modest landholding elite developed in Corrientes and Paraguay, and estancias and smaller cattle stations (*ranchos*) became permanent features in the region. The estancia allowed for a more rational exploitation of cattle that balanced the killing rate with the needs of reproduction.

Corrientes supplied cattle to the rest of the Upper Plata until the end of the colonial period. Meeting this need would have been impossible without improved techniques. In domesticating their herds, Correntinos employed two main practices: the *rodeo* and the brand. On the estancia, the rancher's foreman (*capatáz*) and his men herded the cattle into pastures called rodeos. They brought the cattle together perhaps once a week in this manner in order to accustom them both to the cowhand on horseback and to the designated rodeo area. Once they branded stray cattle with an official mark, the owners could reclaim their own stock when all cattlemen in the vicinity assembled their herds on the fenceless range. The castration of bullocks took place in the autumn months, but in other respects the animals were left alone. This rudimentary husbandry stimulated greater reproduction of herds; from a low of only 8,000 head held on Correntino ranches in 1738, the herds increased to around 160,000 head held in 1760.[1] The estanciero needed cowhands to watch his herds all year long; itinerant cowboys provided most of the labor, some coming from as far away as Montevideo. With the expulsion of the Jesuits in 1767, many former mission Indians joined the labor pool.[2]

Cattle needed little extensive handling. Félix de Azara claimed that only one capatáz and ten cowhands could run an estancia of some 10,000 head of cattle, enough to assure an increase in the size of the herd by one-third each year.[3] Labor was also required, however, for driving livestock from one spot to another, a specialized task given the environmental conditions of the northeast. The tropical climate bred ticks, worms, screwflies, and mites of all kinds. Predatory animals presented even more of a problem. When swimming across piranha-infested waters, for example, the vaqueros would often kill a calf and throw its body downstream. While the piranhas devoured it, the troop crossed elsewhere. Even with such tricks as these, it was common to lose many head of cattle on the drive.

Paraguayan demand for beeves proved consistently high during the colonial era. On repeated occasions, this demand actually placed the stability of the Correntino economy in danger, since, as the cabildo noted at the beginning of the century, "roundups of Correntino cattle [to sell] in the city of Asunción . . . [are effected] in such high numbers that their continuation threatens the fecundity of the remaining herds and promises the total ruin of [Corrientes]."[4] The incentive of high prices also spurred the northward flow of cattle, and the efforts of the Correntino government to stem this tide initially met with little success. Vaquerías were outlawed in the province at the beginning of the century; in 1716 an official outcry arose over the export of tallow and grease.[5] Nevertheless, Correntino cattle continued to be driven across the Paraná.[6]

It seems unlikely that the depletion of Correntino herds in this period resulted solely from incessant Paraguayan demand. Between 1718 and 1739, renewed Indian raids from the Chaco forced the evacuation of villages near the port of Corrientes. Decades passed before this zone was effectively resettled.[7] At the same time, a series of persistent droughts served to shrink the herds still further.[8]

Faced with a near-disastrous situation, local authorities passed tough measures. In 1750, Governor José de Andonaegui announced the absolute prohibition of cattle exports from Corrientes, a decision slightly modified three years later to authorize only the exit of those oxen used as draft animals.[9] This conservationist stance had its origin, however, in the fact that taxes on livestock supported the colonial administration, and government officials wanted the herds to expand to guard this source of revenue. The ranchers, after experiencing the deleterious effects of the vaquerías, now willingly pursued a more rational course, one that ensured regular profits from hide exports without depleting the herds. Thanks to this change, and to more favorable weather conditions, Corrientes realized a steady rise in hide exports throughout the remainder of the century.[10]

Correntino ranching enjoyed increased access to Porteño markets after the creation of the viceroyalty. The traffic in this case was largely confined to hides, tallow, and animal by-products rather than cattle on the hoof. Correntinos drove cattle in large numbers to slaughtering establishments along the Paraná and later to the Arroyo de la China (Concepción) along the Uruguay. The extant registers usually mention these two locations as final destination, though they generally add that there the animals "will be stripped of their skins to be sent on to Buenos Aires."[11] In this manner, 438,662 hides from Corrientes reached the Porteño market during the 1780–97 period.[12]

Corrientes also had to meet the rising demand for livestock from Misiones. Before the expulsion of the Jesuits, Misiones had enjoyed near self-sufficiency in livestock. Jesuit estancias had ranked among the largest and best-managed operations in the Plata.[13] Pablo Hernández recorded the number of livestock belonging to the eleven mission settlements as 381,304 in 1768.[14] Antonio Sepp reported that the mission that did not have 3–4,000 horses was considered poor.[15] The 1750 Treaty of Madrid, however, and the Guaraní War (1754–56) brought Jesuit stockraising to a standstill. The treaty temporarily transferred valuable Jesuit ranching lands to the Portuguese. Indian refugees from the seven missions now in Portuguese territory east of the Río Uruguay crowded into the one community of Yapeyú during 1769. There they were maintained only through massive assistance from Corrientes.[16]

Ranching in Misiones decayed still further over the next decades, leaving secular authorities with little choice but to continue the importation of Correntino livestock. The exact number of animals driven to Misiones between 1770 and 1779 cannot be determined, because licences for those years covered only cattle imported by river.[17] Relatively complete accounting does exist for the 1780–97 period, and from these figures it seems clear that an erratic state of supply and demand characterized livestock trade between the two areas. The number of live cattle legally dispatched to Misiones was 3,185 in 1780. Exports climbed to 18,703 seven years later, but then quickly dropped by one-half in 1788. Exports rose and fell in this irregular manner for almost a decade.[18] The mission establishments never recovered. They soon faced an all-encompassing poverty and were finally abandoned by their Indian occupants. The livestock trade with Corrientes likewise diminished and by the turn of the nineteenth century had nearly disappeared.[19]

Not so the commerce with Paraguay, where the demand for livestock remained constant. Paraguayan herds never proved sufficient to meet local needs, in part because ecological factors limited stockraising. The Spanish naval officer Juan Francisco Aguirre, a noted expert on Paraguay, put it this way: "Unlike the [provinces] of the Río de la Plata, this is not the place for the raising of animals. All such attempts will be impaired by the [poor quality] of the soil and by the climate. The vermin, the heat, the rains, and the frosts all make an impact and the cattle are invariably infested with worms."[20]

Between 1780 and 1797 more than 149,000 head of cattle passed into Paraguay from Corrientes, mostly along the Itatí-Pilar route.[21] The herds generally crossed the river on rafts, with inhabitants on both sides of the river reaping some benefit from the imposition of transit fees, usually a total of 10 percent of assessed value.[22] At low water, the animals could swim to the other side, thereby reducing the transit fee by half. When the river rose to any significant height, as occurred in 1785–86, the passage could prove difficult. In those years, a full 50 percent of the cattle and nearly a third of the horses perished in the crossing.[23]

The final destination for much of the livestock was the northern rangelands adjacent to the Jejuí and Ypané rivers, the main centers of yerba production in Paraguay. Some Correntino cattle reached communities in eastern Paraguay and thereby reduced demand for imported livestock, since the grasslands near these settlements could support sizable herds without the need for further imports. As Azara noted in 1801, "When I went to Paraguay in 1783, we ate for the most part meat that had come from Corrientes; today there are 2,000,000 head of cattle in the country."[24] The holdings of certain Indian pueblos confirm Azara's observations and indicate a growth in Paraguayan stockraising in the viceregal period. In 1794, Caazapá possessed sixteen estancias with a total of 60,000 head; Yaguarón, 30,000; Itapé, 25,000; Itá, 20,000; Yuty, 18,000; and Atyrá, 17,000.[25] The shift to livestock self-sufficiency in Paraguay, so often associated with the Francia era, was already apparent at the end of the eighteenth century.

TABLE 5.1: Paraguayan Hide Exports, 1781–1814

Year	Rawhides	Tanned hides	Year	Rawhides	Tanned hides
1781			1798	7,584	
1782	n/a	n/a	1799	n/a	n/a
1783			1800	4,831	
1784			1801	5,980	
1785	n/a	n/a	1802	6,218	1,600
1786			1803	1,509	1,866
1787		72	1804	3,205	5,376
1788	252		1805	580	1,824
1789			1806	200	7,818
1790			1807		3,538*
1791	75		1808		600
1792			1809		1,557
1793			1810	240	975*
1794	3,549	30	1811		626
1795	2,400		1812	132	1,200
1796	9,200		1813	n/a	n/a
1797	7,227		1814		3,062*

*Approximations based on incomplete registers.
Sources: Registros de guías y tornaguías, 1783–1814, ANA-NE 11, 80, 115, 188, 418, 1149, 1159, 1167, 2536, 2900, 3089, 3337, 3341, 3356, 3360; and Azara, *Geografía física y esférica del Paraguay*, p. 434.

Export statistics, as shown in Table 5.1, confirm the healthy status of Paraguayan ranching. Few of these hides, however, entered the overseas market; the majority of Upper Platine rawhides arrived at Buenos Aires in appalling condition, partly decomposed and overrun with worms. Such hides could serve only as packing material. Tanned hides fared somewhat better, but because of poor curing standards could rarely compete for the foreign hide market. Porteño demand for inferior grades of leather for use in artisan work remained the key element in the Upper Platine hide trade.

The more open commercial climate of the late 1700s, because it stimulated Porteño demand, also resulted in an increased output of cattle by-products throughout the region. Upper Platine artisan industries reflected this growth. The presence of *curupay* trees, whose bark yielded tannic acid, ensured the success of any number of small tanneries in the region. Workers scraped the hair from skins with hot ashes or lime and then treated them with tannin. The lustrous rosy color of the treated hides made them perfectly suitable for artisan work. Ready-made saddlery, candles, shoe soles, and hide whips, while primarily intended for local consumers, were also shipped to Buenos Aires.

The small port of Goya, previously little more than a ranch house on a tributary of the river, had become the center for the export of finished leather goods on the Paraná by 1811.[26] The growth of Goya was linked to the thriving contraband trade. As we have seen, the rural zones of Corrientes often acted as if provincial authority did not exist, largely ignoring legal restraints on trade. Hide traffickers and rustlers had no difficulty in meeting their needs, and fragile craft, often filled to capacity, carried to Buenos Aires the hides acquired in the course of a successful expedition. Correntino ranch hands seldom concerned themselves with the interests of their patrón, and the forests and swamps offered easy refuge for smugglers and escaped slaves.[27]

The viceregal government addressed this problem by forbidding the loading of ships anywhere between Esquina and Corrientes, an order issued in 1792 and again in 1795 without success because the movement of vessels along the rivers remained unsupervised.[28] The estimated number of hides smuggled out of Corrientes at that time was put at 20,000 annually, a figure equal to one-third of the legal commerce.[29]

The only solution left to fiscal-minded authorities was to establish provincial customs houses (receptorías) in the towns of Goya and Esquina in 1802 and 1803 respectively.[30] This measure being equally ineffective, the illegal export of cow- and horsehides continued at an alarming rate. As in the previous century, the cabildo of Corrientes in 1803 warned of the imminent extinction of the region's livestock should the slaughter go on unabated, estimating the annual outflow of hides at 80,000.[31]

In fact, the reduction in trade with Paraguay and Misiones was already serving to curb Correntino exports. Then came the British invasion and occupation of Buenos Aires in 1806–1807. The ensuing war left a large number of hides to accumulate at Goya. When shipment south again became possible, Corrientes responded with the highest volume of hides exported in the colonial period. The provincial trade registers for 1805–1809 recorded over 320,000 cowhides shipped to Buenos Aires, nearly a third of these in the last year alone.[32]

As the colonial period drew to a close, the cattle-producing areas of the Upper Plata underwent some profound changes. Vaquerías were much the exception rather than the rule. The labor base for the estancias had also grown due to the emigration of Indians from Misiones. As this was happening, new trade policies opened the region to wider demand from the lower provinces. These trends helped crystalize the estancia as a major productive unit in the Upper Plata, and they placed the estanciero in an advantageous position vis-à-vis other regional elites. Unlike the urban-based merchants, the estancieros could usually claim a long-term presence in the Upper Plata. They could also appeal, in many cases, to the traditional loyalty of the rural masses, and thus they remained a potent political force during the civil wars of the early nineteenth century.

Stockraising in the Early National Period

The ranching industry escaped few of the ravages of independence and war. Passing troops could easily confiscate animals, ruining in one day what had taken years to build. Unlike the sites for logging and the gathering of yerba, which enjoyed the advantage of being located in the isolated northern zone of the region, the principal ranching zones lay on the southern frontiers. The herds were within easy reach of rustlers from Entre Ríos and Rio Grande, who multiplied in numbers with the lawlessness of the times. In districts adjacent to the provincial capital, the situation was ordinarily more stable, but ranchers still had few commercial options. With the river passage uncertain, most preferred to stay outside of the trade and let their herds reproduce. This was eminently sensible; unlike cosecheros, who had little choice but to sell their tobacco, ranchers could afford to wait, to use leather in place of imported calicoes, and watch their prospective earnings grow. For much of the time, the only safe outlet for their livestock was within the Upper Plata itself, with Paraguay, as in colonial times, absorbing the bulk of Correntino cattle exports. This phenomenon, however, was conditioned by an unfavorable political climate that allowed for little flexibility.

Until 1821, the civil struggles forced a decline in Correntino cattle production. First came the disorder associated with the Belgrano expedition. Soon thereafter followed Portuguese invasions along the Río Uruguay that destroyed what remained of the Guaraní missions. Then, in rapid succession, came the campaigns of Artigas and of Francisco Ramírez. These events left the countryside "infested with wicked deserters and invaders whose common attributes include[d] murder, theft, and abduction."[33] The devastation was widespread. Certain stockraising areas, such as Curuzú Cuatiá, faced destruction on several occasions, first at the hands of the Portuguese and then the Artiguistas.[34] The only cattle-raising areas within the Upper Plata that avoided this destruction were central and eastern Paraguay.

Ranching in Paraguay received a boost after the mid-1810s because other lucrative activities, especially the export of yerba mate and tobacco, had become impractical. Individuals who had previously worked in menial capacities in the yerba trade now found stockraising the most palatable of limited choices. Francia enjoyed considerable support among these men and among the chacreros of the Paraguayan interior. He rewarded their fealty by generally leaving them alone, though on two occasions he enacted legislation on their behalf. In 1830, having for several years realized large surpluses from his state holdings, the Dictator decided to abolish the diezmo—the 10 percent tax on agricultural production (normally paid by ranchers in livestock)—replacing it with a 5 percent tax. Two years later, Francia decreased still further the burden of the rural sector by also eliminating the nominal tax on livestock (*cuatropea*).[35]

The new Paraguayan state inherited from the colonial regime some forty royal ranches (*estancias del rey*). A number of these had been formed previously from lands taken from the Jesuits in 1767.[36] Renamed *estancias de la república* in 1813, these ranches varied in size and productivity and were scattered throughout the central region. They were not broken up and sold, as in other parts of Spanish America, but were, under Francia, augmented and made more efficient. As one observer noted, while colonial officials had basically ignored the royal ranches, the Dictator "has endeavored since the commencement of his sway, to render the domains productive, and has, by so doing, created a branch of revenue, which aided in time, and a wise government, may be found sufficient of itself alone, for all the wants of the state."[37]

Given the external threat, Francia felt he needed such ranches to provision his soldiers. The ranches supplied mounts for the cavalry, charqui for the frontier garrisons, meat on the hoof, and hides for saddlery and chaps. The Dictator wanted his state estancias to produce all foodstuffs needed to support the local troops, including manioc root, yerba, and meat. The army itself supplied the necessary labor.

The state estancias also produced an important share of the items traded by the government at Itapúa and Pilar, where Francia procured the commodities that local sources failed to provide. Even during the earliest days of his dictatorship, Francia conducted a trade in livestock and cured hides.[38] Though hides were not monopolized like yerba or construction woods, the Paraguayan state did play the principal role in their export. Foreign merchants routinely purchased a thousand or more hides from the government at a peso each.[39]

The state estancia system expanded steadily as the years went by. In 1816, Francia received word that the prosperous ranch at Surubiy— formerly Jesuit—had attracted rustlers who had seized many head of cattle. He soon established military posts in the area to protect the state herds. Francia also resettled many of the local inhabitants at other sites and created a subsidiary ranch, where the burgeoning herds were accommodated.[40] Surubiy became a flourishing community in its own right, a major source of remounts for Indian campaigns in the far north and salted meat for the prisons of the capital. At times, large cattle drives left Surubiy for the northern frontier, where they aided settlers whose own herds had been decimated in Indian raids.[41]

By the mid-1830s, a government summary indicated the existence of fifty state ranches (three of which were clusters of several) and twenty-two small military posts, or *puestos*, with enough cattle on hand to provision the garrison. While the majority were located beyond the Cordillera in the east, some five estancias and six puestos were located along the northern banks of the Río Paraná.[42] Fourteen more were situated within ten leagues of Asunción (the site of the largest garrisons), ten near Villarrica, seventeen along the Río Tebicuary in the former Jesuit zone of the south, four in the district of Pilar, and several more close to the yerba center of San Pedro. In the isolated interior, smaller ranches were found alongside such settlements as Yhu and San Estanislao.

Already impressive by the 1810s, the state estancia network increased substantially as a result of political unrest. In 1820, Francia uncovered a conspiracy against his regime on the part of the Montiel, Yegros, and Acosta families and other members of the creole elite. These individuals owned major holdings in cattle and had an interest in expanding the outside market for their hides. Unlike the chacreros, who were unperturbed by the ramifications of a closed economy, these estancieros were antagonistic toward the Francia regime. Within a year, after having jailed hundreds, he had sixty-eight of the conspirators executed and all their properties confiscated.[43] Those shot included some of the wealthiest men in Paraguay, men whose wealth and power derived from huge ranches and from the Porteño trade connection generally.

In this manner, Francia added many of the best private estates in Paraguay to the national domain. While some of this land was sold or leased, much of it Francia placed directly into the state estancia system. One such case involved Manuel Atanacio Cabañas, estanciero, militia officer, and participant in the Paraguayan independence movement. Implicated in the 1820 plot, Cabañas escaped execution only to die in prison several years later. At the time of his death, a partial inventory showed that his considerable wealth included two estancias at Tebicuary, 23 slaves, 3,727 cattle, 1,680 horses, and 21 mules. All of this passed to the state.[44] Other families, such as the Yegros and the Montiel, forfeited even larger properties.[45]

Aside from the use of livestock in the official trade at Pilar and Itapúa, state cattle were sometimes sold on the open market to the Paraguayan public for cash.[46] This was done, it seems, less out of financial necessity than as an expedient to trim the growing state herds, which at times exhausted available pasturage at certain estancias.

The surplus of animals, particularly after 1820, allowed the Dictator to put them to other uses. Villarrica experienced frequent crop failure and for this reason, Francia sometimes dispatched herds of cattle from neighboring state estancias to care for the needs of the town's poor.[47] The state estancias also provided cattle in partial payment of salaries to rural public school teachers. The eight teachers in the Concepción area, for instance, each received one beef a month in addition to a low cash salary.[48]

Historians have assumed that private enterprise in Paraguay suffered greatly during the 1814–40 period. There is clearly much truth to this with regard to foreign trade. In ranching, however, the expansion noted for the estancias de la república was paralleled by growth in the private sector. Francia's land confiscations never extended far into the countryside after the 1820 episode ran its course. As long as ranchers took care in their dealings with the government, he left them to their own devices. This was true even for the remaining wealthy landowners. Many years later, a foreign observer noted the case of José Mauricio Casal, a rich estanciero of Caapucú:

> The father of Don Mauricio had been one of the richest
> estancieros in the country under the old Spanish regime, being
> possessed of as many as eight very large estancias. These
> estancias varied in size, being from three to eight leagues square,
> each of them numbering their cattle by thousands. . . . The silver
> plate which the house contained was to be estimated by
> hundreds of pounds, if not by the ton. The richest silks,
> brocades, and damasks wrought with gold and silver threads
> were bought and stored away [there]. . . . It was in the early days
> of Francia's reign that Don Mauricio became heir to this large
> estate. . . . During the long period of Francia's power, Don
> Mauricio managed so as to avoid the fate of nearly all his class in
> the country, and survived the Dictator. He never provoked the
> enmity or suspicion of Francia, but, on the contrary . . .
> ingratiated himself with him by his liberal donations of cattle
> and horses to the state.[49]

With the rise of Carlos Antonio López in the mid-1840s, "the affairs of Señor Casal seemed no longer to prosper. . . . One estancia after another was sacrificed to the tribunals of López, and the best of them soon after worked into the hands of that family. His silver plate went next by installments, and it all went in the same direction."[50] Casal was hardly alone in sharing this fate.

Improvements in Corrientes

As I have noted, in 1821, the situation in Corrientes took a turn for the better. The civil wars momentarily subsided, the Artiguistas had been banished, and the ranchers of the province looked forward to duplicating the successes enjoyed in Paraguay.

This presented no easy task. The wars had left the province destitute, and the Correntino government felt that only through sweeping measures could ranching recover. Juan José Fernández Blanco proved particularly active on this issue. He regarded the health of the province's herds as being at least as important as the reestablishment of the Paraguay trade. In 1820–21, decrees had appeared that forbade the slaughter of cows and mares. Fernández Blanco reinforced these measures and extended the restriction to colts as well.[51] Such actions constituted the first real attempts to bolster Correntino stockraising since independence. Such legislation, which tapered well with the province's protectionist leanings, remained in place for nearly two decades and was only abandoned with renewed civil war in the late 1830s.

The governorships of Pedro Ferré, Pedro Dionísio Cabral (1827–30), and Rafael Atienza (1833–37) brought a further degree of sophistication to the regulation of Correntino ranching. Ferré proved especially insightful. In 1825, he promulgated a law that allowed the export of horses to the Banda Oriental, while obligating the exporters to return a third of their profits to Corrientes in the form of live cattle.[52] He also decreed a prohibition on the export of cowhides, a temporary measure that supposedly benefitted "not just the public at large, but the individual propietario as well."[53] In fact, it is unclear how the decree was received and what its real effects were.

The governorships of Ferré and Cabral witnessed the Cisplatine struggle with Brazil, a conflict that did nothing to hinder Correntino ranching. Quite the contrary. The province actually gained from the forced removal of Riograndense herds to Corrientes.[54] Though precise figures are lacking, some historians regard this cattle transfer as a major element in the recovery of Correntino ranching.[55] The policy of the provincial government, as reflected in the official government record, the *Registro Oficial*, continued to promote stockraising. Temporary prohibitions on the slaughter of cattle were enacted in 1829 and 1834, as well as new laws in 1838 regulating brands and roundups. The government also facilitated the importation of salt through the elimination of tariffs.[56]

Perhaps the most far-sighted resolution of this period involved the sponsorship of provincial *saladeros*.[57] Salted beef in great quantities was needed for slave rations in Brazil and Cuba, and while salting plants had existed in the Plata for several decades, these were still confined to the province of Buenos Aires and the Banda Oriental. These saladeros tended to be primitive affairs. An animal's body was placed on a flatbed cart and pulled over rails to the flayers, whose knives removed the hide and meat, which was then stacked and dried over poles in the sun. Workers placed the fat, bones, and excess flesh in primitive steam vats to extract tallow and grease.[58]

The kind of salting plant envisioned by Correntino authorities involved newer methods and technologies. Some innovations had made their mark in Buenos Aires during the late 1820s and had rapidly gained acceptance throughout the Plata. An immigrant French chemist, Antoine Cambaceres, had already introduced assembly-line techniques. He designed cattle chutes in the corrals, a truck and rail system to move carcasses within the sheds, and steam vats to render the animal fat from bones and flesh. Cambaceres's workers in Buenos Aires even utilized dried bones as fuel and then packed the ashes, along with manure from the pens, to be exported as fertilizer.[59] In addition to the usual hides and tallow, *saladeros* could process salted meats, mare's grease (much in demand for soap and fuel for street lighting), bones, and horsehair (for upholstery). This kind of salting plant Ferré and others hoped to see in Corrientes.

The Correntino governing elites had reason for feeling optimistic about ranching in the province. Their conservationist stance had achieved some success as herds multiplied in all parts of the Upper Plata. Even with large herds, however, the Correntinos could never hope to compete with the tremendous advantage enjoyed by Buenos Aires in the overseas markets. Only under a system that strictly limited output of hides in the lower provinces could Corrientes hope to garner a share of the foreign trade. The Bonaerense ranching elite was a powerful group, however, and it would have been unthinkable to expect them to work against their own commercial interest. Corrientes had to content itself with a tertiary role in the hide trade, behind Paraguay. This meant that Correntino hides were used chiefly by Porteño cobblers and leather artisans for patchwork. Despite the limitations this implied, the Correntinos were determined to enjoy the fruits of peace. Whether absentee estanciero or merchant, they looked forward to growing profits.

The economic upturn promised some fiscal benefits, and in July 1827, the provincial government decreed a new tax on ranches as part of a plan to provide rural security.[60] The new tax required that estancieros who possessed between 100 and 200 head pay two pesos annually; those with 200 to 500, four pesos; those with 500 to 1,000, eight pesos; and those with more than 1,000, ten pesos. The new tax structure necessitated an accurate accounting for all cattle in Corrientes on a presumed year-to-year basis, and under the auspices of this law, cattle censuses were conducted in 1827, 1829, 1832, 1834, 1835, 1836, and 1838 (see Appendices II and III).

Taken together, these censuses revealed much about Correntino ranching. For one thing, they demonstrated a steady increase in the number of both cattle and sheep over the eleven-year period covered (see Table 5.2). The number of horses, on the other hand, fluctuated considerably, due to military requirements and perhaps to the uncontrolled slaughter of mares, which were considered valuable only for their grease. The fact

TABLE 5.2: Livestock Holdings, Corrientes, 1827–38

Year	Cattle	Horses	Sheep
1827	171,800		
1829	219,118	61,938	59,847
1832[a]	317,684	72,984	70,402
1834	338,415	67,947	86,216
1835	403,984	74,114	88,108
1836	432,152	73,871	96,222
1838	466,590	81,147	107,958

[a]Does not include figures for Bella Vista department.
Sources: Manifiesto de haciendas, 1827, AGPC-Censos, legajo 3; Manifiesto de haciendas, 1829–38, AGPC-EA, legajos 27–54; Maeder, "La evolución de la ganadería en Corrientes," 13.

that sheep received mention at all indicated a minor diversification of stock, though wool remained a marginal export.[61]

The censuses also permit some analysis of the estancieros themselves, whose numbers increased from 523 in 1827 to over 1,000 in 1838 and eventually reached 2,373 in 1854.[62] There was, however, only slight growth in the wealth of individual ranchers. In 1827, no estanciero possessed more than 2,000 head. Within five years, twenty men were in this category, and by 1837, thirty-eight, of whom two, Pablo Bernal and ex-governor Cabral, held more than 10,000 head each.[63] These thirty-eight individuals, however, comprised only 4 percent of the total number of Correntino ranchers in 1837. Small and middle-level estancieros dominated the pastoral economy of Corrientes.

Ranching, it appears, was overwhelmingly a Creole activity. Out of 729 estancieros in the 1832 listing, only one, the North American John Hayes, had a non-Spanish surname.[64] He was, at the same time, the only recognizable merchant, thus demonstrating the mutually exclusive nature of the two groups. While some ranchers were related to merchants (as with the Pucheta family), this was not the general rule, and few traders invested in land at this time. The ranchers and merchants held the reins of political control in Corrientes. They reinforced one another's stake in the region and set the standard for the political participation of other groups, but they remained separate. Despite the secure position of Correntino ranching elites, progress in increasing hide exports was only moderate, as revealed in Table 5.3. Hide exports might have played a more significant role in Upper Platine trade had the most productive ranching zones been safe from recurrent civil war. By the late 1830s, this was no longer the case.

TABLE 5.3: Exports of the Port of Corrientes, Hides and Cattle By-Products, 1826–41.

Years	Tanned hides	Cured cowhides	(in units) Cured horsehides	Rawhides	Cowhorns
1826	3,122	320	372	4,819	11,060
1827	4,626	267	365	18	5,400
1828	5,594	137	804	4,164	6,425
1829	4,249	129	1,211	17,203	5,143
1830	1,914		90	97,208	11,300
1831	5,498	328	484	21,703	34,830
1832	4,480	459	473	22,238	48,221
1833	4,901	400	54	18,924	48,057
1834	6,098	174	412	22,115	56,261
1835	9,104	211	519	11,931	54,010
1836	5,934	416	101	34,183	40,923
1837	3,423	484	806	32,824	36,131
1838	2,225	223	1,058	11,617	6,928
1839	1,725	64	769	55	
1840	2,679	567	859	21,962	6,900
1841	6,707	640	524	26,697	

Sources: AGPC-Toma de Razón, 1826–1841; and Chiaramonte, "El Caso del Corrientes," 91.

Some Reverses

The 1838–47 period brought a temporary halt to the growth of Correntino ranching. War again proved to be the chief obstacle, though in 1834–40 a tick-based disease (*garrapata*) swept through Rio Grande do Sul. The disease, which seems to have caused splenic fever, entered into Paraguay via Itapúa and ravaged livestock herds on a huge scale. The consequences for ranching in nearby Corrientes are difficult to gauge, though the epidemic clearly alarmed Paraguayan authorities. Francia reacted angrily towards the private ranchers and state officials who had allowed herds of potentially infected animals to enter the country. He quarantined the cattle at Itapúa and had them closely inspected for the disease. All sick or suspected animals were destroyed. These were "consumed without delay, using them to feed the laborers engaged in public works, or those in garrisons, or . . . dividing the meat among the poor."[65]

Fearing the inadequacy of these actions, the Dictator shortly thereafter demanded the slaughter of all cattle in and around Itapúa, "no matter to whom they belonged."[66] Tens of thousands of cattle eventually went under the knife before the disease had run its course, and many smaller private estancias vanished in the process.[67]

Farther south, war placed an even greater strain on the countryside than garrapata. The Farrapo Rebellion in Rio Grande often spilled into the borderlands, and rustling increased on both sides of the Uruguay. The combatants found horses and mules for military use far more attractive than cattle, since each mounted soldier required three to five horses. Imperial Brazilian forces attacking from the north generally brought their horses with them, but the rebels had to depend on local supply and what they might get from Corrientes, Paraguay, and the Banda Oriental. Sometimes troops purchased horses from a sympathetic rancher, though, just as often, they simply took horses "on loan" or seized them outright.[68] Imperial cavalry crossed the Uruguay on just such a mission in early 1844 and confiscated nearly 1,200 horses in the Correntino district of La Cruz. Protests made to the Barão de Caxias apparently went unheeded. Seizures of mules were also common.

The general turmoil of the 1830s and early 1840s cost many lives in the Upper Plata and resulted in the near ruin of Correntino ranching. The provincial government's benevolent attitude toward ranching meant little to estancieros who saw their precious stock stolen by each passing army. In addition, new treaty provisions with the Rosistas further depleted the Correntino herds. After his victory over Corrientes in the battle of Arroyo Grande in 1843, Urquiza imposed on the province an indemnity of 320,000 head of cattle and 20,000 mares.[70] In order to comply with the agreement, all estancieros possessing more than fifty head were instructed to survey their herds and present an accurate accounting to the government.[71] Although only a portion of the requisitioned livestock ultimately reached Entre Ríos, the indemnity payment had a negative impact on livestock holdings in Corrientes, so much so that the provincial government imposed new prohibitions on the export of livestock in 1845.[72]

Despite the frequent river blockades occasioned by the civil war, Corrientes managed to maintain some trade in hides and animal extracts. For example, in 1840, Goya registered a total of 21,562 hides exported by convoy to Montevideo. In late colonial times, yearly exports were, on average, nearly three times higher.[73] When convoys were unavailable, exports traveled down the Río Uruguay to the Banda Oriental. This easterly route for Upper Platine exports gave some support to cattle towns like La Cruz, Curuzú Cuatiá, and Restauración.

The end of hostilities in Rio Grande in 1845, and three years later in Corrientes, permitted the implementation of new laws for the promotion of ranching in Corrientes. These included declaring unclaimed cattle the property of the estanciero upon whose land they grazed (15 February 1849); establishing standards for branding and shearing practices (30 June 1849); and prohibiting the forced confiscation of beeves for the army (10 August 1851). Other decrees set export duties on colts, mares, and mules (4 December 1851) and allowed the renewed export of live cattle (6 January 1852).[74] The enactment of these measures illustrated the Correntino government's desire to bring provincial ranching practices more in line with modernizing trends in the lower provinces. And in all of this, the Correntino authorities, like their Paraguayan neighbors, kept a steady eye on potential fiscal returns.

Recovery in Corrientes

The relative tranquility of the post-1848 period permitted an upswing in Upper Platine ranching that benefitted ranchers and merchants alike. As herds recovered, so did the trade in animal products, especially when the fall of Rosas permitted free navigation to Buenos Aires. Even the town of Corrientes, which had never been prominent in hide exports, claimed an important share of that commerce. Between 1848 and 1850, the legal export from that port amounted to 123,069 hides.[75]

The decade of the 1850s brought the first real peace that Corrientes had enjoyed since 1835. Moreover, the province experienced the boon of honest and efficient government, first under the nominal Rosista Benjamín Virasoro (1848–52) and then under the far-sighted Juan Pujol (1852–59). The Correntino economy grew more during the administration of Pujol than under any regime since independence. This was demonstrably true for ranching. The provincial census of 1854 recorded for Corrientes totals of 673,390 cattle, 365,124 horses, 202,621 sheep, and 3,849 mules, a substantial increase over totals for the 1830s.[76] Growth was also evident in the number of individuals engaged in private stockraising in 1854—four times the number noted twenty-seven years earlier.[77] As before, the great majority (some 88 percent) were small ranchers who possessed less than 2,000 head each.

The greatest advances, however, were made in technology. During the 1830s, Ferré could only dream of saladeros functioning within the province, while Pujol saw several in operation in the mid-1850s. One was located on the outskirts of the city, by the banks of the Paraná. Owned by an Englishman, Richard Bannister Hughes, this new salting plant offered the business community of the port an ample opportunity for investment.[78] The North American naval officer Thomas

Jefferson Page visited the establishment in 1855 and was favorably impressed:

> The corral was large and well-stocked, Mr. Hughes having a few days before purchased from the southern part of the province a fine lot of cattle, for which he paid nine [pesos] the head, a threefold increase in price within a few years. In the Buenos Aires market the hides were worth six and one-half [pesos] each; the jerked beef—about 200 pounds to the animal—twelve [pesos]; and the tallow—from twenty-five to fifty pounds—about three [pesos]; the latter, intestines, bones, head and feet, are thrown into immense wooden vats, and subjected for some time to steam pressure, which extracts nearly every particle of grease; it is then drawn off clean and put in hogsheads ready for shipping. The refuse of the vats is used for fuel.[79]

Despite Page's optimism, the Hughes saladero apparently failed to turn a profit, and by April 1858, it was put up for sale along with its machinery and adjoining land.[80] Saladeros in Goya had better luck: By 1863, two such plants spurred the town's "thriving" economy.[81]

The Pujol administration placed emphasis on ranching as an industry. To further modernization, the provincial government encouraged European colonization in Corrientes, and foreign experts, like Aimé Bompland and Jean Martin de Moussy, were contracted to advise the government on innovations in raising and processing livestock. Once contacts had been established with the outside, elites in the interior of the Plata rapidly learned the advantages of modern organization and methods. Indeed, as time wore on, ranchers behaved less like rustic cowpunchers and more like rural capitalists. The official newspaper reflected this change. No longer was it emblazoned with crossed swords and mottoes such as "Death to the unitario savages!" The paper offered its readers listings of current market prices in Buenos Aires and articles on "The Proper Conservation of Meats."[82] For Correntinos, the horizons seemed limitless.

Foreign visitors often commented on this show of enthusiasm, usually attributing it to Juan Pujol. Page regarded the governor as "far in advance of his countrymen . . . liberal, intelligent, a fine gentleman."[83] As an adherent of laissez faire and liberal economics generally, Pujol carefully defended the right of property. Yet he was pragmatic enough to reestablish controls on exports when such edicts served the interests of the Correntino state.[84]

Stockraising in the Brazilian Borderlands

Generally speaking, we know little of the history of the São Borja-Itaqui region aside from occasional reports to the provincial government at Pôrto Alegre. Luckily, these communications often analyzed the state of stockraising in the borderlands. In one such summary of 1858, the government measured growth in this sector, noting a total of 568 ranches for the São Borja area, a figure in keeping with landholding patterns on the Correntino side of the Uruguay. As in the neighboring zone, small and middle-level ranchers dominated the scene, and no single estanciero possessed more than 2,000 calves. Of the fourteen most prominent ranchers, only two personally oversaw their estates; the remainder entrusted their herds to overseers and Indian peones. A tiny number of black slaves augmented this workforce. As for nationality, all involved had Brazilian surnames. Clearly, as in Corrientes and Paraguay, the pastoral economy of the borderlands remained in the hands of long-time residents.[85]

The total cattle holdings of São Borja provided an interesting contrast to the situation in Corrientes. The summary noted a figure of 87,820 calves and 43,205 colts. It further noted an average of twenty-five calves per one-hundred cows. This yields an approximate total of 438,840 head of cattle for the São Borja region alone, a number well in excess of 60 percent of the figure noted for all of Corrientes in 1854. Even if we assume that totals were underestimated for Corrientes and overestimated for São Borja, the final tallies still appear exaggerated in favor of the latter. It is possible that Riograndense herds were more productive, though this contradicts what is known from secondary sources, which all found Riograndense stockraising decidedly backward.

Perhaps the central importance of the 1858 summary lies in its very existence. The recognized need for such a survey demonstrates that even in Rio Grande the modern age had started to penetrate ranching activities. Beef-processing technology appeared primitive by Platine standards, but since security had been assured along the Uruguay, an active trade in hides and livestock was sure to follow. As in the rest of the Upper Plata, the ranchers of São Borja rode a wave of optimism.

Paraguayan Ranching: The López Era

Paraguay shared the success enjoyed by other parts of the Upper Plata. With the rivers open, external markets had developed for Paraguayan products, and hides and animal extracts could enter the mounting trade. Paraguayan stockraising had extended into previously unexploited areas

This phenomenon was in part caused by the need to stave off Indian and Brazilian incursions in the north, to which purpose Carlos Antonio López established some thirty forts and puestos between the Apá and Aquidaban rivers. Rather than provision these directly from Concepción or the capital, López decided to promote stockraising in the region itself. The Belgian traveller Alfred Marbais DuGraty remarked with an exaggerated optimism that the "area to the north of the Aquidaban is well suited to ranching and now that security (in the form of military posts) has been assured by the present government, [the region] has rapidly filled with large rural establishments. . . . Everything has come together to give great importance to this vast territory."[86] So much importance, in fact, that in 1858, López ordered a census of the ranches in the department of Concepción. Four state estancias and one puesto were noted, possessing a total of 5,447 head of cattle and 463 horses. Private estancias numbered eighty-eight, with 40,321 head of cattle and 1,671 horses.[87] The private ranches generally maintained smaller individual herds, though they far outshone the state establishments in aggregate totals. The basic pattern set in Francia's time thus continued under López, the difference being that while Francia encouraged state acquisition of private lands, López seemed more interested in using the state to augment the private holdings of his family.[88]

Though López expressed keen interest in technological innovations of a military nature, he showed little concern for updating stockraising. Since Paraguayan herds grew by 25 to 27 percent each year, he saw no need for change.[89] This situation was fraught with irony; left alone, cattle populations reproduced quickly and enriched their owners even when the traditional markets in the lower provinces were cut off. In this, cattle was superior to agricultural produce, which was subject to spoilage. This inherent advantage resulted in little incentive for change. At the same time, low maintenance costs more than compensated for the primitiveness of the ranching sector.

Yet, private ranchers in Paraguay could never afford to feel complacent; López was not their ally in the way that Francia had been. López made his feelings on this clear in 1842, when he reintroduced the diezmo.[90] This measure added some revenues to the state, but at the expense of the estancieros.

The internal pricing system of Paraguay reflected the specific prejudices and values assigned different livestock during the López era (see Table 5.4). Mares received no mention in the listing owing, no doubt, to "an absurd prejudice against their use, even as beasts of burden; a man mounted on one would create as great a sensation and excite as much ridicule as a dandy upon a donkey in one of our thoroughfares of fashion."[91] Throughout the Upper Plata, ranchers kept mares only for breeding and for their grease.

TABLE 5.4: Livestock Prices, Paraguay, circa 1859
(in pesos fuertes)

Cow (range), 2–4 years old	8
Cow (domesticated), 2–4 years old	12
Cow (fattened for slaughter)	22
Ox (fattened for slaughter), 400–500 pounds	24
Ox (for draw-cart)	28
Swine	21
Mule	20
Horse	10
Donkey	7
Sheep	1
Goat	1

Source: Marbais du Graty, *La república del Paraguay*, p. 332. Calculation is based on exchange rate of 4 francs to the peso fuerte—see p. 361.

Hides generally ranked third in importance in the Paraguayan export structure, after yerba mate and tobacco. Hides, however, remained free of monopoly control by the state and therefore received less regular attention. Nevertheless, the state export registers do reveal a stable, though limited, trade in hides from Paraguay between the early 1850s and 1865 (see Table 5.5). López and private Paraguayan speculators knew that they could not compete with Corrientes in this commodity, much less with the lower provinces, and they did not much try.

The 1860s

At the beginning of the new decade, prospects for the expansion of ranching appeared bright in all parts of the Upper Plata. The defeat of Rosas had brought an end to the rural anarchy that so frequently plagued the region, and with the rivers opened to all flags, foreign hide merchants soon sailed northward. In a few spots, especially in Corrientes, European immigrants began to appear, bringing with them new attitudes towards pastoral work. Indeed, until mid-decade, the successful economic pattern of the 1850s continued and was surpassed: Trade was booming, new saladeros were built, and stockraising looked more profitable than ever.

In the ranching areas along the Uruguay, a marked movement had developed at the behest of Entrerriano cattle interests. Between January and September 1864, the district of Curuzú Cuatiá sent 33,720 head of cattle and 5,046 horses to saladeros in Entre Ríos.[92] This suggests some

TABLE 5.5: Hide Exports, Paraguay, 1851–65

Year	Rawhides (in *pesadas* of 35 pounds)	Tanned hides (number of hides)
1851	1,044	
1852	17,535	
1853	39,545	
1854	39,966	15,566
1855	35,000(?)	12,000(?)
1856	36,424	10,353
1857	38,605	8,230
1858	21,246	3,952
1859		
1860	46,947	5,715
1861	36,567	5,455
1862	38,382	8,113
1863	26,736	3,608
1864	46,263	2,345
1865 (Jan.-June)	15,904	1,893

Sources: Calculations based on *El Semanario*, 1 October 1853; 8 October 1853; 24 December 1853; 11 January 1855; 16 February 1861 through 8 July 1865; Page, *La Plata*, p. 243; Marbais du Graty, *La república del Paraguay*, pp. 346–50; Herken Krauer, "Proceso económico," 83–116.

rationalization of regional options instead of the more well-defined Porteño outlet. The development of Rosario as an alternative port to Buenos Aires served a similar function, albeit limited, on the Paraná. The real effect of these new export possibilities remained uncertain, however, because of the continued dominance of the Porteños in matters of shipping and credit and primarily because of the War of the Triple Alliance.

Before the seizure of the *Marqués de Olinda* in November 1864, a "business as usual" attitude held sway in all matters affecting Upper Platine trade. The stable flow of Paraguayan hides to markets in the lower provinces demonstrates this clearly. The low level of hide exports for 1865 originated in the establishment of the near total blockade of the Río Paraguay in July of that year. Any new shipments had to await the conclusion of the war.

Ranching in other parts of the Upper Plata was hit hard by the conflict, particularly when Paraguayan troops spilled over the border into the stockraising areas of Corrientes and Rio Grande do Sul. As previously noted, the Paraguayans seized livestock and burned ranches as they pushed south along the rivers. The Allies acted in much the same fashion during their counteroffensive. The 100,000 head of cattle the Paraguayans brought from Corrientes during their retreat evidently did their army little good. A British military engineer working for the López government noted that these cattle had "almost all died, either of fatigue, want of food (there being very little pasturage near Paso de la Patria), or from eating a poisonous herb . . . which abounds in the South of Paraguay, and which only animals reared in the district have the instinct to avoid. The number of dead animals on the ground about Itapirú and a few leagues beyond it was terrible during some months."[93] Ranching in the Upper Plata suffered a heavy blow, leaving estancias to the south of the Paraná greatly exhausted and those to the north destroyed. According to one fairly reliable source, Paraguayan cattle holdings plummeted from 2,000,000 head at the outbreak of the conflict to only 15,000 six years later.[93]

Cattle: A Secondary Commerce

During the late colonial period, the Upper Platine cattle industry grew as a result of the general expansion of the regional economy. We have already seen how the yerba trade brought about positive changes for ranching, especially as regards the opening of new cattle frontiers in the north. Increased outside demand also encouraged some export of hides, though few evidently entered the overseas market. Because of unfavorable geographic position, more than the poor quality of its product, the Upper Plata simply failed to compete with the great cattle-producing areas to the south, a trend that became still more pronounced after independence. At the same time, this modest market share failed to inhibit the influence of the ranchers, who remained critical in the political affairs of the region. Able to supply horses and other livestock at short notice, the ranchers made a difference in any military situation—this explains the many efforts made by regional governments to woo them. In the uncertain environment of nineteenth-century South America, the ranchers were central political actors, despite the fact that in many areas—such as the Upper Plata—stockraising was hardly a dynamic sector of the economy.

Hides, tallow, and other cattle by-products invariably ranked behind yerba and tobacco as export commodities of the Upper Plata. Buenos Aires had little need for items that its own ranchers could supply in abundance, nor, of course, was the port city interested in sponsoring a commerce in hides other than its own. As for regional trade, except for a periodic flow of cattle from Corrientes to Paraguay, the general picture in the Upper Plata was one of self-sufficiency. This circumstance suited such leaders as Francia, whose policies bolstered the ranching sector, but whose attitude towards external trade remained ambivalent. This was only sensible, given the influence of the ranchers and the limited potential of Upper Platine hides in the wider market. The economic development of the region, for better or worse, would not be based on ranching.

6

Timber and
Associated Industries

Esta vida algo salvaje que lleva
el obrajero, le hace que adquiera
gran confianza en si mismo, y
es casí fatalista. Nada le
sorprende y está siempre
preparado para la lucha.
Vicente G. Quesada

Compared to tobacco, yerba, and hides, lumber and finished wood products played only a minor part in Upper Platine trade. Consumers in the lower provinces held bulk timber from the northeastern forests in high regard, especially when housing booms fed demand for building material in Buenos Aires and Montevideo. Wooden mallets, furniture, carts, and wheel axles also found a ready market in the south. The domestic market, however, absorbed the greater part of the region's annual output of wood, and the processing of timber encompassed as many risks as the transport of wood downstream. Further, the wood trade only rarely produced profits like those of yerba, so merchants in the Upper Plata ordinarily concentrated on the latter export.

Notwithstanding this state of affairs, in some areas, such as the forested zone adjacent to the town of Corrientes, loggers managed to create a lucrative timber industry. Sawyer pits and shipyards also appeared. As with other aspects of Upper Platine trade, political realities determined the success or failure of these operations. On all levels, from the production of lumber to the manufacture of simple furniture and fully constructed wooden sailing ships, the forest industries of the Upper Plata had to accept the erratic politics of the lower provinces and the limitations their disorder imposed. Within the northeast itself, border disputes further complicated matters by turning Correntinos and Paraguayans into competitors.

Resources

The pre-Columbian Indians recognized the wealth of the Upper Platine forests. Indeed, their mythology teemed with jungle monsters and wood spirits, for the Indians regarded the forests as their home, as well as a source of tools, shelter, and water transport.[1] When the Europeans arrived in the region, they adapted woods to many other functions: carts, furniture, gunstocks, housing materials, and ocean-going ships. By the 1600s, the Upper Plata had gained a reputation for fine hardwood products. Thereafter, raw timber and finished wood items appeared in the lower provinces in increasing quantities.

Sixty varieties of wood furnished timber of all kinds and colors, in many degrees of elasticity, durability, and buoyancy. The most valued wood was Paraguayan cedar (*Cedrela fissilis*), easily worked, desired throughout the Río de la Plata for its strength and variegated color, and known in Spain and elsewhere in Europe. Next in demand came *lapacho* (*Tabebuia*) of several varieties. Artisans used this strong and durable but also workable wood as beams in construction and shipbuilding.[2] *Yvyraró* (*Paterogyne nitens*) served a similar purpose, used especially for axles, wheel spokes, and strong, flexible planking. Artisans prized *urundey* (*Astronium urundeuva*) for its color, veining, and resistance to deterioration. Although dense and difficult to work, it was valued for furniture.[3] *Timbó* (*Enterolobium timbouva*), in part because of its resistance to rot, was favored for ship planking; workers often fashioned large canoes from whole trunks of these trees. Several varieties of *petereby* (*Cordia*) were utilized for masts and yards of vessels. *Palo Santo* (*Phyllostyllon rhamnoides*) provided strong, flexible cart axles, while *tataré* (*Pithocolobium scalate*) provided sturdy ribbing. *Tataí* (*Chlorophora tinctorea*) and *ajuí* (*Ocotea acutifolia*) made excellent furniture. *Curupay* (*Piptadenia rigidia*) not only supplied strong, flexible handles for various tools, but its bark yielded tannin, used throughout the Platine region for the curing of hides. Palms, bamboo (*tacuara*), and other woods provided fence posts, gunstocks, rafters, planking, furniture, and firewood.[4]

During the early nineteenth century, Buenos Aires received charcoal exclusively from ports on the Paraná delta and the lower Uruguay. As the demand for this product rose, however, Upper Platine sources also contributed to the supply.[5]

Logging depended on available labor and access to river transport. Rivers feeding into the Paraguay-Paraná system crisscrossed the Upper Plata. In north-central Paraguay, the muddy Río Jejuí served as a prime artery for transporting Paraguayan cedar. Farther south, forests near the settled areas around the Tebicuary supplied a variety of woods. Loggers in Corrientes made a sustained effort to exploit the woodlands near Empedrado, on the island of Apipé, on other lands contiguous to Paso de la Patria (on the Alto Paraná), and, as the new century wore on, in the remote Chaco forests. As a general rule, Paraguayans refrained from working their section of the Chaco, which they consequently abandoned to hostile Indians. *Quebracho* wood (*Schinopsis lorentzii*), which eventually provided the basis for a substantial industry in the Paraguayan Chaco, was as yet little known or used.

Methods of Exploitation

During colonial times, the Laws of the Indies and the Spanish Laws of the Forest (*ley de montes*) governed logging practices as well as the timber trade in the Upper Plata. These legal codes allowed communities to exploit the forests of the province as common lands. Residents (vecinos) had full use of these lands for their subsistence, as in gathering firewood, but the government refused to concede the right to engage freely in commercial logging.[6] By law, royal authorities permitted municipalities to grant leases to private individuals for logging in return for a stipulated sum paid to the town treasury. Nevertheless, the illegal extraction of timber by vecinos was evidently rather common in the Upper Plata during the late colonial period. In Paraguay, illegal logging seems to have tapered off in Francia's time, though it remained a feature of the Correntino economy, where even during troubled periods it assured some profit.

The custom of leasing logging rights in the Upper Plata changed little with independence. The governments at Asunción and Corrientes continued to act under modified versions of the ley de montes, which gave final authority over woodlands to the state or sovereign. In Corrientes, the state exercised minimal control over logging, exerting its authority only in the actual sale of woods. The Paraguayan state went much further, arrogating to itself a complete monopoly on the export of hardwoods.[7] Unlike the Correntinos, the Paraguayans imposed a strict regulation of logging activities after independence, which normally required a series of licenses (addressed on stamped paper), internal passports, and detailed inventories of all timber to be harvested. These controls served to minimize private logging operations, leaving the state as the only real backer for such enterprises.

The expertise of skilled woodsmen proved necessary for any successful expedition into Upper Platine forests. The brush was often so thick as to render the sun nearly invisible, its gleams only occasionally reaching through the creepers, ferns, and rotting stumps. Workers easily got lost. Danger, in the form of hostile Indians or wild animals, could lie behind every outcropping of trees. The experience of a first-rate axman was also necessary to accurately judge the quality of standing timber and to know how to fell trees efficiently. Thus, a logger with previous time in the forests could command a substantial wage.[8]

To assist these axmen, labor contractors recruited unskilled workers among unmarried men of the rural population and, in Paraguay, from the various pueblos de indios. During the colonial period, provincial governors frequently directed pueblos to supply Indian labor to private entrepreneurs with the understanding that these laborers be paid the same as other unskilled workers and that half of their wages be credited to the pueblos' treasury.[9] Francia never bothered to alter this system. It continued more or less unchanged until 1848. In Corrientes, on the other hand, Indian loggers were the exception. This activity remaining more commonly in the hands of mestizos.

Once recruited, the logging gang made its way either overland or by canoe from the base camp (obraje), situated on a major river or tributary, to the cutting areas, which might be twenty miles away. Because desirable trees grew dispersed throughout the backlands rather than in stands, it often proved necessary to cut a series of paths away from the main trail.[10]

Loggers cut selected trees and then, on high-wheeled carts drawn by oxen, carried the trunks to the obraje or another convenient place on the river. When a sufficient number of logs had been gathered and sawyers at the base camp had finished shaping the timber into rough-squared beams, the men fashioned them into rafts (jangadas). A mid-eighteenth-century cleric, Pedro José de Parras, who happened to sail the Río Paraná, gave a clear description of these logbooms:

> [The jangadas] are composed of various timbers fastened together
> with ropes, iron clasps, and many nails. Among these crafts are
> some very large ones, such that they are fifty-five to eighty yards
> in length and of corresponding width. It is customary, upon
> these joined timbers, to construct a platform which serves as a
> base for the cabin of wood and hides, in which is carried the
> cargo of yerba, tobacco, sugar, etc. However, these craft are not
> made especially for transport but to be broken up for the timber
> from which they are constructed.[11]

Loggers worked in the drier seasons of the year when paths had yet to be rendered impassable by mud. The hard work taxed the health of workers. In addition to vagaries of climate, they faced many dangers in the forest. The seemingly peaceful streams that divided the bush sometimes held crocodiles or razorfish (palometa). Snakes inhabited the trees, along with wasps and other stinging insects. Perhaps the most formidable animal of all was the jaguar, the yaguareté:

> He is afraid of nothing and challenges his prey unmindful of the number of men against him. He will begin to eat [a man] without having completed the kill. He is a brave enemy; the loggers always keep dogs to warn them of his presence and, at night, they light huge bonfires and sleep very close at hand, secure in the knowledge that the jaguar fears the fire. Yet in the darkness [you can see] his eyes shining like sparks.[12]

Indians constituted another hazard, especially in the Chaco. Certain native groups, such as the Toba, maintained amicable relations with the loggers, sometimes acting as guides to virgin woodlands.[13] Other groups, like the Monteses and the Mbaya, raided obrajes with impunity, carrying off the few female camp followers that might accompany the loggers and killing the men they found. In the extreme north, these Indians often had the tacit support of the Brazilians who coveted the same territories.[14] Fear of the Guaicurú prevented the establishment of sizable logging operations in those areas of the Chaco across from Asunción before the time of Carlos Antonio López. Even an arrangement with friendly Indians sometimes went sour. In March 1857, for instance, the Correntino lumberjacks at the Chaco obraje of Riacho Guaicurú abandoned their operation after the accidental shooting of an Indian peon. The loggers, believing that the Toba would read premeditation into the event, fled in terror at the prospect of a general uprising.[15]

Life for loggers in the forests of the Upper Plata was difficult. Cut off from centers of human activity, they developed sharp eyes, a fatalistic character, and a trust for one another that extended beyond the woodlands. The loggers spent months at a time working beneath a burning sun, ferrying massive tree trunks (with the help of oxen where possible) from the base camp down to the river.

The work in the river came next. Swimming, many fathoms of water beneath them, workers assembled the logs into jangadas. After five or six hours, the exhausted men would climb onto the completed rafts or, more often, would be pulled up onto them, half-frozen from the cold water. Their only reward for such a day's work was several cups of yerba mate, a piece or two of charqui, and a ration of tobacco.[16]

Like the yerbateros, the loggers were inured to isolation and self-denial. Changadores sometimes supplied the woodsmen with spirits and contraband goods, but at most logging camps, the chances for any diversion, even drink, remained scant. The only outlet for the loggers' frustrations lie in still more work, hewing out measure after measure of timber, and likely becoming more depressed in the process.[17] Desertion was frequent.

A paucity of archival documentation, particularly for the post-independence era, hampers any comprehensive knowledge of these timber operations. I assume that most practices remained the same throughout the period under study. The obrajes of Corrientes, for instance, were organized in the mid-1800s according to one of several patterns. Some were financed by individual entrepreneurs or business partners who paid woodcutters by the month. Just as often, loggers received payment by the piece, the dimensions and rates being fixed in advance. Two men could fell two trees daily; four trunks made up 25 to 28 varas (a vara is 33 inches in length) of wood, or one complete *carga*. The carga might bring 35 pesos on the Corrientes market.[18] Those woodcutters without specific financial backing formed mutual associations that sold the wood through middlemen. After accumulating three or four cargas, they usually arranged transport downriver with a ship captain who in turn received 50 percent of the profits.

The isolation of the obrajes led to abuses that the Correntino government was powerless to remedy. This did not prevent the promulgation of some fine-sounding, naive legislation. In 1853, the port authorities at Corrientes enacted regulations designed to prevent work stoppages in the Chaco obrajes. These measures included the licensing of loggers and sponsors, the guarantee of mutual obligations between the two, and the effective banning of strikes. In an effort to control runaway debtors, the government prohibited the employment by one sponsor of loggers still indebted to another.[19]

The Upper Platine Timber Industry: The Commercial Dimension

Paraguay presented wood exporters with many opportunities during the final years of the colonial period. In the main, these opportunities came as adjuncts to other, more profitable commerce. After all, jangadas were temporary craft used to haul yerba, tobacco, and hides to the lower provinces. The first two commodities were the real moneymakers in this arrangement; the wood that made up the jangadas was sold almost as an afterthought. Nonetheless, given the growth of all Upper Platine trade, it is little wonder that quantities of bulk timber from Paraguay moved south in the form of jangadas.[20] Sawn lumber also frequently accompanied these shipments. As seen in Table 6.1, the yearly export of Paraguayan timber varied greatly in volume, a likely outcome of problems in supply.

Under the colonial regime, Paraguayan logging operations were relatively free of strict government controls. Francia, however, rejected the idea of allowing unrestrained exploitation of a resource that he deemed

TABLE 6.1: Paraguayan Timber Exports, 1781–1812

Year	Varas	Year	Varas
1781	11,508	1797	1,926
1782	n/a	1798	34,100
1783	30,036	1799	n/a
1784	67,413	1800	19,084
1785	n/a	1801	23,753
1786	14,670	1802	38,101
1787	13,602	1803	9,287
1788	16,035	1804	12,308
1789	31,404	1805	31,935
1790	27,339	1806	22,143
1791	1,080	1807	14,004 approx.*
1792	19,617	1808	31,146
1793	4,329	1809	70,725
1794	17,628	1810	16,632 approx.*
1795	11,916	1811	120
1796	8,448	1812	10,200

*These approximations are based on slightly incomplete registers.
Sources: Libros de asiento de guías y tornaguías, 1783–1812, ANA-NE 11, 80, 115, 188, 418, 1149, 1159, 1167, 1186, 2536, 2900, 3089, 3337, 3341, 3345, 3356, 3360; and Azara, *Geografía física y esférica del Paraguay*, 434.

valuable. State revenues were potentially at risk, and the Dictator jealously guarded the exchequer. During his regime, military forces along the Jejuí and Yhaguy maintained surveillance of private obrajes and, at the same time, conducted substantial logging on their own to supply state needs. In this, as in so much else, Francia played a personal role. He showed great concern that loggers be treated properly and paid on time: "Workers must be paid in cash and be given [daily] maintenance with cattle and provisions from the [state] estancia. An account of the work completed will be kept so that each lumberjack be paid his due. I am to be notified immediately if further assistance is required."[21]

Jangadas coming down the Paraguay to Asunción were often destined for local markets or, by the 1850s, for the state shipyards. If not ultimately bound for the lower provinces, the rafts were broken up in Asunción and the logs and sawn timber passed into the hands of the operation's merchant-financiers. Lumber awaiting shipment to the south accumulated on the riverbank at Asunción or Pilar, marked by the brands of owners or consignees.[22]

Asunción sawyers fashioned logs destined for internal consumption into planks and beams. Sawyers preferred the two-man sawyer stand as the best method for processing logs of lapacho and cedar.[23] Dating from

the early colonial period, these stands remained so common in the settlements of the Upper Plata that their operation often interfered with
other urban activities. This was hardly surprising, given the large size
of these structures, which were constructed over pits dug to accommodate the lengthy motion of the saw. A local official in 1806 complained
to the provincial governor of Paraguay that, contrary to repeated orders,
heaps of sawn timber still obstructed the streets of Asunción and the
sawyer stands endangered the passage of the citizenry at night.[24]

Logs and wood products leaving the Upper Plata theoretically underwent inspection by revenue officials who assessed export duties and
issued exit permits. In practice, the Paraguayans proved more thorough
in the exercise of these regulations than the Correntinos. Even so, tax
evasion and the smuggling of contraband hardwood plagued Paraguay.

The postindependence governments were eager for revenues from forest products, but political disturbances limited outside trade dramatically. Indeed, aside from ready-made oxcarts, few finished wood products
of any kind were exported from Paraguay during the Francia era.[25] The
export of raw timber became a state monopoly. Francia granted export
licenses for wood only in exchange for arms and munitions. While this
policy worked against the growth of the Paraguayan timber trade, it nevertheless managed to secure some needed armaments.[26] In fact, the
exchange of "wood for guns" outlasted the Francia regime. In 1842,
George J. R. Gordon discussed this point with Carlos Antonio López:

> If exported [Paraguayan timber would] be retained in the hands of
> the government as a premium to encourage the importation of
> munitions of war. Señor López expressed, in reference to the
> subject, a strong desire of obtaining supplies of gunpowder and
> arms and assured me that the government would be ready to
> contract for such articles, to be either exchanged for timber,
> which would be cut to order and delivered at Pilar or be paid for
> in cash—though the former would be much preferred by him.[27]

On the other side of the Alto Paraná, the Ferré government in Corrientes also attempted to maintain a measure of control over the harvesting and sale of timber. An 1831 decree reaffirmed the basic tenets
of the Spanish ley de montes.[28] Such enactments, however, held little
force in the Chaco or even in the Correntino hinterland. Meanwhile,
timber shipments to the south aroused the interest of foreign entrepreneurs who saw ample possibilities in the development of obrajes and in
the wood trade generally.[29] The government gave such investment free
rein in Correntino territory. The denuding of woodlands on the left bank
of the Río Paraná resulted, and, as the demand for wood increased, for-

est exploitation shifted to the Chaco and to the island of Apipé.[30] Foreign-born capitalists like Tomás Lubary, Pedro Samson, and Juan Etchegaray invested heavily in these operations.[31]

The export of Correntino timber, like all other exports, was directly affected by the disordered politics of the early nineteenth century. The uncertainty of shipping mandated that commodities earn high profits to offset the high risk. Woods could rarely generate such returns. Thus, as seen in Table 6.2, the volume of wood shipped from Corrientes remained low, subject to wild, war-related fluctuations, as in 1838–41.

As discussed earlier, all Correntino commerce experienced an upturn after the 1845–46 visit of the merchant convoy from Montevideo. The trade figures for the port of Corrientes indicate an enormous increase in the volume of wood exports (see Table 6.3). Such impressive growth was clearly due to the easing of tensions on the rivers and, in particular, the defeat of the Rosistas in Buenos Aires. While sawn timber constituted the greater part of these exports, certain finished items, like mallets and cartwheel axles, were also sent south.

Corrientes was not the only port of consequence engaged in wood exports. The area around Empedrado, a smaller port just to the south, had until this time escaped the ravages of large logging operations. But during the first six months of 1854 alone, the town shipped nearly 70,000 varas of wood to Buenos Aires along with another 6,500 pieces northward to Corrientes.[32]

With the opening of the rivers, the market in the estuary for Upper Platine wood products grew appreciably. The private sector absorbed wood for ship repairs and general construction. A housing boom in Buenos Aires increased demand for solid, dependable building materials. The precise ramifications of the Porteño housing boom are as yet uncertain, but apparently construction in Buenos Aires constituted the single most important element in the new demand.[33] The various provincial and confederal governments also served as important customers, particularly for hardwoods for gunstocks, flagpoles, and the like.

Competition from Porteño artisans reduced the profit margin on finished items, so that the Upper Plata was chiefly important to the Buenos Aires consumer only for sawn timber. Even in this trade, some competition existed. Thomas Jefferson Page, visiting Corrientes in the mid-1850s, noted:

> A vessel of the country arrived with a small lot of American pine boards and scantling, which was sold at 12½ cents the foot [sic yard]—the price I paid both here and at Asunción per yard for sawing plank of native woods. This lumber had been shipped to Buenos Aires from the United States, disposed of, purchased

TABLE 6.2: Exports of Corrientes, Timber and Wood Products, 1826–41

Years	1826	1828	1830	1832	1834	1836	1838	1840	1841
Timber (in varas)									
Tie beams	2,411	2,160	2,181	4,529	4,206	6,919	6,065	1,071	303
Logs	4	11		45	17	121	215		
Beams	100	228	90	28	16	104	40	2	
Planks	925	1,535	254	147	175	152	64		
Total timber	3,451	3,934	2,525	4,749	4,414	7,296	6,384	1,175	322
Other wood products (in units)									
Bamboo	1,424	36	4,498	36	12		100		
Wooden mallets	2	84	291	663	402	322	235	221	44
Cartwheel axles	1,034	554	607	14	179	204	470	254	104
Palm fronds*	3,685	2,770	3,163	2,328	2,644	1,660	524		

*These fronds, commonly used for roof thatching, were also woven together to form a break to stretch across rivers to stop floating timber.
Sources: AGPC-Toma de Razón de Guías, 1826–41; Chiaramonte, "El caso de Corrientes, 92.

TABLE 6.3: Wood Exports, Port of Corrientes

Years	1848	1849	1850	1855
Timber (in varas)				
Tirantes (tie beams)				
of urundey	29,821	98,497	92,388	90,132
of laurel	834	260	436	
of petereby	145			
of lapacho	214	1,534	6,396	
Tirantillos (small beams)	7,956	3,497	6,396	71,451
Trozos (logs)	1,869	4,248	1,270	6,716
Vigas (beams)	1,060	3,799	690	20,941
Alfajías (window frames)	1,525		750	28,526
Tablas (planks)	1,501	1,525	12,316	8,307
Total timber	44,925	113,360	114,943	226,073
Other wood products				
Palmas tijeras (fronds)	418	5,086	312	2,954
Mazos (wooden mallets)	42	420	261	
Ejes (cartwheel axles)		589		
Tacuaras (bamboo)		50	540	
Picanillas (spikes)		93,000	1,300	
Tarugos (wooden pegs)			198	

Sources: Comprobantes, AGPC-CLC (1848) legajos 57–58, (1849) legajos 59–61, (1850) legajos 62–63; El Comercio, 6 January 1856.

again, and reshipped to Corrientes, where it sold for less than native lumber, paying at each change of hands a reasonable percentage. And yet timber is one of the export articles of this Province.[34]

If the shipment mentioned by Page came to South America as ballast and therefore was not meant to earn much profit, then its low price is easily explained. Page also remarked, however, that North American wood had gained fame in the Plata for use in the construction of doors, window frames, and flooring.[35] One can speculate, therefore, that steam mechanization in Maine lumber mills permitted the opening of markets far afield indeed. Merchants brought quantities of North American wood into Buenos Aires, driving the price far below that of the Upper Platine equivalent. Pine imported from Prussia, Sweden, and the Baltic coast of Russia also affected the Porteño market.

The Paraguayan export sector faced many of the same constraints. Entry into outside markets was hampered by high export duties, which reached as high as 20 percent on private shipments of wood.[36] Foreign observers constantly warned Carlos Antonio López and his ministers of the detrimental effects of these export duties. George F. Morice, a British naval engineer under contract to the Paraguayan government, was specific in his advice: "I would strongly recommend to reduce all duties on imports and exports one half!! I have no doubt the revenue would not suffer, as the trade would be doubled by the reduction of duties."[37]

Despite the short-sighted tax structure, evidence suggests that the Paraguayan state wished to expand the country's commerce in woods beyond the Río de la Plata. The government sent samples of different woods to European capitals in order to promote the trade, but the advent of the War of the Triple Alliance doomed these efforts.[38] Wood shipments to the lower provinces continued to bring some profits to the Paraguayans, though never on the scale of tobacco and yerba mate. López and his ministers knew that timber would be an unlikely focus for a major Paraguayan export; yet, since the state itself was the largest consumer of woods within the country, it was also natural for López to take an interest in the timber trade.

Table 6.4 records the various changes in Paraguayan timber exports. Totals during the 1850s shifted considerably, from a high in 1855 of over 55,000 pesos to a low in 1859 of less than one-tenth that amount. In the 1860s, exports stabilized at around 22,000 pesos a year, but it remains unclear why totals for the previous decade were so erratic in terms of volume.

The Upper Platine forest industries grew in importance from the mid-1850s to the early 1860s, though Correntino timber earned far more

TABLE 6.4: Timber Exports, Paraguay

Year	In varas	In pesos fuertes
1852		4,861
1853	32,671	8,234
1854	80,313	49,050
1855		55,000
1856		46,200
1857	17,645	16,325
1858		8,430
1859	7,574	4,102
1860		14,795
1861	23,354	21,055
1862	24,408	22,536
1863	24,867	22,760
1864	22,486	20,872
1865 (Jan.-June)	5,434	4,566

Sources: *El Semanario*, 1 October 1853, 8 October 1853, 24 December 1853, 11 January 1855, and 16 February 1861 through 8 July 1865; Marbais du Graty, *La república del Paraguay*, pp. 346–50; Herken Krauer, "Proceso económico," 83–116.

profit than that of Paraguay. The increase in outside demand provided the key inducement to growth. Trade penetrated even the smallest communities along the Paraná, permitting the exploitation of hitherto underutilized resources on a large scale. Empedrado, for example, exported over 190,000 varas of timber in 1864, a surprisingly large quantity.[39]

Little thought was given to conservation; loggers commonly stripped clean the forests of the Upper Plata for immediate gain. Indeed, in nearly all the reports and memoirs one reads of "limitless resources of woods." But the woodlands were not infinite. As early as the 1790s, Félix de Azara complained of the excesses of the arrendamiento system. With few limitations placed on logging, *arrendatarios* could "cut all the wood they desire . . . so that these men leave the forests . . . in a state of not being able to produce a useful tree."[40] Governments enacted no serious conservation measures, however, and the common view treated the forests as inexhaustible. In time, this attitude would have a tragic effect.

One wood product that received a minor degree of protection was tanbark (*cáscara*). Peeled from the sides of curupay and timbó trees, this bark yielded tannic acid for curing leather. Since the process of stripping trees presented no special difficulties, workers could quickly exhaust the entire holdings of a region. Governments passed conservationist legislation, therefore, under both colonial and independent regimes, with the result being a relatively steady, though limited, supply of tanbark for the tanneries of the estuary.[41] In 1854, the Paraguayans exported a full 15,920 arrobas of this item.[42]

Logging provided several occasions when the interests of Paraguay and Corrientes conflicted. Both parties claimed some of the best woodlands along the Paraná. In 1779, the governor of Paraguay, Pedro Melo de Portugal, sent an expedition to found the settlement of Curupayty near the confluence of the Paraguay and Paraná rivers. This tiny puesto had as its initial function the garrisoning of a zone constantly plagued by Chaco Indian raids. The incursions had long interfered with the active exploitation of nearby forests, which were among the richest in the Upper Plata. Appropriately, of the eighty men who participated in the 1779 expedition, fifty were Correntinos and the rest Paraguayans.[43] From the beginning, legal jurisdiction proved a thorny issue.[44]

The same was true of Apipé after independence. Located on the Alto Paraná to the northeast of Corrientes, this large island was heavily forested with the better varieties of Upper Platine woods. From the Paraguayan viewpoint, however, the island lay in a strategic position: The rapids along its southern shore guarded the approach to Candelaria, Itapúa, and Misiones.[45] The Paraguayans feared that their overland trade with Brazil could be interdicted if Apipé fell into the orbit of Corrientes, and thus, the presence of Correntino loggers on the island remained a sore point for Paraguayan authorities.

Correntino woodcutters had frequented both Apipé and Curupayty since the colonial period.[46] With independence, however, their forays occurred only sporadically. This was just as well, since with Francia in power in Asunción, Correntino logging in disputed territories became decidedly dangerous.

In 1832, a major incident took place on Apipé. A sizable party of Correntino loggers, financed by entrepreneurs Antonio Puyol and Vicente Garay, had established itself on the island, setting up a small obraje and gathering tanbark. One night, five members of this group crossed by canoe to the Paraguayan shore, where they stole a bullock and a quantity of maize and manioc. The Dictator responded to this trivial incident by dispatching troops to the island, who apprehended fourteen of the workmen. The soldiers executed one of these men on Francia's order, and the remainder were sent north in chains to Concepción.[47]

Governor Ferré retaliated by deploying his cavalry in Misiones, seizing the outposts of Loreto and Candelaria. As the Correntino hold over the Candelaria area was, at best, precarious, he also appealed for aid from Domingo Cullen, the governor of Santa Fé.[48] When no help proved forthcoming from the south, Ferré withdrew his troops, contenting himself with occasional raids on Paraguayan puestos and with molesting the Brazilian trade caravans coming from São Borja.[49]

While the Apipé incident must be considered in the light of a general border dispute, it is significant that it was sparked by logging activities. In the years that followed, exploitation of the island stagnated; in the absence of a political settlement, loggers feared Paraguayan raiding parties.[50] In 1852, a treaty between the two sides effectively ended the dispute.[51] The Correntino government was free to grant logging licenses along the banks of the Paraná and Paraguay as far north as the Bermejo and as far east as Brazil.[52]

These border conflicts greatly affected logging because so many fine woodlands lay in disputed areas. The timber there was of excellent quality. More important, these sites had easy access by water to outside markets; i.e., they were commercially viable. Forests abounded on all sides—in the far north, in the Chaco, and in Misiones—but there the terrain was too rough and markets too distant for profitable exploitation. The Río Uruguay provides a case in point. On the map, the river appeared suitable for logging.[53] In fact, the river became uncomfortably narrow in spots and at two places, Butuí and Salto Grande (Santa Rosa), its flow was interrupted by rapids, necessitating a land carriage around the obstacles. These problems might have warranted attention if the cargo being shipped were yerba mate or textiles, but timber and finished wood items simply were not worth the effort in a labor-scarce area. With some small exceptions, therefore, the region of the Río Uruguay had to wait many years before logging became practical.[54]

Shipbuilding

Domestic demand for Upper Platine woods sparked another kind of economic expansion, thanks to shipyards at Asunción and Corrientes. Shipbuilding was by no means new to the Upper Plata. As early as the 1540s, a vessel built in Paraguay had sailed to Spain.[55] The shipyards (*astilleros*) of Corrientes, Itatí, and Asunción continued to function throughout the colonial period, producing canoes and other vessels of small size and limited draft that required little skill to build but satisfied local needs.

The Bourbon Reforms of the 1780s opened commerce along the rivers, and within a decade shipping within the region increased nearly five-fold. The great majority of the vessels involved in this intraplatine trade were constructed in the Upper Plata.[56] Though their experience was confined to rivercraft, the native shipwrights proved equal to the task of building ships. Basque craftsmen in the ports designed and built large vessels. Caulkers, employing native fibers such as *caraguatá* and *guembé*, also were well versed in their trade.[57] In Paraguay, and at Itatí, a ready reserve of semi-skilled labor was drawn from the pueblos de indios. These Indians knew well how "to wield the ax and adze."[58] They also served as crewmembers on downriver voyages, providing the muscle power to push ships off sandbars and the expertise necessary to effect minor repairs.

Before independence, the shipyards of the Upper Plata were all privately owned and operated. The colonial regime helped promote the industry by granting reductions on export duties for goods carried on locally produced vessels.[59]

The various keeled and unkeeled vessels produced in Upper Platine shipyards during the late colonial period included brigs, *garandumbas*, *bergantines*, *sumacas*, *polacras*, *balsas*, and *falúas*. Perhaps the most curious ship constructed during this era was the *piragua*. J. P. Robertson, expelled by Francia from Paraguay, had to sail south aboard a particularly poor specimen of this type of vessel. He described it as

> a huge box, perfectly square and flat at the bottom and the four sides coming out in angular directions, so as to form a square surface on the top, equal to nearly double the size of the corresponding square of the bottom. A sort of gangway or rim is then run around the box, sufficiently broad to allow rowers to stand conveniently upon it. The box being then loaded with bales, square with the top of it, a flooring is laid over them, and on this a hide-house, or *troja*, some eight or nine feet in height, is constructed, and this, again, with the exception of room for passengers and crew, is loaded with produce. The machine of this description, which I purchased and loaded, carried about 1500 bales of yerba, equal to about 200 tons, leaving space for [myself, the] master, pilot, and nineteen or twenty peons. . . . The piragua had neither prow nor stern, and sails are of no use in so unmanageable and unwieldy a body as it presents. We were, in nautical, and in the case literal phrase, obliged to *box* about the river the best way we could, assisted by oars.[60]

The favorable atmosphere for trading in the 1790s enhanced the expansion of shipbuilding. While Porteño capital appears to have dominated the industry, local merchants sometimes ordered vessels for use in their own river trade. By the turn of the century, astilleros existed in Concepción, Asunción, San Antonio, Villeta, Angostura, Pilar, and Curupayty, all on the Río Paraguay; Alfonso on the Río Yhaguy; San Cosme and Itatí on the Alto Paraná; and Corrientes and Goya on the Río Paraná proper.[61] Between 1780 and 1810, Upper Platine shipyards even constructed some thirty-five oceangoing vessels with keels from 36 to 85 feet in length. They also produced a great many smaller vessels, canoes, and launches.[62]

In Paraguay, the tiny navy built several vessels during the Francia years. Soldiers constructed one gunboat toward the end of 1815. Canoes for expeditions against the Indians were prepared at about the same time. The work at the military astillero at Asunción was directed by Antonio Iturbe, "senior master builder of war vessels," under whose orders functioned 23 journeymen, 41 workmen, 11 caulkers, and various sailors.[63] Several Englishmen apparently worked among this group.[64] Unfortunately, few details remain about these operations.

The extent of shipbuilding in Corrientes during the same period is difficult to gauge. Given the pre-independence role of astilleros at the port of Corrientes, it seems likely that some small ships were constructed.[65] Civil war affected Corrientes far more than Paraguay, however, and it is doubtful that shipwrights produced many vessels between independence and the 1850s.[66]

Things slowly began to change in the Upper Plata around the mid-1840s. In Paraguay, the Dictator's death found private shipping in advanced decay. As Robertson had noted,

> even the lapacho tree—indurated, impervious as it is to external
> attacks—is not proof against a decree or a system which, for
> fifteen or twenty years, leaves a vessel to exposure on the beach
> of Assumption, without awnings, without caulking, without
> watering of the decks, without, in short, any one of the
> precautions usually taken to retard decay, in either river-craft,
> or ships that sail on the high seas.[67]

That situation changed. The cautiously expansive Carlos Antonio López held the reins of power in Paraguay, and with revived trade came a renewed growth in shipbuilding.

Ship design, in the meantime, had changed considerably. Following developments in the estuary, new types of river craft (or improved versions of older designs) had come into common use. As a rule, these vessels were decked and larger than before, with piraguas, garandumbas, and other smaller ships becoming outmoded and disappearing from use.

The schooner (*goleta*) was the most important merchant vessel up to the 1860s. With two masts and ample cargo space, it was the ideal ship for the river trade. The chalana, another common river boat in the early days, was rapidly being replaced by the larger *paylebot*, whose increasing use during the 1850s reflected a trend toward larger vessels. By 1860, almost two dozen varieties of smaller vessels were still in use, but together they carried no more than one cargo in ten.[68] Larger vessels carried nine-tenths of Upper Platine exports.

Paraguayan state astilleros at Asunción and Pilar built a fair number of river vessels of small tonnage—*bombardas, balandras* (sloops), *queches*—between 1843 and 1854. All were constructed of native hardwoods in shipyards that employed scores of workers.[69] The government also constructed some vessels called "state war schooners," such as the *República del Paraguay*, whose bowsprit was affixed in July 1850.[70] Other than some canoes and jangadas, private shipbuilding in Paraguay never prospered under López.

In Corrientes, shipyards remained completely in private hands. Between 1849 and 1855, the shipyards at the port of Corrientes constructed 76 chalanas, 21 canoes, and 178 other vessels of various dimensions. Among the latter were bergantines and patachos capable "not only of navigating the swift-flowing Paraná . . . but all the seas of [the globe] as far as India and California."[71] Shipyards also operated at Goya and on the island of Apipé.

The European journey of Francisco Solano López in 1853 inaugurated a new stage in regional shipbuilding. Before this time, Paraguayan state shipyards essentially ran on an ad hoc basis. Thanks to the efforts of the younger López, they began to receive full state support as part of an overall plan of naval preparedness. Although a thorough examination of the construction of Paraguayan warships during the 1850s and 1860s goes beyond the scope of this study, certain features should be mentioned.[72]

First, all large vessels of up to 548 tons produced in the Paraguayan state astilleros were steamers, the advent of which constituted a great innovation. Until then the journey to Buenos Aires had taken two months and the return passage upstream considerably longer. Without favorable winds, sailors had to enter the shallow water to tow the craft with ropes. If trees were available along the banks, these were used to wrench the vessel forward; if not, human effort alone had to suffice. Steamers cut in half the time required for a return voyage and thus eliminated much of this backbreaking labor.

Second, although the steamers had a commercial capacity—which they exercised by shipping state-owned yerba—their primary function was naval, to guard the river approaches to Asunción. This goal was inadequately met by ships constructed in Paraguay, where total tonnage produced in this period failed to exceed 2,500 tons.[73] This explains the purchase of three large steamers easily converted to naval purposes, the *Río Negro, Río Blanco,* and *Tacuarí,* the latter being built to order in Britain. Commercial shipbuilding, then, was clearly subordinated to military concerns in Paraguay.

Third, unlike colonial efforts, non-Spaniards oversaw the post-1852 shipbuilding operations. British engineers and machinists, contracted by the Paraguayan government, installed the foreign-built engines into the steamers and constructed a modern wharf and floating drydock at Asunción. Many of the Britons worked in the engine rooms of the

Paraguayan flotilla for ten years or more, well into the war. Nonetheless, even with foreign expertise, the work proved difficult at times. As the chief engineer for the project remarked: "a complete shipbuilding establishment with its slips, sheds, stores, steam apparatus for bending planks, and a multifarious list of details which make no show on paper, is not to be improvised in a week."[74] Even in the best of times, the repair and maintenance of existing ships claimed most of the time of the 180 workmen on the shipyard's payroll. The activities in Paraguay nevertheless made an impact elsewhere. In 1864, the Buenos Aires *Standard* published a laudatory article praising the progress of the shipyards under the management of John W. K. Whytehead, the chief British engineer, "who had converted the river Paraguay into another Clyde."[75]

Corrientes never duplicated the progress of the Paraguayan astilleros, as Correntino shipyards had neither funds with which to pay foreign technicians nor access to solid government backing. Like their cousins to the north, however, the Correntinos had fine craftsmen and ample supplies of timber. These elements resulted in many fine vessels, such as the patacho *Presidente*, with a 28-vara keel, which was launched in September 1855.[76]

A few steamers also emerged from the shipyards of Corrientes. In 1857, the steamship *General Urquiza*, whose chief shipwright was a Frenchman, M. Girot, was christened at the port. Its maiden voyage to Paraná took only fifty-four hours.[78] Although it was not recognized at the time, the advent of steamers presented Corrientes with a dilemma, since the port could effectively be bypassed as a link in the Paraguay trade. Even if the construction of vessels benefitted certain Correntino shipwrights and port workers, such construction likely harmed provincial trade as a whole. In general, however, the northeast lacked energy and capital for such projects throughout the 1850s and 1860s.[78] This lack the Correntino trading community recognized in 1863 in no uncertain terms: "Would it not be more useful if the [National] government, instead of spending vast sums of money to purchase foreign-made steamships, purchased only the machinery [and expertise] instead, and constructed the vessels in this province, as they do in the neighboring Republic of Paraguay? We certainly believe so!" This opinion, expressed as an editorial in the state newspaper, went on to stress the primacy of Corrientes in the construction of river vessels, noting that of the fifty vessels built annually in the Argentine Litoral, thirty-five were of Correntino manufacture.[79]

And unlike those of Paraguay, the shipyards of Corrientes remained relatively unaffected by the war. Despite the short-lived Paraguayan occupation, shipbuilding resumed quickly to supply Allied troops in the Humaitá campaign (1866–68). The 1869 census mentions five master shipwrights resident in the port of Corrientes.[80] This was no small number given the volume of trade and spoke well for the future of the industry in Corrientes.

The situation was different in Paraguay. Between 1865 and 1868, work at the Asunción shipyard continued at a brisk pace. The strains of war made it impossible to resume the construction of large steamers, but in March 1866, work was still in progress on a new steamer, the keel of which had been laid in 1863. By July, the vessel was ready for caulking.[81] With the Allied blockade at the mouth of the Paraguay, however, it became increasingly difficult to obtain spare parts. Thus, only minimal maintenance was attempted during the later war years, and when the Allies took Asunción in 1869, all work at the shipyard ceased. The remaining Paraguayan ships sought refuge in anchorages out of enemy reach, waiting for a victory that never came. Shipbuilding in Paraguay would only be conducted on a most modest scale from then on.

Carts and Finished Goods

Archival sources shed little light on the trade in Upper Platine finished wood items. Clearly, the region exported all manner of such goods—mallets, fenceposts, window frames, flagpoles, and so on—but together these products represented a minuscule proportion of the Upper Plata's exports. One item is of particular interest, however, in that its export promoted the rest of the commerce: carts. Ox trains provided a key adjunct to the river trade. Many a fine bale of tobacco or box of Manchester goods traversed the Upper Platine interior in oxcarts, and, in the case of the Itapúa commerce, such caravans proved absolutely essential to successful trafficking. The sale of Paraguayan-made carts to traders further to the south reinforced these commercial links.

The carts common to the Plata were extremely rude in design. As one North American observer noted in the 1850s, they comprised "a body, tongue, and two solid wooden wheels. Little or no iron is used in their construction, all bands being composed of green hide, which, put on wet, by contraction becomes nearly as strong and hard as metal. The covers are straw and green hide, and occasionally canvas."[82]

In any event, carts could never make the same impact on trade in the Upper Plata as did sailing vessels. Carts were unsuitable for long-distance commerce in the swampy districts of the region. Moreover, since drivers rarely greased the wooden axles or inner hubs of the wheels, a caravan produced a loud noise that could be heard at a great distance. On the trail across Corrientes, or to and from São Borja, this sometimes attracted the attention of bandits who showed little mercy to an unescorted tropa. More so than sailors, therefore, the cart drivers and muleteers had to follow Adam Smith's advice to "join the trade of soldier" to all the other activities they happened to pursue.

Woods: A Stillborn Trade

In many ways the Upper Platine logging, carpentry, and shipbuilding industries never had a chance. They seemed healthy enough during the viceregal period when private promoters encouraged timber exports as an adjunct to the yerba trade. Though northeastern hardwoods were admired in Buenos Aires and elsewhere, their transport southward along the rivers and subsequent sale only resulted in moderate profits. Merchants preferred more lucrative commodities. Timber exports accounted for little of their overall earnings and few were willing to invest in order to increase the percentage. As for the colonial government, it limited itself solely to some abortive efforts to support ropemaking.

The disruption of colonial ties with Spain brought few changes. The Dictator of Paraguay initially permitted a continuation of colonial patterns insofar as timber exports were concerned. But Francia also sought an economic option that was free of Porteño dominance, even if that meant isolation. Within a short time, a general stagnation of forest industries and a cessation of shipbuilding had set in. Francia's successors sponsored the construction of vessels as a government concern. Still, this project was narrowly naval in scope, depended completely on foreign expertise, and failed to fulfill even the modest goal of keeping secure the river approaches to Paraguay. Few Paraguayans were ever involved. The Correntino state, for its part, spent little time promoting ship construction (although a provincial governor himself was a shipwright) and no effort expanding timber exports. All this the government left to the private sector.

What does the case of timber demonstrate? Above all, it shows that this export could never provide a major focus for the economic development of the region. While some growth might periodically occur, little change took place. By the 1840s, foreign competitors matched certain Upper Platine woods in quality for a cheaper price in the Buenos Aires market. Regional governments were uninterested in commodities with low profit margins and never squarely met this foreign challenge. In all of this, Corrientes appeared more flexible than Paraguay, but hardly enough to offset the negative trend. Hence, though the opening of the rivers in 1852 brought a general improvement of the Upper Plata's trading potential, for forest products it signified only a limited commerce.

Conclusion

They carry on their lives of
alternate violence and lethargy
with a pleasurable contempt for
outside opinion.
Katherine Anne Porter

The Upper Plata took a circuitous route to economic development. Despite the proven wealth of its human and natural resources, the region was a prisoner of its politics and its geography. The economic well-being of the Upper Plata depended on access to markets in the lower provinces, especially Buenos Aires. Politics, however, often made such access difficult or impossible.

The last decades of the colonial era witnessed an export boom in the Upper Plata. This rapid growth was associated with the reforming zeal of Crown bureaucrats and with the activities of peninsular entrepreneurs who formed the first major mercantile elite in the region. These traders introduced specie into the Upper Plata, which made possible a cash economy. They also brought new technologies and credit arrangements. The merchants' influence with key royal officials, including the viceroy in Buenos Aires, also smoothed the way for continued affluence in the future.

The result was nothing short of spectacular. Exports of yerba mate from the Upper Plata rose above 150,000 arrobas a year and the entire region benefitted, not the merchants alone. The desire for still further profits led chacreros to leave subsistence farming to work as yerbateros, ranch hands, day workers, or stevedores in the ports. Those who stayed on the land also participated in the growing trade by raising tobacco for export. New immigrants arrived to take advantage of opportunities as artisans, shopkeepers, loggers, and shipwrights. In all, the viceregal period was a golden age for the Upper Plata.

The Upper Plata had never enjoyed more than a peripheral role in the economy of Spanish South America; now regional exports reached consumers not just in the estuary, but as far away as the Andes. In this new circumstance, the traditional power-brokers of the Upper Plata—the landowners, encomenderos, and wealthy ranchers—increasingly had to share their authority in the region with the merchants. Many merchants and landowners forged profitable relations, but in the main, the Upper Platine elites remained divided, with the newcomers never completely accepted by local society. The prosperity that the region experienced effectively masked this division, but it did not undo it.

Without question, political harmony was the prerequisite for sustained economic growth in the New World, and without stability in the political realm, trade, investments, and other economic benefits could not ensue. Those areas that enjoyed stable politics after the first years of independence, such as Chile, and for the most part, Brazil, consistently gained from greater commercial opportunities. More commonly, as with the Upper Plata, political unrest brought a collapse of bureaucracies and credit structures, followed by economic decline, and ultimately a retreat to older patterns of organization—mercantilism and barter.

The early national period in the Upper Plata clearly represented an extension or revival of colonial attitudes and economic practices. This suited the many conservative elements among the chacreros and rural elites. They feared the centralizing tendencies of the Porteño revolutionaries, and, at the same time, they distrusted the few royalists in their midst. Neither group inspired much confidence among the people of the northeast. The civil wars that erupted in neighboring provinces in the mid-1810s fed this feeling of suspicion, which ultimately found expression in a palpable isolationism.

With all of the limitations implicit in such an aloof stance, how did traders in the Upper Plata continue to work at all? Ingenuity was a key factor. To meet the challenges presented by civil war in the south, merchants created new routes around the trouble spots, sometimes falsifying cargo manifests as to point of origin. They forsook the prospect of overseas and long-distance trade and confined themselves to such nearby markets as Montevideo and Buenos Aires. This permitted a modest return and kept their activities within the boundaries allowed by political reality. Even so, their position remained risky.

The governments of Paraguay and Corrientes took pains to promote commerce and thus revenues earned on trade, while carefully keeping these exchanges subordinate to overall political objectives. Contradiction between these two goals proved inevitable.

In Corrientes, the government reflected an odd blend of liberal politics and conservative marketing practices. Unlike many Argentine provinces, Corrientes avoided the long cycle of military regimes led by caudillos. This left the reins of state power in the hands of an established elite of merchants and ranchers who attempted to keep Correntino trade afloat. In this, they had some success in the 1820s and 1830s. They made only minor headway, however, on the three issues that most concerned them: protection for local artisan industries; a prohibition on uncontrolled dumping of foregin goods into provincial markets; and a permanent opening of Argentina's inland waterways to foreign commercial vessels. Buenos Aires, which for selfish reasons had little love for the mercantilist hankerings of the Litoral provinces, opposed all three of these propositions. Largely due to such differences, Corrientes moved away from its initial pro-Porteño stance and, as the century wore on, became a frank proponent of provincial autonomy. This, in turn, transformed Corrientes into a battleground, and only in the late 1840s was economic stability restored.

In Paraguay, Francia restricted external trade to the two peripheral ports of Itapúa and Pilar. By limiting foreign contacts in this manner, the Dictator monitored carefully the collection of duties—a classic mercantilist approach. Ironically, this scrupulous inspection failed to bring an end to the foreign presence, since, at both locations, Brazilian and Correntino traders dominated the scene. Francia's correct relations with these merchants revealed that he was not unconcerned with commerce, but that he saw politics as being more important. Francia was neither a Bonapartist, nor a popular, proto-socialist revolutionary, nor the founder of an alternative development model for Paraguay. He governed his country along patrimonial lines, like a skillful Bourbon administrator. Francia strictly regulated trade so as to strengthen his regime, but he left alone the basic fabric of Paraguayan society. In this fashion, he secured independence for his country, though at a high price. Francia's paternalism stood in the way of any economic development. Of course, the Dictator could always invoke, as a justification for his peculiar absolutism, the long peace that Paraguay had preserved, while the rest of the Plata sank into a bloody mire of internal conflict and international crisis. Peace, however, was no guarantee of progress. Paraguay underwent little meaningful development until after Francia's death; the self-sufficiency so frequently lauded in the dependency literature failed to provide a substitute for economic development.

The isolation of the Upper Plata in the early nineteenth century had its origin less in the stubborn attitude of Francia than in the disordered state of Platine politics. Buenos Aires consistently tried to play a hegemonic role in the Litoral. The provinces responded by treating the Argentine nation as little more than a superstructure created by the Porteños in order to maintain their economic privileges. Between these two positions existed little room for compromise. Buenos Aires continued to control the customs house and to exploit its comparative advantage in the world market. The Upper Plata continued to be isolated, but did preserve in haphazard fashion most of the trade links it had known during the viceregal period.

The average inhabitant of the region had little difficulty in adjusting to a condition of minimal intercourse with the outside. The fertility of the soil promised a satisfactory standard of life, and the absence of any major class conflict assured a tranquil, if somewhat dormant, social environment. This was enough for many. Still, this cannot be called progress. No mechanism existed to encourage much in the way of economic growth. The governments of the region refused on political grounds to permit an open commerce with the lower provinces. The populace of the Upper Plata, therefore, had little chance to obtain goods from the outside and had to be contented with locally produced articles. These latter were not such as to make a large market possible, and native entrepreneurial skills accordingly decayed over time. Meaningful economic development had to wait for another day.

Cracks in the veneer of isolation came only in the late 1840s with the Anglo-French blockade of Buenos Aires. With the fall of Rosas in 1852, foreign merchants poured into the Upper Plata as never before, bringing with them a huge quantity of goods and a new outlook on river trade. With the rivers opened and Argentina finally reconciled to Paraguayan independence, the opportunities for trade looked substantial. In a matter of months, Upper Platine exports quadrupled.

These events led to a basic economic shift in the region. Subsistence farmers and ranchers, accustomed to long years of isolation, moved swiftly to produce cash crops alone. Little remained of the earlier reluctance to participate in a wider economy.

As before, yerba led the way, though it never recaptured the commanding position it had once held. Brazilian yerba had made impressive gains in Buenos Aires since the 1820s, and any imports from Paraguay had to contend with this competitor. Porteño consumers had grown accustomed to the cheaper Brazilian product. Though they realized that Paraguayan yerba was superior in quality, they were wary of its high price. The Asunción government never grasped that demand for its yerba was relatively inelastic, that without more moderate pricing policies, little headway could be made in the marketplaces of the lower provinces, not to mention the former colonial markets of Chile and beyond.

Tobacco was another matter. In this commodity, the Upper Plata had the chance to expand its share of the market in Buenos Aires, without the burden of heavy state interference. With the rivers opened, Paraguayan cosecheros rushed to supply tobacco, the region's chief cash crop. On at least two occasions during the 1850s, this almost frenzied production for export caused local food cultivation to fall precipitously and was only remedied by direct government action.

Still, this one bright spot for the individual producer did not of itself promise a balanced export picture. Other commodities, such as timber and hides (as well as tallow, oranges, and earthenware), made little impact on the region's export potential. Yet even these minor exports would have fared better had official policy in the Upper Plata shown more understanding of modern commercial practices.

The government of Paraguay failed to manifest any real enthusiasm for free trade. Eager to safeguard the state sector of the export market, Carlos Antonio López made explicit Francia's vague notions of state authority in commerce. He proclaimed government monopolies over the export of yerba and timber. He maintained high fees for import-export licenses. Whereas Francia had purposely circumscribed trade links with the outside, López boasted of a modernization program based on profits from state trading ventures. Despite the defects and shortsightedness of this program, the new attitude was strikingly different. Unlike his predecessor, López insisted that foreign trade ought to be encouraged because it directly supported the exchequer. Nonetheless, his narrow insistence on mercantilist policies effectively slowed the emergence of a native class of traders other than the members of his own family. For Carlos Antonio López, mercantilism ultimately became less a deeply felt ideology than a vehicle for barely disguised nepotism. Paraguay would have experienced greater economic development had not the state so frequently inserted itself into commerce.

In Corrientes, Juan Pujol's government rejected the mercantilism of López and instead welcomed the chance to enter a wider market with few controls on trade. Pujol had good relations with foreign merchants and national politicians and even sponsored a colonization project for French settlers in the north of his province—the latter effort a candid recognition of Corrientes' need to overcome its labor shortage. Pujol's willingness to work with the national government guaranteed the Correntinos a small share of the now peaceful river trade throughout the 1850s.

Regional commerce recorded an active traffic during the first years of the next decade. Merchants, government officials, growers, ranchers, habilitados—all were satisfied with this trend. No one clamored for a return to a "closed economy." Indeed, the inhabitants of the Upper Plata began to diversify their production; cotton was again grown as a cash crop, and tanneries and saladeros were founded. Whole new industries, such as the distillation of orange and palm liqueur, were created. In every meaningful way, the region had embarked on a classic course of economic development with outside trade providing the necessary catalyst.

The War of the Triple Alliance was the great watershed of Upper Platine history. The dependency interpretation of this conflict paints a picture of a gallant Paraguay defending its economic autonomy (and its alternate path to development) against the voracious capitalists of Brazil and Buenos

Aires, covertly manipulated by Britain. No such autonomy existed. By the 1860s, Paraguay, like the rest of the Plata, depended almost completely on the Porteño market, and no one, least of all Francisco Solano López, wanted to see that valuable trade link severed, except on a temporary basis. He thought he would gain the adherence of those Argentines and Uruguayans who opposed Mitre and the Brazilians with a short military campaign. With an easy victory, he could realize his ambitions. López miscalculated, and in the process, led the region to disaster.

The commerce of the Upper Plata in the 1780–1870 period was highly influenced by factors other than supply and demand. Under normal circumstances, the region enjoyed a stable, even prosperous, market in the lower provinces. Times were rarely normal after the mid-1810s, however, and the meticulously constructed web of interregional trade failed to withstand the recurrent civil conflicts. The commercial ties that supported economic growth in the Upper Plata were repeatedly obstructed, leaving governments in the region with few options outside of extreme fiscal conservatism. Development was never generated internally. Real economic change only came at the end of the nineteenth century, when North Atlantic demand, accompanied by massive transfers of capital and technology, transformed regional trade, linking it still more directly to the Porteño market and making great profits along the way. In the end, the integration of the Upper Plata into the larger pattern of Latin American development was only a matter of time.

Appendices

APPENDIX I. Paraguayan Tobacco Exports—The Lopez Era

Year	En rama (arrobas)	Value (in pesos fuertes)	Cigars (1,000s)	Value (in pesos fuertes)	Combining value (pesos fuertes)
1844	n/a	n/a	n/a	n/a	n/a
1845	23,072	34,221	60	430	34,651
1846	n/a	n/a	n/a	n/a	n/a
1847–48	125,708*	n/a	390*	n/a	189,283*
1849	n/a	n/a	n/a	n/a	n/a
1850	n/a	n/a	n/a	n/a	n/a
1851	28,907	56,743	191	1,434	58,177
1852	125,195	161,757	556	3,535	165,292
1853	143,695	157,026	2,086	6,535	163,461
1854	103,866	148,172	5,264	12,573	160,745
1855	225,168*	418,855	4,926*	18,065	436,920
1856	207,810	349,575	4,234	16,935	366,510
1857	250,182	586,120	4,378	17,570	603,690
1858	272,801	500,135	4,159	16,635	516,770
1859	229,009	595,775	2,504	10,016	603,690
1860	124,637	270,370	6,000	22,460	292,830
1861	152,638	308,504	5,445	19,439	327,943
1862	322,562	904,103	3,948	9,782	913,885

(continued)

APPENDIX I. Paraguayan Tobacco Exports—The Lopez Era *(continued)*

Year	En rama (arrobas)	Value (in pesos fuertes)	Cigars (1,000s)	Value (in pesos fuertes)	Combining value (pesos fuertes)
1863	181,056	515,166	4,171	12,868	528,034
1864	322,533	821,846	16,103	30,978	852,824
1865	114,685	263,539	12,741	26,523	295,606

*Minimum figure.
Sources: ANA-SH 274; NE 866; *El Semanario*, 1 October 1853, 24 December 1853, 11 January 1855, 16 February 1861 through 8 July 1865; Du Graty, *La república del Paraguay*, pp. 346–50; Herken Krauer, "Proceso económico," 83–116.

APPENDIX II. Ranching Statistics, Corrientes (1832)[a]

Department	Number of ranchers	Cattle	Horses	Sheep
Ensenadas	47	11,134	3,429	3,890
Itatí[b]	38	11,319	1,444	1,116
Palmar	85	19,863	3,673	2,879
Empedrado	57	13,642	2,863	3,094
Saladas	85	27,814	9,760	8,760
San Roque	65	34,660	7,021	10,486
Caa Catí	68	22,600	3,600	2,900
San Miguel	22	9,700	1,100	700
Yaguareté Cora	39	19,199	9,616	3,220
Goya	92	39,468	9,793	8,748
Esquina	45	16,491	7,819	9,909
Curuzú Cuatiá	86	91,065	12,866	14,700
Total	729	317,684	72,984	70,402

Note: Of the 729 estancieros listed, almost none appear also as merchants, though many are clearly related—the Pucheta family, for instance. An exception is the North American John Hayes, the only non-creole surname in the listing. He owned an estancia in Esquina department that boasted 190 head of cattle, 30 horses, and 240 sheep.
[a]Does not include figures for Bella Vista department.
[b]1833 figure.
Source: Manifiesto general de las haciendas existentes en toda la provincia según la razón particular del corriente año presentada a la policía para los Comandantes de cada Depto., año 1834 [sic], Juan F. Gramajo, Corrientes, 4 March 1833, AGPC-EA 1833, legajo 38.

APPENDIX III. Ranching Statistics, Corrientes, 1834

Department	Number of ranchers	Cattle	Horses	Sheep
Ensenadas	43	9,508	2,094	4,838
Itatí	38	14,914	2,271	1,336
Palmar	89	23,194	3,037	3,121
Empedrado	50	15,554	2,210	3,098
Saladas	56	19,485	5,435	9,971
San Roque	58	36,115	7,928	10,478
Caa Catí	73	25,300	3,500	3,300
San Miguel	22	6,400	1,400	300
Yaguareté Cora	41	24,038	4,634	2,710
Goya	97	47,025	6,897	12,091
Esquina	50	20,153	9,414	8,984
Curuzú Cuatiá	105	69,700	14,600	20,360
Mburucuya	41	11,019	1,060	2,254
Bella Vista	42	16,010	3,467	3,375
Total	805	338,415	67,947	86,216

Note: As in 1832, criollo surnames dominate the listing of ranchers (e.g. Cabral, Esquivel, Ojeda, López, Vallejos). The foreign surnames that do appear are, at the same time, the only merchants of note—

David Spaulding	500 cattle	Bella Vista
	100 horses	
Marcelino Deniz	400 cattle	Goya
José Lopetegui	993 cattle	Esquina
John Hayes	1,530 cattle	Esquina
	125 horses	
	1,025 sheep	

Source: Copia de manifiestos de haciendas correspondientes al presente año de 1834, Juan F. Gramajo, Corrientes, 31 December 1834, AGPC-AE 1834, legajo 44.

Abbreviations

ABPBA	Archivo del Banco de la Provincia de Buenos Aires
AHAER	Archivo Histórico y Administrativo de Entre Ríos
AHRGS	Arquivo Histórico do Rio Grande do Sul
-CV	Coleção Varela
AGN	Archivo General de la Nación (Buenos Aires)
-DBN	Documentos de la Biblioteca Nacional
AGPC	Archivo General de la Provincia de Corrientes
-AC	Actas Capitulares
-CLC	Cuadernos de Libros de Caja
-CO	Correspondencia Oficial
-DG	Documentos del Gobierno
-EA	Expedientes Administrativos
ANA	Archivo Nacional de Asunción
-CJDB	Colección José Doroteo Barreiro
-CRB	Colección Rio Branco
-NE	Nueva Encuadernación
-LC	Libro de Caja
-SH	Sección Historia
-SCD	Sección Copias de Documentos
-SJC	Sección Judicial Criminal
-SPT	Sección Propiedades y Testamentos
MG	Manuel Gondra Collection (Austin, Texas)

PRO   Public Records Office (London)
      -FO   Foreign Office
ROPC   Registro Oficial de la Provincia de Corrientes

Notes

Preface

1. For surveys of this literature, see Ronald H. Chilcote, "Dependency: A Critical Synthesis of the Literature," *Latin American Perspectives* 1 (1974): 4–29; C. R. Bath and D. D. James, "Dependency Analysis of Latin America: Some Criticisms, Some Suggestions," *Latin American Research Review* 11 (1976): 3–54; and Tulio Halperín Donghi, "Dependency Theory and Latin American Historiography," *Latin American Research Review* 17 (1982): 115–30. For a criticism of the historical applicability of the dependency model, see D. C. M. Platt, "Dependency in Nineteenth Century Latin America: An Historian Objects," *Latin American Research Review* 15 (1980): 113–30.

2. In asserting this thesis, we owe an intellectual debt to Carlos Sempat Assadourian, whose *El sistema de la economía colonial. Mercado interno, regiones y espacio económico* (Lima, 1982) has redrawn the analytical parameters of Latin American economic history. See also Steve J. Stern, "Feudalism, Capitalism, and the World-System in the Perspective of Latin America and the Caribbean," *American Historical Review* 93:4 (October 1988), 829–72.

3. For a brilliant discussion on this concept of region, see Eric Van Young, "Doing Regional History: Methodological and Theoretical Considerations," paper read before the Seventh Conference of Mexican and U.S. Historians, Oaxaca, Mexico, 23–26 October 1985.

Chapter One

1. Clifton B. Kroeber, *The Growth of the Shipping Industry in the Río de la Plata Region, 1794–1860* (Madison, 1957), pp. 10–12.

2. Regarding the problem of rapids on the Río Uruguay, see Gabriel Carrasco, *Cartas de viaje por el Paraguay, los territorios nacionales del Chaco, Formosa y Misiones y las provincias de Corrientes y Entre Ríos* (Buenos Aires, 1889), pp. 191–93; the southernmost of the two formations has today been converted into a massive binational hydroelectric facility called Salto Grande.

3. These figures are imprecise as no reliable census was carried out anywhere in the Upper Plata, save in the former Jesuit missions, at any time in the late colonial period. Odin Alf Toness, "The Political and Social History of a Paraguayan Town," Ph.D. dissertation, University of Illinois (Urbana, 1973), 42–45, utilizes Félix de Azara and assigns totals that may be slightly low. The Correntino figures, based on incomplete census materials, were supplied by Ernesto J. A. Maeder, *Historia económica de Corrientes en el período virreinal, 1776–1810* (Buenos Aires, 1981), pp. 103–13.

4. Toness, "Political and Social History"; see also James Schofield Saeger, "Survival and Abolition: The Eighteenth-Century Paraguayan Encomienda," *The Americas* 38:1 (July 1981): 59–86.

5. Maeder, *Historia económica*, p. 128.

6. Jonathan Brown, *A Socioeconomic History of Argentina, 1776–1860* (Cambridge, 1979), p. 222.

7. Juan Carlos Garavaglia, "Un capítulo del mercado interno colonial: el Paraguay y su región (1537–1682)," *Nova Americana* 1 (1978): 29–30.

8. These figures are based on receipts in Santa Fé and are incomplete for the whole of the downriver traffic. Juan Carlos Garavaglia, "El mercado interno colonial y la yerba mate (siglos XVI-XIX)," *Nova Americana* 4 (1981): 182–83.

9. Chilean demand for Upper Platine yerba remained high throughout the eighteenth century. For an example of one particularly large yerba shipment, see Guía of José Coene (2,832 arrobas de yerba con destino a Santiago de Chile). 4 June 1784, ANA-NE 3337, item no. 163.

10. Regarding the puerto preciso, see Oscar Luis Ensinck, "El puerto preciso de la ciudad de Santa Fé. Proceso Historico," *Anuario*. Facultad de Derecho. U. N. Rosario, 5 (1983): 139–204.

11. *Ibid.*; see also Libros de aduana de Buenos Aires. AGN XIII–35-3-1; 35-3-5; 35-4-1; 35-5-4; and 35-11-5.

12. Juan Francisco de Aguirre, "Diario del capitán de fragata de la Real Armada Don . . ," *Revista de la Biblioteca Nacional de Buenos Aires* 17–20 (1949–51), no pagination.

13. Félix de Azara, *Descripción e historia del Paraguay y del Río de la Plata*, 2 vols. (Madrid, 1849), 1:329.

14. *Ibid.*, 1:70. Another source lists 330,480 arrobas exported. See Registro de Despacho de Guías. 29 December 1798, ANA-NE 80.

15. Azara, *Descripción e historia*, 1:329.

16. Ernesto J. A. Maeder, *Historia económica*, p. 121.

17. Ernesto J. A. Maeder, "La ciudad de Corrientes descripta por viajeros y cronistas entre 1750 y 1828," *Nordeste* 1 (1960): 83–112.

18. Azara, *Descripción e historia*, 1:335, 344.

19. Jerry W. Cooney, "Foreigners in the Intendencia of Paraguay," *The Americas* 39 (January 1983): 347–48.

20. *Ibid.*; see also Expediente of José Coene. Asunción, 4 April 1807, ANA-SPT 839.

21. Juan Carlos Garavaglia, *Mercado interno y economía colonial* (Mexico, 1983), p. 80.

22. Libro de asiento de guías para el año de 1800. ANA-NE 3360.

23. Richard Alan White, *Paraguay's Autonomous Revolution, 1810–1840* (Albuquerque, 1978), p. 226. Estanco records indicate a slightly lower total.

24. Maeder, *Historia económica*, pp. 274, 297.

25. See Manuel García de Arce to Cristobal de Aguirre. Villarrica, 18 December 1793. ABPBA 031-2-1, no. 24. It should be noted that, by then, tax payments were commonly made in coin. See Actas del Cabildo de Asunción. 22 April 1793, ANA-Actas del cabildo.

26. Hernán Félix Gómez, *La ciudad de Goya* (Buenos Aires, 1942), p. 31.

27. Kroeber, *Shipping Industry*, p. 31.

28. Cited in John Hoyt Williams, "Dr. Francia and the Creation of the Republic of Paraguay, 1810–1814," Ph.D. dissertation, University of Florida, 1969, 172.

29. *Ibid.*, pp. 173–74.

30. *Ibid.*, p. 192.

31. *Ibid.*, p. 193.

32. Testimony against Captain don Miguel Montiel. Concepción, June 1812, ANA-CRB I-29, 22, 19–20.

33. Triumvirate of Buenos Aires to the Junta of Paraguay. Buenos Aires, 24 March 1812, AGN X-1-9-13.

34. Julio César Cháves, *Historia de las relaciones entre Buenos Ayres y el Paraguay, 1810–1813* (Buenos Aires, 1959), p. 192. Jerry W. Cooney, "The Rival of Doctor Francia: Fernando de la Mora and the Paraguayan Revolution," *Revista de Historia de América* 100 (July-December 1985): 222.

35. Acuerdo of Fulgencio Yegros, Pedro Juan Caballero, and José Gaspar de Francia. Asunción, 16 November 1812, ANA-SH 216.

36. R. A. Humphreys, "British Merchants and South American Independence," in *Tradition and Revolt in Latin America* (London, 1969), pp. 106–129; J. P. and W. P. Robertson, *Letters on Paraguay*, 3 vols., (London, 1838–39), *passim*. Archival materials on the Robertson brothers in Paraguay include J. P. Robertson to the Junta Gubernativa. Asunción, 20 October 1812, ANA-SH 220 no. 4; Demanda of J. P. Robertson. Asunción, 7 March 1812, ANA-SJC 2047; and especially Libro de sobordo de la balandra San Juan Bautista, 1812–1815, AGPC-EA 1810, legajo 1.

37. Robertson, *Letters on Paraguay*, 2:279–80.

38. White, *Paraguay's Autonomous Revolution*, p. 82.

39. Robertson, *Letters on Paraguay*, 3:20–21.

40. For decrees prohibiting the export of coin, see Decreto of Francia. Asunción, 13 November 1814, ANA-SCD 23, no. 38; Bando of Francia. Asunción, 8 August 1816, ANA-SH 226, no. 16 (in this case, he made an exception for shipments of

munitions). In 1823 and 1829, he reiterated his position on the export of coin; see ANA-CRB I-29-23-28, no. 80, and ANA-SH 240, no. 3.

41. Smuggling was prominent throughout the Francia era. For examples, see Causas contra Francisco Aguilar. Asunción, 31 October 1815, ANA-SJC 1513; and Francia to ?. Asunción, 1 September 1827, ANA-SH 239, no. 1.

42. White, *Paraguay's Autonomous Revolution*, pp. 171–72; Eduardo Galeano, *The Open Veins of Latin America* (New York, 1973), pp. 206–16; E. Bradford Burns, *The Poverty of Progress* (Berkeley, 1981), pp. 128–29; Christian Lalive D'Epinay and Louis Necker, "Paraguay (1811–1870): A Utopia of Self-Oriented Change," in Johan Galtung, Peter O'Brien and Roy Preiswerk, eds., *Self-Reliance: A Strategy for Development* (London, 1980), pp. 249–68; and Vivian Trias, *El Paraguay de Francia el Supremo a la guerra de la Triple Alianza* (Buenos Aires, 1975); see also Edy Kaufman, "Authoritarianism in Paraguay: the Lesser Evil?," *Latin American Research Review* 19:2 (1984), 193–207; and Vera Blinn Reber, "Commerce and Industry in Nineteenth-Century Paraguay: the Example of Yerba Mate," *The Americas* 42:1 (1985), 29–53.

43. The North American attraction to the dependency paradigm has been traced in Fernando Henrique Cardoso, "The Consumption of Dependency Theory in the United States," *Latin American Research Review* 12 (1977): 7–24, and in Halperín Donghi, "Dependency Theory," *passim*. In a thought-provoking departure, Soviet and Eastern European historians have distanced themselves from the dependency school per se, yet they, too, have argued that autonomous development occurred in Francia's Paraguay. In their interpretation, however, the Dictator's "experiment" was designed to pave the way for capitalism, rather than some variety of state socialism, in the country. It is unfortunate that these historians evidently have been working without access to primary documents. See Moises Samoilovic Al'perovich, *Revoluciia i Diktatura v Paragvai. 1810–1840* (Moscow, 1975); Jan Szeminski, "Rewolucja i dyktatura w Paragwaju. 1810–1840," *Przeglad Historyczny* 68 (1977), 567–574; and Henryk Szlajfer, "Against Dependent Capitalist Development in Nineteenth-Century Latin America. The Case of Haiti and Paraguay," *Latin American Perspectives* 13:1 (Winter, 1986), 45–73.

44. John Hoyt Williams, "Paraguay's Nineteenth-Century 'Estancias de la República,' " *Agricultural History* 47 (July 1973): 206–15.

45. For an interesting analysis of the Bourbon bureaucratic style, see Susan Socolow, *The Bureaucrats of Buenos Aires, 1769–1810* (Durham and London, 1987), *passim*.

46. José Carlos Chiaramonte, "Coacción extraeconómica y relaciones de producción en el Río de la Plata durante la primera mitad del siglo XIX: el caso de la provincia de Corrientes," *Nova Americana* 2 (1979): 257–58.

47. J. P. and W. P. Robertson, *Letters on South America*, 3 vols. (London, 1843), 1: *passim*. Artigas was nearly always sympathetic toward British trade. See Artigas to Méndez. Cuartel general, 10 September 1815, AGPC-CO 1815, legajo 7.

48. Robertson, *Letters on South America*, 1:51–54.

49. *Ibid.*, 59–67; see also John Postlethwaite to Méndez, Curuzú Cuatiá, 22 January 1818, AGPC-CO 1816–19, legajo 8; and Manuel Mantilla y los Ríos to Juan Francisco Brest. Corrientes, 22 November 1819, AGPC-EA 1819, legajo 4.

50. Robertson, *Letters on South America*, 1:174–98.

51. *Ibid.*, 1:282–87.
52. *Ibid.*, 1:107.
53. Contract between J. B. Méndez and William P. Robertson. San Roque, 22 July 1817, AGPC-CO 1816–19, legajo 8.
54. Even at the end, Méndez tried to coax Postlethwaite into staying, offering him various concessions. See Decreto of Méndez. Corrientes, 25 April 1819, in *ibid.*
55. Johann Rudolph Rengger and Marceline Longchamp, *The Reign of Doctor Joseph Gaspard Roderick de Francia in Paraguay* (London, 1827), pp. 37–39.
56. Efraím Cardozo, "Artigas y el Paraguay," *Revista del Instituto Histórico y Geográfico del Uruguay*, 30 (1952): 11–52.
57. Azara, *Descripción e historia*, 1:330.
58. Guías de aduana, 1817–19. AGN X-37-1-16-18.
59. Pedro Nolasco Torres to Francia. Pilar, 30 January 1822, ANA-SH 383.
60. See, for example, Francia to José Tomás Gill, comandante de Pilar. Asunción, 12 December 1825, ANA-NE 708; Francia to Gill. Asunción, 24 January 1827, ANA-NE 3411.
61. Francia frequently went into minute detail on these matters. On one occasion in 1825, he noted that a recently arrived shipment of flour "is passable, though it has already taken on a bad odor." Francia to Gill. Asunción, 22 December 1825, ANA-NE 708.
62. John Hoyt Williams, *The Rise and Fall of the Paraguayan Republic, 1800–1870* (Austin, 1979), p. 72.
63. Regarding the foreign presence in Ñeembucú, see Pedro Nolasco Torres to Francia. Pilar, 17 March 1822, ANA-SH 383; Bando of Francia. Asunción, 14 July 1825, ANA-SH 442, no. 1; Francia to Gill. Asunción, 18 July 1826, ANA-NE 1242.
64. Alfredo Viola, "El diario de Nicolás Descalzi," *Anuario del Instituto de Investigaciones Históricas Dr. José Gaspar Rodríguez de Francia* 4:4 (1982): 43–44 and *passim.*
65. Gill to Francia. Pilar, 20 February 1827, ANA-SH 394, no. 1.
66. Cited in John Hoyt Williams, "Paraguayan Isolation under Dr. Francia: A Reevaluation," *Hispanic American Historical Review* 52 (February 1972): 108.
67. Viola, "El diario de Nicolás Descalzi," 42–43.
68. For examples, see Guía of Miguel Gerónimo Nuñez. Pilar, 23 December 1822, and Guía of José Mariano Núñes. Pilar, 15 August 1828, both in ANA-NE 1847, and Juan Tomás Gill to Francia. Pilar, 13 June 1827, ANA-NE 2568. Wool imports to Pilar were also evident through the mid-1830s; see Guía of José Ramón Benítez. Pilar, 3 October 1833, ANA-SH 233, no. 1.
69. This is the present site of the Argentine city of Posadas. Alejo Peyret, *Cartas sobre Misiones* (Buenos Aires, 1881), pp. 34–35.
70. V. Martin de Moussy, *Description Geographique et Statistique de la Confédération Argentine*, 3 vols. (Paris, 1860–64), 3:693.
71. Williams, "Paraguayan Isolation," 109–114.
72. Subdelegado Norberto Ortellado to Francia. Itapúa, 27 July and 7 August 1823, ANA-CRB I-29, 23, 28; José Mariano Morínigo to Ortellado. Itapúa, 2 September 1823, *ibid.*
73. Regarding Misiones and the Cisplatine War, see Alberto Palomeque, *El*

general Rivera y la campaña de Misiones (Buenos Aires, 1914); Hernán Félix Gómez, *Corrientes en la guerra con el Brasil* (Corrientes, 1928); and Agustín Beraza, *Rivera y la independencia de las Misiones* (Montevideo, 1971). The active character of the Itapúa commerce at this time is attested to in José León Ramírez, delegado of Itapúa, to Francia. 28 October and 6 December 1829, ANA-CRB 1-30, 2, 6, nos. 3–4.

74. White, *Paraguay's Autonomous Revolution*, p. 257.

75. In May 1838, one citizen of Yuty, Roque Romero, attempted to introduce 600 pesos worth of goods illegally obtained in Itapúa. Contraband passed in the opposite direction as well; many bales (tercios) making their way south, as the records show, "sin guía." Expediente of Roque Romero. Yuty, 17 May 1838, ANA-SH 243, no. 16; Fernando Yturburo, smuggler, to Francia. 9 May 1839, ANA-NE 2611.

76. Jean Etienne Richard de Grandsire, "Briefe aus Paraguay, mitgetheilt von Alexander von Humboldt," *Hertha, Zeitschrift fuer Erd-, Voelker-, und Staatenkunde* (Stuttgart and Tuebingen, 1825), 702–4. Demand for these items, while limited, remained relatively steady in the period under discussion. See Francia to Delegado of Itapúa. Asunción, 17 March 1832, ANA-SH 241, no. 12; Francia to Delegado of Itapúa. Asunción, 19 and 30 May 1837, ANA-SH 243, no. 7.

77. Libro de la receptoría de la capital (año de 1836). 31 December 1836, ANA-NE 2977 (lists 268 traffickers who made the trek to Itapúa, only 6 of whom made the trip more than once).

78. Francia to Subdelegado of Itapúa. 2 November 1831, ANA-SH 241, no. 7.

79. The grief expressed by these merchants at the death of Francia in 1840 was reported as far away as Buenos Aires. *British Packet and Argentine News*, 19 December 1840.

80. Blas José Márquez to Pedro Ferré. Santo Tomé, 9 November 1840, AGPC-CO 1840, legajo 71. A similar incident in 1833 found Francia willing to indemnify a merchant whose goods had been stolen by Indians in an area near Tranquera de Loreto. Francia to Delegado of Itapúa. Asunción, 15 February 1833, ANA-SH 242, no. 7.

81. They were so described on a 1771 map commissioned by the Marqués de Avila. Ernesto J. A. Maeder, "La formación territorial y económica de Corrientes entre 1588 y 1750," *Folia Histórica del Nordeste* 1 (November 1974): 61.

82. Marco Tulio Centeno, "San Juan de Hormiguero. Crónica de su orígen y desarrollo. Antecedentes de la refundación de Santo Tomé (Corrientes)," *Primer encuentro de geohistoria regional. Exposiciones* (1980): 98–103; John Hoyt Williams, "La guerra no-declarada entre el Paraguay y Corrientes," *Estudios Paraguayos* 1:1 (November 1973): 35–43.

83. Decreto of Juan José Fernández Blanco. Corrientes, 8 May 1823, AGPC-CO 1823, legajo 18.

84. Pedro Ferré, *Memorias del brigadier general Pedro Ferré, octubre de 1821 a diciembre de 1842*, 2 vols. (Buenos Aires, 1921), *passim;* Manuel Florencio Mantilla, *Estudios biográficos sobre patriotas correntinos*, reprint (Corrientes, 1986), pp. 32–47.

85. Pedro Ferré to José María Rojas y Patrón. Santa Fé, 25 July 1830, cited in Ferré, *Memorias*, 1:374; see also Ferré to Governor of Cordoba. Corrientes, 13 April 1832, AGN X-5-7-2.

86. Manuel Florencio Mantilla, *Crónica histórica de la provincia de Corrientes*, 2 vols. (Buenos Aires, 1928–29), 1:266.

87. José Carlos Chiaramonte, "Finanzas públicas de las provincias del Litoral, 1821–1841," *Anuario IEHS* 1 (1986): 159–97.

88. ROPC II: 358-359 (Law of 20 January 1830); III: 9–10 (Law of 4 January 1831), 105–106 (Law of 29 October 1832), 187 (Decree of 1 February 1833).

89. ROPC III: 223-224 (Laws of 20 January and 23 January 1834).

90. Razones de efectos of the Englishman Diego Davison (vecino of Goya). 13 January 1830, AGPC-EA 1830, legajo 28; the North American John Hayes (vecino of Esquina). 17 May 1831, and the Englishman John King (also of Esquina). 28 June 1831, AGPC-EA 1831, legajo 32. Four Frenchmen were living in tiny Saladas in 1832 and another three in even tinier Mburucuyá. These two hamlets boasted foreign communities that included Portuguese, Catalans, Paraguayans, Santafecinos, Englishmen, and Porteños. See Lista de extrajeros residentes. Mburucuyá. 23 July 1832. Saladas. 27 July 1832. AGPC-EA 1832, legajo 35.

91. ROPC II: 359-356 (Law of 22 January 1830). In regard to the establishment of Bella Vista, see Hermán F. Gomez, *Fundación de Bella Vista 1825* (Corrientes, 1925).

92. See petition of Juan Achinelli, Italian. November 1832, AGPC-EA 1832, legajo 36; and José Lopétegui, Basque. 17 June 1834, AGPC-EA 1834, legajo 43.

Chapter Two

1. Only pardos retained a distinct ethnic category within the 1846 census, though the number of individuals listed as retainers (*agregados*) still seems to have been high at this late date—another indication that the Francia period saw little social progress. See John Hoyt Williams, "Observations on the Paraguayan Census of 1846," *Hispanic American Historical Review* 56:3 (August 1976): 424–37.

2. Alexandre Baguet, *Rio Grande do Sul et le Paraguay. Souvenirs de Voyage* (Anvers, 1873), p. 40.

3. Report of George J. R. Gordon to Lord Aberdeen on his visit to Paraguay, 1842. Hampton Wick, 29 April 1843, PRO-FO 13/302, p. 101.

4. *Jornal do Commercio* (Rio de Janeiro), 27 July 1841. See also Spencer Lewis Leitman, *Raízes Sócio-Económicos da Guerra dos Farrapos* (Rio de Janeiro, 1979), p. 37.

5. Saturnino de Souza e Oliveira to José Clemente Pereira. Pôrto Alegre, 28 May 1841, AHRGS, caixa 8, no. 34. Between March and June the previous year, the receptor of Curuzú Cuatiá reported the export of 486 horses to Rio Grande. Many more probably slipped through clandestinely. See Comprobantes. Curuzú Cuatiá, March-June 1840, AGPC-EA 1840, legajo 62.

6. Joaquín de Madariaga, governor of Corrientes, to Barão de Caxias. Corrientes, 1 October 1844, AGPC-EA 1844, legajo 71. Similar raids were conducted against refugees living under Paraguayan protection. See Miguel Ferreira de Pampayo to José Gabriel Valle. Itapúa, 6 May 1842, ANA-SH 247, no. 4.

7. See Francia to Receptor of Itapúa. 18 September 1836, ANA-NE 2605; Francia to Receptor of Itapúa. 22 August 1837, ANA-SH 243, no. 7; Francia to

Receptor of Itapúa. 13 December 1837, ibid.; Derechos de introducción y extracción. Itapúa, 31 December 1841, ANA-NE 1325.

8. Williams, *Rise and Fall*, p. 130. (Williams gives the name as "Trayo"); Jordan Luiz de Araujo to the Consuls of the Republic. Itapúa, April(?) 1841, ANA-SH 247, no. 4.

9. Pleas for some sort of political union between Rio Grande and the Platine states were frequent during these troubled times. Even before the outbreak of the Ferrapo Rebellion, the Argentine intellectual Juan Bautista Alberdi mused on the necessity of such a union to oppose the pretensions of the Porteño federalists. See Juan Bautista Alberdi to Juan Lavalle. Montevideo, 31 October 1833, in the Academia Nacional de Historia, Enrique Fitte Collection, Sección Organización Nacional, VIII-30. As late as 1844, Bento Gonçalvez proposed the creation of a federation that would link Rio Grande not only to Brazil, but also to Uruguay, Corrientes, and Entre Ríos; cited in Joseph L. Love, *Rio Grande do Sul and Brazilian Regionalism, 1882–1930* (Stanford, 1971), p. 265, n. 15.

10. Secret Convention of Friendship. Corrientes, 29 January 1842, AHRGS Arquivo Alfredo Ferreira Rodrigues, caixa 213, no. 17.

11. José Miguel Galán, commandant of Santo Tomé, to Justo Díaz de Vivar. 7 March 1843, AGPC-CO 1843, legajo 77; Galán to Pedro Dionísio Cabral. Santo Tomé, 29 march 1843, *ibid.*

12. Love, *Rio Grande do Sul*, pp. 14–15.

13. Woodbine Parish, *Buenos Ayres and the Provinces of the Río de la Plata* (London, 1852), pp. 237, 251. As early as 1819, one British merchant uttered words of warning on this same point that were still applicable more than twenty years later: "The state of civilization in Paraguay is too infantine [sic] to allow an immediate demand for articles of European manufacture. . . . we conceive that in Paraguay such articles are not wanted, because they are not known; and their necessities must be created before supplies for them can be asked for." Report to Commodore William Bowles by an anonymous merchant, Buenos Aires, 25 December 1819, in G. S. Graham and R. A. Humphreys, eds. *The Navy and South America, 1807–1823: Correspondence of the Commanders-in-Chief on the South American Station* (London, 1962), p. 290.

14. Jonathan Brown, *A Socioeconomic History of Argentina*, p. 213.

15. William Hadfield, *Brazil, the River Plate, and the Falkland Islands* (London, 1854), p. 305.

16. Regarding the reaction of the merchant community of Buenos Aires to Francia's death, see *British Packet and Argentine News*, 16 July 1842.

17. Treaty of Boundaries. Asunción, 31 July 1841, ANA-SH 245. The tendencies expressed in this treaty had been evident for several months. In March, Correntino frontier guards were instructed to maintain "perfect harmony and friendship" with their Paraguayan counterparts. See Instructions to Captain Félix Cabrera. Corrientes, 11 March 1841, AGPC-CO 1841, legajo 74.

18. A census of 1841 listed 320 inhabitants for the district of Santo Tomé, including 37 Brazilians, 3 Paraguayans, 2 Italians, 1 Spaniard, and 1 Uruguayan. Federico Palma, "Santo Tomé. Crónica de su restablecimiento," *Revista de la Junta de Historia de Corrientes* 4 (1969): 16.

19. *El Nacional Correntino*, 1 August 1841.

20. Derechos de extracción. Pilar, 31 December 1841, ANA-NE 1905. At first glance, 817 pesos seems paltry, but it was nevertheless significant in an economy still dominated by barter. Introducción de especie. Pilar, 31 December 1841, ANA-NE 1905.

21. Guías otorgadas. Pilar-Asunción (1841), ANA-NE 724–727, 936–937, 1327, 1919, 1923–1924, 1986. For an example of how barter was conducted at this time, see Comprobantes of Manuel Fernández. 8 October 1841, and Esteban Rams y Rubert. 28 December 1841, ANA-NE 1905.

22. The anticipation of foreign shipping was quite real; in Corrientes, the government received a note from the U.S. consul in Montevideo, in which the latter promised to make known to his government that the ports of Corrientes we now open to ships of all flags. See William Hamilton to Minister Secretary of State for Foreign Affairs of Corrientes. Montevideo, 21 December 1841, AGPC-CO 1859, legajo 104.

23. Mantilla, *Crónica histórica*, 2:83–84.

24. George J. R. Gordon, Report to Lord Aberdeen. PRO-FO 13/202, p. 126.

25. Rosas to López and Alonso. Buenos Aires, 26 April 1843, cited in Hebe Clementi, *Rosas en la historia nacional* (Buenos Aires, 1970), pp. 164–65.

26. The exact text of the decree of blockade has not come to light, though it is clearly in evidence from various notes and letters of the era. See Bando of Pedro Dionísio Cabral and Justo Díaz de Vivar. Paraná, 22 April 1843, AGN X-5-7-6; Francisco Lizardo Garayo to Manuel Peña, Paraná, November 1843; Peña to Carlos Antonio López. Buenos Aires, 12 November 1843, in ANA-CRB I-29, 24, 10, nos. 16, 20.

27. Decree of Joaquín Madariaga. Corrientes, 7 October 1844, ROPC V, pp. 213–16.

28. Decree of Carlos Antonio López. Asunción, 14 October 1844, ANA-CRB I-29, 24, 6, no. 3.

29. Pedro F. Ribeiro, *A Missão Pimenta Bueno, 1843–1847*, 2 vols. (Rio de Janeiro, 1965), pp. 74, 134–40.

30. Treaty of 7 December 1844, *El Paraguayo Independiente*, 5 July 1845.

31. Decree of Juan Manuel de Rosas. Buenos Aires, 8 January 1845, ANA-CRB I-29, 25, 15, no. 6.

32. Rosas to López. Buenos Aires, 22 March 1845, ANA-CRB I-29, 25, 15, no. 7.

33. Regarding the complexities of the blockade, see John F. Cady, *Foreign Intervention in the Río de la Plata, 1838–50* (Philadelphia, 1929), *passim*; Alfred de Brossard, *Considerations Historiques et Politiques sur les Republiques de la Plata dans leur rapports avec la France et l'Angleterre* (Paris, 1850), pp. 240–407.

34. *Comercio del Plata* (Montevideo), 22 October 1845 and 1 December 1845; L. B. MacKinnon, *Steam Warfare on the Paraná: A Narrative of Operations by the Combined Squadrons of England and France, in Forcing a Passage Up That River*, 2 vols. (London, 1848), *passim*.

35. *Britannia* (Montevideo), 5 December 1846.

36. *British Packet and Argentine News*, 2 January 1847.

37. *Ibid.*

38. A. Demersay, "De l'Avenir des Relations Commerciales entre la France et le Paraguay," *Journal des Economistes* 1, ser. 37 (1853): 384–86; Julio Cesar

Chaves, *El presidente López. Vida y gobierno de Don Carlos* (Buenos Aires, 1955), pp. 96–98.

39. One Montevideo journal found it astounding that the province of Corrientes, "With such a tiny and impoverished population," could still consume 300,000 pesos worth of goods, returning at least three times its value. *Comercio del Plata,* 18 July 1846.

40. Manifesto general de los cargamentos. Capitanía del puerto de Corrientes. 1 June 1846, *El Pacificador* (Corrientes), 18 June 1846.

41. Colectoría general de la provincia. Corrientes, 4 January 1845, AGPC-CLC 1844, legajo 86; 13 January 1847, AGPC-CLC 1846, legajo 88.

42. Efectos introducidos. Pilar, 30 September 1848, ANA-NE 866. A large community of foreign merchants was now at the latter port. See Robert Kerr to Santiago Oscariz. Pilar, 28 April 1847, ANA-NE 1010, foja 121. By 1849, the number of foreign traders resident at Pilar amounted to about forty. See Félix Barboza, list of foreign merchants. Pilar, 7 August and 17 November 1849, ANA-SH 278, no. 5.

43. Cited in *British Packet and Argentine News,* 28 October 1848.

44. See, for example, *La Revolución* (Corrientes), 9 March 1845 and 13 April 1845.

45. López to Francisco Wisner. 23 June 1849, ANA-SH, no. 14; see also *El Paraguayo Independiente,* 10 June 1848.

46. Wisner von Morgenstern to Hipólito Sonnleithner. Hormiguero, 8 July 1849, ANA-NE 1449.

47. López (?) to Colonel Basilio Antonio Ojeda. Paso de la Patria, 15 September 1849, ANA-NE 2003.

48. The figure of 11,000 animals is derived from a cattle census taken earlier in the year. Informe of Pedro Virasoro. Santo Tomé, 9 June 1849, AGPC-EA 1849, legajo 102. On the overall destruction of the Río Uruguay settlements by Wisner's troops, see Centeno, "San Juan de Hormiguero," 159–62.

49. Cuaderno de cargo y data. Receptoría de Restauración, 1850–1851, AGPC-EA 1850–51, legajos 105–112.

50. Higinio Arbo, *Libre navegación de los ríos. Régimen jurídico de los ríos de la Plata, Paraná, y Paraguay* (Buenos Aires, 1939), pp. 114–15.

51. Treaty of Limits, Friendship, Commerce, and Navigation. Asunción, 17 July 1852, ANA-SH 298, no. 17.

52. Mantilla, *Crónica histórica,* 1:378.

53. Reglamento de Aduana. Asunción, 13 January 1842; Reglamento de la comisión del Resguardo de Aduana de la Villa de Pilar. Asunción, 17 January 1842; Reglamento [sobre] buques nacionales y extranjeros. Asunción, 19 January 1842. *El Repertorio National* 3, 5, 6, (1842).

54. Decreto of López. Asunción, 20 May 1845, ANA-SH 272, no. 9.

55. Regarding the businesses of the López family, see, for instance, Contract of Juana Carillo de López and Pedro B. Moreno. Asunción, 13 January 1864, ANA-NE 3266; and, more generally, George Thompson, *The War in Paraguay* (London, 1869), pp. 8–12.

56. Commercial reports of British consul Henderson. PRO-FO 50/13, 1854 Report; FO 59/15, 1855 Report, and General Commercial Report, dated 22 July 1856; FO 59/19, 1857 Report; FO 59/20, 1858 Report.

57. E. N. Tate, "Britain and Latin America in the Nineteenth Century: The Case of Paraguay, 1811–1870," *Ibero-Amerikanische Archiv* 5:1 (1979): 48; Alfred Marbais Du Graty, *La república del Paraguay* (Besançon, 1862), pp. 345–62.

58. Regarding the various modernization projects of the López regime, see Thomas Lyle Whigham, "The Iron-Works of Ybycui: Paraguayan Industrial Development in the Mid-Nineteenth Century," *The Americas* 35 (1978): 201–218; and, more generally, Josefina Pla, *The British in Paraguay, 1850–1870* (Richmond and Surrey, 1976), *passim*. By 1865, the López military establishment had grown to include nearly 40,000 officers and men—a substantial force that drew heavily from the national budget even during peacetime. See "Cuadro del Estado general del ejército." 1865, ANA-SH 344 no. 22; and, for an example of salaries for military men, see ANA-LC 54, entry of 11 September 1856.

59. Frank Safford, "Foreign and National Enterprise in Nineteenth Century Colombia," *Business History Review* 39 (Winter 1965): 503–526.

60. Douglas Friedman, *The State and Underdevelopment in Spanish America* (Boulder and London, 1984), p. 22.

61. Commercial Report for 1855, Consul Charles Henderson. Asunción, 22 July 1856. PRO-FO 59/15.

62. See the case of Italian merchants Giuseppe Ansaldo, Pio Posoli, and Luigi Montefirpo, arrested for the smuggling of wine, tobacco, and yerba. They were unable to pay the heavy fine of 1,000 pesos each. *El Semanario*, 11 October 1856. 1858 seems to have been a boom year for contraband activities; seven smugglers were imprisoned during that year alone. See Tabla demostrativa de los presos de la carcel pública de la capital. Asunción, 1862, ANA-SJC 1675.

63. Commercial Report for 1854, Consul Charles Henderson. Asunción, January 1855. PRO-FO 59/13. Nine years later, foreigners held 44 percent of all business licenses granted in Paraguay. Report of Mariano Gónzalez. Asunción, 13 April 1863, ANA-NE 1579.

64. Williams, *Rise and Fall*, p. 171; José Falcó to Charles Henderson. Asunción, 18 October 1855, PRO-FO 59/12.

65. Francia to Ramírez. 24 March 1824, cited in Ron Seckinger, *The Brazilian Monarchy and the South American Republics, 1822–1831* (Baton Rouge and London, 1984), p. 99.

66. David Wood, "An Artificial Frontier: Brazilian Military Colonies in Southern Mato Grosso, 1850–1867," *Pacific Coast Council on Latin American Studies. Proceedings* 3 (1974): 95–108.

67. Carlos Antonio López to Tomás Guido, Asunción, 14 January 1858. ANA-SH 261; Efraím Cardozo, *El Imperio del Brasil y el Río de la Plata* (Buenos Aires, 1961), pp. 63–64. See also John Hoyt Williams, "The Undrawn Line: Three Centuries of Strife on the Paraguayan-Mato Grosso Frontier," *Luso-Brazilian Review* 17:1 (1980): 17–40.

68. Commercial Report for 1857, Consul Charles Henderson. Asunción, 20 January 1858. PRO-FO 50/19. Thomas J. Page, *La Plata, the Argentine Confederation, and Paraguay* (New York, 1859), pp. 179–95, speaks at length of the primitive state of Mato Grossense settlements just before the opening of the Río Paraguay.

69. Cristina M. Sonzogni and Mirta Beatriz Ramírez, "La población de la ciudad de Corrientes a mediados del siglo XIX," *Cuadernos de Geohistoria Regional* 2 (1980): 21.

70. Pujol's decree of 16 November 1853 declared that all individuals without visible means of support were relegated to the peón class and ordered to obtain a *patrón*, together with a written note, on stamped paper from the district judge, attesting to the relation of peonage. Individuals who could not find a patrón had to report to the police for work assignment. Women were not excepted. See Juan Pujol, *Corrientes en la organización nacional*, 10 vols. (Buenos Aires, 1911), 3:291–94.

71. Hernán Félix Gómez, *Vida pública del Dr. Juan Pujol* (Buenos Aires, 1920), p. 123.

72. Law of 29 December 1849. ROPC VI, pp. 206–8.

73. Law of 13 October 1852. ROPC VI, pp. 444–45; "Memoria escrita por el ingeniero Nicolás Grondona con referencia a las obras del Riacho de Goya," Río de Soto, 25 January 1853, cited in Pujol, *Corrientes en la organización nacional*, 3:16–31.

74. Legal entanglements and lack of adequate infrastructure plagued the colony in its first five years, after which it was largely abandoned. See Augusto Brougnes, *La verdad sobre la colonia de San Juan. Provincia de Corrientes* (Paraná, 1860), *passim*. The Paraguayans also had a colonization scheme in the eastern Chaco. The French immigrants who came to settle the area (called Nueva Burdeos) were particularly unsuited for the harsh conditions they encountered and this experiment, too, failed. See "Sobre el establecimiento de la colonia francesa en la Nueva Burdeos." 4 May 1855, ANA-SH 314, no. 17; and "La Colonisation au Paraguay," *Annuaire des Deux Mondes* 6 (1855–56): 862–65.

75. Mariano González to López. Asunción, 13 July 1853, ANA-NE 2715, foja 25; Bando of López. Asunción, 28 July 1853, ANA-SH 306, no. 28.

76. Decree of López. Asunción, 6 August 1853, *El Semanario*, 6 August 1853; see also Decree of López. Asunción, 24 September 1853, ANA-CRB I-29, 34, 4, no. 4.

77. Sonzogni and Ramírez, "La población de la ciudad de Corrientes," 21.

78. Despacho de aduana. *El Comercio* (Corrientes), 27 January 1856.

79. Nomina de los señores socios pertenecientes a la Sala de Comercio de Corrientes. *El Comercio*, 29 November 1855. Billinghurst lived on until 1897, leaving among his descendants several important provincial officials, educators, and businessmen. For more on the Billinghurst family, see AGN censos 1869, legajo 210 (Corrientes), and M. G. and E. T. Mulhall, *River Plate Handbook, Guide, Directory, and Almanac for 1863* (Buenos Aires, 1863), pp. 187, 225.

80. Victor Silvero to Tiburcio Fonseca. Restauración, 1 June 1859, AGPC-CO 1859, legajo 104; Ernesto J. A. Maeder, "Historia y resultados del censo confederal de 1857," *Trabajos y Comunicaciones* 18 (1968): 147.

81. Espiridiao Eloy de Barros Pimentel, *Relatorio Apresentado pelo Presidente da Provincia de São Pedro do Rio Grande do Sul* (Pôrto Alegre, 1863), p. 58.

82. The activities of this salting plant, called the "Santa Candida," are described in Manuel Macchi, *Urquiza el saladerista* (Buenos Aires, 1971), *passim*.

83. E. Bradford Burns has argued that Francisco Solano López defended a viable, egalitarian, and traditional way of life in Paraguay. But López disdained the rural population, thinking it hopelessly backward. In no way did he regard himself as one of the "folk." Quite the contrary, he was enamored of everything

European. He imported large quantities of foreign luxury goods. He gave his tailors standing orders to copy the latest Parisian fashions. He spoke French whenever possible. López even attempted, through his Irish lover Eliza Lynch, to re-create a salon society in Asunción, an effort that involved some strange contradictions for all concerned. For example, at a ball hosted by López in 1864, there was no dearth of imported gowns for upper-class ladies, but alterations were next to impossible because only two sewing machines were known to exist in the city. This hardly presents a picture of balanced economic development, nor should it, for López never had such a project in mind, and neither had the Asunceño elites. The Paraguay of López, in sum, had little in it of Burns's "inorganic democracy." See Burns, "The Implication of Modernization in Nineteenth Century Latin America," in Virginia Bernhard, ed., *Elites, Masses and Modernization in Latin America, 1850–1930* (Austin and London, 1979), pp. 68–70. Regarding the conspicuous consumption of Paraguayan elites in the 1850s and 1860s, see Caio Senior, "El último baile del Mariscal," *Hoy* (Asunción), 4 December 1988; and especially Ildefonso Bermejo, *Vida paraguaya en tiempos del viejo López* (Buenos Aires, 1973), *passim*.

84. British textile manufacturers never considered Paraguayan cotton an apt substitute, despite the efforts of López. The Paraguayans went so far as to print long articles on cotton cultivation in the state newspaper and even purchased 400 copies of a pamphlet entitled *Manual para el cultivo del algodón* for distribution to farmers. See Juan José Brizuela to Francisco Sánchez. Montevideo, 15 January 1863, ANA-CRB I-30, 22, 1, no. 1.

85. Two reales the arroba was the assigned tax on all yerba grown in the province. Law of 5 April 1861. *Registro oficial de la provincia de Corrientes del año de 1861* (Corrientes, 1886), p. 30.

86. Decree of 23 September 1861. *Ibid.*, pp. 131–32; Decree of 4 November 1861. *Ibid.*, pp. 139–40.

87. H. S. Ferns, *Britain and Argentina in the Nineteenth Century* (Oxford, 1960), p. 329.

88. Mantilla, *Crónica histórica*, 2:270–73.

89. Galeano, *Open Veins*, p. 210. For more on the British conspiracy thesis, see Trías, *El Paraguay de Francia, passim*; León Pomer, *La guerra del Paraguay. Gran Negocio!* (Buenos Aires, 1968); and José Alfredo Fornos Peñalba, "The Fourth Ally: Great Britain and the War of the Triple Alliance," Ph.D. dissertation, University of California (Los Angeles, 1979). In a curious twist of irony, the British conspiracy notion has also found support among Argentine revisionist writers of the right wing. See José María Rosa, *La guerra del Paraguay y las montoneras argentinas* (Buenos Aires, 1964); Ortega Peña-Duhalde, *Baring Brothers y la historia política argentina* (Buenos Aires, 1968); and David Peña, *Alberdi, los Mitristas y la guerra de la Triple Alianza* (Buenos Aires, 1965).

90. Juan Carlos Herken Krauer and María Isabel Giménez de Herken, *Gran Bretaña y la guerra de la Triple Alianza* (Asunción, 1982).

91. F. J. McLynn, "The Causes of the War of the Triple Alliance: An Interpretation," *Inter-American Economic Affairs* 33:2 (1979): 21–43; see also Diego Abente, "The War of the Triple Alliance: Three Explanatory Models," *Latin American Research Review* 22:2 (1987): 47–69.

92. *El Semanario*, 4 February 1865. Paraguayan intentions to maintain free commercial access to Mato Grosso for ships of friendly nations had been guaranteed by Foreign Minister José Berges in 1864 but were never acted upon. Berges to Charles Washburn. Asunción, 17 November 1864, ANA-CRB I-22, 11, 1, no. 456.

93. George Frederick Masterman, *Seven Eventful Years in Paraguay* (London, 1870), pp. 98–99.

94. Efraím Cardozo, *Hace cien años*, 13 vols. (Asunción, 1967–83), 2:21.

95. Walter Spalding, *A Invasão Paraguaia no Brasil* (São Paulo, 1940), p. 328.

96. João Pedro Gay, *Invasão Paraguaia na Fronteira Brasileira do Uruguai* (Caxias do Sul, 1980), pp. 98–103.

97. Urquiza to Mitre, Concepción del Uruguay, 19 April 1864, cited in Pelham Horton Box, *The Origins of the Paraguayan War* (New York, 1967), p. 268.

98. Wenceslao Paunero to J. A. Gelly y Obes. Campos de Possoa, 18 June 1865, AGN-DBN 15.537, legajo 758.

99. A. J. Kennedy, *La Plata, Brazil, and Paraguay during the Present War* (London, 1869), pp. 36–37.

100. Kennedy remarked that "the description of the Paraguayan campaign in Corrientes reads like an incursion of devils, for there was no opposition, no fighting, to excite their fury; all was done in cold blood, under López's immediate and personal command." *Ibid.*, p. 37. For further testimony on the conduct of the Paraguayans, see Richard F. Burton, *Letters from the Battlefields of Paraguay* (London, 1870), pp. 261–62.

101. Burton, *Letters from the Battlefields*, p. 285. Roberto Billinghurst, incidentally, escaped southward rather than deal with the Paraguayan officials, many of whom were his personal friends.

102. *El Independiente* (Corrientes), 18 May 1865.

103. Mantilla, *Crónica histórica*, 2:278.

104. 100,000 head of confiscated cattle accompanied the Paraguayans on their retreat across the river to Humaitá. Thompson, *The War in Paraguay*, p. 97.

105. *Ibid.*, p. 64.

106. AGN Censo 1869, legajos 210–212.

107. F. J. McLynn, "The Corrientes Crisis of 1868," *North Dakota Quarterly* 47:3 (Summer 1979): 45–58.

108. Charles J. Kolinski, *Independence or Death! The Story of the Paraguayan War* (Gainesville, 1965), p. 198. The magnitude of the demographic disaster has recently been called into question, but little hard data has been supplied to contradict the large volume of anecdotal evidence supporting a high death toll. See Vera Blinn Reber, "The Demographics of Paraguay: A Reinterpretation of the Great War, 1864–1870," *Hispanic American Historical Review* 68 (May 1988): 289–319.

Chapter Three

1. Adalberto López, "The Economics of Yerba Mate in Seventeenth-Century South America," *Agricultural History*, 48:4 (1974): 498–99.

2. Magnus Mörner, *The Political and Economic Activities of the Jesuits in the La Plata Region. The Hapsburg Era* (Stockholm, 1953), p. 129. Some of the restrictive laws regarding yerba shipment are listed in AGN IX (Compañía de Jesús) 7-1-1, no. 576. See also Juan Carlos Garavaglia, "Un modo de produción subsidiario: la organización económica de las comunidades guaranizadas durante los siglos XVII-XVIII en la formación regional altoperuano-rioplatense," *Cuadernos de Pasado y Presente* 40 (1973): 161–91.

3. This jealously provoked regional violence on several occasions during this period. Adalberto López, *The Revolt of the Comuneros, 1721–1735: A Study in the Colonial History of Paraguay* (Cambridge, 1976); James Schofield Saeger, "Origins of the Rebellion of Paraguay," *Hispanic American Historical Review* 52 (May 1972): 215–29. Regarding Corrientes, see Mantilla, *Crónica histórica,* 1:89–92; Raúl de Labougle, *Historia de los Comuneros* (Buenos Aires, 1953), *passim.*

4. Cited in Nicolas P. Cushner, *Lords of the Land. Sugar, Wine, and the Jesuit Estates of Coastal Peru, 1600–1767* (Albany, 1980), p. 160.

5. Magnus Mörner, "The Expulsion of the Jesuits from Spain and Spanish America in 1767 in Light of Eighteenth-Century Regalism," *The Americas* 23 (October 1966): 156–64.

6. Félix de Azara to Viceroy Marqués de Avilés, 8 May 1799. Cited in White, *Paraguay's Autonomous Revolution,* p. 28.

7. José M. Mariluz Urquijo, "Los guaraníes después de la expulsión de los jesuitas," *Estudios Americanos* 6 (1953): 323–30; Ramón Gutiérrez, "Los pueblos jesuíticos del Paraguay: reflexiones sobre su decadencia," *Suplemento Antropológico* 14 (December 1979): 179–99.

8. V. Martin de Moussy, "Memoire Historique sur la Decadence et la Ruine des Misiones des Jesuites dans la bassin de la Plata—leur Etat Actuel," in *Description Geographique et Statistique de la Confédération Argentine,* 3 vols. (Paris, 1864), 3:656–716.

9. Azara, *Descripción e historia del Paraguay,* 1:313; Lynch, *Spanish Colonial Administration,* pp. 164–66; Jerry W. Cooney, "An Ignored Aspect of the Viceroyalty of the Río del la Plata," *Intercambio Internacional* 2 (January 1977): 10–13. A recent analysis of the Buenos Aires receptoría suggests that the amount of Paraguayan yerba imported during these years was about one-third less than that recorded in the Paraguayan export statistics. The difference is probably due to spoilage, and more important, to transshipment to other markets. See Claudia Wentzel, "El comercio del Litoral de los ríos con Buenos Aires: el area del Paraná, 1783–1821," *Anuario del IEHS* 3, (1988): 208.

10. Marqués de Sobremonte to Miguel Cayetano Soler, Buenos Aires, 29 August 1804, MG 294; see also Germán O. E. Tjarks, *El Consulado de Buenos Aires y sus proyecciones en la historia del Río de la Plata,* 2 vols. (Buenos Aires, 1962), 2:823–24.

11. See, for example, "Expediente relativo al fomento de la población de Belén y fundación de una estancia en sus tierras, 1768–1771," ANA-SH 136, no. 15. Regarding the northeastern boundary with Brazil, see Félix de Azara, *Correspondencia oficial e inédita sobre la demarcación de límites entre el Paraguay y el Brasil, 1784–1795* (Buenos Aires, 1836), *passim.*

12. Robertson, *Letters on Paraguay*, 3:136.
13. *Ibid.*, 3:136–37.
14. *Ibid.*, 3:142–145; Page, *La Plata, The Argentine Confederation, and Paraguay*, pp. 585–86.
15. López, "The Economics of Yerba Mate," 501; Mariano Antonio Molas, *Descripción histórica de la antigua provincia del Paraguay* (Asunción, 1957), p. 63.
16. Robertson, *Letters*, 2:150.
17. Regarding changadores, see Manuel Gutiérrez to Commandant of Concepción. 15 December 1807, ANA-SH 203, no. 4; and José Espinola, commandant of Concepción, to Governor-Intendant Eustaquio Giannini. Concepción, 10 February 1809, ANA-SH 366.
18. Demanda contra Juan Bautista Almada. Concepción, 30 September 1806, ANA-SJC 1740. Saloons and travelling bordellos were apparently present in the yerbales until at least the 1840s, when one official complained that the yerbateros had given themselves over to "the sordid and indecorous pleasures of the flesh"; see Pedro Ignacio Franco to Carlos Antonio López. Tacuatí, November (?) 1848, ANA-SJC 1514.
19. Azara, *Viajes inéditos*, p. 210.
20. Agustín Fernando de Pinedo, "Informe del gobernador del Paraguay a S. M. el Rey de España," *Revista del Instituto Paraguayo* 6 (1905): 5–6.
21. Azara, *Descripción e historia*, 1:313–14.
22. As late as 1819, regular shipments of yerba were still being sent from Paraguay to Chile via the old Santa Fé route. See José Tomás Ysasi to Administrador de Aduana. Buenos Aires, 29 April 1819, ABPBA 031, 6–2, no. 9.
23. Carlos de Ysasi to Francia. San Pedro, 16 November 1815, ANA-SH 382, no. 4; see also John Hoyt Williams, "The Deadly Selva. Paraguay's Northern Indian Frontier," *The Americas* 33 (July 1976): 1–24.
24. John Hoyt Williams, "Tevegó on the Paraguayan Frontier: A Chapter in the Black History of the Americas," *Journal of Negro History* 56 (October 1971): 72–84.
25. Decree of Francia. Asunción, 12 September 1823, ANA-SH 231.
26. White, *Paraguay's Autonomous Revolution*, pp. 158–60.
27. See Commodore Thomas Hardy to John Wilson Croker, M. P. HMS *Creole* (off Buenos Aires), 22 December 1820, in Graham and Humphreys, eds., *The Navy and South America*, pp. 322–23.
28. *British Packet and Argentine News*, 22 November 1828.
29. For Paraguay, see Solicitud of José Ignacio Gómez. San Estanislao, 7 February 1818, ANA-NE 3228; Francia to the Administrator of Caazapa. Asunción, 11 August 1837, ANA-SH 243, no. 6. For Corrientes, see "Ley autorizando el benefico de la yerba maté." Corrientes, 29 October 1832, ROPC III, pp. 103–4; Decree of Pedro Ferré. Corrientes, 9 November 1832, *ibid.*, pp. 140–42. Both Correntino decrees refer to yerbales located in the most distant reaches of Misiones in an area disputed between Paraguay and Corrientes.
30. The internal trade involved hundreds of yerbateros. See "Guías otorgados." Curuguaty, 1831–32, ANA-NE 2583, 2584. License fees and taxes of all kinds were often paid in yerba. See, for example, Receptoría de la Villa de San Isidro. 1832–33, ANA-NE 1863.
31. Manifestos of Mariano Rivas. Curuzú Cuatiá, 9 February 1830 and 15 Feb-

ruary 1830, AGPC-EA 1830, legajo 29. Similar documentation exists for March 1833. See AGPC-EA 1833, legajo 38.

32. Francia to Delegado of Itapúa. Asunción, 14 June 1828, ANA-SH 240, no. 2. Price fluctuations were generally recorded in the various government gazettes throughout the period under discussion. For Buenos Aires, see *La Gaceta Mercantil* (1823–52) and *British Packet and Argentine News* (1828–48); for Corrientes, see *El Pacificador* (1846), *Corrientes Confederada* (1848), *La Organización Nacional* (1851), *La Libre Navegación de los Ríos* (1853), *El Comercio* (1854–57), *La Opinión* (1857–59), *La Unión Argentina* (1860), *La Nueva Epoca* (1861), *La Libertad* (1862), and *El Progreso* (1863–65); for Paraguay, see *El Semanario de Avisos y Conocimientos Utiles* (1853–68).

33. Cited in Temistocles Linhares, *Historia Económica do Mate* (Rio de Janiero, 1969), p. 84. For details on the Paranaguá yerba trade, see Cecilia Maria Westphalen, "O Porto de Paranaguá no Ano de 1826," *Boletim da Universidade do Paraná* 2 (December 1962): 1–47; Westphalen, "Paranaguá et le Rio de la Plata au XIXe Siècle," *L'Histoire Quantitative du Brésil de 1800 a 1930* (Paris, 1973): 315–34; and Antonio dos Santos Vieira, *Memoria Histórica da Cidade de Paranaguá e seu Municipio* [1850] (Curitiba, 1952).

34. Juan de la Cruz Maydana to the Receptor de Alcabalas. Curuzú Cuatiá, 26 January 1830, AGPC-EA 1830, legajo 28, noting the passage of four sacks of yerba from Itaqui via the Uruguay river to Curuzú Cuatiá.

35. Decree of Pedro Ferré. Corrientes, 1 February 1833, ROPC III, p. 187.

36. Decree of Rafael Atienza. Corrientes, 24 January 1834, ROPC III, p. 224.

37. For example, see Proceso contra Alejandro Caballero (for having transported 368 arrobas of yerba from the city of Rosario without proper license). Limpio, 8 August 1837, ANA-SJC 1711.

38. *British Packet and Argentine News*, 16 July 1842.

39. "Cuaderno de anotaciones de patentes." 1843, ANA-NE 1355.

40. For an 1841 example, see Carlos Antonio López to Commandant of Pilar. Asunción, 19 April 1841, ANA-SH 247, no. 1.

41. Carlos Antonio López to Colector general. Asunción, 22 August 1844, ANA-NE 798.

42. Charles Gary Lobb, "The Historical Geography of the Cattle Regions along Brazil's Southern Frontier," Ph.D. dissertation, University of California (Berkeley, 1970), 148.

43. Decree of Minister of State Domingos José de Almeida. Piratini, 4 April 1830, O Povo (Piratini) 20 October 1838. In this same decree, the importation of armaments was also freed from duties.

44. *Ibid.*, (Caçapava) 10 October 1839.

45. Decree of Carlos Antonio López. Asunción, 2 January 1846, *El Repertorio Nacional* (Asunción), 1846.

46. Adam Smith was the first to outline the injurious effect of monopolies such as that of the Paraguayan government. He demonstrated how such arrangements allow for only transitory profits while, in the long run, monopoly regulations harm the country that establishes them more than others. See *An Inquiry into the Nature and Causes of the Wealth of Nations* (New York, 1965), pp. 592–606.

47. Rosas reduced import duties by one-third. Lynch, *Argentine Dictator*, pp. 149–50.

48. Decree of Carlos Antonio López. 7 October 1848, ANA-SH 282, no. 24.

49. Carlos Pastore, *La lucha por la tierra en el Paraguay* (Montevideo, 1972), pp. 127–32. The Marxist historian Oscar Creydt argues that the seizure of the pueblos liquidated the remnant of a preexisting feudal order. By transforming the Indians into wage-laborers, López set the stage for the growth of capitalism in the country. Thus, according to Creydt, the 1848 decree was a progressive reform, irrespective of the fact that such "progress was achieved at the expense of the masses." Creydt, *Formación histórica de la nación paraguaya* (1963), pp. 42–43.

50. Regarding continued Indian difficulties in the yerbales and the need for troops, see Benedicto Cardoso to Carlos Antonio López. Villarrica, 9 August 1843, ANA-SH 403. For a description of soldiers used as yerbateros, see Page, *La Plata, the Argentine Confederation and Paraguay*, pp. 136–37.

51. Decree of López and Mariano Roque Alonso. Asunción, 5 July 1842, ANA-SCD 26, no. 35.

52. Decree of López. Asunción, 16 September 1848, ANA-SH 282, no. 18.

53. See, for example, Demanda of Gaspar Otazú. Asunción, 10 July 1858, ANA-SJC 1976.

54. Robert Ave-Lallement, *Viagem pelo sul do Brasil ao Ano de 1858*, 2 vols. (Rio de Janeiro, 1953), 2:254; Antonio Eleuterio de Camargo, *Quadro Estadístico e Geográphico da Provincia do São Pedro do Rio Grande do Sul* (Pôrto Alegre, 1868), p. 112.

55. Treaty of Limits, Friendship, Commerce, and Navigation with the Argentine Confederation. Asunción, 15 July 1852, ANA-SH 298, no. 17.

56. Aimé Bompland to Governor and Captain-General Juan Pujol. São Borja, 14 January 1853; Bompland to Pujol. Restauración, 9 March 1854, cited in Pujol, *Corrientes en la organización nacional*, 3:9–11 and 4:68–71. Misionera yerba subsequently became of primary importance to the Porteño market. See Alfredo S. C. Bolsi, "El primer siglo de la economía yerbatera en Argentina," *Folia Histórica del Nordeste* 4 (1980): 119–82.

57. *La Opinión* (Corrientes), 16 December 1857.

58. G. F. Morice to Francisco Solano López. Buenos Aires, 26 December 1859, ANA-CRB I-29, 34, 30, no. 12. Regarding the success of yerba de Paranaguá in the Porteño market at this time, see *Los Debates*, 2–3 January 1858.

59. The monopoly control exercised by the state over Paraguayan yerba (and, thus, over its pricing) was extremely controversial. Foreign observers nearly always condemned it. See William Hadfield, *Brazil and the River Plate in 1868* (London, 1869), pp. 213–14. The Paraguayan government, for its part, went out of its way to deemphasize the monopoly, claiming that it did not hinder trade. *El Semanario*, 24 June 1857.

60. Annual Report on the Commerce, Industry, and Agriculture of Paraguay for the year 1855. Consul Charles A. Henderson. Asunción, 3 February 1856, PRO-FO 59/15.

61. Linhares, *Historia Económica do Mate*, p. 129.

62. Decree of Carlos Antonio López. Asunción, 28 April 1860, ANA-SH 329, no. 4. Negotiations to obtain 5,000 head of Correntino cattle in exchange for

yerba had begun in 1859. See War Minister Francisco Solano López to Colector General Luis Caminos. Humaitá, 30 September 1859, cited in Livieres Argaña, *Con la rúbrica del Mariscal*, 6:738.

63. Decree of Carlos Antonio López. Asunción, 7 June 1862, ANA-SH 331, no. 1; Marbais Du Graty, *La república del Paraguay*, p. 361.

64. "Registro de libranzas de yerba." ANA-NE 1693; "Beneficios de yerba." Asunción, 16 July 1864, ANA-NE 2303.

65. J. and A. Blyth to Francisco Solano López. London, 8 September 1857, ANA-CRB I-29, 35, 36, no. 26. In 1864, the Paraguayans tried to interest Bismarck in the tea, and 5,000 pounds of it were actually delivered for the use of the Prussian army. See José Berges to Candido Bareiro. Asunción, 21 July 1864, ANA-CRB I-22, 11, 5, no. 381.

66. For examples of yerba sales in Montevideo and Buenos Aires, see Félix Egusquiza to Francisco Solano López. Buenos Aires, 15 October 1862, MG 2010a; see also "Correspondencia comercial." Buenos Aires, 17 Octoberr 1863, in *El Semanario*, 13 October 1863.

67. Mariano González to Inspector of Ports Francisco Bareiro. Asunción, 23 August 1864, ANA-NE 2790, foja 61.

68. "Los yerbales argentinas," *La Unión Argentina*, 25 March 1860; Martin de Moussy, *Description Geographique et Statistique*, 1:428–34. See also Vicente G. Quesada to Juan Pujol. Buenos Aires, 21 December 1857, cited in Pujol, *Corrientes en la Organización nacional*, 7:192–94.

Chapter Four

1. Cardozo, *El Paraguay colonial*, pp. 103–4. Governor Jaime San Just in the 1750s brought Brazilian specialists to Paraguay in an attempt to stimulate tobacco production. One of these men was the father of the future Dictator, José Gaspar de Francia. Antonio Zinny, *Historia de los gobernantes del Paraguay, 1535–1887* (Buenos Aires, 1887), pp. 179–80.

2. Fulgencio R. Moreno, *Estudio sobre la independencia del Paraguay* (Asunción, 1912), pp. 45–51.

3. E. de Bourgade la Dardye, *Paraguay: The Land and the People, Natural Wealth and Commercial Capabilities* (London, 1892), pp. 185–87. The author noted that "when raised upon black earth, tobacco never has any aroma; but in Paraguay it is always grown upon the red earth, and there is the best security of its being of superior quality. Connoisseurs are unanimous in praising its delicate flavor." The red coloration of Paraguayan soil results from a high iron content.

4. Bourgade, *Paraguay*, pp. 185–87. Also see "Reconocimiento y clasificación del tabaco paraguayo." Asunción, 17 June 1865, ANA-SH, vol. 334.

5. Bourgade assigned the following nicotine levels: pito, 2.5 percent; buena, 4 percent; doble, 5 percent; and para, 6 or 7 percent. Bourgade, *Paraguay*, pp. 185–87. Nicotine levels for Cuban tobacco are given in Fernando Ortíz, *Contrapunto cubano del tabaco y el azúcar* (Caracas, 1978), pp. 97–100.

6. The landholding system of the Upper Plata in the late colonial era con-

sisted of chacras (small to medium-sized farms), arrendamientos (leaseholds), estancias (ranches), and community-owned Indian holdings. See Carlos Pastore, *La lucha por la tierra en el Paraguay* (Montevideo, 1972), *passim*.

7. Cam Harlan Wickam, "Venezuela's Royal Tobacco Monopoly, 1779–1810: An Economic Analysis," Ph.D. dissertation, University of Oregon, 1975), 43–52; Harold A. Bierck, "Tobacco Marketing in Venezuela, 1789–1799: An Aspect of Spanish Mercantilistic Revisionism," *Business History Review* 39 (Winter 1965): 489–502; Marco Antonio Fallas, *La factoría de tabacos de Costa Rica* (San José, 1972), pp. 57–63.

8. "Bando . . . comunicando la creación del Estanco de Tabaco y Naipes," Intendente de la Real Hacienda Manuel Fernández, Montevideo, 4 August 1778, in Facultad de Filosofía y Letras, *Documentos para la historia del Río de la Plata* (Buenos Aires, 1912), 2:236–37. For the Royal Monopoly in New Spain, see Eduardo Arcila Farías, *Reformas económicas del siglo XVIII. Nueva España. Industria. Minería y Real Hacienda*, 2 vols. (Mexico, 1974), 2:113–38.

9. C. H. Haring, *The Spanish Empire in America* (New York, 1947), pp. 294–95. Also see Guillermo Céspedes del Castillo, "La renta de tabaco en el virreinato del Peru," *Revista Histórica* 21 (1954): 138–63; Edilberto de Jesús, *The Tobacco Monopoly in the Philippines: Bureaucratic Enterprise and Social Change, 1766–1880* (Quezon City, 1980); José Rivero Muñiz, *Tabaco: Su historia en Cuba*, 2 vols. (La Habana, 1964–65); and Agnes Stapff, "La renta de tabaco en Chile de la época virreinal," *Anuario de Estudios Americanos* 18 (1961): 1–63. The situation was not dramatically different in colonial North America; see Jacob M. Price, *France and the Chesapeake: A History of the French Tobacco Monopoly, 1674–1791* (Ann Arbor, 1973), and, more generally, Joseph C. Robert, *The Story of Tobacco in America* (New York, 1949). For an amusing account of tobacco lore generally, see G. Cabrera Infante, *Holy Smoke* (London and Boston, 1985).

10. Herbert Ingram Priestly, *José de Gálvez. Visitor-General of New Spain 1765–1771* (Berkeley, 1916), pp. 142–55.

11. The best survey of the real renta in Paraguay is Jerry W. Cooney, *Paraguay and the Royal Tobacco Monopoly, 1779–1810*, unpublished ms. (University of Louisville, 1990).

12. *Ibid.*; Daisy Ripodas Ardañas, *Francisco de Paula Sanz. Viaje por el virreinato del Río de la Plata. El camino de tabaco* (Buenos Aires, 1977), pp. 5–16, 30–46; Juan Carlos Arías Divito, "Establecimiento de la Renta de tabaco y naipes en el vireinato del Río de la Plata, 1778–1781," *Historiografía Rioplatense*, 1 (1978): 15–26; as well as his "Dificultades para establecer la Renta de Tabaco en Paraguay," *Anuario de Estudios Americanos* 33 (1976): 1–17.

13. Paula Sanz was, in fact, a favorite protegé of Gálvez, and in Buenos Aires rumor had it that he was an illegitimate son of the minister. John Lynch, *Spanish Colonial Administration, 1782–1810. The Intendant System in the Viceroyalty of the Río de la Plata* (London, 1958), p. 298.

14. Decree of Director General Francisco de Paula Sanz, Asunción, 8 May 1779, ANA-SH, 143. The Upper Plata was hardly unique in such prohibitions. In New Granada, contraband sales were impaired by restricting the cultivation of tobacco to four small and relatively compact areas that were easy to police. John P. Harrison, "The Evolution of the Colombian Tobacco Trade, to 1875," *Hispanic American Historical Review* 32 (May 1952): 165.

15. Decree of Paula Sanz, Asunción, 29 March 1779, ANA-SH, 143; and Cabildo of Asunción to Viceroy Manuel Vertiz. Asunción, 23 April(?) 1779, ANA-NE, 89.

16. Governor-Intendant Pedro Melo de Portugal to Minister of the Indies José de Gálvez. Asunción, 13 June 1779, ANA-SH, 144; Moreno, Estudio, 1:61–65. Brazil exported torcido negro to Africa where it was a barter item in the slave trade. Fernand Braudel, Civilization and Capitalism 15th-18th Century (New York, 1981), vol. 1, The Structures of Everyday Life, the Limits of the Possible, 265.

17. Royal Treasury Minister Martin José Aramburu to Director General Paula Sanz. Asunción, 10 September 1783, ANA-SH 142.

18. The powers given renta officials disturbed Governor-Intendant Melo de Portugal. Melo de Portugal to Vertiz. Asunción, 13 July 1779, ANA-SH 144.

19. Juan Francisco de Aguirre, "Diario del capitán de Fragata . . .," Revista de la Biblioteca Nacional de Buenos Aires 28 (1949), 372–77.

20. Viceroy Marqués de Loreto to Fray Antonio Valdez. Buenos Aires, 25 November 1789, MG doc. 859.

21. "Estado que manifiesta los efectos y caudales perteneciente a la Real Renta de tabacos." Antonio Pablo Morin, Buenos Aires, 24 April 1795, MG 16d.

22. Maeder, Historia económica de Corrientes, pp. 352–61.

23. Dispatch of José Fernández Blanco. Corrientes, 25 April 1780, AGPC-DG, libro 22 (1780).

24. Juan José González to Lázaro de Ribera. Asunción, 9 March 1798, ANA-SH 171.

25. The patrones of the river vessels often misrepresented the number of crew members, thus augmenting the ration of tobacco for illegal sale. See letters of 13 August 1779, 25 April 1780, and 24 May 1780. AGPC-DG 21 (1779) and 22 (1780).

26. Maeder, Historia económica de Corrientes, p. 357.

27. AGPC-DG 31 (1791) and 32 (1792–93). These books constitute a massive compendium on smuggled tobacco in Corrientes.

28. At only one guardpost near Corrientes, 1,539 arrobas were confiscated in 1809 and another 2,144 a year later. Yet all reports indicate that these seizures were slight when compared to the amount of tobacco that slipped through. AGPC-DG 42 (1809). Cooney argues that the clandestine trade was equal, if not superior in volume, to that of the renta.

29. "Expendiente sobre el excesivo número de los matriculados." Asunción, 1803, ANA-NE 3399.

30. Disposition of José Fernández Blanco. Corrientes, 29 May 1801, AGPC-DC 36 (1800–1802).

31. Félix de Azara, Viajes inéditos (Buenos Aires, 1873), p. 45.

32. Dispatch of 7 October 1789. AGN IX.3.4.1.

33. "Informe sobre las factorías y cultivo de tabaco en el Paraguay," Azara, Memoria, pp. 129–32; and in same work, "Informe sobre los tabacos del Paraguay que surten a la real hacienda en el virreinato de Buenos Aires," 154–59.

34. Decree of Congress, Asunción, 22 June 1811, ANA-SH, 214. Regarding the Paraguayan independence movement, see Luis Vittone, El Paraguay en la lucha por su independencia (Asunción, 1960), passim.

35. It should be noted that not all of the new Spanish American regimes immediately abolished the estanco. In Mexico, where the institution endured until

the mid-1840s, returns were still large at the time of independence and only gradually declined thereafter. In Colombia, the tobacco monopoly became an important symbolic issue for those favoring free trade, and it was not terminated until 1850. As for Cuba and the Philippines, both of which remained under Spanish colonial rule, we see widely divergent developments. In the former, the estanco died an early death in 1817; in the latter, the institution lingered on until 1880. Priestly, *José de Gálvez*, p. 154; Luis F. Sierra, *El tabaco en la economía colombiana del siglo XIX* (Mosquera, 1971), pp. 87–99; Rivero Muñiz, *Tabaco*, 2:229–40; de Jesús, *The Tobacco Monopoly*, pp. 178–96.

36. Treaty of Friendship, Union, and Borders between Paraguay and Buenos Aires. Asunción, 12 October 1811, in Benjamín Vargas Peña, *Paraguay-Argentina. Correspondencia dipomática, 1810–1840* (Buenos Aires, 1945), pp. 63–66.

37. For relations between Paraguay and Buenos Aires in this era, see Chaves, *Historia de las relaciones entre Buenos Aires y el Paraguay*, passim. For the tobacco "war" between Asunción and Buenos Aires, see Marcela González de Martínez, "El tabaco en la guerra económica contra Paraguay y Santa Fé," in *Tercer Congreso de Historia Argentine y Regional* (Buenos Aires, 1977), 4:329–36.

38. "Guías de Aduana . . . 1819." AGN X-36-1-18.

39. Miron Burgin, *The Economic Aspects of Argentine Federalism, 1820–1852* (Cambridge, Mass., 1946), p. 71.

40. *El Semanario*, 20 August 1853, claimed a 45,000 arroba a year export figure for the 1830s. Alfred Demersay, *Du tabac au Paraguay* (Paris, 1851), pp. 24–27, makes the same claim. The source for both appears to be Aimé Bompland, who depended on guesswork. Robertson, *Letters on Paraguay*, 3:216–18 suggests 40,000 arrobas for the year 1816. Although a reasonable guess, it overestimated the total export by nearly 7,000 arrobas. Perhaps the wildest figure of all was given by the Brazilian diplomat Antonio Manoel Correia da Camara after a brief visit to Paraguay in 1829. He asserted that that republic could within two years of being "opened" to foreign trade produce 800,000 arrobas of unprocessed tobacco a year and 300,000 arrobas of cigars. Antônio Manoel Correia da Camara, "Calculo Aproximado dos Effeitos e Producçcões do Paraguai." Rio de Janeiro, 1 May 1820. Ministerio das Relações Esteriores, *Anais do Itamarati* (Rio do Janiero, 1938), 4:83–85.

41. See Inventories of Portuguese Smugglers. Asunción, May of 1819, ANA-SPT 931.

42. Five smugglers had been executed the previous summer. Williams, "Paraguayan Isolation," 108–10. Also see José Tomás Gil to Francia. Pilar, 28 May 1826, ANA-SH 238; and "Multas." Pilar, 24 August 1827, ANA-LC 27.

43. Williams, *Rise and Fall*, p. 92.

44. "La ley de aduana para 1836," in José M. Mariluz Urquijo, ed., *Estado y industria, 1810–1870* (Buenos Aires, 1969), p. 118.

45. Juan Manuel de Rosas to Governor Rafael Atienza of Corrientes. Buenos Aires, 20 July 1836, in Ricardo Levene, ed., *Historia de la nación argentina*. 2nd ed. (Buenos Aires, 1950), 7:182–83.

46. Alcides D'Orbigny, *Viaje a la América meridional*, 3 vols. (Buenos Aires, 1945), 1:232–33.

47. ROPC III: 106–7 (Law of 15 December 1832).

48. Treaty of 31 July 1841. Asunción, ANA-SH 245; and "Decreto sobre impuestos a la importación de tabaco, yerba y aguardiente del Paraguay." Corrientes, 23 July 1841, El Nacional Correntino, 23 August 1841.

49. Report of George J. R. Gordon. 1843. PRO-FO 13/202.

50. Secretary of State James Buchanan to Charge d'Affaires William A. Harris. Washington, 30 March 1846, in William R. Manning, ed., Diplomatic Correspondence of the United States, Inter-American Affairs, 12 vols. (Washington, D.C., 1932–39), 1:29–32.

51. The role of Hopkins in the economic and political life of Paraguay has been much debated. See Harold F. Peterson, "Edward Augustus Hopkins: A Pioneer Promoter in Paraguay," Hispanic American Historical Review 22 (May 1942): 245–61; and Pablo Max Ynsfrán, La expedición norteamericana contra el Paraguay, 1858–1859, 2 vols. (Mexico, 1954 and 1958), 1:41–104.

52. Rengger and Longchamp, The Reign of Doctor Joseph Gaspard Roderick de Francia in Paraguay, p. 199; Anon., "Manufacture of Tobacco in Paraguay," Hunt's Merchants Magazine (New York) 20 (1849): 353–54.

53. Juan Andrés Gelly to J. A. Gelly y Obes. Asunción, 5 August 1845, AGN-DBN, 15060, legajo 756.

54. Lynch, Argentine Dictator, pp. 149–50. Also see Tulio Halperín Donghi, Guerra y finanzas en los orígenes del estado argentino, 1791–1850 (Buenos Aires, 1982), pp. 237–42.

55. "Resumen de exportación de la república del año de 1845." ANA-SH 274.

56. "Frutos extraídos de Pilar." 20 March 1847 to 30 September 1848, ANA-NE 866.

57. See Hopkins, "The Republic of Paraguay," 255–56.

58. Charles A. Washburn, The History of Paraguay, With Notes of Personal Observations and Reminiscences of Diplomacy Under Difficulties, 2 vols. (Boston, 1871), 1:362.

59. Ibid. See also La Libre Navegación de los Ríos, 8 July 1853.

60. Hopkins was allowed to transport some 800 arrobas of tobacco out of the country when he left. Washburn, History of Paraguay, 1:368.

61. Juan Andrés Gelly to J. A. Gelly y Obes. Rio Grande, 17 August 1848, AGN-DBN 15086, legajo 756. See also Juan Andrés Gelly, El Paraguay: lo que fue, lo que es, y lo que será (Paris, 1926), pp. 137–38.

62. Decree of Carlos Antonio López. Asunción, 21 February 1856, ANA-SH 319. In this respect, the López government arrogated to itself some of the functions of the old estanco.

63. Decree of Carlos Antonio López. Asunción, 16 January 1855, ANA-SH 314.

64. El Semanario, 3 May 1856.

65. Demersay, Du Tabac, pp. 25–27.

66. A Report of the Trade of Paraguay for the year 1857, Consul Charles Henderson. Asunción, 20 January 1858, PRO-FO 59/19.

67. A Report of the Trade of Paraguay for the year 1858, Consul Charles Henderson. Asunción, 20 January 1859, PRO-FO 59/20.

68. Marbais Du Graty, La República del Paraguay, p. 326.

69. John and Alfred Blyth to Francisco Solano López. London, 8 October 1857, ANA-CRB I-29, 35, 56, no. 27. On the open market in Britain, Paraguayan tobacco was selling for nine to ten and one-quarter pence a pound.

70. John and Alfred Blyth to Francisco Solano López. London, 8 August 1857, ANA-CRB I-29, 35, 56, no. 23.

71. Consul Ludovico Tenré to Foreign Minister José Berges. Paris, 24 August 1863, ANA-CRB I-20, 36, 54, no. 1. Notes of Alfredo Marbais Du Graty. Brussels, 7 September 1863, ANA-CRB I-29, 31, 9, nos. 1–2; and John and Alfred Blyth to Minister of War Venancio López. London, 25 March 1864, ANA-CRB I-30, 2, 18, no. 1.

72. Decree of Carlos Antonio López. Asunción, 6 March 1858, ANA-SH 324. Another decree, specific to the port of Itapúa (now Encarnación), reinforced the classification system. Disposition of Treasury Minister Mariano González. Asunción, 4 August 1862, ANA-SH 331.

73. "Razón de los frutos estraídos, año 1855." *El Comercio*, 6 January 1856.

74. Quesada, *La provincia de Corrientes*, p. 57.

75. *La Libertad*, 14 August 1862.

76. *El Progreso*, 13 December 1863; 17 January 1864. Argentine recognition of Paraguayan independence in 1852 brought with it a reclassification of Paraguayan tobacco as foreign rather than domestic produce. For an analysis of the Correntino tobacco trade in subsequent years, see Cristina M. Sonzogni, "Evolución de la actividad tabacalera en Corrientes y en Misiones (1870–1940)," *Cuadernos de Geohistoria Regional* 8 (1983): *passim*.

77. See *El Semanario*, 4 February through 6 July 1865.

78. *El Semanario*, 8 July 1865.

79. Several Bolivian merchants arrived in Asunción in 1867 after having crossed the Altiplano to Mato Grosso on their way to Paraguay. Tobacco was one of the several products they wished to obtain. *El Semanario*, 24 August 1867.

80. In this the Paraguayans were relatively successful. Utilizing a much reduced labor force, farmers planted many thousands of rows of manioc, maize, and beans in the interior between 1865 and the end of the war. Agricultural censuses produced during this period, for all their excessive optimism, demonstrated an impressive output. Olinda Massare de Kostianovsky, *El vice-presidente Domingo Francisco Sanchez* (Asunción, 1972), pp. 85–100, 193–96; and Moises S. Bertoni, "La agricultura en el Paraguay antes de la guerra de 1864–1870. Datos instructivos," *Cuadernos Republicanos* 18 (1981): 117–41.

Chapter Five

1. Ernesto J. A. Maeder, "La evolución de la ganadería en Corrientes (1810–1854)," *Cuadernos de Estudios Regionales* 4 (1983): 10.

2. Jaime Cortesão, ed., *Do Tratado de Madri a Conquista dos Sete Povos (1750–1802)* (Rio de Janeiro, 1969), *passim*; Tulio Halperin Donghi, *Politics, Economics and Society in Argentina in the Revolutionary Period* (Cambridge, 1975), pp. 16–19.

3. Félix de Azara, *Memoria sobre el estado rural del Río de la Plata en 1801* (Madrid, 1947), p. 8.

4. Informe of Cabildo [1701]. AGPC-AC 13 (1698–1704).

5. Bando of the gobernador Manuel Prado Maldonado. 14 July 1701, AGPC-AC 13 (1698–1704); Gobernador Baltasar García Ros to Cabildo of Corrientes. 28 March 1716, AGPC-AC 15 (1715–18).

6. Maeder, *Historia económica*, p. 219–24.

7. Maeder, "La formación territorial," pp. 33–75; Hernan Félix Gómez, *El municipio del Saladas* (Buenos Aires, 1942).

8. Maeder, *Historia económica*, p. 222 mentions two straight years of drought, 1737–39; see also Acta of 19 October 1739. AGPC-AC 20 (1737–49).

9. Maeder, *Historia económica*, p. 223.

10. Aguirre, "Diario," 1:377–78.

11. Aguirre, "Diario," 3:370 notes that in Concepción del Uruguay, "There are now [1796] present in the port eight *lanchas* that carry 1,000 hides each, that do nothing except transport the same to Buenos Aires."

12. Maeder, *Historia económica*, p. 237.

13. Guillermo Furlong Cardiff, *Misiones y sus pueblos de guaraníes* (Buenos Aires, 1962), pp. 402–10.

14. Pablo Hernández, *Misiones del Paraguay. Organización social de las doctrinas de la Compañía de Jesús*, 2 vols. (Barcelona, 1913), 1:544.

15. Anton Sepp and Anton Boehm, *Reisebeschreibung: Wie nemlichen dieselbe auss Hispanien in Paraquarium Kommeni und kurzer Bericht der denchwuerdigsten Sachen selbiger Lanschaft Voelkein und Arbeitung der sich alldort befinden* (Ingolstatt, 1712), p. 233.

16. Cabildo of Corrientes to Francisco de Paula Bucarelli. 6 July 1769, AGN IX-3-3-7.

17. The guías for the 1770–79 period describe only those cattle exported to Misiones by way of the Uruguay and Alto Paraná. See Maeder, *Historia económica*, pp. 227–32.

18. Maeder, *Historia económica*, pp. 231–32.

19. Ernesto J. A. Maeder, "El caso Misiones, su proceso histórico y su posterior distribución territorial," in P. H. Randle, ed., *La geografía y la historia en la identidad nacional*, 2 vols. (Buenos Aires, 1981), 2:153–57.

20. Aguirre, "Diario," 2:383. Azara stressed these same points, noting that as a result of such conditions, "the cows of Paraguay begin to breed only when three years old, whereas those of Montevideo produce young at the age of two." He also stressed that Paraguayan stockraising suffered from the absence of *barrero*, a saline soil devoured by cattle in other parts of the Plata. The lack of salt in the ranching districts presents an example of irrationality in Paraguayan trade patterns, since, in fact, the province exported salt to Buenos Aires throughout the viceregal period. See Azara, *The Natural History of the Quadrupeds of Paraguay and the River La Plata* (Edinburgh, 1838), pp. 64–65.

21. Ernesto J. A. Maeder, "La producción ganadera de Corrientes entre 1700 y 1810," in *Bicentenario del virreinato del Río de la Plata*, 2 vols. (Buenos Aires, 1977), 1:329, 343–45. For an example of an individual shipment, see Guía of Claudio Aguilar. Corrientes, 12 January 1784, AGN IX-3-27-7.

22. Acuerdo of 2 June 1783. AGPC (Papeles de gobernador Alonso de Quesada).

23. Alonso de Quesada to Governor-Intendant Paula Sanz. September 1787, AGN IX-3-4-1.

24. Maeder, *Historia económica*, p. 235.

25. Aguirre, "Diario," 2:438.

26. Robertson, *Letters on South America*, 3:58–59, 82–87.

27. See, for example, Juan José López to the Consulado of Buenos Aires, 3 June 1803, AGN IX-4-6-4 (folio 211).

28. Decrees of 18 June 1792 and 18 May 1795. AGPC-AC 27 (1790–97).

29. Informe of Serapio Benítez. 27 May 1795, *ibid.*

30. AGPC-DG 37 (1803) and 40 (1806–1807).

31. Acta of 19 August 1803. AGPC-AC 28 (1800–1806); cited in Maeder, *Historia económica*, pp. 244–45.

32. Maeder, *Historia económica*, p. 245.

33. José Ignacio Aguirre, commander of San Roque, cited in Mantilla, *Crónica histórica*, 1:182. The problem of bandits and vagabonds within Latin American ranching districts has been much discussed. See Mario Gongora, "Vagabondage et societé pastorale en Amerique Latine (especialmente au Chili centrale)," *Anales E.S.C.* 21:1 (January-February 1966), 159–77; and especially Silvio R. Duncan Barreta and John Markoff, "Civilization and Barbarism: Cattle Frontiers in Latin America," *Comparative Studies in Society and History* 20 (October 1978), 587–620. The political implications of the rural disorder in Corrientes are covered in José Carlos Chiaramonte, "Organización del estado y construcción del orden social: la política económica de la provincia de Corrientes hacia 1821–1840," *Anuario*. Escuela de Historia. Facultad de Humanidades y Artes. U.N. Rosario, 11 (1985): 229–50.

34. Maeder, "La evolución de la ganadería," 9; Hernán Félix Gómez, *La ciudad de Curuzú Cuatiá. Antecedentes de su fundación y su domínio jurisdiccional*, (Corrientes, 1919).

35. Decree of Francia. Asunción, 24 October 1830, ANA-NE 1862; Decree of Francia. Asunción, 26 April 1832, ANA-SCD 25, no. 14.

36. John Hoyt Williams, "Paraguay's Nineteenth-Century '*Estancias de la República*,'" *Agricultural History* 47 (July 1973): 206–15; Luis Armando Galeano Romero, "Unidades productivas agropecuarias y estructura de poder en Paraguay (1811–1870)," *Revista Paraguaya de Sociología* 9 (January-April 1972), 91–105; Manuel Peña Villamil, "Breve historia de la ganadería paraguaya," *Historia Paraguaya. Anuario* 13 (1969–70): 83–97.

37. Rengger and Longchamps, *The Reign*, pp. 174–75.

38. Francia to Commandant Ramírez. Asunción, 17 March 1829, ANA-SH 240, no. 2. The removal of cattle from state estancias to the markets of Itapúa and Pilar in fact preceded Francia's rule. See expediente "Estancia de San Antonio de cuenta de la patria." 1812, ANA-SH 224, no. 13.

39. Mancel Ignacio Pinto, Itapúa (petition to purchase 1,000 hides at 12 reales each), 10 February 1837, cited in Williams, "Paraguay's Nineteenth-Century "*Estancias*," p. 208.

40. Decree of 25 June 1816. ANA-SH 226, no. 1. Rustling was the most common crime in the rural districts. See Proceso of Juan de la Cruz Cano. Concepción, 14 December 1815, ANA-SJC 1818; and Proceso of José Domingo Leiva. Villarrica, 26 January 1820, ANA-SJC 1521.

41. Williams, "Paraguay's Nineteenth-Century *Estancias*," 209. Regarding these

Indian wars, see Williams, "The Deadly Selva"; Francia to the Juez of Capiatá. October 1816, ANA-SH 226, no. 2; José Miguel Ibañez, commander of Concepción, to Francia. 1 July 1816, ANA-SH 367, no. 1.

42. White, *Paraguay's Autonomous Revolution*, pp. 263–64.

43. Chaves, *El supremo dictador*, pp. 271–82; for examples of such confiscations, see Gill to Francia. 7 November 1825, and 22 June 1826, ANA-SH 393.

44. Cited in Williams, "Paraguay's Nineteenth-Century *Estancias*," 210.

45. *Ibid.*; Chaves, *El supremo dictador*, pp. 276–77.

46. Receipt of 606 pesos, 5 reales, Tesoro general (refers to sales of cattle from state ranches). 13 January 1823, ANA-SLC 22.

47. Juan Peralta, commander of Villarrica, to Francia. 21 May 1829, ANA-SH 403, no. 1.

48. Francia to the commander of Concepción. 5 June 1831, ANA-NE 3412; see also Williams, "Paraguay's Nineteenth-Century *Estancias*," 211.

49. Washburn, *The History of Paraguay*, 1:443–44.

50. *Ibid.*, p. 444. The avarice of the López family in matters of land and property is well-documented. See, for instance, Orden suprema del Presidente. 4 April 1853, ANA-NE 2713, in which López ordered that state-owned livestock (of the estancia Yacarey) be transferred to his private estancia.

51. ROPC I, pp. 63 (Law of 29 December 1821) and 115–16 (Decree of 19 May 1822).

52. ROPC I, p. 366 (Law of 7 February 1825).

53. ROPC III, pp. 25–26 (Law of 13 May 1831).

54. D'Orbigny, *Viaje a la America Meridional*, 1:203–5. D'Orbigny, a French traveller who visited the Upper Plata between 1826 and 1833, remarked that the Riograndense herds were originally stolen by mission Indians; the Indians were despoiled of their prize by Correntino troops and subsequently took revenge by raiding Curuzú Cuatiá in 1827.

55. Maeder, "La evolución de la ganadería," 10, considers the incorporation of Riograndense cattle to be a major factor in the recovery of Correntino stockraising.

56. ROPC II, p. 330 (Law of 23 December 1829), which, nonetheless, permitted the extraction of bulls and oxen; III, pp. 229–30 (Law of 31 October 1834); IV, pp. 80–83 (Decree of 26 July 1838); ROPC IV, pp. 76–77 (Decree of 11 May 1838). Regarding salt imports, see ROPC III, p. 268 (Law of 27 January 1835).

57. *Ibid.*; see also ROPC III, pp. 229–30 (Law of 31 October 1834). Mantilla, in the *Crónica Histórica*, 1:287, notes that the Paraguayan merchant José Tomás Ysasi owned the province's first saladero. He does not indicate whether this took place before or after the fallout with Francia.

58. Brown, *A Socioeconomic History*, pp. 110–11.

59. *Ibid.* See also Wilfred Latham, *The States of the River Plate: Their Industries and Commerce* (London, 1866), pp. 6–11, 113–25.

60. ROPC II, pp. 117–22 (Law of 26 June 1827). The tax paid for the upkeep of a rural police force.

61. Twenty years later, the situation for sheep raising had improved in the Litoral provinces, thanks to the expanding carpet and weaving industries of France and Belgium, which fostered an increased demand for Platine wool. Corrientes and Paraguay remained largely unaffected.

62. Provincial census of 1854. AGPC-Censos 8, 9, 10.

63. Maeder, "Evolución de la ganadería en Corrientes," 16.

64. Manifiesto general de haciendas, año 1834 [sic]. 4 March 1833, AGPC-EA (1833), legajo 38.

65. Francia to the commander of Villa de Labrador. 2 April 1839, ANA-SH 244, no. 2; see also Williams, "Paraguay's Nineteenth-Century Estancias," 213–14.

66. Decree of 30 April 1839. ANA-SH 244, no 2.; see also Francia to Commandant of Itapúa. 2 April 1839, ANA-NE 2610.

67. Gelly, Paraguay, p. 55. Gelly argues that the massacre of livestock was a purposeful move by Francia designed to reduce the herds of private estancieros while leaving state estancias untouched. In fact, as Williams ("Paraguay's Nineteenth-Century Estancias," 214) points out, the April 28 decree applied to all animals regardless of ownership.

68. José Mariano de Matos to Ignacio José de Oliveira Guimaraens. Alegrete, 25 August 1839, AHRGS-Coleção Varela, no. XXI; Domingos José de Almeida to José Mariano de Matos. Caleira, 26 July 1841, AHRGS-Coleção Varela, no. XXVIII.

69. Joaquín Madariaga to the Barão de Caxias. Villanueva, 16 March 1844, AGPC-Copiador de Notas, Ministerio de gobierno, no. 9; Leitman, Raízes sócio-económicos, p. 95. Paraguay had been the chief source of mules for Rio Grande do Sul in the early period of the war, but sporadic disputes with the Correntinos cut that trade drastically by 1838.

70. Treaty of Villanueva. 9 February 1843, AHAER-Gobierno III: 1, legajo 13, no. 87–88; El Republicano, 20 August 1843. For consequences of the treaty, see Mantilla, Crónica histórica, 2:88–89.

71. Decree of 20 March 1843. ROPC V, p. 115.

72. Ibid., pp. 301, 303; La Revolución, 7 September 1845.

73. AGPC-EA 1840, legajos 61–62; 1841, legajo 63; Maeder, Historia económica, p. 245.

74. ROPC VI, pp. 112, 232–33, 349–51, 360, 459–60.

75. AGPC-CLC 1848, legajos 57–58; 1849, legajos 59–61; 1850, legajos 62–64.

76. AGPC Censos, legajos 8, 9, 10.

77. Maeder, "La evolución de la ganadería," 13.

78. This was the same Hughes who was instrumental in early attempts to open Paraguay to British commerce. He visited Asunción in October 1841, and was well received by the consular government of Carlos Antonio López and Mariano Roque Alonzo. See also Kiernan, "Britain's First Contacts," pp. 177–80. See notice of 15 August 1855 in El Comercio, 23 August 1855.

79. Page, La Plata, p. 303.

80. La Opinión, 11 April 1858.

81. M. G. and E. T. Mulhall, River Plate Handbook, Guide, Directory, and Almanac for 1863 (Buenos Aires, 1863), p. 225.

82. La Opinión, 25 September 1857.

83. Page, La Plata, p. 295; see also Ernesto Quesada, "Pujol y la época de la confederación," Revista Argentina de Ciencias Políticas 8 (1917): 257–92.

84. For example, on 14 January 1855, Pujol outlawed the export of calves while, at the same time, maintaining that this was a temporary measure that

did not attack the right of property. See Pujol, *Corrientes en la organización nacional*, 5:9.

85. Relação das Estancias que contene o Termo de São Borja. 9 August 1858, AHRGS Câmara Municipães-São Borja 1858, lata 134.

86. Marbais du Graty, *La república del Paraguay*, pp. 144–45.

87. Relación de haciendas. Villa de Concepción, 25 January 1858, ANA-NE 1567.

88. Family members were allowed to obtain state estancias. In this manner, the López family obtained many properties, including ranches in San Joaquín, Catigua, and San Ignacio, together with all the livestock therein. See ANA-CRB I-30, 24, 38; I-30, 8, 54; I-30, 6, 98; and I-29, 30, 46.

89. Marbais du Graty, *La república del Paraguay*, p. 331.

90. Decree of López. Asunción, 24 November 1842, *El Repertorio Nacional*, no. 25. For details on the working of the diezmo in the countryside, see Eberhard Munck af Rosenschöld, *Algunas cartas del naturalista sueco escritas durante su estadía en el Paraguay, 1843–1868* (Stockholm, 1956), *passim*.

91. Page, *La Plata*, p. 269.

92. *El Progreso*, 4 December 1864.

93. Thompson, *The War in Paraguay*, p. 97.

94. W. H. Koebel, *Paraguay*, (London, 1917), p. 275.

Chapter Six

1. For an excellent examination of forest utilization by pre-Columbian Indians, see Julian H. Steward, ed., *Handbook of South American Indians. The Comparative Ethnology of South American Indians*, vol. 5, Smithsonian Institution, Bureau of American Ethnology, Bulletin 142 (Washington, D.C., 1949), *passim*.

2. Lapacho was exported to Spain for use as crushing beams in olive oil extraction. See Thomas Faulkner, S.J., *A Description of Patagonia and the Adjoining Parts of South America* (Chicago, 1935), p. 35. Much later, Edward Augustus Hopkins noted that he had "seen timbers of the lapacho that have supported the roofs of houses in Buenos Aires for more than two-hundred years. They are now as sound as ever, and, to all appearance, capable of performing the same service to the end of the world. A door-sill of the same wood, half-imbedded in the ground, and marked '1632' belonged to the front door of the house which I inhabited in the city of Asunción. Upon the closest inspection, it was in a state of perfect preservation." See Hopkins, "Memoir on the Geography, History, Productions and Trade of Paraguay [1852]," American Geographical Society, Occasional Paper no. 2 (1968): 17–18.

3. Jerry W. Cooney, "Forest Industries and Trade in Late Colonial Paraguay," *Journal of Forest History* 23 (October 1979): 188–89.

4. For a description of Paraguayan woods, see Carlos Antonio López to los comandantes de la costa arriba. 26 June 1854, ANA-SH 311, no. 4; for a corresponding description of Correntino woods (the great majority of which overlap with those of Paraguay), see Quesada to the Intendente. 25 October 1785, AGPC-DG 26 (1785).

5. Kroeber, *The Growth of the Shipping Industry*, p. 57; Jonathan C. Brown, "Dynamics and Autonomy of a Traditional Marketing System: Buenos Aires 1810–1860," *Hispanic American Historical Review* 56 (November 1976): 613.

6. Regarding the Laws of the Forest (*montes*), see *Enciclopedia universal ilustrada europeo-americano* (Madrid, n.d.) XXXVI: 478–79. The laws concerning common lands are to be found in *Recopilación de leyes de los reynos de las indias* (Madrid, 1973) 2:102–104.

7. Creydt, *Formación histórica*, p. 36; Williams, *The Rise and Fall of the Paraguayan Republic*, p. 73.

8. Cooney, "Forest Industries," 190, notes a considerable wage inflation for skilled loggers in the late 1790s. By the early 1800s, a skilled axman might earn as much as five reales a day (more than four times what he could have earned a decade earlier). Basic rations of yerba, tobacco, salt, manioc, and meat were supplied to all laborers independent of wages. See also Aguirre, "Diario del Capitán de frigata," 417–30.

9. *Ibid.*, pp. 443–44, and Providencia sobre sueldos de Indios. Asunción, 22 October 1790, ANA-SH 155.

10. Cooney, "Forest Industries," 191.

11. Cited in Cooney, *ibid.*; see also Fray Pedro José de Parras, *Diario y derrotero de sus viajes, 1749–1753, España—Río de la Plata—Paraguay* (Buenos Aires, 1943), p. 153.

12. Quesada, *La provincia de Corrientes*, p. 109.

13. See D'Orbigny, *Viaje a la América meridional*, 1:273–89.

14. Williams, "The Deadly Selva," 1–24.

15. Cited in *El Comercio*, 2 April 1857.

16. This lifestyle is fictionalized in the imaginative short stories of Horacio Quiroga, *Cuentos completos*, 2 vols. (Montevideo, 1979).

17. The old Spanish measurements for wood applied everywhere in the Upper Plata throughout the period under study. These measures were always rough. Equivalents of the older measures are: One *vara* equals 34.09 inches; one *pie* equals 11.36 inches; one *tercia* equals one pie but only for width in wood measurement; and one *pulgada* equals .946 inches. No standard definition existed in the Río de la Plata for the terms of sawn timber, though beams (vigas) were generally two pies square in cross section.

18. Late 1850s figure. See Vicente G. Quesada, "Impresiones y recuerdos," *Revista del Paraná* 2 (30 September 1861): 99.

19. Aviso de la capitanía del Puerto [de Corrientes]. 5 July 1853, *La Libre Navegación de los Ríos*, 8 July 1853.

20. Examples of wood shipments via jangadas can be seen in Guía of Rafael de Irigoyen. Asunción, 26 May 1784, ANA-NE 3337, no. 160; guía of Nicolás de Gorrosurreta. Asunción, 7 July 1791, ABPBA 031-2-1, no. 27; and recurso of Ramón Ybarrola. Asunción, 26 November 1809, ANA-SJC 1890.

21. Francia to the commandant of Concepción. Asunción, March 1833, ANA-NE 249.

22. The consignees were not always conscientious about brands or their obligation of shipment. Wood could pile up *en depósito* for a year or more, confusing ownership.

23. Cooney, "Forest Industries," 192–93.
24. Soberino Acosta to Lázaro Ribera. Asunción, 9 January 1806, ANA-SH 211.
25. See White, *Paraguay's Autonomous Revolution*, pp. 226–36.
26. An 1818 summary notes a large quantity of rifles, sabres, and gunpowder imported in exchange for full value in hardwoods. The importation of seventeen inferior-quality cannons on the same occasion elicited the comment that "in the future the export of woods will only be permitted by those who bring good and serviceable arms." See Cuenta general, año 1818 . . . January-November (20 January entry), ANA-NE 1224.
27. Report of George J. R. Gordon. PRO-FO 13/202, p. 119.
28. Decree of 9 June 1831. ROPC III, pp. 68–69.
29. Regarding the promotion of Correntino timber in the foreign community press of Buenos Aires, see *British Packet and Argentine News*, 16 February 1839.
30. Some logging did continue around Itatí, however, through the 1860s. See sale of woodlands by Mauricio Sánchez in *El Progreso*. 13 March 1864.
31. Business liaisons were not without controversy. In 1857, Juan Etchegaray notified obrajeros that any timber sales effected by Pedro Samson (of the obraje Riacho Ancho) were void due to cross-litigations. See *La Opinión*. 29 June 1857. Lubary, incidently, made so much profit on the wood trade that he was able to purchase a schooner, the *Rosario*, for the transport of sawn lumber.
32. Quesada, *La provincia de Corrientes*, pp. 21–22. For data on wood production in the department of Saladas, see *La Opinión*. 16 June 1858, 16 July 1858, 13 August 1858, and 15 October 1858.
33. The urban expansion of Buenos Aires is analyzed by Jonathan Brown in *A Socioeconomic History of Argentina*, pp. 97–122; see also Lynch, *Argentine Dictator*, pp. 127–29; and especially José M. Mariluz Urquijo, "Fomento industrial y crédito bancario en el estado de Buenos Aires," *Trabajos y Comunicaciones* 19 (1965): 128–44. Regarding construction per se, see P. Cornelius Bliss, "Buenos Aires in 1864," *River Plate Magazine* 1:6 (June 1864), where he notes that "Lime is imported from the Banda Oriental, Entre Ríos, and Córdoba, Paraguay furnishes wood for carpentry and cabinet work, Russia and North America are laid under construction for white pine and the materials for ship building. Except bricks and sand, all the material of construction are thus brought from abroad. This circumstance has not prevented Buenos Aires from increasing in a surprising manner for ten years past."
34. Page, *La Plata*, pp. 86–87, 302.
35. *Ibid.* Regarding wood imports to Buenos Aires at this time, see *Los Debates*, 2 October 1857.
36. Derechos de extracción [1856]. ANA-NE 2275.
37. G. F. Morice to Francisco Solano López. Buenos Aires, 26 December 1859, ANA-CRB I-29, 34, 30, no. 12. See also Hadfield, *Brazil, River Plate, and the Falkland Islands*, p. 352. The latter suggested that export taxes be reduced to nothing.
38. See, for example, J. and A. Blyth to Francisco Solano López. London, 8 October 1857, ANA-CRB I-29, 35, 45, no. 27; wood samples sent to Ludovico Tenré, cónsul paraguayo en Paris. 21 November 1863, ANA-CRB I-30, 6, 27; and Ludovico Tenré to José Berges. Paris, 7 March 1864, ANA-CRB I-30, 4, 22, in

which Berges was sent a design for furniture to be worked with Paraguayan woods as a sample for the European markets.

39. *Registro estadístico de la república argentina. 1864*, 2 vols. (Buenos Aires, 1865) 1:371.

40. Cited in Cooney, "Forest Industries," 195; see also Félix de Azara, *Diario de la navegación y reconocimiento del Río Tebicuari*, in *Colección de Pedro de Angelis*, 2nd ed. (Buenos Aires, 1910), 2:392.

41. See German Tjarks, "Panorama del comercio interno del virreinato del Río del la Plata en sus postrimerías," *Humanidades* 36 (1960): 33; Decree of Francia, Asunción, 17 March 1826, ANA-SH 238, no. 4; Decreto prohibiendo sacar cáscara de Timbó, *Manual de policía de la provincia de Corrientes* (Corrientes, 1840), p. 56; Decree of 4 August 1840. ROPC IV, pp. 269–70.

42. Page, *La Plata*, p. 343; *El Semanario*, 6 January 1855.

43. Cited in Williams, "La guerra no-declarada entre el Paraguay y Corrientes," 35.

44. See "Documentos relativos a los cuestión de dominio del Partido de Curupayty." ANA-CRB I-28, 35, 62.

45. See Francia to Commandant of Concepción. Asunción, 18 August 1832. ANA-NE 3412. For an incisive look at the Apipé dispute written from a pro-Correntino perspective, see Alberto A. Rivera, "Contribuciones a la historia de la isla Apipé", *Revista de la Junta de Historia de Corrientes* 7 (1976): 79–104. Regarding the rapids of Apipé and their effect on commerce, see Carlos Burmeister, *Memoria sobre el territorio de Misiones* (Buenos Aires, 1890), pp. 14–15.

46. The Actas Capitulares of Corrientes allude to many logging expeditions in the area. See AGPC-AC 23 (1760–1769); 25 (1776–1782); 27 (1790–1799); and the *Papeles del gobernador Quesada*.

47. These events are related in the *British Packet and Argentine News*. 13 October 1832, 3 November 1832, and 1 March 1834; Rivera, "Contribuciones," 84.

48. Pedro Ferré to Domingo Cullen. Corrientes, 1 September 1832, in Ferré, *Memoria*, 1:422–23. See also Raimundo Fernández Ramos, *Apuntes históricos sobre Misiones* (Madrid, 1929), pp. 209–210.

49. Francia to the Subdelegado of Itapúa. 19 February 1833, ANA-SH 242, no. 7.

50. As actually occurred in 1848, when an obraje owned by Martín Dagorret was abandoned to the Paraguayans. The loggers escaped downriver on a single jangada. Alberto A. Rivera, "Poblamiento de las islas Apipé," paper presented at the Tercer Congreso de Historia Argentina y Regional, Paraná, 12 July 1975.

51. Tratado de límites, amistad, comercio, y navegación. Asunción, 15 July 1852, ANA-SH 298, no. 17; *El Paraguayo Independiente*. 24 July 1852.

52. The Paraguayans rarely interfered after this. In 1855, several Correntino ships were detained at the mouth of the Río Paraguay. The vessels returned to port without loading their cargoes of wood. See "Noticia del Paraguay," *El Comercio*, 8 November 1855. Carlos Antonio López later ordered his frontier guards to allow the ships to extract the wood. ANA-CJDB, vol. IX, p. 2536, and *El Comercio*, 24 January 1856.

53. Out of sixty-one islands in the river between the Río Arapehy and the Salto de Macunan, forty-seven were heavily forested with lapacho, algarrobo, and other hardwoods. João Pedro Gay, "Historia de república jesuitica do Paraguai

desde o descobrimento do Rio da Prata até nossos dias, anno de 1861," *Revista do Instituto Histórico, Geographico e Ethnographico do Brasil* (1863): 788–89, 831, appendix 3.

54. Periodic efforts at commercial woodcutting had been evident in the zone since the late colonial period. Few, if any, were successful. In 1803, for example, the lieutenant governor of Misiones authorized an Englishman, John Heaton, to cut woods along the Uruguay. No record remains indicating whether his expedition took place. See Santiago Liniers to Governor Ribera in "Correo 23 de junio de 1802," ANA-SH 190, 1948. Commercial logging began on the Uruguay only in the 1880s.

55. In 1544, the Asunción astillero had launched a caravel, the *Comuneros*, that was destined to carry as a prisoner to Cádiz the same governor, Alvar Núñez Cabeza de Vaca, who had ordered its construction. Juan Natalicio González, *Proceso y formación de la cultura paraguaya* (Asunción, 1948), 1:127–30.

56. Juan Carlos Nicolau, *Antecendentes para la historia de la industria argentina* (Buenos Aires, 1968), pp. 22–24; Aguirre, "Diario" 17:359–96, *passim*.

57. José M. Mariluz Urquijo, "Noticias sobre las industrias del Virreinato del Río de la Plata en la época del Marqués de Avilés (1799–1801)," *Revista de Historia America y Argentina* 1–2 (1957): 116–17; see also Jerry W. Cooney, "A Colonial Naval Industry: The Fábrica de Cables of Paraguay," *Revista de Historia de América* 87 (January–June 1979): 105–26.

58. "Informe del tribunal de Comercio sobre el proyecto de construir una marina mercantil." Asunción, 18 October 1798, ANA-SH 148. See also Juan Bautista de Achad, protector y defensor de pobres, to Gobernador Ribera. Asunción, 6 July 1804, ANA-SH 193 (this last item notes labor shortages at the shipyards).

59. See, for instance, Viceroy Joaquín del Pino to the Ministro de hacienda Miguel Cayetano Soler. Buenos Aires, 11 December 1802, MG 896.

60. Robertson, *Letters on Paraguay*, 3:195–97.

61. Miguel Lastarria, *Colonias orientales del Río Paraguay o de la Plata 1774–1805*, in Facultad de Filosofia y Letras, *Documentos para la historia argentina* (Buenos Aires, 1914), 3:155–56; "Estado de embarcaciones," *Telégrafo Mercantil*, 5 September 1801, p. 398; AGPC-DG 35 (1798–1800); "Declaración de los facultativos." Angostura, 25 September 1798, MG 1691b.

62. Maeder, *Historia económica de Corrientes*, pp. 286–88; Jerry W. Cooney, "Paraguayan *Astilleros* and the Platine Merchant Marine: 1796–1806," *The Historian* 43 (November 1980): 69–70.

63. The gunboat cost some 12,958 pesos fuertes. Bando of Juan Díaz de Bedoya [1815?]. ANA-NE 1209.

64. Plá, *The British in Paraguay*, pp. 37–42.

65. Roberto Zalazar, *El brigadier Ferré y el unitarismo porteño* (Buenos Aires, 1965), pp. 36–47.

66. As part of the civil war, many piratical activities occurred on the Río Paraná, and many Correntinos took part. It is unclear, however, where the vessels involved were constructed. See Luis M. Cora, et al., *Homanaje al general José Joaquín Gregorio Madariaga* (Corrientes, 1972), pp. 151–63.

67. Robertson, *Letters*, 3:207–208.

68. Kroeber, *Growth of Shipping*, p. 45.

69. A summary of work completed at the Asunción shipyard in early July, 1843, reveals 23 carpenters, 24 caulkers, and 9 sawyers. Razón de lo obrado . . . en el obraje del Estado de la ribera. Asunción, 9 July 1843, ANA-NE 744. By 1854, the same establishment boasted 64 carpenters and 17 caulkers. Razón de las obras trabajadas en el obraje del Estado en la Ribera. Asunción, 1 January 1854, ANA-NE 2726, fojas 9–11.

70. Plá, British, pp. 37–38.

71. El Comercio, 23 August 1855.

72. See Plá, British, pp. 37–42, 95–98, and 151–52. See also J. B. Otaño, Datos para la historia del "Tacuarí" (Asunción, 1932); and Juan F. Pérez Acosta, Carlos Antonio López: obrero máximo (Buenos Aires, 1948), pp. 196–243.

73. Otaño, Datos, p. 175.

74. Cited in Plá, British, pp. 39–40; see also ANA-SH 312, no. 2; and Juan Andrés Gelly to J. A. Gelly y Obes. London, 22 October 1853, AGN-DBN [15111] legajo 757.

75. The Standard, 25 May 1864. For examples of the work accomplished in the state shipyards, see the various razones in ANA-NE 2751, fojas 10–11 (for November 1856); 811 (for March 1859); 2807, fojas 41–44, 2808, fojas 5–10 (for December 1864); 2811, fojas 18–24, 137–139 (for May 1865).

76. El Comercio, 6 September 1855.

77. La Opinión, 11 September 1857, 13 September 1857, 4 October 1857, and 30 October 1857. As early as 1834, the Correntino government had granted an exclusive privilege to a German engineer, Friedrich Bauer, to "place a steamship on the waters of the Paraná within twelve months." The German had no success whatsoever. See Mantilla, Crónica histórica, 1:287.

78. Mulhall, River Plate Handbook, p. 255.

79. "Un astillero especial en la República," El Progreso, 20 September 1863.

80. AGN Censos 1869 (puerto de Corrientes), legajos 210–12.

81. John Watts to Vicente Barrios. Asunción, 25 July 1866, ANA-NE 1763. Aside from these efforts, the only vessels constructed in Paraguay during these years were war canoes. See, for instance, Order of Francisco Barreiro. Asunción, 23 October 1865, ANA-SH 344, no. 12, which mentions the building of 446 canoes.

82. Isaac G. Strain, Sketches of a Journey in Chili and the Argentine Provinces in 1849 (New York, 1853), p. 264; J. P. Robertson likened the movement of such carts to "the dragging of heavy artillery through a difficult and harrassing country." Robertson, Letters on South America, 1:183. Regarding the construction of carts, see Francia to the Comandante of Concepción. Asunción, 23 August 1831, ANA-NE 3412.

Glossary

administrador de naturales   royal official in charge of an Indian village.
aduana   customs house; customs duties.
ajuí   a hardwood of the Upper Plata (*Ocotea acutifolia*).
alcabala   sales tax.
amparado   a black slave (usually attached to a religious order) who could not legally be sold.
anclaje   anchorage fees.
arrendamiento   leasehold.
arrendatario   leaseholder.
arroba   measure of weight equal to 25.35 English pounds.
astilleros   shipyards.
balandra   sloop; a one-masted river vessel.
balsa   a minor river vessel, usually single-masted.
bando   proclamation, decree.
baqueano   guide, scout, river pilot.
barbacuá   large trestle used in the curing of yerba.
barrero   a saline soil eaten by cattle in lieu of salt licks.
beneficiador de yerba   yerba concessionaire, also called *habilitado*.
beneficio   yerba concession.
bergantín   a two-masted river vessel, usually of between sixty and 140 tons.
boleadoras   Indian-designed weapon consisting of a number of weighted stones linked by thongs of rawhide, used to throw cattle and other animals; sometimes called *bolas*.
bombarda   two-masted, keeled vessel, of Mediterranean design.

243

bombilla   wooden straw or metal tube used for drinking yerba mate.
buena   a grade of Upper Platine tobacco.
caamini   superior grade of yerba mate, generally free of dirt, stems, and twigs.
cabildante   town council member.
cabildo   town council.
cacique   Indian chief.
camalote   floating island of aquatic vegetation.
capataz   ranch foreman.
caraguatá   species of agave plant useful in the making of rope and substitutes for paper.
carga   a measure of sawn timber equal to approximately four felled trees.
caudillo   military chieftain.
chacra   small farm.
chacrero   owner of a chacra.
chalana   small river vessel of Upper Platine design.
changador   itinerant peddler, liquor runner.
charqui   dried, shredded beef.
chipá   bread made from manioc flour, eggs, and cheese.
chiripá   leather undergarment worn by vaqueros instead of trousers.
comercio libre   free trade within the Spanish empire.
consulado   merchant guild with administrative and judicial authority in commercial matters.
cosechero   tobacco grower.
criollo   Creole, American-born white.
cuatropea   a tax on hooved animals.
curtiduría   tannery.
curupay   a hardwood of the Upper Plata (*Piptadenia rigidia*). Tannic acid for the curing of leather can be extracted from its bark (*cáscara*).
desarraigado   vagrant, also termed *vago*.
diezmo   tithe, agricultural tax.
doble   a grade of Upper Platine tobacco.
encomienda   royal grant of Indian labor.
en rama   "in bulk," term commonly used in reference to shipments of tobacco.
estancia   ranch.
estancia del rey   government-owned ranch, later called *estancia de la república*.
estanciero   rancher, owner of estancia.
estanco   royal tobacco monopoly.
estanquero   employee of the royal tobacco monopoly.
facón   a double-edged longknife used in rural areas.
factura   invoice.
falúa   small river vessel of Upper Platine design.
fanega   measure of capacity equal to 1.6 bushels.
garandumba   a large river craft of Upper Platine design.
garrapata   a cattle disease caused by ticks.
goleta   schooner; a two-masted, keeled river vessel.
Guaicurú   Indian group of the Chaco region.
Guaraní   principal Indian group of the Upper Plata, language of the same.

guembé fibrous reed used as a rope substitute.
guía legal writ granting permission to move cargo.
habilitación a credit in cash or goods.
hoja large leafed tobacco, a colonial term.
indio criollo an Indian resident of a Spanish town, not held in encomienda.
intendencia late colonial administrative division roughly equal to a province.
jangada logboom, raft.
junta committee, often, but not always, military in character.
lapacho a hardwood of the Upper Plata (*Tabebuia*).
libranza bill of exchange, promissory note, letter of credit.
mate gourd-like vessel used for drinking yerba mate.
Mbaya Indian group of northern Paraguay.
media a grade of Upper Platine tobacco.
merced grant, often a land grant.
mitayo encomienda Indian performing personal service for a stipulated period
of time, while residing in an Indian community.
Monteses small Indian group of northeastern Paraguay.
obraje lumber camp.
Oriental Uruguayan.
originario encomienda Indian residing permanently on an overlord's estate.
palometa razorfish.
palo santo a sweet-smelling hardwood of the Upper Plata (*Phyllostyllon rhamnoides*).
para a grade of Upper Platine tobacco.
patrón ship captain, sponsor.
Payaguá an Indian group of the riverine zones of the Upper Plata.
paylebot small schooner.
peninsular metropolitan Spaniard.
pesada a weight of rawhides equal to thirty-five English pounds.
peso fuerte standard monetary unit in the Upper Plata, equal to eight *reales*.
petereby a hardwood of the Upper Plata (*Cordia*).
pety Guaraní term for tobacco.
piragua a river craft of Upper Platine design.
pito a grade of Upper Platine tobacco.
polacra a minor river vessel common in the Upper Plata during the early 1800s.
Porteño inhabitant of the city of Buenos Aires.
pueblo de indios Indian village, usually with semi-independent charters.
puerto preciso port of mandatory discharge.
puesto military post.
pulpería general store.
quebracho a hardwood of the Chaco region (*Schinopsis lorentzii*).
queche ketch; a two-masted vessel.
raído a leather netting used in yerba preparation.
rancho simple adobe and thatch ranch house; small ranching operation.
receptor tax collector.
receptoría customs station.
regular a grade of Upper Platine tobacco.

rodeo   roundup of cattle, usually for castrating and branding.
saladerista   owner and operator of a meat salting plant.
saladero   meat-salting establishment.
sumaca   smack; a small, two-masted river vessel.
tacuara   bamboo.
tatacuá   leather-lined hole, used in the processing of yerba mate.
tataí   a hardwood of the Upper Plata (*Chlorophora tinctorea*).
tataré   a hardwood of the Upper Plata (*Pithocolobium scalate*).
tercio   hide bale; also a measure of weight equal to 188 English pounds.
timbó   a hardwood of the Upper Plata (*Enterolobium timbouva*).
Toba   Indian group of the Chaco region.
toldería   Indian encampment.
torcido negro   Upper Platine chewing tobacco, darkened and sweetened with molasses.
tornaguía   landing certificate.
tropa   oxcart caravan.
unitario   an adherent of the centralist political movement in the Plata.
urú   foreman at yerba operation.
urundey   hardwood of the Upper Plata (*Astronium urundeuva*).
vaquería   expedition to hunt wild cattle.
vaquero   Upper Platine cowboy.
vara   measure of length equal to 2.843 English feet.
vecino   resident holding full municipal rights.
vecino feudatario   holder of an encomienda grant.
yaguareté   jaguar.
yataí   a palm tree of the Upper Plata known for its edible fruit (*Areca olerácea*).
yerba mate   Paraguay tea (*Ilex paraguaiensis*).
yerba de palos   poorer grade of yerba mate.
yerba de Paranaguá   Brazilian-grown yerba from the province of Paraná.
yerbales   wild stand of yerba, also called *minerales de yerba*.
yerbatero   yerba worker, also called *yerbero*.
yvyraró   hardwood of the Upper Plata (*Paterogyne nitens*).

Bibliography

I. Archives Consulted
Archivo del Banco de la Provincia de Buenos Aires
Archivo Histórico y Administrativo de Entre Ríos
Arquivo Histórico do Rio Grande do Sul
Archivo General de la Nación (Buenos Aires)
Archivo General de la Provincia de Corrientes
Archivo National de Asunción
Manuel Gondra Collection, Austin (on microfilm)
Public Records Office (on microfilm)
Registro Oficial de la Provincia de Corrientes
Academia Nacional de la Historia (Buenos Aires)
University of California Riverside Library, Juan Silvano Godoi Collection
II. Newspapers
Asunción:
   El Repertorio Nacional (1842–45)
   El Paraguayo Independiente (1845–52)
   El Semanario de Avisos y Conocimientos Utiles (1853–68)
Corrientes:
   El Nacional Correntino (1841)
   El Republicano (1843)
   La Revolución (1845)
   El Pacificador (1846)
   Corrientes Confederada (1848)
   La Organización Nacional (1851)

247

La Libre Navegación de los Ríos (1853)
El Comercio (1854–57)
La Opinión (1857–59)
La Unión Argentina (1860)
La Nueva Epoca (1861)
La Libertad (1862)
El Progreso (1863–65)
El Independiente (1865)
Buenos Aires:
    Telégrafo Mercantil (1801)
    La Gaceta Mercantil (1823–52)
    British Packet and Argentine News (1828–48)
    Los Debates (1857–58)
    The Standard (1864)
Rio de Janeiro:
    Jornal do Commercio (1841)
Piratini and Caçapava:
    O Povo (1838–41)
Paraná:
    El Nacional Argentino (1852–56)
Montevideo:
    Comercio del Plata (1845–47)
    Britannia (1846)
III. Books and Articles
Aguirre, Juan Francisco de. "Diario del capitán de fragata de la Real Armada Don. . . . "Revista de la Biblioteca Nacional de Buenos Aires 17–20 (1949–51).
Alberdi, Juan Bautista. Historia de la guerra del Paraguay. Buenos Aires, 1962.
———. Sistema económico y rentístico de la confederación argentina según su constitución de 1853. Buenos Aires, 1921.
Al'perovich, Moises Samoilovic. Revoluciia i diktatura v Paragvai 1810–1840. Moscow, 1975.
———. "Revolution von oben in Paraguay? (Zur Frage de historischen wertung der Diktatur Francias)." In Rolle und Formen der Volksbewegung im Burgerlichen Revolutionszyklus, edited by Manfred Kossok, pp. 101–121. Berlin, 1976.
Anna, Timothy E. Spain and the Loss of America. Lincoln, 1983.
Arbo, Higinio. Libre navegación de los ríos. Régimen jurídico de los ríos de la Plata, Paraná, y Paraguay. Buenos Aires, 1939.
Arías Divito, Juan Carlos. "Dificultades para establecer la Renta de Tabaco en Paraguay." Anuario de Estudios Americanos 33 (1976): 1–17.
Assadourian, Carlos Sempat. El sistema de la economía colonial. Mercado interno, regiones y espacio económico. Lima, 1982.
———. Modos de producción, capitalismo y subdesarrollo en América Latina. Buenos Aires, 1973.
———. "El sector exportador de una economía regional del interior argentino. Córdoba, 1800–1860. (Esquema cuantitativo y formas de producción)." Nova America 1 (1978): 57–104.

Ave-Lallement, Robert. *Viagem pelo Sul do Brasil ao ano de 1858.* 2 vols. Rio de Janeiro, 1953.

Azara, Félix de. *Correspondencia oficial e inédita sobre la demarcación de límites entre el Paraguay y el Brasil, 1784–1795.* Buenos Aires, 1836.

———. *Descripción e historia del Paraguay y del Río de la Plata.* 2 vols. Madrid, 1847.

———. "Diario de la navegación y reconocimiento del río Tebicuarí." In *Colección de Pedro de Angelis.* 2d ed. Vol. 2, pp. 379–412. Buenos Aires: 1910.

———. *Geografía física y esférica del Paraguay.* Montevideo, 1904.

———. *Memoria sobre el estado rural del Río de la Plata en 1801.* Madrid, 1947.

———. *Viajes inéditos.* Buenos Aires, 1873.

———. *Viajes por la América meridional.* Madrid, 1969.

Báez, Cecilio. *Ensayo sobre el Doctor Francia y la dictadura en Sudamerica.* Asunción, 1910.

Bagú, Sergio. *Estructura social de la colonia.* Buenos Aires, 1952.

Baguet, A. *Rio Grande do Sul et le Paraguay. Souvenirs de voyage.* Anvers, 1873.

Benítez, Justo Pastor. *Carlos Antonio López. Estructuración del estado paraguayo.* Buenos Aires, 1949.

———. "La política internacional paraguaya 1850–1862. Las gestiones de José Berges." In *Temas de la Cuenca del Plata,* pp. 91–121. Montevideo, 1949.

Beraza, Agustín. *Rivera y la independencia de las Misiones.* Montevideo, 1968.

Bermejo, Ildefonso Antonio. *Vida paraguaya en tiempos del viejo López.* Buenos Aires, 1973.

Bosch, Beatriz. "Las provincias del interior en 1856." *Investigaciones y ensayos* 13 (1972): 343–70.

———. "Urquiza y la guerra de la Triple Alianza." *Boletín de la Academia Nacional de Historia* 34 (1963): 819–35.

———. *Urquiza y su tiempo.* 2d ed. Buenos Aires, 1980.

Bose, Walter B. L. "Las postas en las provincias de Santa Fé, Entre Ríos, Corrientes y Misiones 1772–1820." *Trabajos y Comunicaciones* 20 (1970): 87–129.

Bourgade La Dardye, E. de. *Paraguay: The Land and the People, Natural Wealth and Commercial Capabilities.* London, 1892.

Box, Pelham Horton. *The Origins of the Paraguayan War.* New York, 1967.

Braudel, Fernand. *Civilization and Capitalism, 15th-18th Century.* Vol. I, *The Structures of Everyday Life, the Limits of the Possible.* New York, 1981.

Brossard, Alfred de. *Considerations historiques et politiques sur les Republiques de la Plata dans leur rapports avec la France et l'Angleterre.* Paris, 1850.

Brown, Jonathan. *A Socioeconomic History of Argentine, 1776–1860.* Cambridge, 1979.

Burgin, Miron. *The Economic Aspects of Argentine Federalism, 1820–1852.* Cambridge, 1946.

Burton, Richard F. *Letters from the Battlefields of Paraguay.* London, 1870.

Bushnell, David. *Reform and Reaction in the Platine Provinces, 1810–1852.* Gainesville, 1983.

Cabral, Salvador. *Andresito Artigas en la emancipación americana.* Buenos Aires, 1980.

Cabrera Infante, G. *Holy Smoke.* London and Boston, 1985.

Cady, John F. *Foreign Intervention in the Río de la Plata 1838–50: A Study of French, British and American Policy in Relation to the Dictator Juan Manuel Rosas.* Philadelphia, 1929.

Camargo, Antônio Eleuterio de, *Quadro Estadístico e Geográphico da Provincia de São Pedro do Rio Grande do Sul*, Pôrto Alegre, 1868.

Cardozo, Efraím. *Hace cien años. Crónicas de la guerra de 1864–1870.* 13 vols. Asunción, 1967–83.

————. *El imperio del Brasil y el Río de la Plata. Antededentes y estallido de la guerra del Paraguay.* Buenos Aires, 1961.

————. "Urquiza y la guerra del Paraguay." *Investigaciones y Ensayos* 2 (January-June 1967): 141–65.

Castelo, Antonio Emilio. *Historia de Corrientes.* Buenos Aires, 1984.

Cattaneo, Cayetano. "Comunicación fluvial del litoral argentino en el siglo XVIII." *Revista de Buenos Aires* 11 (1866): 321–50.

Centeno, Francisco. "Viajes al Paraguay, 1844–1846." *Revista de Derecho, Historia y Letras* 37 (1910): 392–420.

Centeno, Marco Tulio. "San Juan del Hormiguero. Crónica de su origen y desarrollo. Antecedentes de la refundación de Santo Tomé (Corrientes)." *Primer Encuentro de Geohistoria Regional. Exposiciones* (1980), pp. 94–211.

Céspedes del Castillo, Guillermo. *Lima y Buenos Aires. Repercusiones económicas y políticas de la creación del virreinato del Plata.* Seville, 1947.

Chaves, Julio César. *Historia de las relaciones entre Buenos Ayres y el Paraguay, 1810–1813.* 2d ed. Buenos Aires, 1959.

————. *El presidente López. Vida y gobierno de Don Carlos.* Buenos Aires, 1955.

————. *El supremo dictador.* 4th ed. Rev. Madrid, 1964.

Chiaramonte, José Carlos. "El caso de Corrientes. Mercado de mercancías, mercado monetario y mercado de capitales en el Litoral Argentino de la primera mitad del XIX." *Siglo XIX* 2:4 (July-December 1987): 81–111.

————. "Coacción extraeconómica y relaciones de producción en el Río de la Plata durante la primera mitad del siglo XIX: el caso de la provincia de Corrientes." *Nova Americana* 2 (1979): 237–62.

————. "Finanzas públicas de las provincias del Litoral, 1821–1841." *Anuario IEHS* 1 (1986): 159–98.

————. "Organización del estado y construcción del orden social: La política económica de la provincia de Corrientes hacia 1821–1840." *Anuario.* Escuela de Historia. Facultad de Humanidades y Artes. U.N. Rosario, 11 (1985): 229–50.

Coni, Emilio A. *Historia de las vaquerías del Río de la Plata (1555-1750).* Madrid, 1930.

Cooney, Jerry W. "A Colonial Naval Industry: The *Fabrica de Cables* of Paraguay." *Revista de Historia de América* 87 (January-June 1979): 105–126.

————. "Forest Industries and Trade in Late Colonial Paraguay." *Journal of Forest History* 23 (October 1979): 186–97.

————. *Paraguay and the Royal Tobacco Monopoly: 1779–1810*, unpublished ms., University of Louisville, 1990.

———. "Paraguayan Astilleros and the Platine Merchant Marine, 1796–1806." *The Historian* 43 (November 1980): 55–74.

———. "The Rival of Doctor Francia: Fernando de la Mora and the Paraguayan Revolution." *Revista de Historia de América* 100 (July-December 1985): 201–229.

———. "A Riverborne Society: Life and Labor on the *Carrera del Paraguay,* 1776–1811." *SECOLAS Annals* 20 (March 1989): 5–19.

Creydt, Oscar. *Formación história de la nación paraguaya.* n.p., 1963.

Demersay, Alfred. "De l'avenir des relations commerciales entre la France et le Paraguay." *Journal des Economistes* 1, ser. 37 (1853): 382–89.

———. *Du Tabac au Paraguay.* Paris, 1851.

———. *Histoire physique, economique et politique du Paraguay.* Paris, 1864.

Domínguez, Wenceslao Nestor. *La toma de Corrientes el 25 de mayo de 1865.* Buenos Aires, 1965.

D'Orbigny, Alcides. *Viaje a la América meridional.* 3 vols. Buenos Aires, 1945.

Duncan Baretta, R. Silvio, and John Markoff. "Civilization and Barbarism: Cattle Frontiers in Latin America." *Comparative Studies in Society and History* 20 (October 1978): 587–620.

Ferns, H. S. *Britain and Argentina in the Nineteenth Century.* Oxford, 1960.

Ferré, Pedro. *Memoria del brigadier general Pedro Ferré. Octubre de 1821 a diciembre de 1842.* 2 vols. Buenos Aires, 1921.

Figuerero, Manuel V. *Lecciones de historiografía de Corrientes.* Buenos Aires, 1929.

Fitte, Ernesto J. "Apuntamientos para una historia de la navegación en el Río de la Plata." *Investigaciones y Ensayos* 13 (July-December 1972): 211–66.

Flickema, Thomas O. "The Settlement of the Paraguayan-American Controversy of 1859: A Reappraisal." *The Americas* 25 (July 1968): 49–69.

Flores, Moacyr. *Modelo Político dos Farrapos.* Pôrto Alegre, 1978.

Furlong Cardiff, Guillermo, S.J. *Misiones y sus pueblos de guaraníes.* Buenos Aires, 1962.

Gálvez, Jaime. *Rosas y la navegación de nuestros ríos.* 2d ed. Buenos Aires, 1955.

Garavaglia, Juan Carlos. "Las actividades agropecuarias en el marco de la vida económica del pueblo de indios de Nuestra Señora de los Santos Reyes de Yapeyú: 1768–1806." In *Haciendas, latifundios y plantaciones en América Latina,* edited by Enrique Florescano, pp. 464–85. Mexico, 1975.

———. "Un capítulo del mercado interno colonial: el Paraguay y su región (1537–1682)." *Nova Americana* 1 (1978): 11–55.

———. "El mercado interno colonial y la yerba mate (siglos XVI-XIX)." *Nova Americana* 4 (1981): 163–210.

———. *Mercado interno y economía colonial.* Mexico, 1983.

———. "Un modo de producción subsidiaria: la organización económica de las comunidades guaranizadas durante los siglos XVII-XVIII en la formación regional altoperuano-rioplatense." *Cuadernos de Pasado y Presente* 40 (1973): 161–91.

———. "Soldati e contadini: due secoli nella storia rurale del Paraguay." *Annali della Fondazione Luigi Einaudi* 14 (1980): 527–79.

García Mellid, Atilio. *Proceso a los falsificadores de la historia del Paraguay.* 2 vols. Buenos Aires, 1963.

Gargaro, Alfredo. "Antecedentes de la guerra del Paraguay y reacciones en las provincias." *Trabajos y Comunicaciones* 10 (1961): 83–120.

Gay, João Pedro. "Historia de República Jesuita do Paraguai desde o descobrimento do Rio da Prata ate nossos dias, anno 1861." In *Revista Trimensal do Instituto Histórico, Geographico y Ethnographico do Brasil,* 1863, pp. 589–883.

———. *Invasão Paraguaia na Fronteira Brasileira do Uruguai.* Caxias do Sul, 1980.

Gelly, Juan Andrés. *Paraguay: los que fue, lo que es, y lo que será.* Paris, 1926.

Gilberti, Horacio C. E. *Historia económica de la ganadería argentina.* 2d ed. Buenos Aires, 1961.

Gil Navarro, Ramón. *Veinte años en un calabozo; o sea la desgraciada historia de veinte y tantos argentinos muertos o envejecidos en los calabozos del Paraguay.* Rosario, 1863.

Gómez, Hernán Félix. *La ciudad de Curuzú Cuatiá. Antecedentes de su fundición y su dominio jurisdiccional.* Corrientes, 1929.

———. *La ciudad de Goya.* Buenos Aires, 1942.

———. *La ciudad de Santo Tomé.* Buenos Aires, 1942.

———. *Corrientes en la guerra con el Brasil.* Corrientes, 1928.

———. *Corrientes y la República entrerriana, 1820–1821.* Corrientes, 1929.

———. *Historia de la provincia de Corrientes desde la fundación de la ciudad de Corrientes a la Revolución de Mayo.* Corrientes, 1928.

———. *Historia de la provincia de Corrientes desde la Revolución de Mayo al Tratado de Cuadrilatero.* Corrientes, 1929.

———. *Vida pública del Dr. Juan Pujol.* Buenos Aires, 1920.

González, Luis J. *Paraguay: prisonero geo-político.* Buenos Aires, 1947.

González de Martínez, Marcela. "El tabaco en la guerra económica contra Paraguay y Santa Fé." *Tercer Congreso de Historia Argentina y Regional.* Buenos Aires, 1977. 4: 329–36.

Hadfield, William. *Brazil, River Plate, and the Falkland Islands.* London, 1854.

———. *Brazil and the River Plate in 1866.* London, 1869.

Halperín Donghi, Tulio. *Argentina de la revolución de independencia a la confederación rosista.* Buenos Aires, 1980.

———. "La expansión ganadera en la campaña de Buenos Aires (1810–1852)." *Desarrollo Económico* 3 (April-September 1963): 57–110.

———. *Politics, Economics and Society in Argentina in the Revolutionary Period.* Cambridge, 1975.

———. "La revolución y la crísis de la estructura colonial en el Río de la Plata." *Estudios de Historia Social* 2 (1966): 78–125.

Heckscher, Eli F. *Mercantilism.* 2 vols. London, 1935.

Herken Krauer, Juan Carlos. "Proceso económico en el Paraguay de Carlos Antonio López: la visión del consul británico Henderson (1851–1860)." *Revista Paraguaya de Sociología* 19 (May-August 1982): 83–116.

Herken Krauer, Juan Carlos, and María Isabel Giménez de Herken. *Gran Bretaña y la guerra de la Triple Alianza.* Asunción, 1982.

Hopkins, Edward A. "The La Plata and the Paraná-Paraguay." *De Bow's Commercial Review* 14 (1853): 238–51.

———. "The Republic of Paraguay since the death of the Dictator Francia." *The American Review* (September 1847): 245–60.

———. *La tiranía del Paraguay a la faz de sus contemporáneos.* Buenos Aires, 1856.

Hutchinson, Thomas Joseph. *Buenos Ayres and Argentine Gleanings.* London, 1868.

———. *The Paraná, with Incidents of the Paraguayan War, and South American Recollections, from 1861 to 1868.* London, 1868.

Kahle, Günter. "Die Diktatur Dr. Francias und ihre Bedeutung für die Entwicklung des Paraguayischen Nationalbewusstseins." *Jahrbuch für Geschichte von Staat, Wirtschaft und Gesellschaft Lateinamerikas* 1 (1964): 238–82.

Kennedy, A. J. *La Plata, Brazil and Paraguay during the Present War.* London, 1869.

Kiernan, V. G. "Britain's First Contacts with Paraguay." *Atlante* 3 (1955): 171–91.

Kolinski, Charles S. *Independence or Death! The Story of the Paraguayan War.* Gainesville, 1965.

Kossok, Manfred. *El virreinato del Río de la Plata. Su estructura económica social.* Buenos Aires, 1959.

Kroeber, Clifton B. *The Growth of the Shipping Industry in the Río de la Plata Region, 1794–1860.* Madison, 1957.

Kuznesof, Elizabeth. "The Role of Merchants in the Economic Development of São Paulo, 1765–1850." *Hispanic American Historical Review* 60 (1980): 571–92.

Lalive D'Epinay, Christian and Louis Necker. "Paraguay (1811–1870): A Utopia of Self-Oriented Change," in Johan Galtung, Peter O'Brien, and Roy Preiswerk, eds., *Self-Reliance: A Strategy for Development.* London, 1980, pp. 249–68.

Lavarden, Manuel José de. *Nuevo aspecto del comercio en el Río de la Plata.* Buenos Aires, 1955.

Leitman, Spencer Lewis. *Raízes Sócio-Económicos da Guerra dos Farrapos.* Rio de Janeiro, 1979.

Linhares, Temistocles. *Historia Económica do Mate.* Rio de Janeiro, 1969.

Livieres Argaña, Juan I. *Con la rúbrica del Mariscal: documentos de Francisco Solano López.* 6 vols. Asunción, 1970–71.

López, Carlos Antonio. *La emancipación paraguaya.* Asunción, 1942.

López, Francisco Solano. *Pensamiento político.* Buenos Aires, 1969.

———. *Proclamas y cartas del Mariscal Francisco Solano López.* Asunción, 1957.

López Luján, Bernardino. "Descripción histórica y geográfica de la ciudad de San Juan de Vera de las siete Corrientes." *Revista de Buenos Aires* 25 (1865): 160–86.

Lynch, John. *Argentine Dictator. Juan Manuel de Rosas, 1829–1852.* Oxford, 1981.

———. *Spanish Colonial Administration, 1782–1810: The Intendant System in the Viceroyalty of the Río de la Plata.* London, 1958.

MacKinnon, L. B. *Steam Warfare on the Paraná: a Narrative of Operations by the Combined Squadrons of England and France, in Forcing a Passage up that River.* 2 vols. London, 1848.

McLynn, F. J. "The Causes of the War of the Triple Alliance: An Interpretation." *Inter-American Economic Affairs* 33 (Autumn 1979): 21–43.

Maeder, Ernesto J. A. "El caso Misiones, su proceso histórico y su posterior distribución territorial." in *La geografía y la historia en la identidad nacional*, edited by P. H. Randle, vol. 2, pp. 153–57. Buenos Aires, 1981.

———. "La evolución de la ganadería en Corrientes (1810–1854)." *Cuadernos de Estudios Regionales* 4 (1983): 7–21.

———. "La formación territorial y económica de Corrientes entre 1588 y 1750." *Folia Histórica del Nordeste* 1 (1974): 33–75.

———. "Guerra civil y crísis demográfica en Corrientes. El censo provincial de 1841." *Folia Histórica del Nordeste* 4 (1980): 55–90.

———. *Historia económica de Corrientes en el período virreinal, 1776–1810.* Buenos Aires, 1981.

———. "Historia y resultados del censo confederal de 1857." *Trabajos y Comunicaciones* 18 (1968): 137–62.

———. "La población del Paraguay en 1799. El censo del gobernador Lázaro de Ribera." *Estudios Paraguayos* 3 (1975): 63–86.

———. "La producción ganadera de Corrientes entre 1700 y 1810." in *Bicentenario del virreinato del Río de la Plata.* 2 vols. Buenos Aires, 1977.

Maeder, Ernesto J. A., and Alfredo S. C. Bolsi. "La población guaraní de la provincia de Misiones en la época post-jesuítica (1768–1809)." *Folia Histórica del Nordeste* 5 (1982): 61–106.

Manning, William Ray. *Diplomatic Correspondence of the United States. Inter-American Affairs.* 12 vols. Washington, 1932–39.

Mansfield, Charles Blacksford. *Paraguay, Brazil and the Plate. Letters Written in 1852–53.* Cambridge, 1856.

Mantilla, Manuel Florencio. *Crónica histórica de Corrientes.* 2 vols. Buenos Aires, 1928–29.

———. *Estudios biográficos sobre patriotas correntinos.* Buenos Aires, 1884.

Marbais Du Graty, Alfred. *La Confédération Argentine.* Paris, 1858.

———. *La república del Paraguay.* Besançon, 1862.

Mariluz Urquijo, José M. "Los guaraníes después de la expulsión de los jesuitas." *Estudios Americanos* 6 (1953): 323–30.

Martin de Moussy, Victor. *Description Geographique et Statistique de la Confédération argentine.* 3 vols. Paris, 1860–64.

Martínez Montoro, Homero. "El Río Uruguay. Geografía, historia, y geopolítica de sus aguas y islas." *Revista Histórica* 21 (July 1954): 1–328; 22:84–318; 23:327–464; 24:31–223.

Marx, Karl. *Pre-Capitalist Economic Formations.* Edited by E. J. Hobsbawm. New York, 1964.

Molas, Mariano Antonio. *Descripción história de la antigua provincia del Paraguay.* Asunción, 1957.

Montoya, Alfredo J. *La ganadería y la industría de la salazón de carnes en el período 1810–1862.* Buenos Aires, 1971.

Munck af Rosenschöld, Eberhard. *Algunas cartas del naturalista sueco escritas durante su estadía en el Paraguay, 1843–1868.* Stockholm, 1956.

O'Leary, Juan E. *La alianza de 1845 con Corrientes. Aparición de Solano López en el escenario del Plata.* Asunción, 1944.

Ortega, Nestor F. "El tráfico fluvial entre Buenos Aires y Paraguay a fines del siglo XVIII." *Trabajos y Comunicaciones* 1 (1949): 129–41.

Page, Thomas J. *La Plata, the Argentine Confederation, and Paraguay.* New York, 1859.

Palma, Federico. "Un momento en la historia de Misiones, 1832–1882." *Boletín de la Academia Nacional de la Historia* 38 (1965): 3–34.

——. "Orígenes de la ciudad de Goya." *Nordeste* 4 (1962): 159–88.

——. "Santo Tomé. Crónica de su restablecimiento." *Revista de la Junta de Historia de Corrientes* 4 (1969): 11–80.

Palomeque, Alberto. *El general Rivera y la campaña de Misiones. 1828.* Buenos Aires, 1914.

Parish, Woodbine. *Buenos Ayres and the Provinces of the Río de la Plata.* London, 1852.

Pastore, Carlos. *La lucha por la tierra en el Paraguay.* Montevideo, 1972.

Pereyra, Horacio. "Notas sobre la economía del litoral argentino (1820–1836)." *Humanidades* 35 (1960): 123–59.

Pérez Acosta, Juan F. *Carlos Antonio López: Obrero Máximo.* Buenos Aires, 1948.

——. "Gaspar Rodríguez de Francia y Pedro Ferré." *Boletín del Instituto de Investigaciones Históricas* 24 (1940): 112–36.

——. "Gestiones de Carlos Antonio López ante Juan Manuel de Rosas 1842–1844." *Boletín del Instituto de Investigaciones Históricas* 28 (1943–44): 34–61.

——. *López y Rosas: relaciones iniciales.* Buenos Aires, 1944.

Peterson, Harold F. "Edward Augustus Hopkins: A Pioneer Promoter in Paraguay." *Hispanic American Historical Review* 22 (May 1942): 245–61.

Pla, Josefina. *The British in Paraguay, 1850–1870.* Richmond and Surrey, 1976.

Platt, D. C. M. *Latin America and British Trade 1806–1914.* London, 1972.

Poenitz, Erich L. W. Edgar. "La ruta oriental de la yerba. Navegación y comercio en el alto Río Uruguay." *Cuadernos de Estudios Regionales* 1 (1981): 25–60.

Pujol, Juan. *Corrientes en la organización nacional.* 10 vols. Buenos Aires, 1911.

Quesada, Vicente G. *La provincia de Corrientes.* Buenos Aires, 1857.

——. "Reminiscencias." *Revista de Buenos Aires* 3 (April 1864): 584–606.

Ramos, R. Antonio. "Correa da Câmara en Asunción," *Boletín del Instituto de Investigaciones Históricas* 30 (1952): 57–81.

——. *Juan Andrés Gelly.* Buenos Aires and Asunción, 1972.

——. *La política del Brasil en el Paraguay bajo la dictadura del Dr. Francia.* 2d ed. Asunción and Buenos Aires, 1959.

Reber, Vera Blinn, "Internal Trade and Market Towns in Nineteenth-Century Paraguay." *MACLAS. Latin American Essays* 1 (1987): 105–116.

Registro oficial de la provincia de Corrientes (1821–1859). 8 vols. Reprint. Corrientes, 1929–31.

Registro oficial de la provincia de Corrientes del año de 1861. Corrientes, 1886.

Rengger, Johann Rudolph, and Marceline Longchamp. *The Reign of Doctor Joseph Gaspard Roderick de Francia in Paraguay: Being an Account of Six Years' Residence in that Republic from July 1819 to May 1825.* London, 1827.

——. *Reise nach Paraguay in den Jahren 1818 bis 1826.* Aarau, 1835.

Ribeiro, Pedro Freire. *A Missão Pimenta Bueno, 1843–1847.* Rio de Janeiro, 1965.

Ripodas Ardañaz, Daisy. *Francisco de Paula Sanz. Viaje por el virreinato del Río de la Plata. El camino de tabaco.* Buenos Aires, 1977.

Rivarola Paoli, Juan Bautista, "El monopolio de la real renta: el estanco del tabaco y naipes," *El Archivo Nacional* 1:1 (abril 1988), 27–75.

Robertson, J. P., and W. P. Robertson. *Letters on Paraguay comprising an Account of Four Years' Residence in that Republic under the Government of the Dictator Francia.* 3 vols. London, 1838–39.

——. *Letters on South America Comprising Travels on the Banks of the Paraná and the Río de la Plata.* 3 vols. London, 1843.

Rodríguez, Mario. "The Genesis of Economic Attitudes in the Río de la Plata." *Hispanic American Historical Review* 36 (May 1956): 171–89.

Rogers, Rolland C. "The Influence of the Rivers in the Development of Rio Grande do Sul, Brazil." Ph.D. dissertation, Stanford University, 1953.

Romero, Blanca. "La ganadería en la época del Dr. Francia." *Cuadernos Republicanos* 10 (1975): 84–92.

Saeger, James Schofield. "Survival and Abolition: The Eighteenth-Century Paraguayan Encomienda." *The Americas* 38 (July 1981): 59–86.

Saldías, Adolfo. *Historia de la confederación argentina. Rosas y su época.* 9 vols. Buenos Aires, 1958.

Santos Muñoz, Pablo. *Años de lucha (1841–1845): Urquiza y la política del litoral rioplatense.* Buenos Aires, 1973.

Schmitt, Peter A. *Paraguay und Europa: die diplomatischen Beziehungen unter Carlos Antonio López und Francisco Solano López, 1841–1870.* Berlin, 1963.

Schneider, Jürgen. "Wirschaft und Aussenhandel Paraguays in den ersten fünfzig Jahren nach der Unabhängigkeit. Der Mythos der Industrialisierung durch Isolation," in Titus Heydenreich and Jürgen Schneider, eds., *Paraguay. Referate des 6. Interdisziplinären Kolloquiums der Sektion Lateinamerika des Zentralinstituts* (Munich, 1984), pp. 131–46.

Scobie, James R. *La lucha por la consolidación de la nacionalidad argentina, 1852–62.* 2d ed. Buenos Aires, 1979.

——. *Secondary Cities of Argentina. The Social History of Corrientes, Salta, and Mendoza, 1850–1910.* Completed and edited by Samuel L. Baily. Stanford, 1988.

Seckinger, Ron. *The Brazilian Monarchy and the South American Republics, 1822–1831.* Baton Rouge, 1984.

Sepp, Antonio, S. J. *Relación de viaje a las misiones guaraníes.* 3 vols. Buenos Aires, 1971.

Soares de Sousa, José Antonio. *A Missão Bellegarde ao Paraguai 1849–1852: Exposição, Antecedentes e Notas.* Rio de Janeiro, 1966.

Socolow, Susan M. *The Merchants of Buenos Aires, 1778–1810: Family and Commerce.* Cambridge, 1978.

Sonzogni, Cristina M., and Mirta Beatriz Ramírez. "La población de la ciudad de Corrientes a mediados del siglo XIX." *Cuadernos de Geohistoria Regional* 2 (1980).

Spalding, Walter. *A Epopeia Farroupilha.* São Paulo, 1963.

———. *A Invasão Paraguaia no Brasil.* São Paulo, 1940.

Szeminski, Jan. "Rewolucja i dyktatura w Paragwaju 1810–1840," *Przeglad Historyczny* 68 (1977), 567–574.

Szlajfer, Henryk. "Against Dependent Capitalist Development in Nineteenth-Century Latin America. The Case of Haiti and Paraguay," *Latin American Perspectives* 13:1 (Winter 1986), 45–73.

Tanzi, Hector José. "La actividad agropecuaria en el virreinato del Río de la Plata." *Investigaciones y Ensayos* 2 (1967): 261–87.

Tasso Fragoso, Augusto. *Historia da Guerra entre a Triple Aliança e o Paraguai.* 5 vols. 2d ed. Rio de Janeiro, 1956–60.

———. *A Revoluçao Farroupilha (1835–1845).* Rio de Janeiro, 1939.

Tate, E. Nicholas. "Britain and Latin America in the Nineteenth Century: The Case of Paraguay, 1811–1870." *Ibero-Amerikanisches Archiv* 5:1 (1979): 39–70.

Thompson, George. *The War in Paraguay.* London, 1869.

Tjarks, Germán O. E. *El consulado de Buenos Aires y sus proyecciones en la historia del Río de la Plata.* 2 vols. Buenos Aires, 1962.

———. "Nueva luz sobre el orígen de la Triple Alianza." *Historia Paraguaya* 21 (1984): 245–313.

———. "Panorama del comercio interno del virreinato del Río de la Plata en sus postrimerías." *Humanidades* 36 (1960).

Vargas Peña, Benjamín. *Paraguay-Argentina: correspondencia diplomática, 1810–1840.* Buenos Aires, 1945.

Vázquez, José Antonio. *El doctor Francia visto y oído por sus contemporáneos.* Buenos Aires, 1975.

Velázquez, Rafael Eladio. "Navegación paraguaya de los siglos XVII y XVIII." *Estudios Paraguayos* 1 (November 1973): 45–84.

———. *El Paraguay en 1811: estado político, social, económico y cultural en las postrimerías del período colonial.* Asunción, 1965.

———. "Transformaciones de la época de la intendencia en el Paraguay." *Historia Paraguaya* 20 (1983): 75–104.

Vidaurreta de Tjarks, Alicia. "Diario de viaje al Plata de José Bergés, 1851–52." *Trabajos y Comunicaciones* 19 (1969): 205–269.

———. "Los farrapos y el Río de la Plata." *Jahrbuch für Geschichte von Staat, Wirstchaft, and Gesellschaft Lateinamerikas* 24 (1987): 417–54.

———. "Al margen de la guerra del Paraguay." *Trabajos y Comunicaciones* 18 (1968): 243–61.

Villalobos, Sergio. *Comercio y contrabando en el Río de la Plata y Chile, 1700–1811.* Buenos Aires, 1965.

Viola, Alfredo. "El diario de Nicolás Descalzi." *Anuario del Instituto de Investigaciones Históricas Dr. José Gaspar Rodríguez de Francia* 4 (September 1982): 37–64.

———. "Facetas de la política gubernativa del Dr. Francia." *Cuadernos Republicanos* 10 (1975): 93–125.

———. "Moneda y control de cambio durante el gobierno del Dr. Francia."
*Anuario del Instituto de Investigaciones Históricas Dr. José Gaspar
Rodríguez de Francia* 3 (September 1981): 11–22.

———. "La tenencia de la tierra durante el gobierno del Dr. Francia," *Anuario
del Instituto de Investigaciones Históricas Dr. José Gaspar Rodríguez
de Francia* 2 (November 1980): 80–89.

Walker, Geoffrey J. *Spanish Politics and Imperial Trade, 1700–1789.* London,
1979.

Warren, Harris Gaylord. "The Paraguayan Image of the War of the Triple Alliance." *The Americas* 19 (July 1962): 3–20.

Washburn, Charles A. *The History of Paraguay, with Notes of Personal Observations and Reminiscences of Diplomacy under Difficulties.* 2 vols.
Boston, 1871.

Wentzel, Claudia. "El comercio del litoral de los ríos con Buenos Aires: el area
del Paraná, 1783–1821." *Anuario del IEHS* 3 (1988): 161–210.

Whigham, Thomas Lyle. "The Iron Works of Ybycui: Paraguayan Industrial Development in the Mid-Nineteenth Century." *The Americas* 35 (October
1978): 201–218.

———. "Agriculture and the Upper Plata: The Tobacco Trade, 1780–1865." *Business History Review* 59:4 (Winter 1985): 563–96.

———. "Cattle Raising in the Argentine Northeast, c. 1750–1870." *Journal of
Latin American Studies* 20 (November 1988): 313–35.

———. "The Back-Door Approach: the Alto Uruguay and Paraguayan Trade,
1810–1852," *Revista de Historia de América,* 109 (January–June 1990),
45–67.

White, Richard Alan. *Paraguay's Autonomous Revolution, 1810–1840.* Albuquerque, 1978.

Williams, John Hoyt. "The 'Conspiracy of 1820' and the Destruction of the
Paraguayan Aristocracy." *Revista de Historia de América* 75–76 (January-
December 1973): 141–56.

———. "The Deadly Selva: Paraguay's Northern Indian Frontier." *The Americas* 33 (July 1976): 1–24.

———. "Dr. Francia and the Creation of the Republic of Paraguay, 1810–1814."
Ph.D. dissertation, University of Florida, 1969.

———. "La guerra no-declarada entre el Paraguay y Corrientes." *Estudios Paraguayos* 1 (November 1973): 35–44.

———. "Paraguayan Isolation under Dr. Francia: A Reevaluation." *Hispanic
American Historical Review* 52 (February 1972): 102–122.

———. "Paraguay's Nineteenth-Century *Estancias de la República.*" *Agricultural History* 47 (July 1973): 206–215.

———. *The Rise and Fall of the Paraguayan Republic, 1800–1870.* Austin, 1979.

———. "Woodbine Parish and the 'Opening' of Paraguay." *Proceedings of the American Philosophical Society* 116 (April 1972): 343–49.

Wisner, Francisco. *El dictador del Paraguay José Gaspar de Francia.* Buenos Aires, 1957.

Wood, David. "An Artificial Frontier: Brazilian Military Colonies in Southern Mato Grosso, 1850–1867." *Pacific Coast Council on Latin American Studies: Proceedings* 3 (1974): 95–108.

Ynsfrán, Pablo Max. *La expedición norteamericana contra el Paraguay, 1858–1859.* 2 vols. Buenos Aires and Mexico City, 1954, 1958.

Zalazar, Roberto. *El brigadier Ferré y el unitarismo porteño.* Buenos Aires, 1965.

Zinny, Antonio. *Historia de los gobernantes de las provincias argentinas.* 5 vols. Buenos Aires, 1920–21.

Index

rapids, 4, 7, 79, 189, 190
razorfish, 180
receptorías, 45, 159
reexportation, effects of, 48
regional coherence and discord, 36,
40, 56, 57, 60, 64, 67, 78, 88
Registro Oficial, 164
regular, 134
República del Paraguay, the, 193
Restauración, 168
retail stores, 18, 139; shopkeepers, 32
Rhine Convention, the, 56
Riacho de Goya, 19, 77
Riacho Guaicurú, 181
Riachuelo, battle of the, 87
Ribera, Lázaro de, 29
Río Blanco, the, 193
Rio de Janeiro, 41, 53
Rio de la Plata region, 5, 6
Rio Grande do Sul, cattle and, 160,
164, 167, 168, 171, 174; politics
and, 53, 54, 55, 59, 83; yerba and,
121, 123, 126, (table) 128, 131
Río Negro, the, 193
river travel, barriers to, 40, 61; cattle
and, 155, 157; commerce and, 13,
14, 34, 56, 57, 62, 76; timber and,
178, 191, 192, 193. *See also* open
river trade
Robertson, John Parish, 25, 26, 191,
192
Robertson, William, 25
rodeo, 155
Rolón, José María, 81, 82
Rosario, 52, 80, 174
Rosas, Juan Manuel de, *95*; policies
of, 55, 57–67, 124, 125, 143, 144,
146, 147, 168
Rothschild, Lionel Nathan de, 150
royal fifth, the, 12
royal monopolies, 14, 16, 18, 21,
135–41. *See also* monopolies,
Crown
rustling, 161, 168

Saladas, 138, 239 n 32
saladerista, 67
saladeros, 79, 164, 165, 169, 173

salt, 25, 164
salt and saline soil, 233 n 20
Salto, 7, 77, 79
Salto Grande, 190
Samson, Pedro, 185
San Antonio, the, 138–39
San Carlos, 40
San Cosme, 191
San Estanislao, 70, 116, 124, 162
San José, 40
San Javier, 127
San Joaquín, 124
San Juan, 77
San Lorenzo, 62
San Miguel, 150
San Pedro, 70, 123, 162
San Roque, 138, 150
Santa Bárbara, the, 138, 139
Santa Fé, 4, 11, 22, 64, 111, 121, 122,
146, 189
Santa Fé y Animas, the, 142
Santa Lucía, 9, 138
Santa Rosa, 7, *94*, 190
Santiago de Chile, 11
Santiago del Estero, 138
Santo Tomás, 40
Santo Tomé, 40, 54, 66, 79, 86
São Borja, the river at, 7; trade at, 40,
58, 66, 67, 121, 123, 126, 171, 189;
wars and, 42, 53, 54, 55, 86, 189
São Luis de Maranhao, 147
São Paulo, 53
sawyers, 9, 183
sawn timber trade, 182, 185
schooners, 192, 193
separatism. *See* Farrapo Rebellion
Sepp, Antonio, 156
servants, 9
sheep, 166
shipbuilding, 190–95; woods used in,
178
shipyards, 46, *100*, 183, 190–94
shopkeepers, 32; retail stores, 18, 139
slavery, 9, 53, 164
sloops, 193
smallholders, 19, 134. *See also*
chacreros
smallpox vaccine, 59

About the Book and Author

This study addresses the question of how independence affected the Upper Plata, a hinterland region in South America that today comprises Paraguay, northeastern Argentina, and the adjacent Brazilian borderlands. In analyzing the commercial and political history of this pivotal area, Whigham argues that the region's backwardness in the nineteenth century resulted more from political instability than from innate economic disadvantages.

Paraguay emerged from independence with a strongly conservative regime that espoused traditional mercantilist policies in trade matters. Led by the theologian-turned-dictator José Gaspar de Francia, the Paraguayan state successfully avoided the civil wars that engulfed the Argentine provinces, but at the high cost of depressing all outside commerce. A barter economy reappeared throughout the region. After 1852, however, Argentina decreed free navigation on the interior rivers and the Upper Plata experienced a sudden growth in its exports of timber, hides, tobacco, and yerba mate. Yet, just as the region became integrated into the wider South American economy, the disastrous Triple Alliance War (1864–1870) erupted and changed forever the course of Upper Platine development.

This economic history of the Upper Plata will interest all who seek studies that test and challenge dependency theories.

Thomas Whigham, assistant professor of history at the University of Georgia, is the author of *La yerba mate del Paraguay* (1780–1870) (Asunción, 1991), and several important articles on the economic history of the Plata published in such journals as the *Revista Historia de América,*

274 / About the Book and Author

Latin American Research Review, The Americas, Journal of Latin American Studies, and the *Revista Paraguaya de Sociología.* He was educated at the University of California, Santa Cruz, and at Stanford University, where he received the doctoral degree in 1986. He is married and has one child.